P9-CIV-393

AMERICAN CRUCIBLE

GARY GERSTLE

AMERICAN

CRUCIBLE

RACE AND NATION IN

THE TWENTIETH CENTURY

PRINCETON UNIVERSITY PRESS · PRINCETON AND OXFORD

COPYRIGHT © 2001 BY PRINCETON UNIVERSITY PRESS
PUBLISHED BY PRINCETON UNIVERSITY PRESS, 41 WILLIAM STREET,
PRINCETON, NEW JERSEY 08540
IN THE UNITED KINGDOM: PRINCETON UNIVERSITY PRESS, 3 MARKET PLACE,
WOODSTOCK, OXFORDSHIRE OX20 1SY
ALL RIGHTS RESERVED

SECOND PRINTING, AND FIRST PAPERBACK PRINTING, 2002
PAPERBACK ISBN 0-691-10277-5

THE LIBRARY OF CONGRESS HAS CATALOGED THE CLOTH EDITION
OF THIS BOOK AS FOLLOWS

GERSTLE, GARY.
AMERICAN CRUCIBLE : RACE AND NATION IN THE TWENTIETH CENTURY / GARY GERSTLE.
P. CM.
INCLUDES BIBLIOGRAPHICAL REFERENCES AND INDEX.
ISBN 0-691-04984-X (ALK. PAPER)
1. UNITED STATES—HISTORY—20TH CENTURY. 2. UNITED STATES—FOREIGN
RELATIONS—20TH CENTURY. 3. UNITED STATES—POLITICS AND GOVERNMENT—20TH
CENTURY. 4. NATIONAL CHARACTERISTICS, AMERICAN. 5. NATIONALISM—UNITED
STATES—HISTORY—20TH CENTURY. I. TITLE.
E741 .G475 2001
973.91—DC21   00-051680

BRITISH LIBRARY CATALOGING-IN-PUBLICATION DATA IS AVAILABLE

THIS BOOK HAS BEEN COMPOSED IN SABON
TEXT DESIGNED BY CARMINA ALVAREZ

PRINTED ON ACID-FREE PAPER. ∞

WWW.PUPRESS.PRINCETON.EDU

PRINTED IN THE UNITED STATES OF AMERICA

10 9 8 7 6 5 4

FOR DANNY AND SAM

Contents

Figures

Acknowledgments

It is a pleasure to thank those who made it possible for me to write this book. Fellowships from the Institute for Advanced Study in Princeton, New Jersey, the National Endowment for the Humanities, the John Simon Guggenheim Memorial Foundation, and the Graduate Research Board of the University of Maryland provided encouragement and precious time to research, study, and write. I benefited greatly from opportunities to present my work in progress at American University, University of Tokyo, Ritsumeikan University (Kyoto, Japan), University of Massachusetts, Columbia University, Woodrow Wilson Center for International Scholars,

Princeton University, University of Minnesota, Catholic University of America, University of New Hampshire, University of Maryland, Ben Gurion University (Israel), and Michigan State University. I am grateful to the 1995 Social Science Research Council conference in Sanibel, Florida, and to the 1998 *Journal of American History* workshops at the International Institute for Social History in Amsterdam and at Sidney Sussex College, Cambridge University.

The formulation of the book's key ideas also took shape in stimulating graduate seminars on American nationalism and nationhood that I taught at the University of Pennsylvania and the Catholic University of America. Valuable feedback came from many other graduate students as well, including John Allen, Jeremy Bonner, Michael Coventry, Carlos Davila, Mary Beth Fraser, Christopher Gildemeister, Jeffrey Hornstein, Susan Hudson, Russell Kazal, Stephen Nordhoff, and Kathleen Trainor. A special thanks to two former graduate students who have now become colleagues: Jerald Podair scrutinized the penultimate version of my manuscript, filling every page with useful comments, large and small, while Maria Mazzenga assembled much of the research on which the last two chapters and epilogue are based while emerging as one of my best and toughest critics.

The progress and content of this work often depended on the diligence and imagination of research assistants—Jennifer Delton, Ryan Ellis, Michael Peterson, and Kelly Ryan—who uncovered many valuable textual and photographic materials. Photo researcher Lili Wiener was exceptionally generous with her time, advice, and expertise. Dick Blofson, neighbor and documentary filmmaker extraordinaire, enabled me to transform a key film image into a photo that I could use for this book. And historian Nancy Weiss Malkiel made it possible for me to use another important photo by sharing with me her marvelous knowledge of the civil rights movement.

I am indebted to scholars and friends who read chapters and, through their astute comments, helped me to make this a better book: Susan Armeny, Steve Fraser, John Higham, Jennifer Hochschild, Nancy Green, David Levy, Jerry Muller, Robyn

Muncy, Nell Painter, Tom Sugrue, Dave Thelen, and Lt. General Bernard E. Trainor (USMC Ret.). Alan Brinkley, Michael Kazin, Nelson Lichtenstein, and Roy Rosenzweig took time from busy schedules to read the entire manuscript and offer me indispensable advice. I hope that they will find evidence of the many contributions they have made in the pages that follow. Colleagues at two history departments, the Catholic University of America and the University of Maryland, nurtured me and this project along, and I want to thank them for their enthusiasm and support. Special thanks to my family away from home, Robbie Schneider and Sarah Mitchell and their daughters, Kate and Laura.

I can hardly imagine a better home for this book than that provided by Princeton University Press. Brigitta van Rheinberg worked with me on every aspect of the manuscript, not satisfied until we got it right. From start to finish, she has been a superb advocate and critic. Others at Princeton have contributed to the book's design, production, and quality, including designer Carmina Alvarez, production editor Brigitte Pelner, production director Neil Litt, and editorial assistant Mark Spencer. Jim O'Brien expertly assembled the index.

The walls between scholarship and family life are more permeable than they sometimes appear. My mother, Epsie, and sister, Linda, will know that this book is in part an attempt to comprehend how the different generations of our immigrant family made their way and remade themselves in America. I'm sorry that my father Jack didn't live to see this book, for he would have enjoyed it immensely. Whether my sons, Danny and Sam, will enjoy this book is another matter, but they have left their mark on it and on me. Their presence in my life is an extraordinary gift. The joys of parenthood and the complicated connections between work and family will come as no surprise to Liz, my partner in life, love, and intellectual pursuits. Our journey has been remarkable.

AMERICAN CRUCIBLE

INTRODUCTION

"**A**merica is God's Crucible, where all the races of Europe are melting and reforming!" proclaims the protagonist in Israel Zangwill's 1908 play, *The Melting-Pot*. "Germans, Frenchmen, Irishmen and Englishmen, Jews and Russians—into the Crucible with you all! God is making the American." With these words, Zangwill articulated a central and enduring myth about the American nation—that the United States was a divine land where individuals from every part of the world could leave behind their troubles, start life anew, and forge a proud, accomplished, and unified people. Arthur Schlesinger Jr., writing eighty years later, endorsed the same myth, locating the transformative power of the United States not in God but in the nation's core political ideals, in the American belief in the fundamental equality of all human beings, in every individual's inalienable rights to life, liberty, and the pursuit of happiness, and in a democratic government that derives its legitimacy from the people's consent. These beliefs represent a kind of democratic universalism that can take root anywhere. But because they were enshrined in the American nation's founding documents, the Declaration of Independence and Constitution, Schlesinger and others have argued that they have marked something distinctive about the American people and their polity. In the 1940s Gunnar Myrdal bundled these civic rights and principles together into a political faith that he called the "American Creed." Although I prefer to use the more generic term "civic nationalism," which Michael Ignatieff and other students of the contemporary nation employ to denote these beliefs, it is clear that their role in promoting freedom and democracy in American history is indisputable.[1]

Throughout its history, however, American civic nationalism has contended with another potent ideological inheritance, a racial nationalism that conceives of America in ethnoracial terms, as a people held together by common blood and skin color and by an inherited fitness for self-government. This ideal, too, was inscribed in the Constitution (although not in the Declaration of Independence), which endorsed the enslavement of Africans in the southern states, and it was encoded in a key 1790 law limiting naturalization to "free white persons." Although modified in 1870, this 1790 law remained in force until 1952, evidence that America's yearning to be a white republic survived African American emancipation by almost 100 years. As late as the 1920s, members of the House of Representatives felt no shame in declaring on the House floor that the American "pioneer race" was being replaced by "a mongrel one," or in admiring a scientist who told them that Americans "had been so imbued with the idea of democracy . . . that we have left out of consideration the matter of blood [and] . . . heredity. No man who breeds pedigreed plants and animals can afford to neglect this thing, as you know."[2] From the perspective of this racialized ideal, Africans, Asians, nonwhite Latin Americans, and, in the 1920s, southern and eastern Europeans did not belong in the republic and could never be accepted as full-fledged members. They had to be expelled, segregated, or subordinated. The hold that this tradition exercised over the national imagination helps us to understand the conviction that periodically has surfaced among racial minorities, and especially among African Americans, that America would never accept them as the equals of whites, that they would never be included in the crucible celebrated by Zangwill, and that the economic and political opportunities identified by Schlesinger would never be theirs to enjoy. In the words of Malcolm X, America was not a dream; it was a nightmare.[3]

In this book, I argue that the pursuit of these two powerful and contradictory ideals—the civic and the racial—has decisively shaped the history of the American nation in the twentieth century. I show how both ideals influenced critical immigration and war mobilization policies, shaped social reform movements ranging from progressivism and the New Deal to the Congress of Industrial Organizations (CIO) and civil rights, and animated the nation's communal imagination. I give special attention to American liberals: presidents such as Theodore Roosevelt, Franklin Roosevelt, and Lyndon Johnson; congressmen of the 1920s and 1930s such as Samuel Dickstein, Adolph Sabath, and Fiorello LaGuardia; government agencies such as the 1940s Office of War Information; artists such as the filmmakers Frank Capra and Francis Ford Coppola, the comic strip creators Jerry Siegel and Joe Shuster, and the novelist Thomas Bell; and reformers who built the CIO and pushed through the civil rights revolution of the 1960s. These liberals and others, I contend, were the most influential architects of the twentieth-century nation. They were committed to the civic nationalist tradition in general and to equal rights for ethnic and racial minorities in particular. But many of them periodically reinscribed racialist notions into their rhetoric and policies. I examine the antinomies of the civic and racialist traditions in the writings and speeches of Theodore and Franklin Roosevelt, and explore the ways in which these same oppositions figured in many of the moments that defined the nation they built, from Theodore Roosevelt's charge up San Juan Hill in 1898 to Lyndon Johnson's confrontation with the Mississippi Freedom Democrats at the 1964 Democratic National Convention. I am particularly interested in how liberals and their supporters wrestled with the contradictions between the two nationalist traditions, how they managed to adhere to both simultaneously, and why the tensions between them did so little for so long to weaken the authority or cohesion of the nation.

I am also interested in the complexities of each tradition. It is easy to equate racial nationalism with a quest for racial purity, as the Ku Klux Klan did in arguing that the only true Americans are those who have "Anglo-Saxon" blood coursing through their veins. Other racial nationalists, however, have rejected such notions of purity. Theodore Roosevelt, for example, celebrated racial hybridity, believing that the world's most accomplished races—the British, the Americans, and the Australians—drew their strength from the merging together of diverse and complementary racial strains. Roosevelt was constantly seeking situations in which different races of Americans could be brought together in crucibles, mixed with each other, and molded into one people and one race. The most important crucible, in his eyes, was that of war, for the stress and dangers of combat generated pressures to unify that no peacetime initiative could simulate. Yet Roosevelt's melting pots were invariably racialized. They always, and deliberately, excluded one or more races—usually blacks, often Asians and American Indians. Roosevelt believed that such discrimination was necessary to forge an exemplary race. Indiscriminate mixing would inevitably lower a superior race's intelligence, morals, and courage.

Many Americans shared Roosevelt's belief in the superiority of a racialized melting pot. It influenced many writers, who, like Zangwill, often did not think to include blacks, Hispanics, or Asians in their American crucible, and it guided the racial policies of nation-building institutions, such as the military, that brought together whites of varying nationalities, religions, and regions even as they separated whites from blacks. But if the effort to define the nation in racial terms was constant during this era, the precise racial mix of groups that were allowed to contribute to American nationality was not. Early in the century, many native-born Americans thought that eastern and southern Europeans derived from such poor racial stock that they would never metamorphose into Americans. By the 1930s and 1940s, however, these eastern and southern European ethnics were challenging this characterization of themselves as racially inferior and were winning recognition for their worth as white Americans. Achieving inclusion did not mean that they were undermining the tradition of racial nationalism, for other racial groups, such as blacks and Asians, still found themselves on the outside looking in. The questions of why certain groups were able to overcome allegations of racial inferiority and others not and how their struggles for inclusion both challenged and reinforced the tradition of American racial nationalism form an important part of the story that this book tells.

The history of civic nationalism in the United States displays a similar kind of complexity. The promise of economic opportunity and political freedom to all citizens, irrespective of their racial, religious, or cultural background, was a vital component of this tradition. For most of the nineteenth century, it was thought that the mere removal of discriminatory laws would be sufficient to make the promise of opportunity real. But in the early twentieth century, the rise of the corporations transformed the economic and political landscape. The manufacture of new products and the creation of new wealth generated hopes that a society of general affluence was in reach, but the inability of millions to escape industrial poverty spread despair. Liberal reformers began arguing that corporations were occluding individual opportunity for the masses and that a regulatory state was now necessary to restore faith in America or in what the liberal intellectual Herbert Croly called "the promise of American life." Croly coined the term "New Nationalism" to describe a civic nationalist state-building project that he outlined in 1909, and Theodore Roosevelt made it the centerpiece of his progressivism.[4] Other liberal presidents would follow in Roosevelt's steps, arguing that a welfare state, the protection of labor's right to organize, and limitations on industrialists' power were

now necessary to fulfill the nation's civic mission. Civic nationalism even became a tool in the hands of anticapitalist socialists and
Communists who saw in its elastic principles an opportunity to
claim that economic egalitarianism would honor America's civic
creed. In the pages that follow, I reconstruct the efforts to stretch
the meaning of civic nationalism in this way, showing first how
these efforts enjoyed success during the progressive and New Deal
eras and then how the anticommunism of the Cold War snapped
civic nationalism back into an older, and less flexible, form.

A focus on anticommunism allows us to discern an exclusionary
tendency within the civic nationalist tradition itself, one that limited its ideological elasticity and sometimes compromised the atmosphere of openness and tolerance that it bestowed on American
society. Immigrants who refused to absorb and respect America's
civic nationalism, for example, were often treated harshly by neighbors, employers, and the state. Political radicals of a variety of
faiths, including anarchism, socialism, and communism, were also
vulnerable to ostracism, persecution, and the declaration that they
were un-American. During periods of perceived national crisis,
nonassimilating immigrants and political radicals became the targets of state-sponsored coercive campaigns to strip them of their
now alienable rights to free expression and free assembly. Many
of those who attacked these cultural and political dissenters saw
themselves as civic nationalists. They regarded their quarry not just
as political enemies but as the nation's enemies who had squan-
dered their right to be part of God's crucible.

Both racial and civic nationalism, then, were complex traditions,
simultaneously elastic and exclusionary, capable of being altered
in various ways to address new economic and political problems
as they arose. Together these two traditions imparted a clear, if
paradoxical, shape to what I call the Rooseveltian nation, a nation
whose outlines are discernible in the first two decades of the twentieth century and whose character would define American society
from the mid-1930s to the mid-1960s. The advocates of this nation
espoused an expansive civic nationalist creed: political and social
equality for all, irrespective of race, ethnicity, or nationality, and a

regulated economy that would place economic opportunity and security within the reach of everyone. Simultaneously, many of its supporters subscribed to the racial notion that America, despite its civic creed, ought to maximize the opportunities for its "racial superiors" and limit those of its "racial inferiors." Finally, they were prepared to harshly discipline immigrants, political radicals, and others who were thought to imperil the nation's welfare. Such disciplining was expected either to marginalize and punish the dissenters or to tame and "Americanize" them, rendering them suitable for incorporation into the national community. Disciplinary campaigns would lift up some, but not all, groups of racial inferiors into the American mainstream.

The Rooseveltian nation flourished amid the swirl of these contradictory principles for thirty years, commanding the respect of most people who lived within its borders. During its midcentury heyday, and in the thirty years prior to then when it was taking shape, this nation depended on war to achieve its aims: against the Spanish at the turn of the century, the Germans in World War I, the Germans and Japanese in World War II, and the Soviets and their allies in the Cold War. Wars provided opportunities to sharpen American national identity against external enemies who threatened the nation's existence, to transform millions of Americans whose loyalty was uncertain into ardent patriots, to discipline those within the nation who were deemed racially inferior or politically and culturally heterodox, and to engage in experiments in state building that would have been considered illegitimate in peacetime. Americans do not usually think of war as determinative of their nationhood, but in this book I argue that, at least for the twentieth century, war has been decisive. Perhaps no figure illustrates the association of war and the nation more than Theodore Roosevelt, which is why I have accorded him a pivotal role in the story that I tell.

In the 1960s, the Rooseveltian nation fell apart. The trigger was the civil rights revolution that began in the 1940s and reached its climax in the 1960s. In its first two decades, the movement for racial equality was civic nationalist to the core, identifying itself with the Pilgrims, Founding Fathers, and the American dream, and calling on all Americans to respect their democratic inheritance and judge each other—in the words of Martin Luther King Jr.—by the content of their character rather than the color of their skin. But the persistence of racial nationalism bred disillusionment, prompting many black activists to jettison their civic ideals and embrace black power, an ideology that rejected America as hopelessly compromised by racism and that called on blacks to break their affective and cultural ties to it.

The black nationalist renunciation of America was a stunning development. Once it occurred, the contradictions within the Rooseveltian nation overwhelmed its capacity for imparting unity and purpose to a bitterly fractured society. The rapid spread of black nationalist principles to a mostly white and middle-class university population and, then, to far larger segments of white America, including European ethnics often thought to be black power's die-hard opponents, accelerated this nation's collapse. I argue that the disastrous war in Vietnam was the decisive element in this diffusion, as it made millions of whites receptive to a radical critique of state power, nationalist ideals, and cultural assimilation in ways that most Americans had not been since the First World War. The Vietnam War, alone among twentieth-century wars, could not be turned to nation-building purposes. To the contrary, it tore apart the nation to which Theodore Roosevelt and World War I had given birth. By 1970, neither the civic nor racial traditions of American nationalism retained enough integrity to serve as rallying points for those who wished to put the nation back together.

The nation, of course, did not end with Vietnam. In an epilogue I explore the rise of multiculturalism in the 1980s and its significance as an antiracist and anti-American ideology. I also examine the determined efforts, first by Reaganite conservatives and then by Clintonian liberals, to revive affection for the American nation and to launch new nation-building projects. I place this nationalist renaissance into historical perspective and speculate on whether the new nation that is now taking shape will resemble the Rooseveltian one or whether it will rest on a significantly different, and perhaps less contradictory, set of principles.

This is a work of synthetic interpretation that owes a great deal to the labors of other scholars. The notes to my chapters record the fullness of my debt. In conceptualizing this work, I have incurred several more general intellectual obligations that need to be mentioned here. First, I am beholden to those scholars who, in the last fifteen years, have revived the study of nations. Although most of these scholars have written about nationalism in places other than the United States, they have helped me to imagine how a history of the American nation might be written. Most important among them is Benedict Anderson, whose book, *Imagined Communities*, on the origins of nations and nationalist consciousness in Europe and Latin America in the eighteenth century, allowed me to see nations for what they are: invented political and cultural entities whose power rests not only on the acquisition and control of territory but also on their ability to gain the allegiance and affection of the large and heterogeneous populations that reside within their borders. Nations first appeared in Europe when dynastic realms, rooted in an older kind of political and cultural system that generated unity on the basis of vertical ties between subjects and an exalted king or God, were breaking up and changes in the materialist forces of production were making it possible to imagine new politicocultural systems built on the horizontal comradeship of citizens. Once the idea of a nation emerged, Anderson has written, it was "capable of being transplanted . . . to a great variety of social terrains, to merge and be merged with a correspondingly wide variety of political and ideological constellations."[5]

That nations are invented and variable underscores how much they are sociopolitical creations and, as such, historically contingent. Their origins may be purposive or accidental. They can gain or lose strength, expand their territory or lose it, fortify their myths of origin and belonging or see them undermined or altered, celebrate aspects of their history or repress them. Nations can win the allegiance of their people through promises of liberty, prosperity, and immortality or beat them into submission through campaigns of fear and intimidation. They can subordinate, expel, or kill those identified as enemies of the nation and protect and assist those who form the citizenry or the *Volk*. Nationalist sentiment can rest on a series of rational political principles as well as on myth, emotion, and contradiction. To write the history of a nation, then, is to be alert to this range of possibilities and to identify those which seem most important.

I also owe a great deal to a distinguished line of works, stretching from W.E.B. Du Bois's *Black Reconstruction in America, 1860–1880*, through Edmund S. Morgan's *American Slavery, American Freedom*, to David R. Roediger's *The Wages of Whiteness*, that has argued for the centrality of race to American politics and society.[6] The literature on the history of race and racism in America is, of course, enormous. Prior to the past twenty years, however, much of it tended to depict racism as the work of white southerners, the ignorant poor, and aristocratic reactionaries and others who were out of touch with the American mainstream or at least with its dominant, liberal currents. The notion that race might have been constitutive of American democracy, welfare policy, the labor movement, and other progressive developments rarely surfaced. Du Bois and other black scholars had been making this argument for decades, of course. The rescue of their work from the margins, along with the work of scholars such as Morgan and Roediger in the last generation, has now made that once submerged notion difficult to ignore. Just as other scholars have insisted on the centrality of race to notions of American freedom and class consciousness, so I argue for its importance in regard to American nationalism.[7]

I have not followed, however, the lead of some whiteness scholars in seeing race at the root of every expression of American nationalism. This view, in my mind, ignores the strength and autonomy of the civic nationalist tradition and the ways that different groups have used it to advance the causes of both social democracy and racial equality. For this reason, I have been drawn to Eric

Foner's *The Story of American Freedom* and Rogers M. Smith's *Civic Ideals: Conflicting Visions of Citizenship in U.S. History*, both of which acknowledge the full influence of race and other forms of exclusion without slighting the power of civic ideals.[8]

Whether it is now possible to move beyond our long history of racial exclusion and build a strong and tolerant nation on the basis of a civic creed alone, a position currently advocated by prominent liberal intellectuals and policy makers, is an important question that the epilogue addresses. How it is answered carries implications for the kind of society we think Americans of the twenty-first century will inhabit. But that is getting ahead of the story. First we must gain a sense of how the American nation of the twentieth century came to be. For that, we turn to a moment in 1898 when that nation, in a victorious war against Spain and under the spell of Theodore Roosevelt's heroism, can plausibly be said to have been born.

CHAPTER 1

Theodore Roosevelt's
Racialized Nation,
1890–1900

In the 1890s many American nationalists believed that a good war would impart the unity, vigor, and prosperity that they felt their increasingly troubled and fractious society needed. A long economic depression, spanning the years 1893–97, had deepened poverty, exacerbated tensions between the rich and poor, and sown doubts about the virtues of industrialization. Cities were awash in immigrants, many of whom appeared to care little about America and its democratic heritage. Many northerners and southerners still seemed unwilling to let go of the anger and resentments aroused by the Civil War thirty years earlier. And the new industrial and bureaucratic order seemed to be robbing men of precious masculine virtues—independence, strenuous living, patriarchal author-ity—while giving women an expanded role in economic and politi-cal affairs. International developments also appeared to threaten America, especially the rush by European powers for territory, trade, and conquest in Africa and Asia. If America wanted to stay abreast of its economic competitors, many nationalists argued, it had to establish an international military presence, at minimum to protect foreign markets and, at maximum, to demonstrate the power of America and the superiority of its industrious, freedom-loving, and aggressive people.

A victorious war against a European rival could enhance Ameri-ca's international stature. The calls for unity that such a war would inevitably entail might also heal the divisions between North and South, rich and poor, and even between the native- and foreign-born. Men who fought, meanwhile, might be able to recover a manliness that seemed to be slipping from their grasp.

Few wished for such a war more ardently than Theodore Roose-velt, a rising star in the Republican Party who, in the 1890s, had served as a civil service commissioner, New York City police com-missioner, and, by 1897, assistant secretary of the navy. In 1898, when war erupted between the United States and Spain over the latter's increasingly brutal efforts to end an insurrection in Cuba, one of its few remaining colonies, Roosevelt could barely contain his enthusiasm for the coming fight. He resigned his position as assistant secretary, raised a volunteer cavalry regiment that would be immortalized as the Rough Riders, and then rushed to Cuba where he led his troops to victories in battles that decided the out-come of the war. Covering himself in glory, he returned to America a hero, a status he would quickly parlay into political advance-ment. He became governor of New York in 1898, vice-president of the United States in 1900, president in 1901, and leader of the progressive movement that, energized by the American victory in 1898, launched a remarkable crusade to heal the republic's deep economic, social, and political wounds and restore its historic promise.

As we shall see, Roosevelt's progressivism expanded and en-riched American civic nationalism. But first we must reckon with

Roosevelt's racial nationalism, which powerfully informed his conception of what he was doing in Cuba. This racial nationalism was
manifest not only in his attitude toward Cubans and other groups
of Latin Americans, whom he judged to be too racially inferior to
be entrusted with the responsibility of self-government. It was also
evident in his conception of the mission and composition of the
Rough Rider cavalry. This regiment's mission was to throw American men into the kind of racial and savage warfare that earlier
generations, especially the backwoodsmen of the mythic Daniel
Boone era, had experienced in their struggles against the Indians.
In Roosevelt's recounting of that pioneer history, the battles of
these rural warriors against the savage red man had forged them
into a powerful, superior, and freedom-loving race. It also served
the indispensable purpose of uniting disparate groups of Europeans
into one American people. America, in the 1890s, Roosevelt believed, desperately needed to recapture the strength, vitality, unity,
and race consciousness of those pioneer Americans. This belief underlay his eagerness for war and impelled him to envision the
Rough Rider regiment as a crucible that would bring together various groups of Euro-Americans and give them solidarity and purpose that, in his eyes, they so conspicuously lacked. At the same
time, Roosevelt excluded blacks from his regiment, for he deemed
them too base a race to become true Americans. They would pollute his regiment, rob it of its superiority, and prevent Euro-Americans in it from invigorating the "American" race and nation.

In Cuba, Roosevelt and his Rough Riders carried out their reenactment of the nation's founding myth with panache. In two of the
war's most important battles—for Kettle Hill and San Juan Hill,
ridges that guarded the approach to Santiago, the Spanish capital
in Cuba—they had charged into the teeth of tough Spanish defenses
and overran them. But a problem had arisen. As Roosevelt stood
on the crest of San Juan Hill, a moment he would always regard
as the greatest in his life, he saw black Americans everywhere. They
belonged to the Ninth and Tenth Cavalries and the Twenty-fourth
Infantry; they were among the finest regular soldiers in the U.S.
Army, and Roosevelt knew this. In his heart, Roosevelt understood
that the Rough Riders and, by extension, America, would not have

triumphed in this crucial battle without the assistance of these "buffalo soldiers," and in the flush of victory, he admitted as much.

Something extraordinary had happened during those battles, as black American soldiers had fought alongside and intermixed with white ones, demonstrating that racial division could be overcome and that a fighting force including all Americans, not just those of European descent, could operate effectively. Roosevelt possessed the material for constructing a radically new and racially egalitarian myth about the American people. Even though his civic nationalist principles ran deep, he was not prepared for the opportunity that the victory at Kettle and San Juan Hills had handed him. As he wrote the history of his battles in Cuba, he diminished the black contribution to his victory to the point of insignificance. The nation to which he wanted to give birth and lead had to be a white nation. The greatness of America, he believed, could only lie in the exploits of Euro-Americans forged by battle into a single and superior race. Out of such convictions was the twentieth-century nation born.

A HISTORY OF THE AMERICAN "RACE"

If for Karl Marx history was the history of class conflict, for Roosevelt history was the history of race conflict: of the world's various races struggling against each other for supremacy and power. Roosevelt was hardly an accomplished racial theorist, but he had absorbed the racialist thought that permeated literary and academic circles in the late nineteenth century. Like many of his contemporaries, Roosevelt equated race with peoplehood. The British, the Americans, the French, the Germans, the Italians, the Chinese, the Japanese, the Africans—each of these groups was thought by Roosevelt to possess a distinct culture rooted in inborn racial traits that had been transmitted from generation to generation. In his epic work, *The Winning of the West* (1889), Roosevelt traced the process by which the American "race" had come into being and made itself into the greatest English-speaking race the world had even known.[1]

   The history of racial conflict, in Roosevelt's eyes, pointed in the direction of civilization and progress: more often than not, the higher civilized races triumphed over the lower savage or barbaric ones. But this tendency was not an iron law. There had been shattering reversals—the Dark Ages most notably—when the forces of barbarism had overwhelmed the citadels of civilization. No race, no matter how civilized its people or how superior their mental ability, could afford to become complacent about its destiny. Racial triumph came only to those peoples willing to fight for it. Success in battle required the cultivation of manly, warlike, even savage qualities: physical toughness and fitness, fearlessness, bravery, singlemindedness, ruthlessness.

   The fierce Germanic peoples who streamed southward out of the central European forests in the fourth and fifth centuries possessed these qualities, which is why they laid waste to the once mighty Roman Empire, whose warriors and rulers had gone soft. These Teutons possessed the intelligence, the independence, the love of liberty and order, and the intense tribal loyalty (patriotism) necessary to push civilization forward. But they had often failed to impress their qualities or superiority on the peoples whom they had conquered, allowing themselves instead to be absorbed by the Spanish, French, and other "subject-races."[2] These latter races benefited from this infusion of Germanic blood, becoming strong, powerful, and conquering peoples themselves. But after a few centuries, the Germanic elements of these subject races faded for lack of replenishment and the latter then reverted to their more natural, and mediocre, racial condition.

   In Britain, however, the fifth-century Germanic invasion had taken a different course. The conquest of the indigenous Briton and Celtic peoples had not been easy, and large numbers had been killed or driven off. The invading Teutons, as a consequence, formed a large portion of Britain's population and were able to impress their customs, beliefs, laws, and language on the conquered local peoples. The Teutons, in effect, successfully assimilated the indigenous Celts and Britons into their race, and thereby improved the quality of their own racial stock. Here Roosevelt first revealed his own belief in the benefits that could accrue from racial mixing and racial assimilation, provided that these processes were properly controlled by the superior race.[3]

Periodic attempts at invasion from abroad kept the Teutonic instinct for self-preservation razor sharp, while Britain's physical separation from Europe prevented Latin and other continental cultures from penetrating and enervating Britain's Teutonic core. In these circumstances of Teutonic domination, war, isolation, and limited assimilation, a super-Teutonic race incubated, strengthening itself through the incorporation of conquered Celtic and Scandinavian peoples and their customs, and preparing to embark on the greatest adventure the world had ever seen: "the spread of the English-speaking peoples over the world's waste spaces." This adventure lasted three hundred years until the English race, once limited to a small island "between the North and Irish seas," held "sway over worlds whose endless coasts are washed by the waves of the three great oceans."[4] To Roosevelt, it was no accident that the spread of this race had inaugurated an extraordinary period of economic growth, technological innovation, and democracy. The Teutonic-English race had raised the quality of civilization and carried it to the farthest reaches of the globe.

In this saga of worldwide triumph, the most important conquest had occurred on the North American continent, where an English-speaking people had duplicated the feats of the Teutons in Britain, but on a larger and more heroic scale. In Roosevelt's eyes, the settlers who mattered were not the godly Puritans of New England or the virtuous farmers who diligently worked the land or the merchants who made great fortunes by acquiring and trading the continent's abundant resources. Rather, they were the backwoodsmen who bravely ventured forth into the trans-Appalachian wilderness to battle the Indians and clear the land. These backwoodsmen, in Roosevelt's eyes, like the Germans who had invaded Britain, were warriors above all, and their primary task was not placid husbandry but relentless war against the savage Indians who claimed these lands as their own. Roosevelt had no use for a Turnerian view of the frontier as an uninhabited place awaiting cultivation by diligent bands of husbandmen. "A race of peaceful, unwarlike farmers," Roosevelt argued, "would have been helpless before such foes as the red Indians, and no auxiliary military forces could have protected them or enabled them to move westward. . . . The West would never have been settled save for the fierce courage and the eager desire to brave danger so characteristic of the stalwart back-woodsmen."[5]

Roosevelt loathed the savage red man but admired him, too, for his bravery, cunning, and, most of all, ferocity. The backwoodsman achieved his greatness as a result of the extraordinary battles he had fought to subdue the remarkable Indian foe. Here is a typical Rooseveltian account of the terrifying but ennobling character of the backwoodsmen–red men encounters:

> Often the white men and red fought one another whenever they met, and displayed in their conflicts all the cunning and merciless ferocity that made forest warfare so dreadful. Terrible deeds of prowess were done by the mighty men on either side. It was a war of stealth and cruelty, and ceaseless, sleepless watchfulness. The contestants had sinewy frames and iron wills, keen eyes and steady hands, hearts as bold as they were ruthless. . . . The dark woods saw a myriad lonely fights where red warrior or white hunter fell and no friend of the fallen ever knew his fate, where his sole memorial was the scalp that hung in the smoky cabin or squalid wigwam of the victor.[6]

On the field of battle, the Indian was every bit the backwoods-man's equal.

Roosevelt regarded the conquest of the Indians and the winning of the West as "the great epic feat in the history of our race." The relentless westward march was "a record of men who greatly dared and greatly did, a record of wanderings wider and more dangerous than those of the Vikings; a record of endless feats of arms, of victory after victory in the ceaseless strife waged against wild man and wild nature."[7] And just as the struggle to subdue the Celts had given rise to a super-Teutonic race in Britain, so too the war to exterminate the Indian created the "Americans," the fittest English-speaking race yet to appear on earth.

The backwoodsmen could not assimilate the Indians as the Teutons had done to the Celts, for the racial gap between them and the Indians was simply too great to be bridged. Those Europeans who had mixed with the Indians—the French and the Spanish—had merely created new, inferior races.[8] But the war against the Indians had accelerated a different kind of assimilatory process, one that fashioned a single American people out of many European strains. The backwoodsmen, according to Roosevelt, were primarily the descendants of two British races—the Scotch Irish and the English—but included in their ranks significant numbers of Germans, Huguenots, "Hollanders," and Swedes. Although these distinct "racial" groups were still conscious of their differences when they arrived in the wilderness, they had become oblivious to them within the course of their lifetimes. "A single generation, passed under the hard conditions of life in the wilderness," Roosevelt wrote, "was enough to weld [them] together into one people." And so, "long before the first Continental Congress assembled, the backwoodsmen, whatever their blood, had become Americans, one in speech, thought, and character." "Their iron surroundings," Roosevelt continued, "made a mould which turned out all alike in the same shape."[9] Here, for the first of many times, Roosevelt referred in a positive way to the melting-pot origins of the American people.

This assimilation was different from the sort undertaken by the conquering Teutons in Britain, for there the Teutons assimilated the Celts into their own culture. Roosevelt might have claimed that the American culture was essentially English or Anglo-Saxon; and, at times, he came close to labeling the backwoodsmen culture Scotch Irish.[10] But he pulled back from both claims, perhaps because either would have put him into the awkward position of having to admit that his own heritage—mixed but primarily Dutch—lay outside the core American culture. Instead he stressed the mixed, hybridized character of the American, unconsciously reiterating the perspective expressed 100 years earlier by J. Hector St. John de Crèvecoeur. "What then is the American, this new man?" Crèvecoeur had queried in a famous passage in his 1782 book,

Letters from an American Farmer. "He is either an European, or
the descendant of an European, hence that strange mixture of
blood, which you will find in no other country. I could point out
to you a family whose grandfather was an Englishman, whose wife
was Dutch, whose son married a French woman, and whose present four sons have now four wives of different nations."[11] This
statement precisely anticipated Roosevelt's view regarding the origins of the American people.

There was, however, one important similarity between the melting-pot character of assimilation in the United States and the Teu-
tonic-conformity assimilation that had occurred in Britain. Both
were controlled processes. The control in Britain lay in making sure
the Celts assimilated to a dominant Teutonic culture; the control
in America lay in limiting the American mix to European strains.
Both Crèvecoeur and Roosevelt only included in their American
brew races emanating from Europe. They excluded all nonwhite
races—not only Indians but Africans as well.[12]

Roosevelt did not worry much about the proper place of Indians
in the nation, for the savage wars with the Americans had culminated in their expulsion or extermination. But he was troubled by
the place and role of blacks. Roosevelt regarded the importation
of African slaves to the North American continent as a racial
and national catastrophe. The European races who conquered
America, Roosevelt intoned, "to their own lasting harm, committed a crime whose short-sighted folly was worse than its guilt, for
they brought hordes of African slaves, whose descendants now
form immense populations in certain portions of this land."[13]
These "hordes" could never be truly assimilated into American
society: the distance separating them from the white races was
simply too great. Nor could they play the role of the proud
savage foe against whom American warriors defined their race and
peoplehood, for the Africans were already a bowed and conquered
people when they arrived, forced to obey their masters' every
command. Regrettably, the black man could "neither be killed
nor driven away."[14] He had to be found a place in the nation.

But where? Giving blacks an equal place would violate the racial order of things, while hemming them into a subordinate status vitiated the American commitment to democracy and equal opportunity.

Roosevelt blamed this dilemma not on his heroic backwoodsmen but on the "trans-oceanic aristocracy" of the seventeenth and eighteenth centuries that had allegedly created and sustained the international slave trade.[15] The racial crime committed by these aristocrats had already triggered one national disaster—the Civil War—that almost destroyed the mighty nation that the backwoodsmen had so painstakingly and courageously built. And even emancipation, an act that Roosevelt supported, provided no simple cure to the race problem because Negroes, Roosevelt believed, would not take well to democracy, a form of government that depended on the kind of self-control and mastery that only the white races had attained.[16] As president, Roosevelt would struggle to devise what were, in his eyes, decent remedies to the race problem. But he would always regard the Negro as an indelible black mark on the white nation that had so gloriously emerged in the mid-eighteenth century, a constant reminder of America's racial imperfection, of an opportunity compromised by the nefarious dealings of corrupt, antidemocratic, and immoral aristocrats. There would never be, Roosevelt once conceded in private correspondence, a true solution to "the terrible problem offered by the presence of the negro on this continent."[17]

In his frettings about the Negro problem, Roosevelt admitted what is everywhere implicit in his racialist history of America: that democracy was a form of government appropriate only to the European or white races. This view appeared, too, in his occasional writings in the 1890s about Chinese immigrants. Roosevelt applauded the 1882 Chinese Exclusion Act (as well as similar legislation passed in Australia): "From the United States and Australia the Chinaman is kept out because the democracy, with much clearness of vision, has seen that his presence is ruinous to the white race." "Had these regions been under aristocratic governments,"

Roosevelt wrote, "Chinese immigration would have been encouraged precisely as the slave trade is encouraged by any slave-holding oligarchy, and the result in a few generations would have been even more fatal to the white race." Fortunately, "the democracy, with the clear instinct of race selfishness, saw the race foe, and kept out the dangerous alien" and thus preserved "for the white race the best portions of the new world's surface."[18]

In his probe of the process through which democracy had actually taken root in the "best portions of the world's surface," Roosevelt subscribed to some of the same views about the socially leveling and purifying effects of the frontier that Frederick Jackson Turner would soon popularize. The harsh wilderness, Roosevelt argued, stripped people of their Old World ranks and privileges. In the backwoods of Kentucky and in what would become Tennessee, conditions of rough equality prevailed. A sense of entitlement or privilege was worthless; a man could get only what he worked for. Self-reliance was perhaps the most important ingredient of success, but each man also depended on the labor of his family and the support of his neighbors. A democratic ethos emerged from this sense of mutual interdependence, an ethos that prompted the settled backwoodsmen to devise institutions of self-government that would bring security, justice, and equality to the wilderness.[19]

But Roosevelt, unlike Turner, refused to base his entire account on environmental factors. "It has often been said that we owe all our success to our surroundings; that any race with our opportunities could have done as well as we have done." This view, Roosevelt asserted, was demonstrably false. "The Spaniards, the Portuguese, and the French, not to speak of the Russians in Siberia, have all enjoyed, and yet have failed to make good use of, the same advantages which we have turned to good account." The Americans had made plenty of mistakes and missed more than their share of opportunities. But "we have done better than any other nation or race working under our conditions." For Roosevelt the explanation for the rise of democracy in the wilderness rested ultimately on the racial superiority of the English-speaking peoples.[20]

WAR, RENEWAL, AND THE PROBLEM OF THE "SMOKED YANKEE"

Roosevelt's *The Winning of the West* brims throughout with confident superiority. But, even as he was writing this treatise, Roosevelt was beset by worry that past achievements had set processes in motion that could yet ruin the American race. By the early 1890s, the wild frontier of the eighteenth century had vanished and the Indians had been routed. The conquest of the West and the invention of democracy had triggered industrial and cultural revolutions that were rapidly making America into an urban, industrialized society. While the backwoodsmen had set these changes in motion, their very success had forced them to the margins of American society. Roosevelt worried that America, as a result, would lose its racial edge. "A peaceful and commercial civilization is always in danger of suffering the loss of the virile fighting qualities without which no nation, however cultured, however refined, however thrifty and prosperous, can ever amount to anything."[21]

Everywhere, Roosevelt spotted signs of racial degeneration: in an overly refined elite that had abandoned "the strenuous life" for the effete manners and habits of European aristocrats; in a falling birthrate among this same elite, an unmistakable sign to Roosevelt that the vigor of this mighty race was slipping; in the impoverished urban masses whose loyalty to the nation was questionable and whose growing involvement in lawless strikes Roosevelt regarded as signs of barbarism; in a society so preoccupied with material gain and "ignoble ease" that it no longer knew how to pursue the heroic life. In short, the unique and racially superior civilization that the backwoodsmen had assiduously created was in danger of going the way of Rome: opulence, complacency, effeminacy, military collapse.[22]

Roosevelt conceived of his personal life as a crusade against the enervating effects of excessive civilization. He was determined to excel at hunting and ranching, as a way of developing in himself

the qualities that made the Scotch Irish backwoodsmen such a vigorous race. By fathering six children, Roosevelt provided not only
ample demonstration of his own virility but also an example that
other members of his race could emulate. He preached against the
complacent life, whether it took the form of the poor beggar content to live off charity or of the railroad tycoon obsessed with
money. He called incessantly for the pursuit of a "higher life" of
glory such as achieved by Washington, Lincoln, and Grant. Each
of these heroes had distinguished himself in war, and Roosevelt
believed that true eminence would elude him until he, too, had
proved his worth on the battlefield.[23]

Just as he expected his program for a strenuous life to bring him
personal greatness, so Roosevelt believed that an emphasis on muscular and racialized nationalism would reinvigorate America. By
the early 1890s he had cast his lot with Admiral Alfred Thayer
Mahan and other imperialists who argued that America should
contest Britain, France, Germany, Russia, and Japan for territory,
military might, and world power. Social Darwinist to the core,
these imperialists believed that America had to prove itself the military equal of the strongest European nation and the master of the
"lesser" peoples of Asia, Africa, and Latin America.[24] Hankering
for a fight, they strove to turn emergent power struggles in the
Caribbean and the Pacific into armed confrontations. Fights with
barbarian races abroad could replace the fight with the savage Indians at home and thus keep Americans racially fit. As Roosevelt
declared in 1897, "No triumph of peace is quite so great as the
supreme triumph of war."[25] The imperialists' opportunity came in
1898, when the explosion of the battleship Maine in Havana harbor set Spain and the United States on the path to war.

At the first opportunity, Roosevelt resigned as assistant secretary
of the navy to accept the lieutenant colonelcy of the First Volunteer
Cavalry, a regiment that would soon be immortalized as the
"Rough Riders." Many did not want him to leave his navy post
for active duty. Newspapers throughout the country called on him
to remain in Washington where, in only a year, he had substantially
improved the navy's battle readiness. President William McKinley

urged him to stay, as did his good friend Henry Cabot Lodge and his own ailing wife, Edith. But Roosevelt would not be swayed. True men, he believed, proved themselves on battlefields, not in bureaucracies.[26]

Receiving a commission in a volunteer unit was the perfect opportunity for Roosevelt, for it meant he would be able to surround himself not with regular soldiers, themselves the routinized product of a bureaucratic and regimented institution (the army), but with the very best of America's citizen warriors. More than 20,000 men applied for the 1,000 available places in the First Volunteer Cavalry, and Roosevelt filled a majority of places with cowboys, hunters, and prospectors of the West and Southwest, men who bore the closest resemblance to his fabled backwoodsmen. "They were a splendid set of men," Roosevelt would later exclaim, "tall and sinewy, with resolute, weather-beaten faces, and eyes that looked a man straight in the face without flinching." "In all the world," he added, "there could be no better material for soldiers than that afforded by these grim hunters of the mountains, these wild rough riders of the plains." Having come from lands that had been "most recently won over [from the savage Indians] to white civilization," these men were among the few remaining Americans who still possessed the ferocity, the independence, and the warlike skills of the Kentucky backwoodsmen.[27]

Just as the predominately Scotch Irish backwoodsmen of old had benefited from the mixture of their majority with minority streams from France, Germany, and elsewhere, so the quality of the Rough Riders was enhanced by the inclusion of complementary American strains. Most important were the fifty men, most of them athletes, who had come from Harvard, Princeton, and Yale and who possessed a refined sensibility and a capacity for leadership that many of the rowdy southwesterners lacked. Roosevelt chose an equal number of Indians, a few of pure blood but most a powerfully disciplined mixture of red and white. He selected a smattering of Irishmen and Hispanics, at least one Jew, one Italian, four New York City policemen, and a group "in whose veins . . . blood stirred with the same impulse which once sent the Vikings overseas." Like the frontier, the regiment created the conditions for a carefully regulated process of racial mixing, one meant to generate the finest possible American fighting force. Three cups of southwesterners, leavening tablespoons of Ivy Leaguers and Indians, and a sprinkling of Jews, Irish, Italians, and Scandinavians yielded, in Roosevelt's eyes, a sterling, all-American regiment.[28]

The inclusion of even limited numbers of Indians, Jews, and Italians made this regiment a more diverse group than the bands of backwoodsmen who had conquered the West had been, a sign, perhaps, that Roosevelt had become somewhat more liberal in his racial attitudes.[29] Yet, Roosevelt was not prepared to welcome every racial type into the Rough Rider crucible: he had neither sought nor accepted any black or Asian volunteers, demonstrating once again his conviction that the inclusion of the "most inferior" racial ingredients would pollute the American brew. The melting pot continued to depend for its success as much on exclusion as on inclusion.[30] And, of course, there were to be no women in this regiment. The welfare of the nation depended, as it always had, on fraternities of male warriors, ready to engage in savage warfare.

The Rough Riders quickly achieved a camaraderie that, in Roosevelt's eyes, justified his efforts to regulate the processes of racial mixing and male bonding. The Ivy Leaguers brought civility to a regiment full of rowdy spirits while the roughness and physicality of the southwesterners compelled the elite easterners to abandon their aversion to hard and "disagreeable" labor.[31] The regiment somewhat uneasily absorbed the few Irishmen, Italians, and Jews, giving them belittling (although affectionate) nicknames such as "Sheeny Solomon" and "Pork-chop."[32] The social equality that Roosevelt encouraged also shaped relations between officers and enlisted men. Roosevelt craved a close relationship with his troops. He got to know each of his 1,000 men by name, greeted them with waves rather than formal salutes and bought them beer after a long march. He took his sergeants to dinner at a restaurant reserved for the army's top brass and commandeered officers' rations for his enlisted men. Often reprimanded by his superiors for such transgressive fraternizing, Roosevelt was quick to offer the authorities the necessary apologies. But, in truth, his flouting the rules of military conduct was calculated. Here was a way for him to recreate a frontier-type environment, where social distinctions and rank counted for little. A man was judged for his ability as a man, and that was all.[33]

Getting his carefully groomed regiment to the front lines required all of Roosevelt's organizational abilities and Washington influence. The job of mobilizing for war quickly overwhelmed an American military that counted only 28,000 regular soldiers in its ranks. Every task of provisioning (horses, guns, bedding, food) and transportation—moving the troops by train from the San Antonio training grounds to Tampa's debarkation point and by ship from Tampa to Cuba—proved an ordeal. Any slipup along the way could mean the failure of the Rough Riders to get the tools of warfare or to reach the field of battle. Fortunately, the Rough Riders' commanding officer and Roosevelt's immediate superior, Colonel Leonard Wood, a consummate military insider, knew how to procure what the regiment needed. Still, the Rough Riders might have missed their appointment with destiny on San Juan Hill had not Roosevelt and his troops seized a transport ship that had been reserved for another regiment and thereby forced their way to the head of the troop convoy heading for Cuba. The Rough Riders, as a result, were among the first troops to disembark at Daiquiri and to begin marching toward the expected engagement with Spanish troops in the heavily fortified hills east of Santiago.[34]

The Spanish, as it turned out, were in no mood for a long war and gave up after only three weeks and four rather small battles. But the Rough Riders played important roles in three of the four conflagrations—Las Guasimas, Kettle Hill, and San Juan Hill— and came home military heroes. Roosevelt, by muscling his way to the front of the convoy that left Tampa in June, had literally willed his regiment to the battlefield and to glory.[35]

It had taken considerable propaganda work to turn the light-complexioned and highly cultured Spanish enemy into the dark and savage foe, but the American tabloids, led by the Hearst and Pulitzer papers, proved equal to the task. These newspapers fed

Fig. 1. "The Spanish Brute," 1898. Depicting the Spanish rulers in Cuba as a dark and savage race, illustrations such as these, appearing in American newspapers and magazines in 1898, helped to make the case for war. (From *Judge*, 1898)

American civilians and troops alike a steady diet of sensational stories about atrocities that the Spanish had committed against the freedom-loving Cubans. They focused on the sinister Catholicism of the Spanish as a way of explaining to their Protestant nation the autocratic and ruthless character of Spanish rule. Visually, the Spanish were often depicted in the simian form that Americans used to portray the races they most despised.[36]

The Rough Riders' first encounter with Spanish troops seemed to confirm the latter's savage racial nature. Expecting to meet the Spanish in a civilized engagement on an open field of battle, the Americans were ambushed in heavily forested terrain at Las Guasimas. The battle revealed that the Spanish army had adopted the guerrilla tactics favored by their Cuban adversaries, an intelligent adaptation of military technique to the Cuban terrain and foe that the Americans would come to respect. But initially it seemed to

Roosevelt and others steeped in frontier lore that they had encountered at Las Guasimas a savage enemy. Roosevelt's recounting of the battle could have been lifted from narratives he had already written about eighteenth-century Indian attacks in the Kentucky backwoods: "The Spaniards knew the trails by which we were advancing, and opened heavily on our position. Moreover, as we advanced, we were, of course, exposed, and they could see us and fire. But they themselves were entirely invisible. The jungle covered everything, and not the faintest trace of smoke was to be seen in any direction to indicate from whence the bullets came."[37] Fortunately the Rough Riders included many experienced Indian fighters in their ranks, and their expertise gave the whole outfit the skill and confidence to prevail. Roosevelt's troops advanced inch by inch through the dense vegetation, fighting fiercely, and ultimately forcing the Spanish to retreat.[38]

In this first battle, by Roosevelt's telling, the Rough Riders had shown the same pluck, resourcefulness, and courage as the Kentucky backwoodsmen. And just as the tough conditions of the American wilderness had welded together the frontiersmen, "whatever their blood," into one superior people, so too the rough encounter at Las Guasimas had been a mold that forged the motley Rough Riders into a truly American shape. Roosevelt took note of the melding process at a funeral service held the morning after the battle at the common grave in which the seven Rough Riders who had died at Las Guasimas were buried: "There could be no more honorable burial than that of these men in a common grave— Indian and cow-boy, miner, packer, and college athlete—the man of unknown ancestry from the lonely Western plains, and the man who carried on his watch the crest of the Stuyvesants and the Fishes, one in the way they had met death, just as during life they had been one in their daring and their loyalty."[39]

Las Guasimas was only a prelude to the furious battles at Kettle and San Juan Hills, the high and heavily fortified ridges that guarded the approach to Santiago. The Rough Riders had been assigned a support role behind several regiments of regular troops, but as the casualties mounted and as communications between the generals in the rear and the front lines broke down, Roosevelt moved his Rough Riders into the thick of the action. Roosevelt demonstrated extraordinary heroism and recklessness. He inspired a wild charge up Kettle Hill that overran Spanish defenses. He then organized the fragments of several regiments that had made it to the top into a reserve force that provided critical support to the regulars who were assaulting the adjacent San Juan Hill. Roosevelt spent much of the battle on horseback, riding among his troops, urging them up the hill, disregarding danger and death. His daring and impulsiveness resembled those of General George Custer, but Kettle and San Juan Hills were to be the sites of no last stands. Sheets of bullets rained down upon the American troops, and shells exploded everywhere. All around Roosevelt saw men being killed and wounded or collapsing from exhaustion. By the time the fighting had ended, 90 of the 450 Rough Riders who had entered the battle lay killed or wounded. Many more would later succumb to illness arising from their exhaustion. One bullet grazed Roosevelt's wrist but none wounded him. Virtually alone among the officers and men, he escaped sickness. In this climactic battle that Roosevelt had long wished for, he seemed as immortal as a Greek god, especially to the awestruck journalists who were reporting this fight to the millions of avid newspaper readers back home. "Mounted high on horseback, and charging the rifle-pits at a gallop and quite alone," rhapsodized Richard Harding Davis, the famed *New York Herald* and *Scribner's* reporter, Roosevelt "made you feel that you would like to cheer."[40]

In the Cuban campaign, Roosevelt brought to life the mythic past that he had invented for the American people in *The Winning of the West*. In the climactic Kettle Hill–San Juan Hill battles that symbolized the triumph of America over savagery and the forging of the many streams of humanity into one American people, Roosevelt himself played the starring role. But there was a problem. Just as the arrival of the black man on the North American continent had compromised the great white nation that was taking shape there, so, too, the presence of black U.S. troops on Kettle Hill and

Fig. 2. Theodore Roosevelt and His Rough Riders, 1898. Roosevelt poses with his Rough Riders on a hill overlooking Santiago, Cuba, after their victories at Kettle and San Juan Hills. (Courtesy Library of Congress)

San Juan Hill interfered with the nation's triumph—or at least with Roosevelt's enjoyment of that triumph.

Roosevelt had been able to keep blacks out of the Rough Riders, but he could not keep them out of Cuba. Four regular regiments, a substantial percentage of the U.S. army, were all black (although commanded by white officers), and they were among the most experienced and reliable American troops.[41] For years they had been stationed west of the Mississippi, where they had become skilled at Indian warfare. When the United States declared war on Spain, the U.S. military rushed the black troops to Tampa and then to Cuba, raising tensions along the way between the black soldiers

Fig. 3. The Ninth or Tenth Cavalry, Cuba, 1898. These soldiers played a key role in the taking of Kettle and San Juan Hills, a contribution acknowledged by Roosevelt and other white soldiers at the time but later denied. (Courtesy National Archives)

and whites who watched the troop trains pass through southern train depots. The Ninth and Tenth Cavalry Regiments played an important role at Las Guasimas and an even more vital role in the taking of Kettle Hill and San Juan Hill. The Tenth Cavalry had been the front-line troops on Kettle Hill and, in the process, lost more of its officers (eleven of twenty-two) than any other regiment. When Roosevelt had called for a charge up the hill, they had eagerly joined in. Meanwhile, several platoons of the Negro Ninth Cavalry had reached the summit of Kettle Hill from a different direction at the same moment as had Roosevelt. Black troops from both regiments and, even more important, from the Twenty-fourth Infantry Division, fought hard for San Juan Hill as well.[42]

When Roosevelt reached the top of San Juan Hill he found himself the effective commander of the Rough Riders, the Ninth and Tenth Negro Cavalries, and three other cavalry regiments. The chaos of battle had mischievously produced a true American melt-ing pot—the heterogeneity of the Rough Riders itself further diver-sified by the presence of both white and black regulars—and the pot had worked its magic, as all these diverse troops had fought as a single, cohesive unit. White regulars, the heavily southwestern Rough Riders, the journalists, and even Roosevelt himself all heaped praise on the black soldiers, who returned to America as heroes. The Tenth Cavalry participated in a parade down Washing-ton's Pennsylvania Avenue and received President McKinley's sa-lute. When Roosevelt bid farewell to the Rough Riders in October, he toasted the black soldiers: "The Spaniards called them 'Smoked Yankees,' " he said, "but we found them to be an excellent breed of Yankees. I am sure that I speak the sentiments of officers and men in the assemblage when I say that between you and the other cavalry regiments there exists a tie which we trust will never be broken." The Rough Riders, reported a black soldier of the Tenth Cavalry, roared their approval.[43]

Roosevelt certainly spoke for Lieutenant John J. Pershing, then an officer of the Tenth Cavalry: "White regiments, black regi-ments, regulars and Rough Riders, representing the young man-hood of the North and South, fought shoulder to shoulder, un-mindful of race or color, unmindful of whether commanded by an ex-Confederate or not, and mindful only of their common duty as Americans."[44]

Roosevelt might have seized on evidence of intermixing of black and white troops to celebrate the melting pot as a mechanism that could fashion a single nation out of all the different racial, ethnic, and regional groups who resided in America. But Roosevelt was never entirely comfortable with the way in which blacks had fought alongside whites in the critical battles on Kettle and San Juan Hills. In fact, he was alarmed by the mixing, by "the different regi-ments being *completely intermingled* [emphasis added]—white reg-ulars, colored regulars, and Rough Riders."[45] He believed that complete and unregulated mixing, as had occurred in Mexico and other Latin countries, produced mediocre races. The indiscriminate interpenetration of black and white troops in the heat of battle, moreover, threatened to explode his mythic view of the regulated assimilatory process that produced racially superior Americans and to disrupt the reenactment of that process that Roosevelt had so carefully orchestrated. The black troops had to be put in their place—a place separate from, and subordinate to, the one occupied by white Americans.[46]

Roosevelt took on this task when he began publishing his history of the Rough Riders in *Scribner's* magazine in 1899. In recounting the heroic seizure of San Juan Hill, Roosevelt interrupted his triumphalist narrative to criticize the shortcomings of the Negro troops. Although these troops were excellent fighters, "they were peculiarly dependent on their white officers."[47] Left on their own—as many had been by the time they arrived on the summit of San Juan, given the high casualty rate among the officers of the Ninth and Tenth—they faltered, even ran. Roosevelt recalled an incident in which he had had to draw his revolver on black troops who seemed to be leaving their positions without permission. Only after he had threatened to shoot them did they return to the forward lines.[48]

Presley Holliday, a black soldier of the Tenth Cavalry, remembered this incident differently. He described a chaotic situation as night was falling on San Juan Hill and recalled many requests for soldiers to carry the wounded to the rear and to procure rations and trenching tools for the troops at the summit. Both Rough Riders and black soldiers responded to these calls, which created the impression of many soldiers leaving the battle scene. This is what Roosevelt apparently saw when he drew his revolver and aimed it at the black troops. But, according to Holliday, Lieutenant Fleming of the Tenth (a white officer) quickly reassured Roosevelt that the black soldiers had been following orders. The next day, Roosevelt even visited members of the Tenth Cavalry and apologized to them.[49]

It is, of course, difficult to know exactly what went on at dusk, when all the soldiers, including Roosevelt himself, were exhausted from the fight and may have had difficulty seeing and thinking clearly. Perhaps some black troops had been too quick to leave the still insecure summit for the safety of the rear when the opportunity arose. Holliday, himself, admitted that some of the Tenth Cavalry's newer recruits became nervous at being separated from the bulk of their regiment and at being in such close proximity to white soldiers.[50] But even if this nervousness prompted them to look for opportunities to leave the summit, it was not, in itself, adequate reason for Roosevelt to challenge the worth of the black fighting man. There had been many instances in Cuba of white soldierly cowardice and of blacks proving themselves to be the more stalwart and reliable troops. Indeed, the colored Twenty-fourth Infantry had been called upon to charge San Juan Hill—and did—only after the white Seventy-first New York had panicked and refused to attack.[51] Roosevelt ignored this and other incidents of white cowardice and black valor, determined as he was to charge that only black troops lacked the self-reliance and hardy individualism to become their own men, to become true Americans. In that dark, chaotic, and confusing moment on San Juan Hill, Roosevelt was certain that he had "uncovered" incontrovertible evidence of the black soldiers' "peculiar dependence" on white officers. The Rough Riders, in Roosevelt's eyes, had shown themselves to be the Kentucky backwoodsmen's equal in every respect, whereas the black cavalrymen troops had demonstrated once again what Roosevelt had "always known": that blacks were not truly fit for combat, that they lacked the necessary qualities to participate as equals in the great nation that Daniel Boone and his fellow frontiersmen had willed into existence in the eighteenth century.

These were devastating charges in 1899, especially when leveled by a person of Roosevelt's stature. Emboldened by the 1896 Supreme Court decision in *Plessy v. Ferguson*, the South was disfranchising blacks and excluding them from institutions that had been designated white—schools, restaurants, stores, parks, and many places of employment. In the North, whites were pushing blacks out of the skilled trades and a wide range of service jobs that had long supported a small but vibrant black middle class.[52] The Spanish-American War took on special significance in this context, for it gave blacks an opportunity to demonstrate their loyalty to America and to demand an end to discriminatory treatment. African Americans hoped that their impressive record of service would compel the U.S. military to open officer ranks to them, and that the achievement of this status could then become a powerful symbol of their quest for equality, integration, and belonging.[53] How could a nation permit officers of its own army to be denied the right to vote, to sit on juries, or to use public accommodations? Most whites, Roosevelt among them, evidently agreed that the nation could not tolerate this blatant contradiction. They sought to resolve it, however, not by tearing down racial barriers but rather by reinforcing and justifying the ones already in place. Just as most blacks could not successfully discharge the responsibilities of citizenship, so, too, Roosevelt and others argued, they could not be entrusted with leading troops into battle. The black demand for officer status was rebuffed. In this climate of racial separation and discrimination, it did not take long for whites to challenge the fighting abilities of black soldiers, even when they were commanded by white officers. By the First World War, few blacks were even permitted to represent America in combat. The nation had stripped virtually all blacks of the right to fight and die for their country. The sacrifices and heroism of the Ninth and Tenth Cavalries had become but a dim memory to whites.[54] White southerners, meanwhile, were reintegrating themselves into the military. As a result of the Spanish-American War, efforts to recreate America as a white nation had borne fruit.[55]

The centrality of race to the definition of Roosevelt's America was apparent, too, in the treatment of the Cubans and Filipinos, ostensible American allies in the fight against the Spaniards. Finding a savage foe in the Spanish-American War proved a more difficult task than Roosevelt and others had anticipated. Despite their "savage" behavior at Las Guasimas, the Spanish soldiers soon revealed that they were far whiter and more civilized than the Americans had expected. Meanwhile, U.S. troops were unnerved by their encounters with Cuban troops. The latter were often poorly dressed, inadequately provisioned, and lacking in regimental discipline. American soldiers were particularly upset by the Cuban practice of stripping corpses—friend and foe alike—of clothing, food, guns, and any other usable items, and of their annoying penchant

Fig. 4. Artist's Rendition of the Great Charge. The heroic role of black soldiers in the taking of San Juan Hill not only disappeared from Roosevelt's own account of the war in Cuba but from paintings such as this one and other commemorations of the great charge. (Courtesy the Granger Collection, New York)

for begging. And they were stunned that Cuban troops were overwhelmingly dark in complexion. The U.S. troops knew little about the long Cuban struggle for independence, of the hardships they had had to endure, and of why they had chosen guerrilla tactics against the Spanish. Americans, influenced by the Hearst and Pulitzer newspapers, had imagined that Cubans were a people much like themselves—freedom-loving, civilized, and white. Hence, they were shocked to discover that the Cubans exhibited traits they could define as primitive and undignified. The black Cubans, not the Spanish, were the island's true savages.[56]

The Cubans never became the savage foe against whom the Americans were compelled to fight a war of extermination; that honor went to the Filipinos.[57] The Cubans instead became the childlike ally in need of American mentoring, assistance, and protection. On these grounds, the United States justified its refusal to grant the Cubans the full political independence they so desperately sought. Instead it made the island into a virtual colony, taking on the "white man's burden" of uplifting one of the world's darker and more savage races. In such ways the Spanish-American War reinforced Americans' sense of themselves as a white and superior people.[58]

Roosevelt would always regard his fight on Kettle and San Juan Hills as his finest hour. The war had elevated America to world-power status, bringing the country influence or direct control over Cuba, Puerto Rico, Hawaii, and the Philippines. America's soldiers had shown that the nation could still produce the hardy, fierce, and self-reliant men who had willed the country into existence a hundred years before. Roosevelt had demonstrated the kind of courage and leadership that he had so admired in such leaders as Washington and Grant. It did not seem to matter to him or to most others that America's success had come against a feeble foe with a disintegrating empire that had given up the fight almost as soon as the serious combat had begun. An impressively large cross section of Americans gloried in the achievements of their male warriors, seeing in them not simply evidence of individual virtue but also of a national reconciliation and rebirth. Southerners had fought alongside northerners, poor cowboys alongside rich Ivy Leaguers, Jews and Catholics alongside Protestants. The traumatic class, sectional, and ethnic antagonisms of the 1890s seemed to vanish, at least momentarily, as white Americans of all kinds pulled together for a common cause. The enthusiasm for war even penetrated isolated communities of immigrant Catholics and Jews who had carefully guarded the cultural and political gulf separating them from the American mainstream.[59]

Roosevelt came back from the war, in the words of one biographer, "the most famous man in America."[60] The Rough Riders, aided by Roosevelt's efforts to fashion and publicize their deeds, indelibly stamped themselves onto American memory. Their exploits were celebrated in print, on stage, and in the Buffalo Bill show, one of the most popular entertainments of its day.[61] Their achievement lay not simply in the heroism they had shown on Kettle Hill and San Juan Hill. It lay also in demonstrating that the frontiersmen had survived the passing of the frontier and could still be called on to serve the nation. Their service extended beyond battle; it entailed as well creating a milieu—in this case, the Rough Rider regiment—in which Americans from the densely populated and industrial East could escape the excessive gentility, effeminacy, and regimentation of civilization and make themselves over into the hardiest of Kentucky backwoodsmen.

The number of easterners actually involved in this makeover was, of course, minute. But the Rough Rider experience worked its transformative magic on far larger numbers as myth, for all kinds of Americans could now imagine becoming Rough Riders themselves and charging up a hill to obliterate a savage foe. The Rough Rider narrative, so carefully scripted by Roosevelt, drew its power from stories of frontiersmen-Indian encounters already embedded in the American psyche. The narrative, in turn, gave those old stories—which would come to be known as "Westerns"—new and much-needed authority as America rushed headlong into its urban, industrial age. All kinds of Euro-American males, even those of foreign birth or immigrant parentage who had never come within miles of a cowboy, would quicken their process of becoming American by imagining themselves as Daniel Boone and Davy Crockett, Geronimo and Cochise, Teddy Roosevelt and Rough Rider hero Bucky O'Neil.

Through his creation of the Rough Riders, Roosevelt did more than assure the survival of the frontier myth. He also fashioned a new myth about the making of America and Americans that did not depend on the frontier at all. This was the notion of the army regiment, especially one under fire, as a crucible, as a mechanism that would bring together Americans from different regions, ethnicities, classes, and religions and mold them into one shape. That the hardships and dislocations of war spurred assimilation was not itself a new idea. In *The Winning of the West*, Roosevelt had argued that this process had forged the superior English and American races. But this older process was one that had unfolded in frontier-type conditions where the conquerors could easily dominate the sparsely inhabited civilian areas that had fallen under their control. The notion of an army regiment as an engine of assimilation unto itself was something different, for this engine did not depend for its success on the frontier or on the conquest of dispersed populations. The control over assimilation that a frontier-like environment had given the conquerors of old was now vested in a military chain of command with the power to bend and shape a regiment to its specifications, much as Roosevelt had molded the Rough Riders. This regiment, if thrown into battle, could accomplish its assimilatory work anywhere—in cities as well as the frontier, in civilized as well as primitive societies, at sea as well as on land.

Over the course of the next fifty years, two more wars, and the conscription of 20 million Americans into the armed forces, this myth of the assimilatory regiment would be reworked and refined until it became the story of the heroic and multiethnic platoon. As the nation that Roosevelt had helped to fashion reached the peak of its power and authority in the 1940s and 1950s, no narrative of nation building was more important than that of how platoons of ethnically, religiously, and sectionally diverse American men had sacrificed their lives for each other, fought valiantly against the enemy, and made their nation the most powerful and wonderful society on earth. Roosevelt had been one of the creators of this myth, and it offered crucial sustenance to a nation that had strayed far from its mythic frontier roots.

The success of the male warrior regiment or platoon as an assimilatory institution depended a great deal on the control that its leaders were able to exercise over its composition and behavior. On this point, Roosevelt had been unvaryingly consistent. Controlled assimilation was, to Roosevelt's way of thinking, the one kind of assimilation that worked. Only certain kinds of racial combinations produced superior hybrids; thus, the ingredients of any melting pot had to be carefully chosen. Moreover, the circumstances of their melding had to be regulated, either naturally through the action of the environment, or socially through military organization or political leadership—hence the appeal of a regiment as a mechanism of assimilation, for it drew on military hierarchy and its regulatory power.

This thirst for control revealed Roosevelt's conviction that the nation could only succeed as a carefully ordered and disciplined entity. It expressed as well his abhorrence of anarchy, which he defined as untrammeled liberty. Anarchy came in many forms: in indiscriminate racial mixing of the sort that had produced mediocre races in Latin America and that had caused a dangerous moment of vulnerability on San Juan Hill; in a laissez-faire economy where each buyer and seller ruthlessly pursued his or her own self-interest without regard to the commonweal; in married women making decisions about their future independently of their husbands; in labor strikes that disrupted normal patterns of production and distribution and sometimes degenerated into mob violence; and, of course, in the revolutionary activities of self-professed anarchists who wished to strike down all institutions of centralized authority—corporations, governments, armies, even nations. Roosevelt conceived of himself, and his nationalism, as anarchy's enemy.

This did not make him a reactionary. To the contrary, his celebration of controlled hybridity and of a marketplace regulated for the commonweal made him, in the early years of the twentieth century, a leading progressive. But it did impel him to distrust popular movements of all sorts (except those that he himself led) and to emphasize order, hierarchy, and control as integral features of politics and nation building.

No aspect of national order mattered more to him than that of race. America's destiny lay in sustaining the finest English-speaking race the world had even known. Sustenance depended on melting together Americans and members of other European races, preferably in circumstances of war. Sustenance involved, too, proscribing the intermingling of the white and nonwhite races. America's future as a nation depended, in other words, on a complex blend of racial hybridity and purity, of racial inclusion and exclusion. In such ways would race define Roosevelt's nation.

CHAPTER 2

Civic Nationalism and

Its Contradictions,

1890–1917

It is tempting to interpret Roosevelt's nationalism as simply an American expression of what European scholars label "ethnic," or "romantic," nationalism, one that locates the essence of the nation in the *Volk*, defined as a people who share the same blood, history, language, and land. The *Volk*, in the eyes of racial and ethnic nationalists, did not change much, if at all, over time. Indeed it was thought to be an entity standing outside history, a force of moral and biological purity that could eradicate the alleged evils of modernity: corruption, materialism, promiscuity, and racial mixing.[1]

Many individuals and groups in the United States subscribed to such racially charged nationalist notions, the Ku Klux Klan being the best-known and most successful example.[2] But Roosevelt was not among them. The notion that European peoples represented pure biological entities made no sense to him, for he keenly understood that war and conquest had made Europeans far more hybridized a people than most cared to admit. Roosevelt celebrated hybridity: the world's greatest peoples, after all—the British, the Americans, the Australians—had emerged from melting pots. Even prior to the American Revolution, Roosevelt had once written, "we were then already, what we are now, a people of mixed blood."[3] The smelting, Roosevelt believed, had to be controlled by a skilled puddler if it were to produce the best and most efficient result; but if this requirement were met, then racial mixing would always produce peoples superior to those that had remained pure. In his celebration of hybridity, Roosevelt was very much a modern and deeply at odds with members of his gentry class, such as Henry Cabot Lodge, Henry Adams, and Frederic Remington, who longed for a pure, Anglo-Saxon, America. Nowhere in Roosevelt's voluminous writings, in neither his published work nor his private letters, is it possible to find the kind of indiscriminate revulsion against "outsiders" expressed in this passage from a Remington letter: "Jews, Injuns, Chinamen, Italians, Huns—the rubbish of the earth I hate—I've got some Winchesters and when the massacring begins, I can get my share of 'em, and what's more I will."[4]

Roosevelt instead was a kind of civic nationalist, someone who imagined the nation, to use Michael Ignatieff's words, "as a community of equal, rights-bearing citizens united in patriotic attachment to a shared set of political practices and values."[5] Such a national community was open, in theory at least, to all those who resided in a nation's territory, irrespective of their ethnicity, race, or religion. It was democratic, for it vested "sovereignty in all of the people."[6] In practice, Roosevelt's national community was open to anyone who could claim European origins or ancestry. Roosevelt paid little attention to whether these Europeans had come from eastern or western Europe, from Catholic, Protestant, or Jewish backgrounds, or from the ranks of the rich or the poor; to all he extended the invitation to become American. He assumed a quite different posture toward blacks, Asians, and other nonwhites. He did not attempt to exclude them from the political community as thoroughly as he had excluded them from his nationalist mythology. In fact, on numerous occasions he passionately defended the political rights and aspirations of African Americans and Asians who, to his thinking, had achieved a requisite level of intellectual and moral competence. But he also believed that the vast majority of nonwhites would not achieve those levels during his lifetime or for several lifetimes thereafter.

Although racism compromised Roosevelt's civic nationalism, it would be a mistake to dismiss the sincerity of his civic declarations. He felt his civic nationalism, or what he called "true Americanism," deeply, and it allowed him to welcome into American society "lowly" and "racially inferior" European immigrants whom most people of his class and cultural background despised. It is easy to belittle the progressive character of Roosevelt's inclusionary attitudes toward European immigrants, now that anti-Catholicism and anti-Semitism have largely vanished as significant American ideologies and all Euro-Americans are thought to belong to the same white race. But Roosevelt's embrace of Catholic and Jewish Europeans was not popular among many native-born Protestant Americans of his time. In fact, the arrival of so many of them, especially from "primitive" regions in eastern and southern Europe, generated hysteria among large numbers of native-born Protestants. Many of these immigrants, in turn, responded to Roosevelt's warmth with appreciation, enthusiasm, and votes. His civic nationalism also gave nonwhite Americans something to work with, for its democratic and egalitarian ethos allowed them to believe that they could yet find a way to gain full citizenship rights and thus to include themselves in the great national experiment. The American creed of a Gunnar Myrdal and the integrationist dream of a Martin Luther King Jr. sprang from the same taproot of civic nationalism that Theodore Roosevelt espoused in the early years of this century.

"TRUE AMERICANISM"

Roosevelt's civic nationalism emerged in the course of thinking through how America should respond to the millions of European immigrants entering American society in the late nineteenth and early twentieth centuries. He began articulating his views in response to nativists who, in the 1890s, were clamoring for immigration restriction and discriminatory treatment of immigrant Catholics and Jews.[7] "It is a base outrage," Roosevelt declared in 1894, "to oppose a man because of his religion or birthplace. . . . A Scandinavian, a German, or an Irishman who has really become an American has the right to stand on exactly the same footing as any native-born citizen in the land, and is just as much entitled to the friendship and support, social and political, of his neighbors."[8] On another occasion, he extended the same support specifically to Jews: "I should . . . have been ashamed to discriminate against a good man just because he was a Jew."[9] He took pride in his cabinet, the first in American history in which "Catholic and Protestant and Jew sat side by side." "I would have broken the neck of any one of them," he declared, "if I had found he was acting toward any American citizen in an un-American manner. . . . But I would have stood by him to the last if he himself had been attacked because of his creed or because of his national origin; and this I would have done as regards every man in this Republic whether he was Protestant or Catholic or Jew, whether he was of English or Irish, French or German origin."[10]

Roosevelt's civic nationalism was rooted both in his Republicanism and in his love of the cosmopolitan city in which he had grown up. Since the 1860s, the Republican Party cast itself as the foe of discrimination and favoritism. In 1866, party radicals had pushed through Congress the Fourteenth Amendment, meant to protect

U.S. citizens from racial and other forms of discrimination. Shortly thereafter, the party staked its reputation on civil service reform. From the earliest days of his political career, Roosevelt had wanted to purge government of favoritism, cronyism, and corruption and to insure that government appointments would be reserved for the best qualified. That meant adopting civil service procedures that relied on impartial merit tests rather than on ties of party, friendship, or nationality. As civil service commissioner from 1889 to 1895, Roosevelt had significantly increased the number of federal jobs governed by civil service regulations. As police commissioner in New York City from 1895 to 1897, he appointed numerous Irish, German, Jewish, Scandinavian, Italian, and Slavic cops, making the police force "a body thoroughly representative of the great city itself."[11] As president, he would use the same principles to appoint large numbers of Jews, Catholics, and African Americans to federal posts.[12]

For Roosevelt, this commitment to merit uncompromised by prejudice or cronyism was more than a matter of abstract principle; it reflected, too, what he had learned as a denizen of what he called "huge, polyglot, pleasure-loving" New York, where people from all walks of life had found a way to live together.[13] Roosevelt valued what he saw as New Yorkers' inclination to put aside their prejudices, and he believed that city leaders ought to encourage this broad-mindedness. To be sure, Roosevelt's early encounters with Tammany Hall had left him with suspicions about Irish politicians and a lifelong enmity toward the Democratic Party. But this coolness hardly affected his eagerness to mix with New Yorkers of all sorts. He was proud to call himself a friend of Otto Raphael, a Jewish policeman, who, like Roosevelt, was " 'straight New York.' "[14] As police commissioner, Roosevelt became famous for his midnight strolls with the photojournalist Jacob Riis (himself an immigrant), ostensibly to catch deadbeat cops who were asleep on the job or otherwise neglectful of their duties. But Roosevelt loved just as much the exposure these excursions gave him to the hidden communities and activities of New York City life. "These midnight rambles are great fun," he once wrote. "My whole work brings me in contact with every class of people in New York. . . . I get a glimpse of the real life of the swarming millions."[15]

There was a voyeuristic element to this, just as there had been in Riis's sensationalist exposé, *How the Other Half Lives*.[16] But there was also a strong desire to break down barriers that had separated New Yorkers from each other and to prod all citizens of the "great city" to cross neighborhood and ethnic boundaries. One Sunday in the summer of 1895, 30,000 New Yorkers, many of them German Americans, staged a giant parade to protest Roosevelt's enforcement of the New York State law forbidding the sale of alcohol on Sundays. Roosevelt was not terribly concerned with Sunday drinking—temperance was not one of his crusades—but he felt that he, as police commissioner, could not condone the extensive bribing of policemen by saloonkeepers intent on opening their doors. His stance angered New York's German Americans, for whom a "continental Sunday" was a time honored tradition, and their fury mounted as, week after week, the saloons stayed closed. They imbued their mammoth parade with a light spirit, full of satire and mirth, as befitted a group that would have preferred to be drinking rather than protesting. The parade organizers even sent Roosevelt a mock invitation to attend. But the 30,000 who mobilized for the parade were deadly serious about their desire to punish Roosevelt and his allies for their hard-line policy.[17]

To everyone's surprise, Roosevelt accepted the "invitation" to attend the parade. Arriving at the event, he immediately claimed for himself a choice spot on the reviewing stand and then behaved as though the entire parade had been organized in his honor. He waved to the marchers and applauded the floats and costumed marchers who passed by. When one incredulous and nearsighted marcher shouted "Wo ist der Roosevelt?" Roosevelt gleefully exclaimed, "Hier bin ich!" Everyone within earshot broke into laughter. Roosevelt had won the crowd to his side.[18]

This was a man who reveled in his contacts with the many different nationalities of New York. He viewed New York as yet another melting pot, performing the same kind of assimilative work that his regiment would soon accomplish on San Juan Hill. And, as his presence on the reviewing stand suggests, Roosevelt wanted to be the skilled puddler who stirred and regulated the pot's mixture of people, imparting to it an unambiguously American character.

Some scholars have argued that Roosevelt's openness to immigrants extended only to the so-called old immigrants from Great Britain, Germany, and Scandinavia who were thought by many to belong to superior and easily assimilable races. The new immigrants from eastern and southern Europe, in this view, received no welcome at all, for they were considered to lack the racial makeup necessary to succeed in America.[19] Some evidence supports this view. When Roosevelt talked about the diverse immigrants who were becoming American, he usually drew his examples from the ranks of the old immigrants—Irish, German, and Scandinavian. He wrote little about Italians, Poles, Slovaks, and others who composed the new immigration. And the one apparent exception to that pattern—Jews—may not have been an exception at all, for most of the Jews he held up as exemplary Americans were immigrants (or the children of immigrants) from Germany.

But other evidence does not support this interpretation of Roosevelt's beliefs and inclinations. Consider, for example, his enthusiastic embrace of Israel Zangwill's play, *The Melting Pot*, when it opened on Broadway in 1908.[20] The play's protagonist, David Quixano, belongs to a Russian Jewish family that can only be described as new immigrant. David's mother, father, and sisters had been slain during the 1903 Kishinev pogrom. David flees to New York, where he is taken in by his uncle, Mendel Quixano, who is depicted by Zangwill as the stereotypical eastern European Jewish immigrant, "wearing a black skull-cap, a seedy velvet jacket."[21] Mendel lives with his mother, Frau Quixano, a forlorn soul who speaks only Yiddish and for whom America is a graveyard for her religion and culture. Mendel and David, both talented musicians, desire to escape the provincialism and tragedy that envelop Frau Quixano. While Mendel is a bit too old and too tied to his mother to succeed in this quest, David possesses the necessary talent, drive, and independence. He seizes the opportunity that America gives him, writes his American symphony, marries the Gentile girl of his dreams, and becomes a proud American.[22]

Roosevelt, of course, endorsed Zangwill's depiction of America as a land of unlimited opportunity. But, even more important, he applauded Zangwill's insistence that even immigrants like David, whose origins lay in the allegedly inferior races of eastern Europe, could become the most successful and best of Americans. It mattered, too, that David succeeds in America not by maintaining his Jewish heritage but by assimilating into American culture. The words that Zangwill puts in David's mouth could have come from Roosevelt's own pen: "America is God's Crucible, the great Melting-Pot where all the races of Europe are melting and reforming! . . . Germans and Frenchmen, Irishmen and Englishmen, Jews and Russians—into the Crucible with you all! God is making the American."[23] No wonder Roosevelt wrote Zangwill, "I do not know when I have seen a play that stirred me as much."[24]

An even more impressive demonstration of Roosevelt's comfort with the new immigrants occurred in 1913, in the midst of a strike by women garment workers in New York City. Roosevelt traveled to Henry Street and St. Mark's Place to witness the strike firsthand and to interview the strikers about their grievances and ambitions. On Henry Street he encountered young women who would have been described by some observers as the most pathetic examples of the new immigration: They were the "lowest and poorest paid workers that we saw," Roosevelt noted.[25] Their racial background was equally "base," for many were Turkish Jews who could not even speak Yiddish, let alone English. They were thus cut off not only from American culture but also from the comparatively mainstream Yiddish-speaking Jewish community and labor movement in New York City.

It would have been easy for Roosevelt to find fault with these women and to deplore an immigration policy that had let them in. A Henry Cabot Lodge or Madison Grant would likely have responded to a close encounter with these Turkish Jewish women with horror rather than empathy, with demands for their deportation or

Fig. 5. Theodore Roosevelt Visits a Brooklyn Garment Shop, 1915. Roosevelt demonstrates his concern with the conditions under which immigrant women workers labored. (Courtesy Library of Congress)

exclusion rather than for their protection. But this was not Roosevelt's reaction. He was moved by their plight, feeling "deep sympathy for them personally." Moreover, Roosevelt noted, "there is the
larger question of the social good of the whole race." We must take
care of them, he argued, for they represent the "mothers of . . . *our*

American citizenship for the next generation [emphasis added]."
One can discern in Roosevelt's reaction a Victorian paternalism that
stressed the need to save these poor damsels from their distress (although his preferred remedy, unionization of the women, was not
paternalist at all). Such a judgment, however, too readily ignores
Roosevelt's unambiguous invitation to these women to become part
of the American nation. In going out among these poor Turkish
Jewish women, mixing easily with them ("gather around me and
tell your stories," he implored at one point), and treating them as
the mothers of future Americans, Roosevelt was showing the same
solicitude to and ease with a group of new immigrants as he had to
the old immigrant Germans who had staged the saloon-closing parade nearly twenty years earlier.[26]

There was, of course, a catch to Roosevelt's solicitude: the diverse streams of European humanity flowing into New York had
to Americanize. "We must Americanize them in every way, in
speech, in political ideas and principles, and in their way of looking
at the relations between Church and State."[27] Roosevelt did not
mince words: The immigrant "must not bring in his Old-World
religious[,] race[,] and national antipathies, but must merge them
into love for our common country, and must take pride in the
things which we can all take pride in. He must revere our flag; not
only must it come first, but no other flag should ever come second.
He must learn to celebrate Washington's birthday rather than that
of the Queen or Kaiser, and the Fourth of July instead of St. Patrick's Day. . . . Above all, the immigrant must learn to talk and
think and be United States."[28]

These were tough statements, for they denied the Americanizing
immigrant the right to maintain even a nostalgic affection for his
or her homeland. Why couldn't an Irish immigrant continue to
celebrate St. Patrick's Day while becoming a true American? True
love of country, Roosevelt answered, was a powerful and jealous
emotion, "an elemental virtue, like love of home, or like honesty
or courage," that could not be compromised without severely damaging a man's character. Then this Victorian man hurled what
he regarded as his most devastating criticism: "A man who loves

another country as much as he does his own is quite as noxious a member of society as the man who loves other women as much as he loves his wife."[29]

In singling out for criticism those who claimed to love more than one country, Roosevelt was targeting not only immigrants but also native-born Americans, many from Roosevelt's own class, who had become Europeanized, seeking a kind of refinement, social status, and culture unavailable to them in America. Roosevelt loathed these would-be aristocrats and sought to expose the effeminacy that, he argued, lay at the root of their behavior: they were "undersized," unable to "play a man's part among men," possessing "that flaccid habit of mind which its possessors style cosmopolitanism."[30] Effeminacy was a kind of treason, for it meant that a man had betrayed his true nature, an act as contemptible and dangerous as that of a citizen who betrayed his country.[31] Aristocrats, cosmopolitans, and immigrants who loved two nations were all traitors to Roosevelt's America.

The Spanish-American War had eased Roosevelt's worries about the Europeanizing American aristocrat and the non-Americanizing European immigrant, for it had reinvigorated American manhood and drawn into the nation those who had been slow to demonstrate patriotic ardor.[32] But in his writings and speeches in the five years prior to war Roosevelt had made clear his readiness to discipline any male who refused to become a real American man. America, he declared, had "no use for the German or Irishman" who retained his culture, "no room for any people who do not act and vote simply as Americans." "We have a right to demand," Roosevelt declared, that the immigrant "become thoroughly Americanized."[33] And this sense of right only increased after the century's turn, as the number of immigrants arriving each year reached and then exceeded 1 million.

And what if the immigrant refused to become "thoroughly Americanized?" Roosevelt was prepared to subject such a person to comprehensive, even coercive, Americanization campaigns. The Constitution, however, limited the range of Americanization policies that the federal government could enact in peacetime, so

Roosevelt turned first to social and political processes that the federal government was authorized to control, immigration and naturalization. During his presidency, he worked hard to winnow the immigrant stream of "undesirables" and compel a greater degree of Americanization among those wishing to become American citizens. He supported efforts to exclude prospective immigrants who, in his eyes, lacked the ability—physical, moral, or mental—and will to Americanize.[34] In 1903, he signed a law that barred the insane, the impoverished, prostitutes, and anarchists from entering the United States. The law also authorized the government to deport any immigrant who became an anarchist within three years of his arrival; this was the first time the federal government had made political ideas legitimate grounds for expulsion.[35] In 1907 Roosevelt signed another law that made it even more difficult for pauperized immigrants to gain admission to the United States and that empowered the president to deny entry to immigrants who were considered a threat to American labor standards.[36] This same law also declared that any American-born woman who married a foreigner would be stripped of her U.S. citizenship and declared an alien, a provision meant, among other things, to punish women thought to be indifferent to their Americanness.[37] Finally, the 1907 law established a commission to study whether certain nationality groups who seemed slow to Americanize should have their ability to enter the United States curtailed or eliminated altogether. This became the famous Dillingham Commission, which delivered a forty-two volume, prorestrictionist report in 1911, after Roosevelt had left the presidency.[38]

Roosevelt also raised the bar for becoming American by winning congressional approval of a law stiffening naturalization requirements. To be considered for citizenship, an applicant now was expected to have resided in the United States at least five consecutive years, speak English, prove that he was neither a polygamist nor an anarchist, and produce two witnesses who could vouch for his or her "moral character" and "attachment to the principles of the Constitution."[39] Roosevelt, in short, had put into law his demand that immigrants "thoroughly Americanize." To make sure that the new citizenship requirements would be enforced, Roosevelt established the Bureau of Immigration (1906). This agency quickly gained a reputation as one of the most coercive institutions of the federal government, its actions largely exempt from judicial review.[40]

Roosevelt did not always make clear what steps he would take to disrupt those ethnic communities that showed little interest in naturalization or citizenship. On the one hand, he did not publicly advocate using federal power to shut down foreign-language parochial schools or to restrict the rights of assembly and speech among groups who brazenly declared their devotion to their native lands. Such interference would have violated the Constitution and thus could not have been easily justified except in moments of national emergency. But Roosevelt wanted to use public schools to force "hyphenated Americans" to become "Americans pure and simple."[41] He endorsed legislation that would have compelled future immigrants to settle in the South and other areas far removed from established ethnic communities in the Northeast and Midwest; such dispersion of immigrants, it was thought, would accelerate their assimilation.[42] And he regarded coercion, or discipline, as a positive social good, and one that fell within the legitimate boundaries of state action. He wielded disciplinary power—or what he liked to call his "Big Stick"—with relish, and looked for opportunities to clobber not only recalcitrant immigrants but Caribbean nations, corporate monopolists, and political radicals who refused to accede to his wishes.

Roosevelt did not see himself as a bully, as someone who compulsively beat up on weaker parties. Instead he viewed coercion as a process that enhanced the commonweal and strengthened the nation. Those who did the disciplining, Roosevelt believed, would sharpen their own fitness; for them, the act of disciplining was a kind of "strenuous living" that, like war, regenerated the superior race. Those who were targeted for disciplining, meanwhile, would find themselves uplifted to a higher plane of existence. It "is an immense benefit to the European immigrant to change him into an American citizen," Roosevelt declared.[43] The wonders and opportunities of America would then unfold before the Americanized immigrant's eyes, for "no other land offers such glorious possibilities to the man able to take advantage of them, as does ours."[44] The loss of Europeanness that such a change would have entailed did not trouble Roosevelt, for what the immigrant gained as an American would be far superior to what had slipped away.[45]

In insisting upon the superiority of Americanness to ethnic and regional identities, Roosevelt revealed his ideological proximity to many European nation builders, liberal and radical, who wanted to turn peasants into Frenchmen, Scots and Welsh into Britons, and Ukrainians, Lithuanians, and Armenians into new Soviet men. All were civic nationalists who believed that to become a citizen of a democratic republic (or a workers' state) and to identify as a patriot willing to defend the republic at all costs was to ascend to the highest stage of humanity. Most believed that some degree of coercion would be necessary to turn residents of their lands into citizen-patriots. Those civic nationalists who were more sensitive than was Roosevelt to the coercion or cultural loss that such transformations entailed (and many were not) justified their nationalist path by embedding it in a narrative of emancipation: people who tossed off their "stunted" inherited culture, who made themselves over into citizens, would become free. This narrative was compelling, for it had the power of the Enlightenment and of the American and French revolutions behind it. These seminal events of the seventeenth and eighteenth centuries had arguably shown that democracy and prosperity lay within the grasp of any man who shook off—or was liberated from—superstition, irrationality, and blind obedience to monarchs, clerics, and demagogues, and became a free and self-governing individual.[46]

And what about women? Could they become free and self-governing individuals? Not, really, in Roosevelt's eyes. The centrality of the male warrior to Roosevelt's narratives of nation building, his admiration for muscular individuals willing to use force, and his abhorrence of effeminacy in all its guises underscore the deeply gendered nature of his nationalist thought. Men, Roosevelt believed, were society's natural leaders; nations rested on the intense homosocial bonds arising among men sharing the perils of combat. Women's nature, to Roosevelt's way of thinking, did not allow them to succeed at men's work, and the admission of females to the army and other sacred institutions of male comradeship would only compromise the work of nation building.

Women's inferiority did not mean, however, that they, or at least the Euro-Americans among them, were to be excluded from the nation. Their contributions as wives and mothers were essential both to the creation of new male citizens and to these citizens' moral education. Women were, as Roosevelt had declared of the New York City Turkish women on strike, the "mothers . . . of our citizenship." An interesting ambiguity attaches itself to Roosevelt's use of the word "our" in that phrase. It is possible that Roosevelt meant "our" to refer to all Americans, male and female; but it seems more likely that the "our" refers only to men, and expresses Roosevelt's belief that women's primary role was to create male citizens while accepting their own exclusion from, or subordination within, citizenship ranks.

Roosevelt enlarged his conception of women's roles over the course of the first two decades of the twentieth century. His interest in the conditions of workers and the immigrant poor not only led him to advocate unionization for women workers but brought him into contact with women progressives such as Jane Addams and Florence Kelley who advocated woman's suffrage and other reforms likely to increase women's political influence. And when Roosevelt formed the Progressive Party in 1912 (a subject that the last part of this chapter takes up), he welcomed into the party a large contingent of these women reformers, who proceeded to play a prominent role in convention proceedings and the ensuing political campaign. Roosevelt's embrace of these women activists reflected more than just expediency, more than the simple fact that he desperately needed all the support, male or female, he could muster. At a time when many men, in Roosevelt's estimation, were suffering the effects of effeminacy and thus failing as fathers, leaders, and soldiers, the female role in building the nation had assumed greater importance. By improving the living and familial conditions in which male children were born and raised, women reformers could help to insure that the next generation of men would be better skilled in manly virtues. Roosevelt, at times, even accepted the need for a modified conception of masculinity that accorded with the female reformers' emphasis on cooperation, service, and social welfare, qualities that other men of Roosevelt's time derided as fatal to the male pursuit of "rugged individualism." As a sign of the growing political role that Roosevelt envisioned for women, he became a supporter of woman suffrage. Women suffragists and feminists, in turn, found in Roosevelt's civic nationalism the language to justify their struggle for equality.

But Roosevelt never became a feminist, or a believer in the fundamental equality of men and women. He supported suffrage because he believed that it would ultimately strengthen men, by enlisting women to cleanse the political process of corruption and vice, thus enhancing the ability of men to pursue national virtue and glory. In this way, Roosevelt's civic nationalism retained its gendered cast, reserving for men the opportunity and responsibility to become free and self-governing individuals. And thus during the years when the Rooseveltian conceptions of nationhood held sway, feminists would find full equality an elusive goal.[47]

RACIAL DILEMMAS

In the abstract, the task of reconciling civic nationalism with racial nationalism was quite straightforward. Roosevelt simply argued that certain races—notably Asians and African Americans—could not meet the fundamental requirements of American citizenship. "Only the very highest races have been able" to make a success of self-government, and it would be foolish, even contemptible, to assume that "utterly undeveloped races" could function on an even footing with whites in a democracy.[48]

The practical work of exclusion was, in some cases, as easily accomplished as the ideological work. This was certainly true in regard to the Chinese, whom Roosevelt despised. The Chinese

Exclusion Act of 1882, which barred Chinese immigrant laborers from entering the country, insured that the Chinese American population would not become large enough to pose a real problem to American democracy. Congress kept this 1882 exclusion in place until the 1940s.[49]

But, in other cases, the work of reconciling civic and racial nationalism proved more difficult. The Japanese, for example, should have been near the bottom of Roosevelt's racial hierarchy: they were not white and they resided thousands of miles from the European peninsula, where all the great races had been born. But, in fact, Roosevelt admired the Japanese, for they had built a strong nation that successfully competed with the Europeans and Americans for territory, markets, and mastery of the "lower races." Roosevelt was especially impressed by the Japanese victory over the Russians in the Russo-Japanese War of 1905. Soon after negotiating an end to this war (an intervention that brought him the Nobel Prize for Peace), Roosevelt wrote: "I think Japan has something within itself which will be good for civilization in general. If she is treated fairly and yet not cringed to, I believe she will play her part honorably and well in the world's work in the Twentieth Century. Most certainly we have a good deal to learn from her."[50]

Did this mean that Americans could learn from Japanese immigrants and that the Japanese had a role to play in American democracy? Yes, it did. Roosevelt believed that the "heartiest friendship and goodwill" had been generated by encounters between Japanese and American travelers, students, scientists, artists, professionals, and merchants. These and other "gentlemen" composed the educated and commercial classes of the two countries. He further believed that all Japanese who resided in the United States were to be treated "on an exact equality with the people from Europe."[51] Indeed, he supported their right to naturalize. But there was a problem: the American laboring classes had shown no ability to get along with Japanese immigrants, chiefly because the former feared economic competition and depressed living standards. The hostility of West Coast American workers and their allies to Japanese laborers was so intense that it held out the prospect of a race war on the Pacific slope. Roosevelt regretfully confided to the Japanese ambassador in 1907 that "as yet we are not at the point where it is possible that the classes of citizens of the two countries who are more suspicious and less broad-minded [than the educated classes] should feel in the same way about one another; and above all this is true when they compete in their labor."[52] For the sake of peace, both on the West Coast and between the United States and Japan, Roosevelt felt compelled to insist in 1907 on a policy barring the further immigration of Japanese workers. By the terms of the Gentlemen's Agreement of 1907, the Japanese government halted the immigration of male Japanese laborers to the United States, while Roosevelt prevailed upon the San Francisco School Board to rescind its policy of segregating Japanese children in separate schools.[53]

On the surface, this exclusion policy resembled the Chinese Exclusion Act of 1882. But Roosevelt saw more differences than similarities: he had hailed the 1882 act as a long overdue measure, whereas he considered the 1907 agreement a "disagreeable policy of exclusion," one forced on him by the "criminal stupidity" of Americans who were always raising the spectre of the "yellow peril."[54] In Roosevelt's eyes, the underlying principle of the 1882 act had been race, the alleged inability of the "Chinaman" to assimilate into the American race, whereas the principle of the 1907 agreement was class, the inability of the lower classes of both races to get along. Roosevelt's turn to class analysis as a way of explaining racial animosity is an interesting move in its own right. But what matters is how Roosevelt's explanation violated the principles of his racial nationalism, for it forced him to concede that at least some members of a nonwhite race deserved admission to the American crucible. He had allowed his civic nationalist belief that each immigrant ought to be considered on his own merits, irrespective of his racial or cultural origins, to score a small, but significant, victory over his racist conviction that certain groups could never be integrated into the American nation. In so doing, he had challenged the racialized nationalism that he had worked so hard to construct on San Juan Hill.

The work of reconciling civic and racial nationalist principles in regards to black Americans was harder still for Roosevelt, because the relatively easy remedy of an exclusionary immigration law was not something that could solve the "Negro problem." The corollary to immigration exclusion—the repatriation of blacks to Africa—seemed too impractical even to propose as public policy.

That Roosevelt tolerated blacks' subordination to whites, and thought of them as an inferior race, is beyond dispute. He never deviated from the words he wrote to his good friend Owen Wister in 1906: "I entirely agree with you that as a race and in the mass they are altogether inferior to whites."[55] As president, he actually appointed fewer blacks to federal positions than had his predecessor McKinley.[56] During these years, he continued his assault on the fitness of black soldiers that he had begun shortly after the conclusion of the Spanish-American War. The climax of this campaign occurred in 1906 when he ordered the dishonorable discharge of 167 men of the all-black Twenty-fifth United States Infantry Regiment. They were allegedly covering up for a few renegade soldiers who may have assaulted a white woman and may have participated in a raid on the white residents of Brownsville, Texas. The facts of the case were hotly debated at the time and were never truly clarified. But this did not stop Roosevelt from dismissing scores of innocent black soldiers, including five who had been awarded the Congressional Medal of Honor for their heroism in Cuba and the Philippines. It is unlikely that Roosevelt would have meted out an equally harsh treatment to a group of white soldiers accused of a cover-up.[57]

Yet this same man earned the loyalty of blacks and the enmity of southern whites because on occasion he violated the color line in sensational and highly publicized ways. He enraged southern whites when he appointed a black man, William D. Crum, to the collectorship of the port of Charleston, South Carolina, a prestigious federal post, and he infuriated them again when he shut down the post office in Indianola, Mississippi, to punish local whites who had run their African American postmaster, Minnie M. Cox, out of town. Roosevelt's greatest sin against southern whites occurred

Fig. 6. Booker T. Washington and Theodore Roosevelt, 1903. The heads of the two men appear to be photographs pasted onto their drawn bodies. It is not known where this image appeared, but it is easy to imagine it evoking hope among various black publics and rage among many white ones, especially in the South. (Courtesy Library of Congress)

within months of his inauguration, when he invited Booker T. Washington to dine with him at the White House. Not only did he thus become, in the words of the *Washington Bee*, "the first President of the United States to entertain a coloured man." He also committed, in the words of one keen observer, "the one unpardonable violation of the Southern racial code"—"the breaking of bread between the races on equal terms." With the exception of interracial sexual intercourse, there could be no more "ultimate and positive expression" of a commitment to social equality. Many southern whites never forgave Roosevelt for this transgression.[58]

Those wanting to believe in Roosevelt's commitment to racial equality could find many other examples of good deeds. As civil service commissioner, he had eliminated from exams given in southern cities questions regarding applicants' religion, political orientation, and race; the result was that greater numbers of black applicants were able to enter government service.[59] As governor of New York, he had pushed through a measure that outlawed racial discrimination in the state's public schools and repealed a law that had allowed individual towns to place white and black children in separate educational institutions.[60]

As president, however, it is more difficult to find similar evidence of Roosevelt's commitment to social equality. He never directly attacked the system of segregation that, during his presidency, took root in the South and prevented, among other things, blacks and whites throughout the region from eating together in public places. Why, then, did Roosevelt dine in so public a manner with Washington? And why, in a similar vein, did he go to great lengths to appoint black officials to coveted federal positions in the South? Recently, historians have treated these events as part of an elaborate and cynical game of political posturing in which Roosevelt was attempting to secure his southern base among black Republicans. Once he decided that the political payoff of this base was too small, he stopped appointing blacks and began courting southern whites instead.[61]

Roosevelt no doubt made these sorts of calculations, but it would be a mistake to interpret his entire approach to the race question through this Machiavellian lens. Such an approach assumes that Roosevelt's civic nationalist principles were superficial and easily tossed aside when they got in the way of political ambition. But this was not the case. Roosevelt took his civic nationalism seriously. On many occasions and at great length, he declared his personal commitment to treating "each black man and each white man strictly [according to] . . . his merits as a man, giving him no more and no less than he shows himself worthy to have."[62] And thus he had to find a way of reconciling these views with his low opinion of blacks as a race.

His preferred mode of resolution was the one he had applied to the Japanese problem: class analysis. Just as Japanese gentlemen had to be treated differently than the Japanese laborers, so, too, earnest, educated, and economically successful blacks had to be given a decent, even equal, place at the dinner table, in federal employment, and at the ballot box. In defending his action in Indianola to enraged southern whites, Roosevelt wrote: "All I have been doing is to ask, not that the average Negro be allowed to vote, not that there be Negro domination in any shape or form, but that these occasionally good, well-educated, intelligent and honest colored men and women be given the pitiful chance to have a little reward, a little respect, a little regard, if they can by earnest useful work succeed in winning it."[63]

Roosevelt's repeated use of the adjective "little" revealed the limitations of his commitment to the cause of racial equality. The numbers of blacks granted the full rights of citizenship would be few; their rewards slender. Nevertheless, Roosevelt's admission that some blacks would have to be treated as citizens—with rights, respect, and opportunity—and thus welcomed into the nation challenged his mythological and racialized view of America. And this challenge carried more serious consequences than the one posed by the Japanese, for the masses of Negroes resided in America—unlike prospective Japanese immigrants, who did not—and they would themselves have a voice in determining how many of them would be admitted to the nation and on what terms. Roosevelt had inspired blacks with his talk of a "square deal for black and white alike," of "all men up, not some men down," and of opening "the door of hope" to the Negro race.[64] And these egalitarian sentiments continued to motivate them, even as the limitations of Roosevelt's agenda became frustratingly clear. If Roosevelt's civic nationalist principles did not truly destabilize his racial nationalism, they did roil it and helped to set the stage for future battles.

THE NEW NATIONALISM

Roosevelt's New Nationalist program, announced in 1910 and codified in the Progressive Party platform of 1912, once riveted popular and scholarly attention. For historians of George Mowry's and Arthur Link's generation, this program, with its calls for the regulation of capitalism and the establishment of a welfare state, signaled the emergence of modern liberalism. This dimension of Rooseveltian nationalism is now all but ignored. But we need to look at it again.[65]

The phrase "New Nationalism" was coined in 1909 by the writer-journalist Herbert Croly, in his book, *The Promise of American Life*, to describe a progressive political philosophy and program. Croly viewed America with dismay. Industrialization had widened the gulf between rich and poor and dimmed America's historic promise to give everyone within its borders the opportunity to make something of himself or herself. And the Jeffersonian idea that Croly saw as America's traditional political philosophy— that liberty and equality would be best achieved by every man pursuing his own self-interest—no longer worked. It simply enabled the rich to get richer while denying the masses the assistance they needed to climb out of their poverty.[66]

America, in Croly's eyes, had to be reconstructed; the nation had to be reimagined and rebuilt—economically, politically, and culturally. His plan for reconstruction was as thoroughgoing as that advocated by socialists, but he emphatically rejected socialism, because its calls for class struggle and internationalism entailed the destruction of the nation and, with it, the bond "upon which actual human association is based."[67] Croly offered a New Nationalism in socialism's place, and he presented it to his readers not as the lastest European import but as a sensible reworking of American political traditions. His program would preserve the Jeffersonian goal of a society dedicated to democracy even as it rejected the Jeffersonian commitment to individualism and self-interest. Instead, Croly proposed a revived Hamiltonianism, by which he meant the building of a strong state that would regulate the overly powerful economic institutions and assist the poor masses in their efforts to improve their condition.

Croly's book was too long and too steeped in the language of European social science to become a best-seller. But it garnered attention from influential politicians and thinkers, including Theodore Roosevelt, just back from his African safari and looking for a way to reenter American politics after his premature retirement from the presidency in early 1909. Roosevelt promptly embraced Croly's New Nationalism as his own. Roosevelt's action did not really signal a radical departure in his politics. Roosevelt had inherited a tradition of state building from his predecessors in the Republican and Whig parties. Moreover, Croly's creed gave Roosevelt a name for the efforts he had already taken as president (1901–9) to establish a large federal government with the power to control the corporations and to offer all ordinary Americans, no matter how impoverished or disadvantaged, a "square deal."[68]

The New Nationalism also allowed Roosevelt to address a glaring weakness in his earlier formulations of civic nationalism. Roosevelt's civic creed had always contained within it the promise of economic opportunity and advancement to those who worked hard and lived honorably. But the civic nationalist philosophy that he had formulated in the 1890s, with its focus on equal *civil* and *political* rights for all citizens, could not deliver on that promise. Politically, this philosophy owed a great deal to classical liberalism, especially in its insistence that individual emancipation would follow upon the removal of all artificial constraints on political and civic participation. Thus, Roosevelt had believed that the ending of discriminatory treatment in public and private life would give European immigrants and other disadvantaged groups ample opportunity to partake of the American dream. But Roosevelt had failed to gauge the negative effects of industrialization on individual opportunity and virtue. Belatedly, and after much prodding from New York City's vigorous labor movement, Roosevelt acknowledged that grinding poverty was preventing workers, even those with full political and civil rights, from achieving economic security or the leisure necessary to cultivate their civic virtue.[69] The poor needed what T. H. Marshall would later call "social rights": the right to limit the hours of work, to earn a decent wage, to receive compensation for work-related injuries, and to insure themselves and their families against sickness, old age, and death.[70] Once possessing these and other social rights, citizens would be able to gain economic security and to reach their fullest moral and civic potential. The New Nationalism made the attainment of these social rights central to its program. Every man, Roosevelt declared, would then be able "to make of himself all that in him lies" and "to reach the highest point to which his capacities . . . can carry him."[71] In this way the promise of civic nationalism would be fulfilled.

Roosevelt regarded the unveiling of his New Nationalism as an epochal event. He revealed it in a speech at Osawatomie, Kansas, the bloody spot where, in 1856, John Brown and his men had ignited a civil war in Kansas by hauling five proslavery settlers from their cabins and crushing their heads with broadswords. In recalling Brown's incendiary actions, Roosevelt had no intention of reigniting passions over the race question. To the contrary, he took pains in the early part of his speech to welcome Confederate veterans and their descendants and to make clear that they could become full-fledged Americans without having to recognize the humanity, let alone the civil rights, of black Americans.[72]

What attracted Roosevelt to Osawatomie was the compelling figure of John Brown himself, the unflinching martyr who had sacrificed his life for a great political cause.[73] With his gift for self-dramatization, Roosevelt saw himself as cut from the John Brown mold: as a larger-than-life figure who, through his words and deeds, would oppose truth to power, no matter what the cost. Roosevelt had no intention of sacrificing his life. But he vaguely understood that his Osawatomie speech could ruin his political career. In this respect, he turned out to have been prescient, for the crusade he was about to undertake would drive him out of his beloved Republican Party and compel him to launch a new party that had little chance of bringing him the political power he craved. Before he had exhausted his political possibilities, however, Roosevelt had buoyed the forces of reform and insured that his cause, the New Nationalism, would become one of the most important political crusades of the twentieth century.

The broadsword that Roosevelt unsheathed at Osawatomie struck at "the special interests"—corporations, banks, and "a small class of enormously wealthy and economically powerful men" who had used money "to control and corrupt the men and methods of government for their own profit."[74] "Ruin in its worst form is inevitable," Roosevelt warned, "if our national life brings us nothing better than swollen fortunes for the few and the triumph in both politics and business of a sordid and selfish materialism."[75] The special interests had to be driven out of politics; the government had to be "freed from the[ir] sinister influence . . . [and] control."[76] It was time for Americans to place the welfare of the commonwealth ahead of the welfare of rich individuals. "The man," Roosevelt wrote, "who wrongly holds that every human right is secondary to his profit must now give way to the advocate of human welfare, who rightly maintains that every man holds his property subject to the general right of the community to regulate its use to whatever degree the public welfare may require it."[77] Such an ideological reorientation, Roosevelt acknowledged, would necessitate "a policy of a far more active governmental interference with social and economic conditions in this country than we have yet had." But Americans could not allow themselves to be deterred by this lack of precedent; they had to "face the fact that such an increase in governmental control is now necessary."[78]

In his speech, Roosevelt unfurled a long list of activities that a strong central government ought to undertake: regulating the activities of railroads, meatpackers, oil refiners, coal companies, and other interstate corporations; levying heavy taxes on excessive personal and corporate fortunes; insuring that the nation's natural resources be "used for the benefit of all our people and not monopolized for the benefit of the few";[79] encouraging workingmen to join unions and thus increase their ability to negotiate good terms of employment; and assuming responsibility for general social welfare by regulating the hours of work, offering compensation to workers injured on the job, and improving the nation's schools. Roosevelt delivered a manifesto that went a long way toward defining modern liberalism.

Roosevelt conceived of his New Nationalism as an alternative to, rather than as a fulfillment of, radicalism. He did not want to destroy property and expropriate the propertied. He warned not only about excessive privilege but also about the spirit of mob violence and anarchy that sometimes infected the labor movement.[80] He demanded that labor unions obey American laws, respect property rights, and accept some form of regulated capitalism as the basis of economic life.

Roosevelt had always loathed radical unionists who were intent on revolutionizing American society in order to begin anew, and he had never hesitated to deny them a place in his nation. Radicalism threatened political order and civility, qualities that Roosevelt prized as much as liberty. He had come to the presidency as a result of a bullet fired at McKinley by a deranged anarchist, and he would never forgive the anarchist movement—nor their first cousins, the socialist and syndicalist movements—for this act. "Anarchy," he wrote shortly after the assassination, "was not the outgrowth of unjust social conditions but the daughter of degenerate lunacy, a vicious pest, which threatens to uproot the very foundation of society if it is not speedily stamped out by the death, imprisonment, and deportation of all Anarchists."[81] These were uncompromising words, and indicative of the fury with which Roosevelt often denounced real or imagined radicals.[82] Outside of immigration and naturalization policy, Roosevelt could not easily translate his antiradical sentiments into federal law, for the Constitution protected the rights of radicals—at least those among them who were American citizens—to life, liberty, and freedom of speech and assembly. But in his imagination, Roosevelt was forever battling radicals, determined to vanquish them or expel them from his nation and thus forestall the misery that these "vicious pests" sought to unleash on the American people. The "worst foes," he wrote on another occasion, "are the foes of that orderly liberty without which our Republic must speedily perish. The reckless labor agitator who arouses the mob to riot and bloodshed is in the last analysis the most dangerous of the workingman's enemies."[83]

To underscore his distance from irresponsible radicals and to emphasize the conservative elements of his program, Roosevelt compared himself with his hero, Abraham Lincoln. Just as Lincoln was radical in his ambition to free the slaves and conservative in his determination to preserve the union, so, too, Roosevelt would destroy excessive privilege while preserving the economic order and constitutional system in which that privilege had accumulated.[84] Roosevelt's civic nationalism made it easy for him to assume a conservative posture, for his goal, he argued, was not a radical change in American society but rather the preservation of the first principles of the American republic.

Roosevelt's efforts to align his cause with Lincoln, the nation, and conservatism brought little comfort to true conservatives. They correctly understood that Roosevelt was serious about his desire to use state power against economic privilege. In subsequent speeches, Roosevelt clarified the populist thrust of his program. "The existence of this nation has no real significance," he declared, "unless it means the rule of the people, and the achievement of a greater measure of widely diffused popular well-being than has ever before obtained on a like scale."[85] This was the message that Roosevelt broadcast in Osawatomie and elsewhere in 1910, electrifying the large crowds that had gathered to hear him and shocking conservatives everywhere.[86]

Roosevelt did not speak directly about immigrants at Osawatomie or elsewhere on his New Nationalist tour. He refused to draw sectional or ethnic distinctions: "I speak to you here in Kansas exactly as I would speak in New York or Georgia, for the most vital problems are those which affect us all alike."[87] But European immigrants were never far from Roosevelt's mind. As a New Yorker, he understood how large a proportion of the working class comprised immigrants and their children. His New Nationalist program was meant to bring them into the nation, not just politically and culturally, but economically as well. It promised the immigrants that, if they became American, they would improve themselves. They would acquire power in government; they would gain the wherewithal to improve their economic condition and to reach their fullest human potential. Roosevelt had made clear his intention to use the powers of the state not just to discipline the immigrants who refused to become American, but also to help working-class immigrants realize the "glorious possibilities" of American life. In return for becoming American, immigrants would be offered political and economic power. It was this combination of discipline and opportunity that would make Roosevelt's New Nationalist program so potent a force in American politics.

As his movement gathered momentum, Roosevelt attracted to it the nation's leading social welfare progressives, individuals such as Paul Kellogg, Jane Addams, Frances Kellor, Robert Woods, and Lillian Wald, who had labored intensively with immigrants in their neighborhoods, schools, and workplaces.[88] For these reformers, the plight of the European immigrants—the inadequate wages, the slum conditions in which they lived, the infectious diseases from which they suffered, and the urban vices to which they had succumbed (prostitution, gambling, and political corruption)—symbolized much that was wrong with America. These reformers had not turned on the immigrants. Rather, through extensive contacts with immigrants at settlement houses, in unions, and in politics, they had come to view the immigrants sympathetically and to devise a reform agenda oriented to their needs. The social welfare reformers called for better working conditions, higher wages, improved housing and sanitation, playgrounds to give children more wholesome recreation, Americanization programs to teach immigrants English, and public museums and libraries to cultivate immigrant minds.[89]

The ranks of these reformers had swelled in the first decade of the new century, but they still felt neglected by the national parties and media. All that seemed to change in the summer of 1912. Reform sentiment was rising in the Democratic and Republican parties. When Republican regulars denied Roosevelt the nomination, he bolted the GOP to found a new party, the Progressive Party. So many reformers attended the new party's founding convention in Chicago in 1912 that it felt, to them, like a reunion. They were giddy with the belief that their concerns had moved from obscure charity and academic conferences to the very center of American politics. "A great party," Jane Addams exclaimed in her speech seconding Roosevelt's nomination, "has pledged itself to the pro-

Fig. 7. Theodore Roosevelt Campaigning for the Presidency, 1912. Men, women, and children in New Jersey listen to their candidate expound upon his New Nationalist program. (Courtesy Library of Congress)

tection of children, to the care of the aged, to the relief of over-worked girls, to the safeguarding of burdened men." The Progressive Party had become "the American exponent of a world-wide movement toward juster social conditions."[90]

With the reformer Woodrow Wilson running on the Democratic ticket, and the Republican vote likely to be divided between William Howard Taft and Roosevelt, Roosevelt had little chance of winning the presidency. Nevertheless his Progressive Party helped to define an agenda that would remain central to American reform for fifty years. Three generations of reformers would commit themselves, as did Roosevelt, to the establishment of a large regulatory state that would manage the economy, expand opportunity, and provide social welfare. The economic and political incorporation of European Americans was central to this project. Woodrow Wilson would commit himself to this project as well. As Mowry astutely observed, the New Deal "was in many ways only a step away from the New Nationalism."[91] The founding of the Progressive Party was thus a crucial moment in the development of American liberalism. It was also a key episode in the history of American civic nationalism, for it signified the creed's expansion to include the right of all Americans, including immigrants, to call on the state for help in overcoming poverty and powerlessness. To pursue this right was to promote American ideals and help America become the greatest nation in the world.

The Progressives who advocated this expansive civic nationalism had even cleansed their patriotism of some of its aggressive and antiradical elements. A party with Roosevelt as its candidate had to commit itself to some degree of military preparedness, and the Progressive platform committee obliged the colonel by calling for the addition of two battleships to the navy and the fortification of the Panama Canal. Jane Addams and the other Progressive pacifists did not like this incipient militarism but, after some obligatory protests, they fell into line.[92] Still, the party platform's militarist elements were quite modest.

For a time, moreover, it looked as though the Progressive Party would tear down the wall that Roosevelt had laboriously erected to separate reform from radicalism. Many Progressives were sympathetic to socialism, or at least to that creed's more conservative and democratic formulations. A significant minority traveled back and forth between the Progressive and socialist camps.[93] Most participants in the Progressive Party demonstrated little inclination to practice the kind of socialist-loathing and -baiting that was so common among Democrats and Republicans, adopting a posture of measured respect instead. An affinity with socialism may explain the decision of the party's convention delegates to twirl red bandannas during Roosevelt's stirring address to them. Reports of this scene puzzled the Socialist presidential candidate Eugene V. Debs, who did not know quite what to make of a mainstream party representing itself with miniature versions of the red flag that the socialists had long claimed as their own.[94]

Yet, the waving of the red bandanna was more a flirtation with than an embrace of the left. The Progressives were indeed honoring the socialists, who had done much to rivet the nation's attention on the inequalities that capitalism had spawned. In the process, they widened the political boundaries of the nation to grant socialist discourse a legitimacy it had not previously enjoyed. Still, most Progressives saw their movement as an alternative to socialism, not as its fulfillment; the waving of small red bandannas can be seen as a way of countering the appeal of large red flags. As the historian Martin Sklar has written, Progressives wanted to "contain" socialism in both senses of that term. They wanted to include elements of the socialist agenda within their liberal program, and they wanted to stymie socialism by offering their own movement in its place. Progressives accorded socialists an important role in prodding the polity to confront key economic and social justice issues, but the actual governing was to be left to the Progressives themselves. If antiradicalism had receded as a constituent element of civic nationalism, it had not been eliminated.[95]

Meanwhile, many Progressives were reluctant to rid their movement of racial nationalist tendencies. The Progressive Party had raised black hopes, drawing many African American voters to Roosevelt. Even those who remained suspicious of Roosevelt found in the Progressive pledge to help the most disadvantaged Americans a compelling reason to throw their support behind this new movement. In the summer of 1912, black Republicans in several southern states left their party and put together delegate slates to send to the Progressive Party's convention. But Roosevelt and his supporters refused to seat them, choosing to honor the credentials of lily-white delegations from these same southern states instead.[96]

The black delegates were the properly elected ones; but Roosevelt, seeing an opportunity to build a Progressive base among southern whites dissatisfied with the Democratic Party, brushed propriety aside. The southern whites whom Roosevelt wanted to woo would only join the Progressive Party on the condition that the party endorse the principles of white supremacy, and that meant an acceptance of black segregation and disfranchisement in the South. Roosevelt acquiesced in this demand, prevailing upon the Progressive Party's convention committee to deny southern black delegates their seats.[97]

From the perspective of his civic nationalism, this move should not have been difficult for Roosevelt to have made or justified. He simply could have stressed how few southern blacks had raised themselves to the level at which they were capable of handling the political responsibilities already vested in whites. But Roosevelt felt compelled to mount a far more complex defense, for his decision to subordinate blacks had drawn a firestorm of criticism both from within and beyond the Progressive Party.

Roosevelt stressed the impotence and corruption of black Republicanism in the South, the base from which the Progressives would have drawn their black support. He emphasized his support for black participation in the North and proudly pointed to the black men who had been elected members of delegations from thirteen northern and border states. "The Progressive Party," Roosevelt declared, "is already, at its very birth, endeavoring in these States, in its home, to act with fuller recognition of the rights of the colored man than ever the Republican party did."[98] Finally, he insisted that racial progress in the South would come not from high-handed northern attempts to force a new racial order on that recalcitrant region but from the many well-intentioned "white men in the South sincerely desirous of doing justice to the colored man." Only these "[white] men of justice and of vision as well as of strength and leadership," Roosevelt wrote, can do for the colored man "what neither the Northern white man nor the colored men themselves can do": secure the right of free political expression "to the negro who shows he possesses the intelligence, integrity, and self-respect which justify such right of political expression in his white neighbor."[99] The white delegates to the Progressive convention, Roosevelt implied, were precisely these sort of wise southern men who would work on the Negro's behalf.

Roosevelt's rationalizations could not hide how much his actions had violated the spirit of the Fourteenth and Fifteenth Amendments, which forbade discrimination against citizens on the basis of color, nor how much southern white Progressives—even the "wisest" among them—wanted to perpetuate white supremacy, not upend it. And to ask southern blacks to trust their fate to well-intentioned white neighbors was not only to insult their capacity for political self-mobilization but also to demand that they acquiesce in their own subordination.

Roosevelt's fellow Progressives attacked him on all these grounds, as well as others. But Roosevelt stuck to his guns, and a large majority of Progressives assented to Roosevelt's policy. This was the case even with Jane Addams, a founder of the National Association for the Advancement of Colored People (NAACP), who asked herself, in a searching self-examination published in the *Crisis*, the organization's magazine, whether her "abolitionist father would have remained in any political convention in which colored men had been treated slightingly." Addams knew the answer all too well: her father would have bolted rather than condone such treatment by staying. But Addams could not bring herself to act in this way, and she comforted herself by remembering how much her father had always insisted that she think for herself rather than blindly follow his—or anyone else's—example. The time in which she lived, Addams told herself and the readers of the *Crisis*, was different from his, for "war on behalf of the political status of the colored man was [now] clearly impossible." Moreover, the opportunity to build a movement of "political democracy and social justice" was too great to sacrifice on the altar of race. Addams was confident that the Progressive Party eventually would grapple with racial inequality, once it had gathered enough steam to transfuse the rank and file "with the full scope and meaning of social justice." Then it would "lift the question of the races . . . out of the grip of the past and into a new era of solution."[100]

History would, in some respects, bear out Addams's prophecy. Her ideological descendants, located primarily in the Democratic Party, would play a vital role in the civil rights revolution of the

1950s and 1960s. But not even this fact can remove the stain on liberalism's reputation arising from the Progressives' accommodation to white supremacy in 1912. Addams had earlier insisted that the Progressive Party endorse woman suffrage wholeheartedly and unequivocally, and she successfully resisted Roosevelt's efforts to temporize.[101] Had Roosevelt been successful in his obstructionist tactics, Addams no doubt would have left the party. But the issue of black suffrage was another matter; here she could compromise and capitulate.

The usually decisive Roosevelt engaged in an uncommon amount of public agonizing over his decision to treat southern blacks as a group subordinate to whites. His public pronouncements on the decision were invariably long-winded. They all included lengthy iterations of his civic nationalist conviction that every American be guaranteed "his right to life, to liberty, to protection from injustice" without regard to creed, birthplace, social station, or color.[102] In his communications and speeches, Roosevelt also listed the many efforts made by the Progressive Party in the North to guarantee blacks their political rights. None of this went over very well with white southerners who were contemplating joining Roosevelt's crusade. Then, on the eve of the election, Roosevelt further alienated his potential white southern supporters by committing another "unpardonable violation of the Southern racial code": he dined with two blacks in a Rhode Island hotel, reminding white supremacists everywhere of his original sin—his White House meal, more than a decade earlier, with Booker T. Washington. The Progressive Party's southern campaign was a fiasco, netting Roosevelt many fewer votes than he had won in 1904 and 1908.[103]

In the end, Roosevelt helped himself very little with his expediency. But the failure resulted not simply from a poorly conceived strategy, but also from the divided, contradictory character of Roosevelt's nationalism. His mythic view of America had no place for blacks or other non-Europeans of color. From this perspective, it troubled him little to discriminate against, ignore, or subordinate blacks. But his civic nationalist ideals kept getting in the way, reminding him to treat each individual on his or her own merits.

Roosevelt's civic nationalism was a capacious and democratic creed. Through it, he sought to open the nation to virtually all European immigrants, even those who had come from the "inferior" peoples of southern and eastern Europe. He also insisted that this creed conferred on all disadvantaged Americans, immigrant and native-born alike, a series of "social rights" to economic opportunity and security and emphasized that it was the job of the government to insure universal access to these rights. These rights came encumbered with duties: immigrants had to jettison their Old World cultures and assimilate fully into American life. Those who demurred would be subjected to the coercive powers of the state. Roosevelt firmly believed that a judicious mix of enticement and discipline, of opportunity and coercion, was the best strategy for reconstituting the nation in an age of industrialization. During the heady days of 1912, Roosevelt and his supporters were carried away with the notion that their New Nationalism provided a remarkably comprehensive and just solution to America's problems. Indeed, their program became the template upon which twentieth-century liberalism took shape.

These Progressives, however, could not solve the problem of race. Throughout his life, Roosevelt believed that most nonwhites belonged to "inferior" races with limited capacities for self-government. Only those few individuals within these races who demonstrated that they had lifted themselves to the level of the Europeans were to be rewarded with a full complement of civil and social rights. This kind of thinking permitted Roosevelt and his supporters at the Progressive Party convention of 1912 to reinscribe African American subordination into their liberal politics. Because this convention represented a key moment in the genesis of modern liberalism, the refusal to seat black delegates takes on a significance that extends well beyond progressivism itself.

But the very fact that Roosevelt, Addams, and others were troubled by their actions revealed the power of civic nationalist ideals. So, too, the uncertain terms in which they rationalized their act and the inconsistency of their behavior toward blacks exposed the unstable nature of their racism. In their actions we can discern the true American dilemma—a national identity divided against itself. On the one hand, Roosevelt and others conceived of America as a land meant for Europeans in which blacks had either a subordinate place or no place at all. On the other hand, they subscribed to a civic nationalist ideal that welcomed all law-abiding residents into the polity and disavowed distinctions based on race. How were the opposing conceptions of national identity to be reconciled into a single American creed? Sometimes this dilemma came into full view, as it did in 1912; other times it was obscured, as images of the two Americas developed separately from each other, dominating different political and cultural forms. But both sprang with equal force from the same source—American nationalism—and both would animate liberal politics for another half century.

CHAPTER 3

Hardening the Boundaries

of the Nation,

1917–1929

The First World War seemed to fulfill the Rooseveltian nationalist dream. Americans were being tested in battle against a "savage" foe—the "Hun"—and thus would be able to demonstrate valor and to forge themselves into a hardened and glorious nation. The racial lines had been reaffirmed in ways that largely excluded blacks from combat and thus from important tests of citizenship and manhood. Roosevelt believed that the millions who were drafted into the army in 1917 and 1918, many of them immigrants, would be forged through this experience into true Americans. Anyone on the homefront who refused to participate in what

Roosevelt called "The Crucible" would have to contend with a dramatically enlarged and empowered state ready to discipline recalcitrants through censorship, jail, and deportation. Not since the 1790s had the federal government so curtailed the freedom of expression in the interests of national security. Finally, the government established an array of large, regulatory institutions to direct the private economy. For New Nationalists, this was a dream come true, for the state they had coveted, one that would regulate capital, expand opportunity, and incorporate the downtrodden into American life, seemed to arise overnight.

Roosevelt did not live long enough to evaluate the outcome of these wartime nation-building projects. His hatred for President Woodrow Wilson inclined him to belittle or dismiss the policies that the Democrats were pursuing, even when they hewed closely to the New Nationalist vision he had outlined in 1910. But had he lived into the 1920s, some of the key developments of the war and postwar likely would have satisfied him. Major elements of the disciplinary project, including the subordination and exclusion of "inferior" racial groups, 100 percent Americanization programs, the assault on ethnic pluralism, and the prosecution of political radicals, were all measures that Roosevelt, at one time or another, had deemed necessary to nation building. Not all of these initiatives lasted into the 1920s and beyond. But one did—immigration restriction. A series of anti-immigrant laws passed from 1917 to 1924 halted virtually all immigration on the part of southern and eastern Europeans and East and South Asians to the United States. Alleged racial inferiority or political radicalism, or both, made these groups the targets of this exclusionary legislation. And the legislation's most critical feature—a quota system that marked certain European nationality groups as racially inferior and, as a consequence, allowed each a paltry number of immigrant slots a year—remained a federal law for more than four decades.

This movement for immigration restriction strengthened the racialist tradition of American nationalism precisely at the moment when Americans are often thought to have dispensed with "older" notions of racial hierarchy and embraced the freewheeling thinking and behavior of the Jazz Age. Civic nationalism did not disappear at this time; to the contrary, many Americans turned to this latter tradition as a way of defending those who had been racially stigmatized and of reasserting the egalitarian foundation of American life. In the 1930s this turn would culminate in efforts to sharpen assaults on racism. But civic nationalism was not as central as racial nationalism to the 1920s, a time when overwhelming numbers of congressmen and senators voted to make race determinative of the country's entire immigration policy—and thus to reassert its constitutive role in shaping the American nation.

Roosevelt's response to this legislation likely would have been complex. He would have been discomfited by the degree to which the law stigmatized the Japanese and eastern and southern Europeans, groups that, at an earlier time, he had welcomed into his nation. He would have been dismayed that this restrictive legislation was not accompanied by an effort to carry over the New Nationalist wartime state to peacetime and, through programs of social welfare and economic advancement, to deepen the immigrant masses' attachment to American ideals. But he probably would have been pleased that this restrictive legislation reinforced key principles of his national project—an insistence on the racial superiority of the "American" people, an intolerance of political radicalism, and an opposition to cultural pluralism—at the very moment in which America was entering its modern era. Indeed, the transformations of war and its aftermath invigorated the nation that Roosevelt had been so keen to establish on American soil.

WAR AND DISCIPLINE

Theodore Roosevelt had long been convinced that war revitalized nations. Mortal combat sharpened a people's racial instincts and strengthened its character. And for nations comprising multiple nationalities, regions, or tribes, war served the essential purpose of melting the many into one. This had happened with the Scotch Irish, English, Huguenots, Dutch, and Germans on the American frontier; it had happened with northerners, southerners, Ivy Leaguers, cowboys, Irish, Jews, and Italians in the Rough Riders. And it desperately needed to happen again, and on a large scale, in order to transform the immigrant multitudes, walled off in their foreign colonies, into Americans. The 1910 census had revealed that 32 million Americans, a full third of the nation, lived in immigrant families; in cities of the Northeast, Midwest, and West, these Americans formed majorities.[1] Lamenting the dangerous lack of assimilation among these immigrants, Colonel Leonard Wood declared in 1916 that "some institution should remove" the immigrants from their poor "physical and mental environment and force them to make outside contacts so that they might 'speak American and think American.' "[2] Because the public schools, the churches, and the families and homes had proved inadequate to the task, the army needed to step in. Roosevelt heartily agreed. "The military tent where they all sleep side by side," he wrote, "will rank next to the public school among the great agents of democratization."[3]

America's declaration of war against Germany and its Central Power allies in April 1917 seemed to give the nation the war that Roosevelt, Wood, and others believed it needed. A draft was instituted, and, in only a year and a half, 24 million men eighteen years of age and older had registered for it. A total of 5 million served in some branch of the American military. Foreign-born men constituted an estimated 18 percent of the army, a percentage greater than their share of the total male population. A war on this scale seemed to open extraordinary opportunities for assimilation and nation building. By 1918 Roosevelt was sure that these opportunities were being realized. He concluded one prowar essay he wrote that year with a poem by a doughboy celebrating how the ethnically diverse members of a platoon—Dennis P. O'Leary, Dimitri Georgoupoulos, Vladimir Slaminsky, Garibaldi Ravioli, Van Winkle Schuyler Stuyvesant, Don Miguel de Colombo, Thomas Scalp-the-Bear, and Isaac Abie Cohen—had all fought as Yanks and as "first-class fightin' " men.[4]

The transformation, through propaganda, of the once admired Germans into the dreaded and savage "Huns" seemed to satisfy another requirement of Roosevelt's war program. The Germans had committed atrocities against Belgian civilians as they raced toward France, and this gave Roosevelt and others the opportunity to expose the savagery that allegedly lurked deep within the German race. The large and centralized propaganda machine of President Woodrow Wilson's administration did everything it could to spread images, in newspapers, posters, and movies, of the vicious and threatening Hun, as a way of getting Americans ready to fight. Judging from the ferocious anti-German hysteria that swept the United States and from the doughboys' apparently sincere declarations that they were going to save Europe from barbarism, the Hun propaganda campaign seemed to work. American soldiers would have ample opportunity to prove their mettle and strengthen their nation through heroic combat against a savage foe.[5]

But, in fact, the war itself did not closely follow Roosevelt's prescriptions. Woodrow Wilson was the commander in chief, not Roosevelt, and Wilson was the product of a Democratic Party that, while certainly not averse to war, had long been reluctant to entangle America in European affairs. Faithful to his party's isolationist tradition, Wilson struggled to keep the United States neutral. Another of the Democrats' traditions was a suspicion of a large state and of professional armies; these, many Democrats believed, would inevitably be turned against the people's liberty. So Wilson was slow, to Roosevelt's way of thinking, to gear up for war or to appreciate the fine work of social engineering that a large army could accomplish.[6] When Wilson finally did commit the nation to war, he embraced war aims that made Roosevelt cringe. For Wilson, the glory of the war would derive from the fact that this would be the last war, "a war to end all wars," and it would be achieved by arranging "a peace without victory." America would refuse to savage its enemy either on the battlefield or in peace negotiations; it would triumph by spreading its ideals of peace, liberty, democracy, self-determination, and reasonableness to all the peoples of Europe, including the vanquished. Such magnanimity would usher in a new and peaceful era of international relations. Wilson's crusade attracted the support of millions of Americans, who rightly recognized it as an international expression of their own country's civic

Fig. 8. The "Hun," 1918. Germany, depicted as the Hun in this 1918 Dayton, Ohio, newspaper illustration, looks uncomprehendingly at a document listing President Woodrow Wilson's idealistic peace aims. (Courtesy Library of Congress)

nationalist ideals. Roosevelt never regarded this crusade as anything other than folly and perversity.[7]

Combat itself also diverged from the Rooseveltian plan. Roosevelt's own attempts to raise and lead a volunteer regiment were
rebuffed by Wilson, who rightly understood the political danger of
allowing Roosevelt a chance to reenact the glories of his Rough
Rider days.[8] And the war itself offered precious few opportunities
for deploying the American habit of frontier fighting. This was not
a war in which small, mobile units engaged each other in vicious
fights over a vast terrain, the heroism of an Indian warrior or a
Daniel Boone determining victory or defeat. Rather, armies were
huge and immobile, battles across the trenches were indecisive, and
acts of individual heroism counted for little.

Still, by the time America intervened, the opposing armies had
begun to move out of their trenches and the encounters between
them were growing more decisive. The arrival of more than 2 million American soldiers in France in 1917 and 1918 helped to turn
the battle against the Germans. The American soldiers, on the
whole, fought well, especially given the brief period of their training. A few Daniel Boone types emerged, such as Sergeant Alvin C.
York, who used his skills as a marksman, learned in the Tennessee
backwoods, singlehandedly to kill 17 Germans and capture another 132. News of some stirring American victories, such as the
overrunning of a German stronghold at St. Mihiel, reached the
home front, as did the heroism of the "Lost Battalion," which,
though surrounded by Germans for five days and without food or
water, gamely fought on until the survivors were rescued. The
"Lost Battalion" was as close as America came to achieving a stirring "last stand."[9] But no individual or group achieved the status
Roosevelt or the Rough Riders had in 1898 or that the Marines
and the mythic "multiethnic platoon" would achieve in World War
II. The American soldiers were together for too short a time and
involved in too little combat for the army-as-melting-pot to erase
ethnic and regional differences. Meanwhile, newly invented IQ
tests administered to enlisted men revealed an alarming level of
alleged feeblemindedness and illiteracy that led authorities to

conclude that these individuals, many of them foreign-born, could never be forged into Americans.[10] For all these reasons, the war did not easily lend itself to stories of Americans proving themselves in mortal combat, or of combat fusing Americans of many backgrounds into one hardened and superior people.

These difficulties may have been overcome had Americans continued to regard the war, after the initial victory celebrations, as a great and enduring triumph. This outcome would have allowed writers, filmmakers, and other makers of popular culture to get hold of the soldiers' stories and mythologize them for posterity. There certainly was no shortage of efforts to honor the soldiers' sacrifice and perpetuate memory of their deeds. The government erected a Tomb of the Unknown Soldier at Arlington National Cemetery and declared that Armistice Day, November 11, would henceforth be honored as Veterans Day. A new veterans organization, the American Legion, was formed even before the war ended, and quickly achieved strength and political influence. Writers such as Willa Cather and Edith Wharton found a public eager for books that portrayed the war in idealistic and inspirational terms. Others attempted to tie American success in World War I to the patriotism of immigrant and ethnic soldiers. Finally, the war generated the usual flood of personal memoirs by former doughboys.[11]

But, in terms of popular historical memory, these efforts did not make much of a dent. The failure to arrange a just and enduring peace prompted Americans to reexamine the war, and a growing number concluded that American intervention had been a colossal and costly mistake. Irresponsible elites, they felt, had taken the nation to war against its better interests. By the mid-1920s, the themes of illusion, irresponsibility, authoritarianism, and the destruction of individuality came to dominate in war-related fiction, and peace movements were challenging veterans organizations for control of the war's memory.[12]

On one critical issue, however, Roosevelt's expectations were being fulfilled: the disciplining of an unruly population. Wilson, like Roosevelt, believed the American people had to acquire a unity and a patriotism that they lacked. They needed to learn, in other words, how to behave like a nation. Wilson's idealistic crusade for a "peace without victory" and a "war for democracy" had not been built on magnanimity alone. Wilson worried as much about the unassimilated immigrant presence as had Roosevelt. He recognized that class antagonisms were roiling American society, a division that, as the events of November 1917 had demonstrated in Russia, could eventuate in disastrous social revolution. He also understood how deep opposition to war ran in American society; in 1916, he had been reelected on a slogan declaring "He Kept Us Out of War." Prominent progressives such as Jane Addams and suffragist leader Carrie Chapman Catt opposed the war, as did a large pacifist group that had emerged among the nation's Protestant clergy; so did most of America's socialists and syndicalists. The country's sizable German American and Irish American populations objected to entering the war on Great Britain's side. The opposition to war, in other words, was large, diverse, mobilized, and influential.[13]

Wilson's determination to fight a different kind of war was meant, in part, to neutralize this opposition. If he could rally Americans around their civic nationalist principles—liberty, democracy, and self-determination—then he would give them a reason to fight and achieve political unity.

In 1917 he set up a new agency, the Committee on Public Information (CPI), to publicize and popularize the war. Under the chairmanship of George Creel, a midwestern progressive and muckraker, the CPI conducted a propaganda campaign on a grand scale. The CPI distributed 75 million copies of pamphlets explaining U.S. war aims in several languages. It trained a force of 75,000 "Four Minute Men" to deliver succinct, uplifting war speeches to numerous groups in their home cities and towns. It papered the walls of public and private institutions with posters, placed advertisements in mass-circulation magazines, sponsored exhibitions, and peppered newspaper editors with thousands of press releases on the progress of the war.[14]

The CPI campaign worked, but not as its architects intended. While it sharpened Americans' sense of their country's historic

Fig. 9. "Your First Thrill of American Liberty," 1917. This poster captures the hopeful, civic nationalist side of the government's propaganda campaign to unite immigrants behind the war effort. (Courtesy National Archives)

ideals, it did not secure their unquestioning acquiescence in the war effort. Instead, it prompted many to ask how well the ideals of liberty and democracy had been realized in America, and how many Americans benefited from them. As the war progressed, workers, socialists, women, and African Americans raised these questions with increasing force, striking and protesting to register their anger at class, racial, and gender inequalities. Such militancy not only deepened rather than narrowed awareness of the divisions rending American society. It also threatened, in the eyes of Wilson, America's ability to fight effectively and to achieve the kind of international influence he needed to persuade other nations to subscribe to his plan for peace.[15]

In these circumstances, the federal government turned increasingly from exhortation to repression and, in 1917 and 1918, unveiled a disciplinary project breathtaking in its scope. Government-supported attacks on German Americans as a threat to national unity were broadened in 1918 and subsequent years to include immigrants from southern and eastern Europe and Asia, culminating in a draconian and racialized system of immigration restriction. Anti-immigrant sentiment led to Prohibition, an intrusive use of state power to change the drinking behavior of individuals deemed incapable of changing themselves, and to sharp restrictions on the civil rights of Japanese immigrants in the western states. The government deployed the broad powers given it under the Espionage and Sedition Acts in 1917 and 1918 to break up radical antiwar groups and to imprison or deport their leaders. After the war, many state and local governments adopted coercive Americanization measures, such as requiring the use of English for instruction in all subjects (except foreign languages) in public and private schools. These initiatives, in combination, amounted to an extraordinary effort to reshape the nation in ways that would exclude the unwanted, reform those regarded as social and political degenerates, and punish those who continued to engage in un-American behavior.[16]

A disciplinary project on this scale required a "disciplinary state" to carry out its policies. This federal state had begun to emerge during the Progressive Era and gained size and stature in

World War I. The federal Bureau of Immigration, set up under the Department of Commerce and Labor in 1891 and strengthened by the Immigration Act of 1907, controlled all matters pertaining to the admission, exclusion, and deportation of aliens. Previously these matters had been handled haphazardly by state governments and the courts. In 1917 and 1918, this bureau created a special antiradical division to expedite deportation proceedings against immigrant members of the Industrial Workers of the World (IWW), anarchist groups, and other radical organizations. It pursued alien radicals and illegal immigrants with alacrity and with a free hand, its actions exempt from judicial review.[17] The Bureau of Investigation, founded in 1908, also grew dramatically during the war and, soon after the war ended, set up a General Intelligence Division under the direction of a twenty-four-year-old J. Edgar Hoover to collect information on suspected radicals. By 1919, half the Bureau of Investigation's agents were engaged in antiradical work, quickly assembling an index of 80,000 suspects. This agency also assumed responsibility for enforcing Prohibition.[18]

Bureau of Investigation agents worked alongside those of the army's Military Intelligence Division, which developed from insignificance in 1917 to an agency of more than 1,000 in 1918. Authorized to collect information on anyone or any organization thought to threaten or "impair . . . military efficiency," it investigated a large range of suspected traitors, from anarchists and Communists to the black nationalist followers of Marcus Garvey.[19] The work of these federal institutions was augmented by state and local governmental organizations, such as the New York State Committee to Investigate Seditious Activities, which was established in 1919. Its chair, State Senator Clayton Riley Lusk, frankly enunciated his goal of a "reasonable and wise repression of revolutionary activities [directed] . . . towards the maintenance of law, order, and peace in the community."[20] And its agents, working closely with the New York City Police Department's Bomb Squad and other local enforcement groups, collected information on suspected radicals, raided their organizations to collect literature and membership lists, interrogated their leaders, and prosecuted many under a New York State "criminal anarchy" statute.[21]

Private patriotic groups aided the work of this disciplinary state. Their role had been hammered out in World War I, when members of the American Protective Association (APA), with the blessings of the postmaster general and the attorney general, exposed German loyalists, "Bolsheviks," and other traitors.[22] This cooperative work between the APA and federal departments paralleled the close relationships between federal economic agencies and private corporations that were widely hailed as the most efficient and patriotic way to manage a hugely complex war economy.[23] And just as Herbert Hoover and others labored to sustain these public-private links in the postwar, so, too, did the American Legion and similar groups seek to sustain their ties to public agencies of surveillance and political order. The Legion, working with the Bureau of Investigation, carried on its own campaigns to identify and ostracize suspected radicals and to scrutinize textbooks and teachers in the public schools for signs of dissent, insurrection, and excessive foreignness. In the South, a reborn Ku Klux Klan kept an eye out for miscegenation; elsewhere it drummed up a steady stream of accusations of disloyalty and subversion against Catholics and Jews. In the West, the Native Sons of the Golden West scrutinized the business and social habits of Japanese immigrants, making sure they were not circumventing prohibitions on their right to own land or interacting with whites in "unacceptable" ways.[24]

The number of public agencies and private groups focused on disciplining the American people reveals the intensity and comprehensiveness of these campaigns. But the disciplinary state, even with private adjuncts, was not omnipotent. The traditional American suspicion of state power, suspended during the war, came roaring back after the war ended, hampering the disciplinary state's work. Prohibition had cut alcoholic consumption in half, but limited funds meant spotty enforcement, widespread lawbreaking, and the admission by 1933 that the "noble experiment" had failed.[25] Other initiatives also encountered a resurgent commitment to limiting federal power. Thus, for example, the ferocity of the 1919 antiradical campaign (the so-called Red Scare) disguised a key limitation from which it suffered: it targeted only alien radicals because the attorney general and Bureau of Investigation lacked the statutory power to arrest their native-born counterparts. J. Edgar Hoover desperately wanted to pursue native-born radicals on his subversives list, which, by the early 1920s, had mushroomed to 450,000. But Congress would not give him the peacetime sedition law he needed.[26] The Supreme Court, meanwhile, struck a triple blow against coercive Americanization campaigns by ruling in 1923, 1925, and 1926 that a Nebraska law forbidding the teaching of foreign languages, an Oregon law designed to outlaw Catholic schools and their foreign and "un-American" teachings, and a Hawaii law subjecting private Japanese-language schools to stringent public oversight were all unconstitutional. All three rulings stressed the limits of federal power, especially when interfering with parents' child-rearing decisions.[27] It is this kind of retrenchment of state power that has led some historians to see the disciplinary campaign as ephemeral and to treat its appearance as merely a diversion (albeit an unfortunate one) from Americans' deep attachment to their individual liberties. But in one critical policy area, immigration, the interpretation of the disciplinary campaign as temporary is wrong.

The immigration acts of 1917, 1918, 1921, and 1924, in combination, reduced the level of immigration by approximately 85 percent and virtually cut off immigration from southern and eastern Europe, stigmatizing people from these regions as dangerously radical and as inferior to the "races" of northern and western Europe. At the same time, these acts barred Asian immigrants altogether because their racial stock was deemed either unassimilable or inferior to American stock. Finally, these laws strengthened the sanctions that the government could take against immigrant anarchists or any other immigrant who believed in or advocated the "violent overthrow of government, the assassination of officials, or the unlawful destruction of property."[28] These measures profoundly shaped American society from the 1920s through the 1960s, not only through the establishment of racialized and politicized patterns of exclusion and inclusion, but also through increasing the rewards for assimilation and penalties for cultural difference for those immigrants already here.

The success of immigration restriction stemmed in large part from its capacity to achieve its goals without antagonizing the opponents of federal power. On the one hand, immigration restriction did not require a huge policing apparatus—at least nothing like the manpower and funds that a compulsory Americanization campaign directed at tens of millions of immigrants would have entailed. On the other hand, the courts had exempted immigration policy from the strict constitutional scrutiny it applied to legislation directed at citizens. Because these laws were directed at aliens rather than citizens, the courts had ruled, the usual constitutional safeguards protecting individuals' liberty against government power did not, in many cases, apply.[29] In regard to immigrants, a strong and punitive state could be established and maintained at a relatively low cost. Congress, as a result, possessed extraordinary latitude in devising immigration and naturalization laws.

Immigration restriction is not only important unto itself. It also became a policy site onto which Americans projected their fears about their nation's alleged enemies; here they could translate these anxieties into harsh and repressive legislation. Because the disciplinarians found their Americanization, Prohibition, and antiradical initiatives blocked or limited, they embraced immigration restriction as an alternative way of excluding or subordinating radicals, Jews, Catholics, and other groups whom they feared. Here was an effective way of narrowing the boundaries of the American nation.

"KEEPING PURE THE BLOOD OF AMERICA"

Immigration restriction was not a new idea in 1917. In the previous thirty-five years, the federal government had begun to restrict immigration in two ways. First, it established the principle of group exclusion—restricting or excluding an entire nationality because of unwelcome ascriptive traits or collective behaviors that were alleged to be characteristic of it. The first act to embody this principle was the Chinese Exclusion Act of 1882, which denied Chinese laborers the opportunity to immigrate to the United States. This act was renewed several times in the 1890s and 1900s, and then followed by the so-called Gentlemen's Agreement of 1907 that barred immigration of male Japanese laborers. Second, the government established the principle of individual exclusion—restricting or excluding certain individuals, irrespective of their nationality, because of undesirable physical, mental, or political characteristics. The 1907 Immigration Act exemplified this principle, prohibiting sick, feebleminded, and anarchistic immigrants from entering the United States.[30]

These two principles were increasingly written into law, evidence of the nation's movement toward restriction after a long period of open borders. Until the First World War, however, proponents of restriction were disappointed in the results of their efforts. Three times they had failed to make literacy a prerequisite for prospective adult immigrants. Congressional majorities had voted for such a law on three different occasions, only to see it vetoed each time by presidents Grover Cleveland, William Howard Taft, and Woodrow Wilson.[31] All three presidents were convinced that America both needed immigrants for economic development and that America's obligation to serve as a refuge for Europe's teeming millions was too sacred to renege upon.[32] But with war looming, and America full of immigrants from lands that the United States might soon be fighting, support for immigration restriction grew to the point that Congress was able to override a presidential veto, which it did in passing the Immigration Act of 1917.

Although this act ostensibly excluded any immigrant who could not read, regardless of his or her national origins, it was meant to discriminate against certain Asian and European groups.[33] This intention was most obvious in a clause establishing an "Asiatic Barred Zone"—a huge area covering virtually all of East and South Asia, with the exception of Japan and parts of China. Any Asian national living in that zone was to be denied the opportunity to immigrate to the United States. This clause extended the ban on Asian immigrants from the Chinese and Japanese to virtually all inhabitants of the region.

The immigration act also, however, applied the principle of group exclusion to European immigrants for the first time. The bill's principal targets were the so-called new immigrants, those from southern and eastern Europe who were predominately Catholic and Jewish, and whose literacy rates were far lower than those of the immigrants who came from Great Britain, Scandinavia, Germany, and other regions of northwest Europe. The bill's principal architect, Senator William P. Dillingham of Vermont (Republican), was quite explicit about his desire to reduce the number of new immigrants. In fact, he admitted to embracing the literacy test only after discovering that the application of such a test would reduce the flow from eastern and southern Europe by 30 percent while not affecting the flow from northern and western Europe at all.[34]

The 1917 law, however, did not achieve its goal. It had established no overall upper limit on annual immigration, an omission that became particularly problematic once the war ended and millions of displaced and literate Europeans began looking toward America as a refuge and a place to begin life again. More than 400,000 persons arrived in the second half of 1920 and more than 800,000 in 1921, most of them from southern and eastern Europe; there were predictions of millions more to follow.[35] Japanese immigrants continued to come as well, although their numbers were small. But many white westerners would not be appeased until every Japanese looking to enter the United States was turned away.[36]

Finally, the act of 1917 had failed to anticipate the way in which the Russian Revolution forced a reframing of the immigration problem. Few events exerted as large an impact on the United States, in both the short and long terms, as the Bolsheviks' seizure of power in November 1917. Lenin's Bolsheviks were radical opponents of capitalism, offering the downtrodden communism—the collective ownership of the means of production—as a far more equitable and just social system than the private-property system prevailing in the United States and other capitalist citadels. Upon assuming power, Lenin immediately withdrew Russia from the war, judging it a fight between national capitalist elites that offered no benefits to Russia's or Europe's masses. Further, at the war's end, Lenin encouraged socialist revolutions in Germany, Hungary, and elsewhere that he hoped would topple the existing regimes and replace them with workers' states. These revolutions failed, but not without causing great turmoil and fear. Throughout Europe, Communist parties emerged from these struggles, determined to build their strength for future revolutions.[37]

The numbers of radicals and of Bolshevik sympathizers in the United States did not approach the numbers in Europe, but they were not insignificant. Labor unrest had rippled through American industrial centers during and after the war, with millions joining unions and going on strike. Many of these strikers were inspired by the Russian Revolution, not necessarily because they were themselves Communists (although some were), but because they saw this event as the dawn of a new age, in which workers would gain power and claim a fair share of their country's wealth after decades of capitalist exploitation. Woodrow Wilson feared the Bolshevik challenge acutely, and several of his daring diplomatic initiatives—"a peace without victory," self-determination, and a League of Nations to settle disputes through negotiation rather than war—can be understood in part as attempts to limit Lenin's international appeal. So, too, Wilson's cable to Congress from Versailles in 1919, that "the question which stands at the front of all others amidst the present great awakening is the question of labor," reflected his growing conviction that America risked revolution if it did not attend to its labor problems.[38]

To Wilson, addressing the labor question entailed a wide-ranging program of political reform that would improve the conditions of the country's laborers. "We can meet Bolshevism only with bold liberalism," he wrote his brother-in-law in 1919.[39] But a majority of Americans had turned against reform; fearing Bolshevism, they supported repressive campaigns against suspected radicals. In these circumstances, antiradicalism became a key component of the state's disciplinary project. By 1918 Congress had passed another Immigration Act, this one meant to shut out radical immigrants. It expanded the exclusion of radicals from anarchists to anyone who advocated revolution, assassination, or the unlawful seizure of private property.[40] In 1919 and early 1920 the government and private patriotic groups destroyed the offices of radical organizations, confiscated their printed materials, and imprisoned or deported their leaders. The antiradical forces made few distinctions between the various groups—socialists, Communists, anarchists, and syndicalists—that composed the left, even though these groups often loathed each other. In the popular imagination, they were all Bolsheviks or "reds," so-called because of the red flag that, for years, had been the revolutionaries' banner. There could be no compromise with these revolutionaries, for they would not stop until they had overturned America's capitalist system, seized and collectivized private property, and destroyed American democracy.[41] From 1917 through 1989, resistance to communism, both at home and abroad, became a defining feature of the American nation. To be a Communist, or some other kind of "red," was, by definition, to engage in un-American behavior.

Anticommunism was not an entirely new force in American politics, for it built on the earlier fear of anarchists that Roosevelt and others had felt so keenly in the years prior to World War I. Like antianarchism, anticommunism stressed the sanctity of private property, respect for the law and the Constitution, and an abhorrence of violence. But communism posed a far greater threat than did anarchism. The anarchists may have been dangerous but they were relatively few in number and without substantial resources. The Communists, by contrast, held all of Russia, a sprawling land containing a numerous and proud people. And they possessed a state with the power to organize revolutionary violence on an international scale.

In the minds of many Americans, the fear of communism commingled with the fear of the new immigrant. Even a casual observer of the wartime and postwar strikes would have noticed that a substantial proportion of strikers were immigrants. There was a simple explanation for this. Immigrants, especially those from southern and eastern Europe, formed work-force majorities in most industries: more than 80 percent in sugar refining, 70 percent in clothing manufacture, 60 percent in cotton goods, oil refining, woolen goods, coal mining, and meat-packing, and 50 percent in iron and steel.[42] Thus, heavy southern and eastern European involvement in the strikes simply reflected their domination of the work forces in those industries. But the anticommunists saw the situation differently: foreign workers, they argued, were vulnerable to radical propaganda in ways that American workers were not. The new immigrants' unfamiliarity with English, their illiteracy, and their isolation from American cultural influences and political traditions generated an "almost complete inability," in the words of a petition to Congress from the Kansas legislature, "to understand our institutions of government"; these immigrant workers had no way of determining that the American way was superior to the Communist way.[43] Thus, as Congressman Charles R. Crisp of Georgia (Democrat) put it, "Little Bohemia, Little Italy, Little Russia, Little Germany, Little Poland, Chinatown . . . are the breeding grounds for un-American thought and deeds."[44]

To Crisp and others, the illiterate and pauperized colonies of foreigners formed only half the labor problem. The other half lay in highly educated immigrant revolutionaries who were spreading subversive doctrines. A 1919 attorney general's report on radical newspapers in the United States laid out the dimensions of this problem. The Justice Department identified 327 radical papers, a full two-thirds of which (222) were published in foreign languages. Justice counted another 144 radical newspapers that were published abroad but that circulated in the United States.[45] These newspapers marked the presence of a substantial immigrant, radical population. Unlike the masses of isolated and "dumb" immigrants who supplied the raw labor for American industry, these revolutionists were literate, cerebral, and clever. Against them, the literacy test instituted by the Immigration Act of 1917 was useless.

In the minds of increasing numbers of Americans, these radicals were largely Jewish. Because Russian Jews were overrepresented in Bolshevik ranks, some American anti-Communists treated the Bolshevik Revolution as a Jewish plot. One Congressman even offered the fantastic claim that 75 percent of the Bolsheviks in Russia were Jewish.[46] Much as Adolf Hitler and other right-wing ideologues were beginning to do in Europe, opponents of communism in the United States were drawing on the old stereotype of the devious, cunning, and dangerous Jew to explain the radical new evil that Bolshevism was thought to embody.[47]

In Europe, the tying of Bolshevism to Jewish cunning reinvigorated anti-Semitism. Especially as Europeans tried to recover from the devastation of war, they found in the Jew a convenient scapegoat, as they had done so many times before. This was particularly true in large stretches of central and eastern Europe, and it prompted hundreds of thousands of Jews there to contemplate escape to America. They overwhelmed American consulates with requests for passports and visas.[48] Few among them were Bolsheviks; they were far more likely to be in flight from the Bolshevik regime than carriers of the Bolshevik "virus." But that made them no more desirable to the American representatives abroad who received their petitions. One consular official in Rumania described the refugees in Bucharest as a class of "economic parasites, tailors, small salesmen, butchers, etc.," with "ideals of moral and business dealings difficult to assimilate to our own." Their moral laxity made them, in the words of an American consular official in Poland, "good material for bolshevik propaganda."[49] In the imaginations of many Americans, as in the minds of the authors of these reports, the image of the Jew as parasite merged with that of the Jew as Bolshevik. In either guise, these Jews, if they came to America, would spread disease and disorder.

American anti-Communists were convinced that Jewish revolutionaries had already harmed America. They pointed to the Russian Jewish anarchists Emma Goldman and Alexander Berkman who, twenty-five years earlier, had attempted to assassinate Henry Clay Frick, then Andrew Carnegie's right-hand man.[50] Emma Goldman's fame had only increased since that moment: by 1919, she was one of the best-known and most feared radicals in the

United States.[51] In Congress, anti-Communists pointed their finger at one of their own, Victor Berger, a German Jewish congressman from Milwaukee. Berger had long been a major figure in the American Socialist Party. He was a moderate socialist, in the sense that he wanted to achieve socialism through the ballot box rather than through strikes or revolution. He was no friend of the Russian Revolution. But he had publicly opposed America's entry into World War I, an act for which he had been convicted under the wartime sedition law and imprisoned. His constituents, in defiance, had reelected him to Congress, even though he was headed for jail.[52] His fellow congressmen could not contain their outrage. Congressman Percy E. Quin of Mississippi (Democrat) called him "a more dangerous character . . . within the United States" than anyone else and condemned the "colony of Germany . . . in Milwaukee" for reelecting "that enemy of this Government to the Congress." In Quin's eyes, and the eyes of others, Berger's continued popularity demonstrated how easily foreign Jewish revolutionaries could manipulate isolated "colonies" of immigrant workers. He wanted Congress to solve this double immigrant problem through draconian immigration restriction, and he called on his colleagues "to kick him [Berger] out of the doors" whenever he arrived from jail to assume his congressional seat.[53]

Anti-Communists also feared Italian immigrants. Like European Jews, hundreds of thousands of Italians were eager to emigrate to the United States. Significant numbers among them as well were drawn to radicalism. Italian radicals in this country tended to be anarchists rather than Communists or socialists, but the Bolsheviks' success in Russia had convinced them that their moment of revolution, too, was at hand. The threat of Italian anarchism seized the American public's attention in 1920, when two Italian-born anarchists, Nicola Sacco and Bartolomeo Vanzetti, were arrested in Brockton, Massachusetts, and charged with the robbery and murder of a paymaster at a Brockton factory. Convicted of first-degree murder in a notorious trial, they would eventually be executed for their alleged crime. But even before the verdicts were handed down and long before the execution was carried out, the incident was used to symbolize the vulnerability of America to foreign revolutionists. Calls for the exclusion of Italian immigrants joined with those directed against Jews.[54]

Proponents of such exclusionary measures also hoped to combat the organized crime syndicates that had emerged in some Italian communities. Italian criminals, of course, were interested in wealth and power rather than ideology or revolution. But they appeared like the revolutionists in important ways. Both groups were seen as clever and conspiratorial, manipulating the isolated immigrant masses to serve their own purposes. And both were purported to be ruthless and immoral in their willingness to violate American laws and traditions for the sake of their own advancement. Further, Prohibition was making the gangsters more dangerous by handing them the newly outlawed liquor industry to run.[55]

Something had to be done to keep these people out of the country. Senator Thomas J. Heflin of Alabama (Democrat) succinctly summed up the case: "You have it in your power," he told his fellow senators, "to do the thing this day that will protect us against criminal agitators and red anarchists . . . you have it in your power to build a wall against bolshevism, which is seeking to aid a world movement by spreading its poison here; you have it in your power to keep out of your country criminal hordes of Europe." The Senate and House responded to this sort of pleading by passing the emergency Immigration Act of 1921 by overwhelming majorities.[56]

As in 1917, the bill's purpose was to restrict the number of eastern and southern European immigrants (Jews and Italians in particular). Its method was to limit the immigration from any country to 3 percent of that country's population resident in the United States in 1910.[57] By such calculations, the total number of openings for eastern and southern Europeans would total only about 150,000, an 80 percent reduction from the prewar average of 738,000. Another 200,000 slots would be allocated to immigrants from northwest Europe, thus restoring a more favorable balance between the old immigrants and the new. President Wilson, serving out the final months of his presidency, refused to sign the bill, but President Warren Harding did on May 19, 1921. By an act of Congress on May 11, 1922, the provisions of this emergency legislation were extended to June 30, 1924, by which time Congress expected to install a permanent system of immigration restriction.[58]

Unlike the 1917 law, the 1921 law did its work. By 1923, the number of immigrants from southern and eastern Europe had shrunk from 513,813 to 151,491, from 79 to 49 percent of total European immigration. As a proportion of immigration from all areas of the world, southern and eastern Europeans had fallen from almost two-thirds to a little more than a quarter.[59]

Thus, as Congress contemplated an enduring policy of immigration restriction for 1924, it had an opportunity to congratulate itself on a social policy that had quickly brought about the desired result: shrinking the number of immigrants from eastern and southern Europe. The mood of the country could certainly have permitted a moment of congratulation and relaxation. Prosperity had returned after the depressed years of 1920 and 1921, and worries about crowded labor markets were ebbing. Europe had begun to stabilize itself, easing American anxieties that millions of Europeans were desperate to immigrate to the United States. The Soviet Union was entrenched in the lands of the former Russian Empire, but the fear of an imminent red revolution in the United States was fading. Nevertheless, Congress remained obsessed with the menace that eastern and southern Europeans, especially Jews and Italians, posed to the United States. Both houses of Congress were determined to eliminate that menace altogether if possible. This determination became the driving force behind the Immigration Restriction Act of 1924.

To justify their anxieties about eastern and southern Europeans, the framers of the 1924 act turned increasingly to a new racial ideology, scientific racism, that had taken root in popular, scholarly, and policy-making communities. This racism rested on a belief that the world's peoples comprised many different, and differentially endowed, races. Northwest Europeans and their descendants in America, Canada, and Australia were thought to be the races most gifted with intelligence, character, and capacity for self-government. Eastern and southern Europeans, meanwhile, were depicted as racially inferior and incapable, by reason of heredity, of assimilating American values and beliefs. Many of the scientists who adhered to this racism were eugenicists, in the sense that they wished to maximize America's superior racial stock and minimize the numbers of racial inferiors. Their racist discourse structured debates about immigrants in the popular press, in the courts, and even in Congress, as the 1924 immigration restriction legislation was taking shape.

Thus, the star witness before the House Committee on Immigration and Naturalization, where the 1924 bill was drafted, was Harry H. Laughlin, a prominent eugenicist. The committee had appointed him as its "expert eugenics agent" in 1920 and asked him to study the "degeneracy" and "social inadequacy" of various immigrant groups. For Laughlin, the various forms of social degeneracy—feeblemindedness, insanity, crime, epilepsy, tuberculosis, alcoholism, dependency—were rooted in racial degeneracy. Thus, the best social policy was based not on the care or even, in the case of criminals, incarceration of degenerates, but on their elimination from society. With respect to immigrants, this meant passing a law banning "degenerate" groups. The report Laughlin delivered to Congress in November 1922 purported to find much higher levels of degeneracy among the new immigrants than among the old, and this finding became a central weapon in the restrictionists' arsenal.[60]

Racialist language and eugenicist principles permeated discussions on the House and Senate floor. Congressman Fred S. Purnell of Indiana (Republican) declared: "There is little or no similarity between the clear-thinking, self-governing stocks that sired the American people and this stream of irresponsible and broken wreckage that is pouring into the lifeblood of America the social and political diseases of the Old World." Purnell quoted approvingly the words of a Dr. Ward, who claimed that Americans had deceived themselves into believing that "we could change inferior beings into superior ones." Americans could not escape the laws of heredity, Ward argued. "We can not make a heavy horse into a trotter by keeping him in a racing stable. We can not make a well-

Fig. 10. "I Am the Undesirable Immigrant," 1924. This comic strip by Herbert Johnson satirizes America's dread of eastern and southern European immigrants. It captures both the revulsion against the alleged looks, smell, and stupidity of the new immigrants and the fear that these undesirables would destroy American political institutions ("All gov'ment is tyrants!"). (Courtesy Library of Congress)

bred dog out of a mongrel by teaching him tricks." The acts that Ward dismissed as "tricks" included the learning by immigrants of the Gettysburg Address and the Declaration of Independence.[61]

Congressman J. Will Taylor of Tennessee (Republican), meanwhile, approvingly read to his colleagues a *Boston Herald* editorial warning that America was entering the same period of eugenical decline that had doomed Rome: "Rome had [mistaken] faith in the melting pot, as we have. It scorned the iron certainties of heredity, as we do. It lost its instinct for race preservation, as we have lost ours. It flooded itself with whatever people offered themselves from everywhere, as we have done. It forgot that men must be selected and bred as sacredly as cows and pigs and sheep, as we have not learned." "Rome rapidly senilized and died," the editorial concluded, and so would America unless Congress took note of hereditarian principles and passed the 1924 restriction legislation.[62]

"Mongrelization" emerged as an obsession in these eugenics-inflected discussions. The word described the same sociological process of racial mixing that "the melting pot" did, except that it cast it in a wholly negative light. Restrictionists repeatedly called on their fellow congressmen to rid themselves of the "delusional" and dangerous notion that race mixing might actually be a good thing.[63] Some drew on ingrained nightmares of black-white miscegenation and of the cunning, immoral, and evil offspring that such mixing allegedly produced. Representative Elton Watkins of Oregon (Democrat) declared that "our sturdy pioneer race" was being replaced by "a mongrel one, an unstable and bastardized population, where character and merit would have no recognition to leadership, but might and greed would be supreme."[64] Representative John J. McSwain (Democrat) of South Carolina had been impressed by a section of *America's Race Heritage* in which the author, Clinton Stoddard Burr, had tied Bolshevism to mongrelization. "Many a warped brain that menaces world politics in our modern day," Burr had written, "may be attributed to the mongrel blood of the individual."[65] Another congressman chimed in that all eastern and southern European revolutionaries—"soviets and the socialists and the bolshevists, the radicals and anarchists"—were "mixed bloods."[66] America's salvation from the Bolsheviks, degeneracy, and other evils, declared Congressman R.E.L. Allen of West Virginia (Democrat), lay in "purifying and keeping pure the blood of America."[67] This entailed closing the immigrant gates to all except those individuals who came from northwest Europe and who belonged to the same Nordic or Saxon stock that had originally settled the United States.

Purnell, Taylor, McSwain, Allen, and others in their camp were heirs to the long tradition of constructing the nation in racialist terms. Theodore Roosevelt had imagined the nation in this way; he had drawn racial boundaries more expansively than did 1920s restrictionists (he included the new immigrants within his favored racial circle), but he had never thought that those boundaries could be eliminated altogether if America was to realize its destiny. The restrictionists infused this racialist inheritance with the modern principles of eugenics and thereby hoped to achieve an America of greater racial purity than Roosevelt had thought possible or desirable.

This new emphasis on racial purity and ineradicable racial differences challenged American notions of equality and democracy. Laughlin frankly explained the nature of the challenge: "We in this country have been so imbued with the idea of democracy, or the equality of all men, that we have left out of consideration the matter of blood or natural inborn hereditary mental and moral differences. No man who breeds pedigreed plants and animals can afford to neglect this thing, as you know."[68] Representative Grant M. Hudson of Michigan (Republican) echoed these words when he introduced into the *Congressional Record* this excerpt from a Wisconsin magazine: "We must recognize the danger in the fact that we have armed these heterogeneous American stocks with a political weapon many of them are congenitally unfit to use, and clothed legions of them by legislative fiat with an 'equality' which flies in the face of nature and their history."[69] Hudson and others did not actually propose the jettisoning of democracy and its replacement by the rule of racial superiors, but they did underscore the importance of "race inheritance in self-government." Only by strengthening America's racial stock would American democracy be restored to its potential and "Americanism . . . permitted to expand and develop the freedom and blessing of the human race."[70]

To improve America's racial stock, the framers of the 1924 legislation proposed a quota principle similar to that found in the 1921 act, but one far more discriminatory in intent. They wanted to shift the census year in which the quota was to be determined from 1910 to 1890, and cut the quota from 3 to 2 percent of a country's population living in the United States at that time. These two changes were calculated to reduce the total annual immigration quota from 350,000 to 165,000, and, in the process, to shrink southern and eastern European immigration to insignificance. If it passed, the 1924 law would reduce annual southern and eastern European immigration to only 18,439, a mere 3 percent of its average annual prewar level (738,000). Congress had found a way to dam this unwanted immigrant stream.[71]

Whereas Congress as a whole worried most about the effects of a "degenerate" eastern and southern European presence, agitated western congressmen and senators were preoccupied by the Japanese "threat." White westerners saw themselves as being on the far western edge of the white man's frontier, constantly menaced by the yellow races of Asia, especially the Japanese. For that reason, they insisted, their concerns about the Asians could not be dismissed as a local or regional concern. The future of America as a white nation, indeed the fate of white civilization worldwide, hinged on containing the Japanese threat. The United States, of course, had already responded to this threat: by the terms of the Gentlemen's Agreement of 1907, the Japanese government was obligated to halt the flow of Japanese male laborers to the United States, a policy that had dramatically slowed Japanese immigration. But, in the view of white westerners, it had not cut Japanese immigration enough, given the threat that the Japanese posed.

White westerners feared the energy, diligence, frugality, and ingenuity of the Japanese immigrants. As they pored over Laughlin's congressional report, they noticed that the Japanese suffered less from degeneracy than virtually any other group, including the vaunted British.[72] And some white westerners even conceded that, in virtually every endeavor, white Americans were no match for the Japanese. Congressman John F. Miller of Washington (Republican) declared that the "Japanese can drive any white man out of any production anywhere or in anything into which he enters." In his hometown of Seattle, Miller claimed the Japanese were displacing whites from agriculture, truck farming, small groceries and markets, jewelry stores, dry goods clothing, drugstores, tailoring, and even hotels and banks. Japanese women, Miller alleged, were bearing children at levels that white women could never reach.[73] "The American father, the American mother, the American child," intoned Senator Samuel N. Shortridge of California (Republican), "cannot successfully compete with the oriental."[74] In social darwinist terms, these white westerners were running up the white flag.

In 1913 Chester H. Rowell, a California progressive and editor of the *Fresno Republican*, had written a frank piece on why the Japanese so threatened white Americans. "Injustice has been the only American way of meeting a race problem," he argued. "We dealt unjustly with the Indian, and he died. We dealt unjustly with the negro, and he submits. If Japanese ever come in sufficient numbers to constitute a race problem, we shall deal unjustly with them, and they will neither die nor submit."[75] Picking up the same theme, Congressman Israel M. Foster of Ohio (Republican) noted in 1924 that the Japanese "lacked the docile, subservient qualities that are essential" to being an inferior race in America.[76] The Japanese constituted a racial group over whom whites held no natural advantage; they could not be bullied into submission, nor could they be killed off. "This is the bigness of the problem," wrote Rowell, "and the whole reason for the emotional intensity of California's agitation over a situation whose present practical dimensions are relatively insignificant." For Californians and, by extension, the rest of America and the entire Western world, "the possible crisis takes on the significance of Thermopylae."[77]

Fears of racial commingling between white Americans and Japanese immigrants joined fears of racial competition. Congressman Miller declared all marriages between Japanese men and white girls to be "failures—tragedies, sad and pathetic. Many a white girl has tried it to her undying sorrow. . . . No greater tragedy can befall an American girl" than to marry a Japanese man.[78] The abhorrence of such interracial unions propelled the opposition to "mixed"

Fig. 11. The Japanese "Invade" America, 1920. In this 1920 political campaign poster, the Japanese are depicted as silent but powerful invaders who, left unopposed, will conquer California. The crusade to stop Japanese immigration begun in California soon reached Congress and shaped the restriction legislation passed in 1924. (Courtesy Library of Congress)

schools, where Japanese boys sat alongside "American" girls. Rowell, in his article, reproduced this telling testimony given by a white California farmer to the California legislature. " 'Up at Elk Grove, where I live,' he [the farmer] said, 'on the next farm a Japanese man lives, and a white woman. That woman is carrying around a baby in her arms. What is that baby? It isn't white. It isn't Japanese. I'll tell you what it is—it is the beginning of the biggest problem that ever faced the American people.'"[79]

Separation of the yellow and white races was "in the very nature of things."[80] "Nature's God," declared Foster, "has given the world a brown man, a yellow man, and black man." God "contemplated the existence of separate, independent races, peoples, nations," noted Shortridge, "and civilization would be better served by keeping these races and peoples apart. The opponents of Japanese immigration were willing to trade with Japan and to welcome Japanese visitors to the United States; but any lengthy cohabitation of the same space or commingling in the same families would violate the divine plan and bring social disaster to the United States.[81]

Because the Japanese could be neither assimilated nor made subservient, they had to be excluded altogether from America. For that reason, the restrictionists insisted on including in the 1924 legislation a clause barring from the United States all immigrants who were ineligible for citizenship. In decisions handed down in 1922 and 1923, the Supreme Court had ruled that Japanese, Indian, and, by extension, other East and South Asian immigrants fell in this category by virtue of a 1790 law that reserved citizenship for "free white" immigrants. These decisions buoyed the anti-Japanese congressmen and allowed them to think that their views accorded with racial principles laid down at the very moment of the American republic's creation.[82] Thus these congressmen even refused to grant the Japanese the token quota they had given southern and eastern Europeans. The Japanese, like all South and East Asians, were barred altogether from immigrating to the United States. The 1924 Immigration Law, with its draconian, racialized measures against southern and eastern Europeans and against

South and East Asians, passed both houses of Congress by over-whelming margins.

The law's passage had been made possible, in part, by the with-drawal of corporations from the antirestrictionist coalition. Until the early 1920s, large employers had been convinced that open borders were essential to the health of their businesses, insuring them of a continuous supply of cheap labor, and they had led the campaigns to keep the immigrant gates wide open. But the inter-ruption of the European supply by World War I had forced employ-ers to seek out other sources of labor closer to home and to acceler-ate their plans to mechanize their production so as to reduce their aggregate labor needs. They turned to southern blacks migrating North, Mexican peasants fleeing the turmoil of their nation's revo-lution, and, to a certain extent, young single (and white) women, whose entry into the work force in World War I widened opportu-nities for them in the postwar era. Meanwhile, corporations used a portion of their wartime government subsidies and profits for capital improvements that yielded advances in mechanization and production efficiency. Thus, by the mid-1920s, many had become convinced that they no longer required eastern and southern Euro-pean immigrant labor, and they ceased to voice objections to those intent on restricting immigration. Indeed, the 1924 debates are re-markable for the absence of a corporate voice, pro or con. On only one matter, the question of Mexican immigration, did big business make its desires known, and its insistence that no upper limits be placed on the number of Mexican peasants allowed to enter the United States yielded a provision in the 1924 law that exempted all nations of the Western Hemisphere from the quota system. Thus the absence of corporate interest in the debate on European and Asian immigration arguably played a significant, if invisible, role in the legislation's passage. But if business subtly enhanced the chances for restriction's passage, it did not, in any way, determine the racialized character of the act.[83]

Immigration restriction dramatically shrank the numbers of newcomers, altered the "racial" complexion of the nation, and pressured immigrants already here to assimilate. It also drew on and contributed to virtually all the other initiatives of the disciplinary project. In its characterization of the new immigrants as degenerate and weak-willed, it expressed the same sentiments that fueled Prohibition. In depicting southern and eastern European immigrants as devious, cerebral revolutionaries who were bringing social disaster to the United States, it tapped the vast reservoir of antiradical feeling that had produced the postwar Red Scare. It fed on western anxieties about Japanese grit, cunning, and unassimilability that, in California and Washington, had already yielded laws stripping Japanese immigrants of their civil rights, including the right to own and lease land.[84] Finally, the kind of eugenics-inflected revulsion against "mongrelization" that informed congressional immigration debates in Congress also triggered an expansion and hardening of state antimiscegenation laws. This process culminated with the passage, in 1924 Virginia, of a statute that historian Peggy Pascoe has described as "the most draconian miscegenation law in American history." The law prohibited a white from marrying a black, Asian, American Indian, or "Malay"; and it changed the definition of who counted as a black person from anyone who was at least one-sixteenth black to any individual possessing at least one black ancestor, no matter how remote.[85] The Virginia statute, passed in the same year as immigration restriction, powerfully strengthened the nation's substantial body of racially and eugenically based marriage laws.

We do not usually think of the 1920s, the easygoing Jazz Age, as a time when the racialized character of the American nation intensified, reinforcing the barriers separating blacks and Asians from whites, eastern and southern Europeans from "Nordics," and immigrants from natives. Yet these developments were central to the age. That the proponents of these changes frequently justified their aims in the name of science underscores the modern character of the racial regime they implemented. Indeed this regime, backed by an edifice of race law, would remain in place for forty years, persisting through the Great Depression, World War II, the affluent

1950s, and John F. Kennedy's 1960 election. It must be seen for what it was: a defining feature of modern America.

CIVIC NATIONALISM IN THE NEW RACIAL REGIME

The antiradical and anti-immigrant legislation of the 1920s did not go unchallenged. Immigrant radicals protested on behalf of those who faced deportation. Liberal religious groups decried the racial and political intolerance upon which much of the repression rested. Liberal advocacy groups, such as the American Civil Liberties Union, sprang up to fight the repressive state in all its manifestations. Southern and eastern Europeans began naturalizing and voting in large numbers, hoping to defeat politicians who had passed laws harmful to their interests. These individuals and groups frequently couched their protests in the language of American civic nationalism, declaring that they were fighting for an America that encouraged the free exchange of ideas and that made no distinctions on the basis of race, creed, or religion.[86] In the process, the immigrants and ethnics among them strengthened their ties to a nation that had stigmatized them as racially inferior.

Even Asian immigrants found inspiration in the tradition of civic nationalism, for they benefited indirectly but substantially from the Fourteenth Amendment. By granting citizenship and equal protection to all persons born in the United States, this amendment insured that the Asian immigrants' American-born children would become full-fledged citizens upon birth, with all the individual rights and opportunities for political influence that such a status conferred on its holders.[87] The immigrant groups whom the restrictionists despised would thus never face the danger of becoming a caste of perpetual aliens, marginalized and exploited across the generations by their exclusion from citizenship. Many restrictionists in America and in Congress were unhappy with the access to citizenship that the children of unwanted immigrants would one day enjoy. But while some state assemblies proposed that the terms

of the Fourteenth Amendment be changed to serve the purposes of
Asian exclusion or some other racialist agenda, no one in Congress
dared make this argument, at least not on the Senate or House
floor.[88]

The benefits that the Fourteenth Amendment conferred on
Asian Americans were unintended, for the amendment had been
drafted with the needs of black freedmen, not foreigners, in mind.
And its mere existence, as the case of African Americans during
the era of Jim Crow amply demonstrated, did not insure that racial
minorities would actually possess the equal rights to which they
were entitled. Nevertheless, the Fourteenth Amendment strengthened the liberal character of the nation's constitutional regime. Its
importance was not just practical but symbolic, for in opening the
door to the full inclusion of immigrant offspring it allowed even
those Asian immigrants who were experiencing the full brunt of
the repressive state in the 1920s to think that America could be
redeemed, its civic nationalist tradition strengthened, and its racialized boundaries weakened, even eliminated.

Still, the pressures on immigrants in 1920s America were great.
To be Catholic or Jewish, or to be a Japanese immigrant in these
years was to experience taunts and discrimination. Radicals and
illegals in these groups risked deportation; all had to endure being
cut off from cultures and families that had long nurtured them
while contending with an American environment increasingly hostile to displays of cultural difference. The pressure to Americanize
was enormous, even among radical immigrants who despised much
of American culture as decadent and bourgeois. Sometimes the responses to and the protests against these pressures were brave and
stirring. But at other times, those who had been targeted sought to
avert the worst by siding with the nativist majority and embracing
the very racist values that had done them so much harm. Nowhere
is this tendency toward capitulation clearer than in the small band
of congressmen who opposed the Immigration Restriction Act of
1924. They denounced and ridiculed the racist pretensions of the
1924 act as they applied to Europeans, delivering ringing and eloquent endorsements of the nation's civic nationalist tradition. But

they also acquiesced in the racial denigration of the Japanese, reinforcing the very racialization they so deplored.

The congressional opponents of immigration restriction were small in number and drawn largely from New York City, Chicago, and heavily immigrant districts in Connecticut, Rhode Island, and Massachusetts. Adolph J. Sabath of Illinois (Democrat), and Samuel Dickstein and Emanuel Celler of New York City (both Democrats) were among their leaders. A young Fiorello LaGuardia, also of New York City (Republican), was rising rapidly in their ranks. They had no chance of stopping the restrictionist juggernaut and little chance of eliminating the racist component of the legislation. But they did not smolder in silence: they were outraged by the discrimination against eastern and southern Europeans and determined to let everyone in the Capitol know it. They were emboldened by the knowledge that they stood for a civic nationalism every bit as powerful as the racial nationalism espoused by their opponents.

Thus, Congressman Richard S. Aldrich of Rhode Island (Republican) denounced the 1924 bill as "the worst kind of discrimination against a large class of individuals and absolutely opposed to our American ideas of equality and justice."[89] Congressman John J. O'Connor of New York (Democrat) declared that the stigmatization of certain European races as inferior would render his America unrecognizable: "This is not the America I belong to. That is not the America that I was brought up to love and to worship. That is not the America that I want to be a part of."[90] And Congressman Peter F. Tague of Massachusetts (Democrat) reminded the restrictionists how their proposed bill would sully the memory of all those boys from eastern and southern Europe who had given their lives for America in the Great War. Recalling his trip to Arlington's National Cemetery, he mused, "I stood awhile at the tomb of America's Unknown Soldier, the last resting place of him, whom we know not, nor whence he came. Standing there, with bared head, I wondered if in life he was an Italian, an Irishman, a Jew, a Nordic, a Slav, or what. . . . I thought of what a travesty on American ideals it would be if in passing this bill we would prevent coming to America the unknown mother of our revered unknown soldier."[91]

Like Tague, other opponents of restriction referred to the loyalty and sacrifices of first- and second-generation immigrants from southern and eastern Europe who served in the U.S. Army in World War I. Sabath pointed out that 420,000 such individuals served in the military and fought valiantly.[92] Congressman Nathan D. Perlman of New York (Republican) entered into the *Congressional Record* the names of the ethnic American soldiers who had received the distinguished service cross in World War I.[93] Congressman W. Frank James from Michigan (Republican) exclaimed that the newest immigrant in the army "was as good an American and just as willing to fight and die" as those who claimed descent from the Mayflower.[94] To back up his point, he drew on no less an authority than General E. H. Crowder, the architect and administrator of the military draft: "The great and inspiring revelation here," Crowder had written, "has been that men of foreign and of native origin alike responded to the call to arms with a patriotic devotion that confounded the cynical plans of our arch enemy and surpassed our own highest expectations. . . . No need to speculate how it has come about; the great fact is demonstrated that America makes Americans."[95]

Although the arguments of the antirestrictionists failed to deter the restrictionist majority, their affirmation of a civic conception of nationalism helped to sustain a tradition that would become an important weapon in future fights. But these antirestrictionists did not always stand up for their civic nationalist tradition. Indeed, on the question of Japanese exclusion, they abandoned it altogether.

The Japanese question altered the nature of racialist discourse in Congress. The bias against southern and eastern Europeans stemmed from the conviction that they constituted races that were inferior to those of northwest Europe. But whenever discussion shifted to the Japanese, the racial distinctions among Europeans seemed to disappear. Now only four races in the world mattered: white (Europeans), yellow (Asians), black (Africans), and brown (Indians and nonwhite Hispanics). America's mission, according to the opponents of the Japanese, was to preserve the integrity of the white, European race and the civilization it had so laboriously built.

This racialist discourse put the defenders of the eastern and southern European immigrants in an awkward position. On the one hand, it inclined them to sympathize with and fight for the Japanese who, like their own constituents, experienced the sting of racial discrimination. On the other hand, it allowed them to distance the southern and eastern Europeans from the colored races, and to argue that the former belonged to the same superior European race as the English and Germans. More often than not, the congressional representatives of the eastern and southern Europeans, some of whom were themselves new immigrants, embraced this second option. They thus became complicit in promoting a racialized nationalism that, in other circumstances, they deplored.

Defending Japanese immigrants was not an unimaginable position to take in 1924. Secretary of State Charles Evan Hughes, following in the tradition of Roosevelt himself, laid out a geopolitical argument for granting the Japanese a small annual quota on the basis of the 1890 census and thus putting them on a par with southern and eastern Europeans. Even such a small concession (the annual quota would have allowed only forty-six Japanese to immigrate to the United States each year), Hughes reasoned, would serve the United States well in foreign affairs. It would strengthen the Western-oriented, democratic forces within Japan, weaken the militarists there, and make Japan a force for peace rather than war in East Asia.[96]

Hughes's modest proposal went nowhere. Overwhelming majorities in both Houses regarded the admittance of 46 Japanese immigrants a year (or 246, if the House version of the bill were to be adopted) as unacceptable.[97] The restrictionist James D. Phelan, a former California Democratic senator, explained why in a letter he sent to Hughes: "The ultimate purpose of the Japanese . . . is to establish themselves in this country on an equality with Europeans and thus enjoy citizenship, the voting privilege, the ownership of land, and other benefits they do not now enjoy." This ambition to be treated like European immigrants could not be tolerated, argued Phelan, for it would enable the Japanese "to win their first battle in their campaign for an acknowledgement of racial equality."[98] And winning this first battle would lead to further victories and to eventual social disaster in the United States.

The defenders of the eastern and southern European immigrants might have pointed out how strange it was to hear the Immigration Restriction Act of 1924 invoked as an instrument of racial equality, when the driving force behind it was to stigmatize entire groups of Europeans as racially inferior and undesirable. So, too, they might have shown some solidarity with the Japanese who, by Phelan's clear admission, were fighting for the simple benefits of citizenship. But they did not. Adolph Sabath declared that he, Dickstein, and other minority members of the House Committee on Immigration and Naturalization were "all in favor of exclusion of the Japanese."[99] Dickstein, himself, made the same point in dramatic fashion, interrupting an anti-Japanese tirade by California Congressman John E. Raker (Democrat) to "make it clear" that he shared Raker's point of view.[100] Only LaGuardia showed some sympathy for Japanese plight, but Sabath was quick to cut him off and shut him up. Young and inexperienced, LaGuardia did not challenge Sabath's gag order.[101]

Listening to Raker and other western politicians, Sabath, Dickstein, and others grasped how much a campaign against the Japanese could benefit immigrants from southern and eastern Europe. Whenever talk focused on the Japanese, the racial standing of the southern and eastern Europeans seemed to rise. The latter were no longer racially despised peoples, but simply Europeans, racially and culturally indistinguishable from the Germans, English, and Scandinavians. The designation of the Japanese and, by extension, all "yellow" people as the racial other had magically fused all Europeans into members of a single superior race. The eastern and southern Europeans no longer had to listen to charges that they were degenerate, mongrelized, and unassimilable. Denigrating the Japanese elevated the new immigrants and allowed them to claim identities that some in their ranks desperately wanted—as Americans, white Americans, Caucasians. When they saw how America's fondness for racial distinctions might benefit their people, Sabath, Dickstein, and their supporters made the fateful decision to play America's racial game.

If we deplore this decision, it is not so hard to understand why Sabath and Dickstein made it. Immigrants quickly grasped how much race mattered in American society and how much their future prosperity and freedom depended on getting situated on the right side of the racial divide. The Supreme Court decisions of 1922 and 1923 rendering Asian immigrants ineligible for citizenship, the strengthening of antimiscegenation law, and the growing appeal of eugenics signaled that race was becoming more, not less, important in public policy. And these developments evidently encouraged Sabath, Dickstein, and others to believe that ringing endorsements of America's civic nationalist tradition would not be enough to guarantee the interests of their constituents. When they saw an opportunity to place their constituents on the right, white side of the racial divide, they grabbed it.

They and other antirestrictionists also did so in regard to blacks and Mexicans. In the great debate on immigration that raged from 1920 through 1924, African Americans constituted the invisible racial other, meriting only a handful of mentions in thousands of pages of congressional testimony and debate. But America had learned how to talk about race from its own history of black-white relations, and the resonance of such terms as "race purity," "racial incompatibility," and "mongrelization" drew on this experience. When blacks did become visible, they were marked by virtually all debate participants as inferior, unassimilable, subservient, and lacking the racial instinct for self-government. Restrictionists tended to group the new immigrants with blacks, as a way of demonstrating the former's inferiority. Antirestrictionists, meanwhile, insisted on the vast gulf separating the two groups as part of their effort to demonstrate that southern and eastern Europeans were capable—unlike blacks—of assimilating to American values and institutions.[102] Antirestrictionists also insisted on the superiority of the new immigrants to those from Mexico, and how unjust it

would be to pass a law—as the 1924 legislation proposed to do—
that excluded the former while continuing to admit the latter. As
Congressman John Philip Hill of Maryland (Republican) declared,
"I prefer to have Europeans rather than Mexican peons";
La Guardia concurred.[103]

The new immigrants themselves in the 1930s and beyond would
behave much like their representatives in Congress. Out of their
ranks would come a vigorous movement to oppose racial distinctions and to compel America to live up to ideals enunciated in the
Declaration of Independence and Constitution. Out of their ranks,
too, would come a desire to prove their whiteness and to claim its
privileges. They would carry forward both the civic and racialized
notions of American nationalism.

ABORTING THE NEW NATIONALISM

Had Roosevelt lived until 1924 or 1925, he would not have been
entirely pleased with the outcome of the disciplinary project. He
would have looked approvingly at the pressures brought to bear
on immigrants to give up their Old World cultures. He might have
gloried in the repression of the left and might have regarded the
slamming shut of immigrant gates as a regrettable necessity; even
as it stigmatized groups, such as eastern and southern Europeans,
whom he respected, it nevertheless promised to strengthen the
boundaries of the nation, intensify the demands for loyalty, naturalization, and Americanism, and affirm the whiteness of the American people. He might even have joined the many liberal Americans
of the time in believing that the stiff restrictions on immigration
enacted by the 1924 law would, despite their racially offensive
character, at least allow the melting pot to do its work and the
transformation of eastern and southern Europeans into white
Americans to proceed.[104]

But he would not have accepted the humiliation of the Japanese
nation embodied in Congress's refusal to include its emigrants in
the quota system. And he would have been furious at Congress's

failure to complete the work of nation building by erecting, in the 1920s, an enduring New Nationalist state.

Roosevelt had long been convinced that the success of the American national experiment depended as much on the spread of economic opportunity as on the imposition of cultural, racial, and political discipline. And Roosevelt further believed that a large federal state was essential to regulate capital, to place economic opportunity within reach of the downtrodden, and to insure an economic environment conducive to general prosperity. In such an environment, immigrants would not simply be turned into Americans through the coercive power of the federal government. They would voluntarily affiliate with America, convinced that they stood to benefit from joining a society that offered far more economic opportunity and advancement than did the societies into which they had been born. The act of choosing to become American would give their Americanness a depth and conviction that could never be achieved by disciplinary policies alone.

In World War I the New Nationalist state that Roosevelt and other progressives had long dreamed about seemed to materialize. The Wilson administration established federal agencies to regulate industry, labor, railroads, and agriculture. The immediate objective, of course, was to harness the nation's immense and sprawling economy to maximum and efficient war production. But the progressives in the Wilson administration saw this as an opportunity for the democratic state to rein in the power of capital, to augment the rights of labor, and to spread the benefits of American abundance more equitably throughout the population. If this wartime experiment were to go well, then its principles could be applied to a peacetime economy.

The New Nationalist state succeeded on several levels. The Food Administration and the U.S. Railroad Administrations, under the direction of Herbert Hoover and William McAdoo respectively, performed especially impressively, with Hoover devising an ingenious incentive system that insured the prodigious production of foodstuffs and McAdoo brilliantly managing the complex rail system that had been put under his control. The War Industries Board, charged with supervising American manufacturers, ran into considerable resistance from industrialists and from the War and Navy Departments until Bernard Baruch was able to cajole the various players into working together. The employers and workers whom the National War Labor Board was charged with managing also proved difficult to control, although the board did settle some nasty disputes while granting labor unions a stronger national voice in governmental affairs than they had ever enjoyed before.[105]

Certainly the wartime state had accomplished enough in terms of supervising the economy to provide a solid foundation on which to build its peacetime equivalent. Indeed, the heady wartime experience of imposing public regulation on a private economy would fire the imaginations of progressives and liberals for a generation.[106] But the progressives lost their majority in Congress in 1918; in 1920, they lost the presidency. The Republicans who replaced them were fiercely committed to the proposition that a large government deprived peoples of their liberty. They thus set about dismantling the New Nationalist state; by the early 1920s, barely a trace of it survived.

What did survive, under the direction of Herbert Hoover, first as secretary of commerce and then as president, was a commitment to private-public cooperation. Hoover had taken from his wartime experience not the idea of large-scale public regulation of the economy but rather the more modest conviction that private economic institutions would benefit from cooperating with each other and with the federal government. This was a reasonable reading of the wartime experience, especially since few knew better than Hoover that many wartime government agencies were more powerful on paper than they were in fact. Especially in such agencies as the War Industries Board, success depended on the ability of government officials to persuade private actors to do the government's bidding. Frequently, this meant giving them lucrative financial incentives. But, in Hoover's eyes, success also depended on bringing individual producers together and convincing them of the benefits of cooperation. As a result, he worked tirelessly to impart this ethic of cooperation to widely divergent groups of manufacturers and distributors.[107]

If these tactics contributed to 1920s prosperity, they did little to curtail the power of capital or to help poorer groups of producers contend with the more powerful. They did not strengthen labor or otherwise level an economic playing field that tilted heavily toward the wealthy. To accomplish the latter, the government had to do more than meet with private producers and persuade them of the benefits of cooperation. It had to establish regulatory agencies with the power to enforce the government's will on the economy and to strengthen the weaker groups in their dealings with the more powerful. Hoover was not willing to take this step, and the peacetime New Nationalist state remained a mere blueprint.[108]

Only a minority of 1920s Americans, of course, believed that the economy needed a thoroughgoing reconstruction. By the mid-1920s, prosperity had returned, unemployment had fallen, and real wages were rising. Many Americans, moreover, seemed to be getting quite rich. But there were troubling signs. Throughout the decade, an estimated 40 percent of the working class remained mired in poverty, unable to afford a healthy diet or adequate housing, much less any of the more costly consumer goods. In 1930, 75 percent of American households did not own a washing machine, 70 percent were without a vacuum cleaner, 60 percent had not even a radio, and 50 percent did without a car. The million or more workers who labored in the nation's two largest industries, coal and textiles, suffered the most, for both industries were experiencing severe overcapacity. By 1926 only half of the coal mined each year was being sold. New England textile cities experienced levels of unemployment that sometimes reached 50 percent. Almost everywhere, unions were losing ground, as business and government, backed by middle-class opinion, remained hostile to labor organization.

Labor issues were also immigrant issues. In coal and cotton goods, immigrants composed 60 percent of the work force. In most industrial centers outside the South, immigrants and their children formed working-class majorities. Many were not sharing in 1920s prosperity; the limits on their economic opportunity added to the insecurity that their status as immigrants and as "racial inferiors" had already conferred on them. And this double sense of exclusion complicated their Americanization, at least in terms of how Roosevelt imagined this process of incorporation unfolding. Roosevelt wanted Americanization to produce loyalty and devotion to the nation. But the immigrants' anger at their exclusion might breed a contentious or rebellious Americanism not at all to Roosevelt's liking or in the nation's best interests. Few worried about this outcome in the "roaring 1920s." But the inclination for instability and revolt was incubating and would break upon American society with considerable force in the 1930s.

Developments in the 1920s revealed the complex ways in which the racial and civic nationalist traditions exerted their influence on the American people. Through the immigration restriction act of 1924, racial nationalism achieved a major triumph and insured that it would continue to shape America during its modern era. Ethnic opponents of this legislation, and their congressional supporters, turned to civic nationalist principles as a way of combating the racism they deplored. Moreover, the frustrations with the fragility of working-class life inclined growing numbers in this group to elaborate a set of economic rights as central to civic nationalist fulfillment.

In the process of building a political opposition on civic nationalist principles, European ethnics were, of course, declaring their allegiance to the American nation, a pledge that, prior to World War I, many of them had been disinclined to make. The disciplinary campaign of World War I and its aftermath greatly influenced this transformation in ethnics' loyalty. Only in the 1920s did many begin to imagine themselves as citizens of the American republic. In this way repression had dramatically strengthened the hold that the national imaginary exercised over America's immigrant population. The new consensus on the importance of belonging to the

American nation would not yield political quiescence or stability. To the contrary, furious battles would erupt over the meaning of American ideals. But the disciplinary campaign of the 1920s had done more than simply strengthen the nation. It had also made racialized notions of belonging central to the nation's welfare, and many groups of civic nationalists, even those with frankly liberal or radical agendas, could not entirely free themselves from the taint of racial nationalism's influence. In a variety of ways, some conscious and some not, New Dealers, labor militants, and even Communists would declare that the best Americans were white, Anglo, or Nordic. This would be an enduring legacy of the 1920s and an integral part of the liberal nation that took shape under Franklin Delano Roosevelt's leadership in the 1930s and 1940s.

CHAPTER 4

The Rooseveltian

Nation Ascendant,

1930–1940

The extended emergency of depression and total war presided over by Franklin Delano Roosevelt allowed Americans to engage in an experiment in state building without precedent in their history. During the 1930s and early 1940s, a large state emerged that would regulate America's capitalist system in the interests of general prosperity and of labor-management harmony; that would provide economic assistance to those deemed unable to help themselves and to those—such as veterans—to whom the nation owed a special debt; and that would establish a large military to wage war and protect the peace. Roosevelt and the Democrats in Congress justified this large state in terms of civic nationalist ideas—strengthening the nation, its democratic institutions, and its people during a time of acute distress. Successful in overcoming the antistate sentiments that dominated the 1920s, they completed the liberal nation-building project that Theodore Roosevelt had outlined in 1910.

Because the disciplinary campaign of the 1920s, and especially its immigration restriction component, had been successful in silencing those who might have challenged the cultural and political boundaries of the American nation, FDR and his fellow New Dealers felt little need to emulate TR's commitment to identifying and ostracizing the nation's alleged enemies. FDR liked to stress the openness of American society, not its rigidities. He cultivated a welcoming, rather than a punishing, mien. Perhaps nowhere was his success more evident than in the devotion of the eastern and southern Europeans and their descendants to him and to his New Deal. In word and deed, FDR had welcomed them into the American nation and allowed them to become full-fledged Americans, both in sentiment and in fact. Millions of these ethnics went to the polls for the first time in the 1930s, and they voted for FDR in overwhelming numbers. In a remarkable show of gratitude, nine out of every ten Jews who voted in 1940 cast their ballots for FDR.[1] If the immigration restriction legislation of the 1920s had disciplined this "unruly" and "dangerous" population, the reform legislation of the 1930s and 1940s had opened up opportunities for it—and for Italians, Poles, and others—that had not existed before. Many now counted themselves, as a result, as ardent patriots. Had TR lived until this time, he would have been pleased with how the New Deal supplemented the discipline of the World War I era with opportunities for immigrant European Americans and their children, enabling it to forge a new nation out of heterogeneous stocks.

Devotion to FDR and the New Deal reveals only part of the 1930s story, however, for it ignores the degree to which a popular revolt from below, emerging most forcefully from the ranks of workers, shaped the civic nationalism of those years. Far more combative than FDR himself, and containing many political radicals in its ranks, the labor movement, especially as it was embodied in the Congress of Industrial Organizations (CIO), used civic nationalist principles to fashion a social democratic creed. It portrayed industrial elites as the chief threat to the nation's well-being and depicted ordinary working-class men and women as America's best citizens. It sparked numerous protests and mobilized millions of workers. This popular pressure pushed FDR to the left, forcing him to make the New Deal far more proworker than it had originally been. In the process it demonstrated the capaciousness of the civic nationalist creed and the degree to which insurgents could use it to advance class-based agendas.

But labor's rise did not go unopposed and, by 1937, in the wake of the dramatic success of a wave of sitdown strikes, conservatives began mobilizing to halt labor's and the New Deal's advance. Led by the likes of Martin Dies, a Democratic congressman from Texas, they countered the social democracy that labor had infused into civic nationalism with a conservative patriotism constructed from principles of individualism, states' rights, anticommunism, and suspicion of foreigners. Dies's father had been a leading restrictionist in the 1910s and 1920s. The younger Dies, though not indulging in the eugenics-inflected talk that had been popular then, blamed eastern and southern Europeans for the nation's problems and declared them unfit for membership in his American nation. Dies's emergence in 1938 into a position of political prominence as chair of the newly established House Special Committee on Un-American Activities allows us to glimpse the continued influence of racial nationalism on American politics and culture. The influence of this tradition, it turns out, manifested itself not simply among opponents of the New Deal but among many of its most stalwart supporters—Communists, the CIO, liberal and left-leaning artists, and even in the thoughts of FDR himself. The survival of racial nationalism in liberal and radical circles should not be used as a justification for claiming that the politics of Dies, FDR, and the CIO were indistinguishable. To the contrary, the political differences among these groups and individuals remained substantial. Still, it does reveal how all participants in the political battles of the 1930s lived in the shadow of the 1920s and of the racial regime that had been established at that time.

A KINDER AND GENTLER NATION BUILDER

From a young age, TR was FDR's hero. In 1907, as a twenty-five-year-old law clerk, FDR imagined a career that would duplicate that of his famous cousin. First, he would win a seat in the New York State Assembly, then he would be appointed assistant secretary of the navy, and then he would become governor of New York, vice-president, and then president of the United States. Incredibly, this is almost exactly what happened (except that he became a state senator rather than an assemblyman and he lost his 1920 race for the vice-presidency). That Franklin adopted Theodore's pince-nez and many of the latter's favorite phrases and pronunciations (such as "bully" and "dee-lighted") further evidences how he emulated him. In politics, FDR first made his mark by taking on the Tammany machine in the New York State Assembly, much as TR had done thirty years before.[2]

Yet, FDR would be no carbon copy of TR. He entered the Democratic Party rather than the Republican, in part because of family tradition (his father had been a Grover Cleveland Democrat) but even more important, because he perceived there to be too many young Roosevelts—TR's own four sons—vying with each other to inherit their father's GOP mantle. He drew close to Woodrow Wilson in World War I and became a supporter of the League of Nations and of liberal internationalism and an opponent of territorial aggrandizement; and though he was never a doctrinaire New Freedom man, he would prove willing to experiment with a greater variety of economic policies than TR had been. Finally, while FDR was hardly free of racial prejudice, he did not share TR's belief in the centrality of racial warfare and of racial hybridity to American greatness.[3]

But in one substantive way, he was TR's ideological heir. He was a fervent nationalist who conceived of the nation as an entity nobler than any particular class, region, or interest. During his presidency, FDR lauded TR as someone "able to see great problems in their true perspective because he looked at the Nation as a whole. There was nothing narrow or local or sectional about him. . . . [He] was a great patriot. . . . Everything about him was big and vital and, above all, national."[4]

FDR was particularly contemptuous, as was TR, of groups, but particularly of elites, that seemed consumed by the pursuit of wealth and heedless of the "higher life." This perspective was rooted partly in FDR's class background, as a member of an older gentry experiencing economic displacement by the likes of the Vanderbilts, Carnegies, and Rockefellers. But it was also imparted to him at Groton, his boarding school, through the teachings of Rector Endicott Peabody, a close friend of TR's and a man to whom FDR would retain a lifelong devotion. Peabody was a kind of American Tory who impressed on his young charges the importance of disinterested public service inspired by Christian values and a concern for the commonweal. Peabody had fully absorbed the muscularized Christianity of his day, seeing great virtue, as did TR, in strenuous living and noble war.[5] TR himself was a frequent visitor to Groton, where he lectured the boys on manhood, public service, and national well-being. As FDR came to see his presidency in terms of reinvigorating the nation and its mission, he turned again and again to what he had learned from TR and Peabody as a young man. He would never become the war enthusiast that TR had been, but he placed great stock in what a nation could achieve by cultivating among its people the higher warlike attributes—resolve, courage, discipline, cooperation, and sacrifice. And he looked back with awe at what he thought the nation had accomplished in World War I, when a spectacular government-inspired mobilization of troops, resources, and morale had won the war and made the United States the most powerful and affluent society on earth. FDR understood how consonant war mobilization was with TR's New Nationalism.

Traces of TR's New Nationalism are everywhere in FDR's First New Deal. The very name New Deal, of course, tied this 1930s program to TR's Square Deal. Key advisers, such as Harold Ickes, secretary of the interior, and Henry A. Wallace, secretary of agriculture, had been Bull Moose progressives. TR would have loved the Civilian Conservation Corps, which took 2.5 million young men out of their communities and placed them in rural paramilitary camps where they were instructed in forestation, irrigation, and national pride. And the National Recovery Administration (NRA), the centerpiece of FDR's First New Deal, bore the imprint of TR's economic philosophy. It called on the government to organize industries into self-regulating cartels that would restrain individual capitalists' propensity to pursue the highest profit without regard for its effects on workers, consumers, or the general prosperity. Cooperation between industrialists would replace ruinous competition, and labor-management harmony would replace class warfare. The government would regulate these processes to insure their success. The nation as a whole, and all its residents, would be the beneficiaries. In its endorsement of large corporations and government regulation, the NRA was close to the New Nationalism. For these reasons, the early New Deal, John Milton Cooper has shrewdly commented, marked "something of a Theodore Roosevelt restoration."[6]

This restoration was apparent, too, in FDR's and the New Dealers' belief in the progressive and ennobling effects of war. They looked upon domestic mobilization during World War I as one of the country's finest hours, a period of "great cooperation" in FDR's words, conveniently overlooking the degree to which that mobilization had depended on repression and persecution of real and imagined dissenters.[7] Looking back, they saw only how war mobilization had finally broken the back of laissez-faire, allowing the government to assume powers it had long lacked and thus to replace economic chaos with planning, exploitation with fairness, competition with cooperation, and poverty with abundance. They celebrated the War Industries Board, the War Labor Board, the Food Administration, and the United States Housing Corporation,

Fig. 12. Franklin D. Roosevelt and the Civilian Conservation Corps, 1933. President Roosevelt visits this Civilian Conservation Corps camp at Big Meadows, Virginia, with several key aides including Secretary of the Interior Harold Ickes (seated third from left), Secretary of Agriculture Henry Wallace (sixth from left), and Assistant Secretary of Agriculture Rexford Tugwell (seventh from left). The paramilitary character of the CCC, evident in the soldierlike uniforms of the CCC men, underscores the degree to which early New Deal programs relied on the metaphors and mobilizing techniques of war. Yet the laughter captured in this moment also points to a softer side of the New Deal, one in which Roosevelt used his compassion and skills at communication to knit together diverse groups of Americans into a single national community. (Courtesy Library of Congress)

and built New Deal agencies on similar designs. They extolled, too, the martial values of cooperation, sacrifice, and determination that had given the American people unity and strength. They sought to bring those same values to bear on America's new enemy, economic depression, convinced that such values would enable Americans to triumph in the same way their predecessors had in World War I. For the nation to go forward, FDR declared in his Inaugural Address, "we must move as a trained army and loyal army willing to sacrifice for the good of a common discipline."[8]

Of all the early New Deal initiatives, the NRA depended the most on wartime analogies. Its business provisions drew on the War Industries Board, its labor provisions on the War Labor Board. Its director was a retired army general, Hugh Johnson, who had been the liaison between the War Industries Board and the army in World War I.[9] Johnson launched a massive propaganda campaign modeled on the wartime work of the Committee of Public Information. Memories of World War I combat even inspired the NRA's Blue Eagle campaign, which called on Americans to demonstrate their support for the government's economic recovery program by wearing a blue eagle button on their work clothes and plastering their homes and businesses with blue eagle decals proclaiming "We Do Our Part." "In war," FDR explained, "in the gloom of night attack, soldiers wear a bright badge on their shoulders to be sure that comrades do not fire on comrades. On that principle, those who cooperate in this [NRA] program must know each other at a glance. That is why we have provided a badge of honor," the Blue Eagle, "and I ask that all those who join with me shall display that badge prominently."[10] It is difficult to imagine an economic program more drenched in the language and metaphors of war. This interpenetration of war and reform would have pleased TR.

But the metaphor of war in the New Deal can be pushed too far. FDR and his New Dealers did not attempt to reproduce every aspect of the World War I experience. They showed scant interest in renewing the disciplinary project that the Great War had spawned. They undertook no concerted campaign against immigrants and their hyphenated Americanism. They organized no great assault on Bolsheviks, Communists, or some radical other, at least in the early 1930s, and, of course, they repealed Prohibition, a key component of the disciplinary project that had sought to undermine the cultural practices of Catholic immigrants. Although TR had not been a prohibitionist, he had supported other elements of the wartime disciplinary campaign, believing that the government ought to spearhead the drive for moral discipline. FDR did not subscribe to this view.

FDR was a kinder and gentler nation builder than TR. TR cultivated an image of himself as a tough cop, forever waving his big stick at enemies—internal and external—who dared to challenge his nation. Integral to this image was a parallel one of TR as a man of action, rounding up horses on his dude ranch, exploring dangerous parts of Africa and the Amazon, leading the charge up San Juan Hill, and busting trusts. FDR had hoped to see military action and, as a young man, had become a vigorous outdoorsman in his own right. But his encounter with polio had left him without use of his legs and a manliness much diminished—a blow to his outdoorsman persona that not even a compliant news media could entirely hide. Nor had he ever possessed the same relish for confrontation as had TR. The historian Geoffrey Ward has noted how "the creative uses of indirection . . . were built into . . . [FDR] from infancy," a result in part of being the only child of an overprotective and indulgent mother. "He had learned early," Ward argues, "that the best technique for getting one's way was often to do one thing while chattering pleasantly about something else."[11]

Also in contrast to TR, FDR deliberately softened the image of the presidential office. FDR pioneered in the use of radio, and his signature use of that medium was the "fireside chat," an informal talk by the president to his people who, presumably, were assembled around the radio, near the hearth, listening to their leader. The fireside image suggests qualities of warmth, caring, even intimacy, and the figure of a kind and forgiving grandfather seeking to sustain and protect his family in the home's warmest spot. Absent from this scenario is the figure of the stern patriarch who reprimands, even casts out, misbehaving offspring. Indeed, FDR made remarkably few efforts in the first two years of his presidency to identify enemies of his nation, groups who merited repression or exclusion. He had targeted the Depression as the enemy, of course, but, in FDR's telling, it had no human agents. He singled out no foreign people and no group of immigrants or radicals as being

responsible for America's plight. Except for an attack on "unscrupulous money changers" in his 1933 Inaugural Address, he re-
frained from castigating Wall Street speculators and their allies.[12]
Throughout his military-like campaign against the Depression, he
stressed the value of savaging one's enemies less than the virtues
of community, cooperation, and sacrifice. He had no intention of
replicating the sternness that had been so integral a part of TR's
public persona. And judging from the volume of mail that inundated FDR in his first few years—an utterly new phenomenon in
the annals of the presidency—Americans loved his "accessibility"
and compassion, and wanted as much of them as they could get.

If differences in upbringing and the onset of a terrible disease
account for some of the divergence in leadership styles between TR
and FDR, differences in the time in which they governed account
for the rest. TR was faced with the task both of unifying an unruly
population and of bringing order to the industrial system. The disciplinary project of the World War I era had accomplished the first
task by the mid-1920s. Immigration had been slowed to a trickle,
ethnic diversity had been repressed and tamed, the racial boundaries of the nation secured. By the time FDR entered office, ethnic
unruliness no longer seemed to matter. Cultural disunity was not
a great worry, nor was the collapse of long-standing racial distinctions. Thus there was less of a need to assume the role of the harsh
disciplinarian. The calamity of the Great Depression, meanwhile,
had created a need for a different kind of leader, able to embrace
his constituents irrespective of whether or not they had jobs,
whether or not they had achieved lofty goals in their private and
work lives, whether or not they were "deserving." Herbert Hoover
was oblivious to this yearning. He cultivated the role of the demanding father, reprimanding Americans who failed to find jobs
and denying them federal relief. Americans loathed him for this
posture.[13] A great deal of FDR's popularity, in contrast, lay in his
ability to act compassionately, evident in his willingness to support
relief for the able-bodied poor and, in more general terms, to extend welfare benefits to large numbers of Americans who needed
help. His embrace of this political style did not mean that he was

more liberal in his social attitudes toward ethnic and racial minorities than TR or even Hoover; in some respects he was less so. It means that by upbringing, inclination, and political savvy, he was able to fulfill the role called for by the times.

A clear demonstration of his compassionate style can be discerned in two 1936 speeches he gave in New York City to mark the fiftieth anniversary of the Statue of Liberty's appearance in New York harbor. A little more than ten years had elapsed since a huge majority in Congress had voted to cut off the "dangerous" immigration streams from southern and eastern Europe. FDR had not participated in that debate, although, at the time, he had supported quotas in another venue: as a member of the Harvard Board of Trustees, he endorsed efforts to cut Jewish enrollment at Harvard by one-half to two-thirds. He, too, had been concerned that American culture and civilization would be overwhelmed by foreigners of questionable morals and intentions. Yet, in his 1936 speech, he expressed no worry about the new immigrants. He betrayed none of TR's anxiety—or of his own—about whether these immigrants wanted to become American, and whether they were capable of handling the responsibilities of citizenship. To the contrary, he embraced the new immigrants, drawing them close to his bosom and, by extension, the bosom of the nation. "We gave them freedom," he asserted. "I am proud—America is proud—of what they have given us." They have improved American civilization and culture, he declared. They have become fully American and have come "to appreciate our free institutions and our free opportunity . . . as well as those who have been here for many generations." Roosevelt even suggested that perhaps "in some cases the newer citizens have discharged their obligations to us better than we have discharged our obligations to them."[14]

That FDR could laud the new citizens in this manner rested on his conviction that the new immigrants had fully Americanized. Rejecting the views that had prevailed among large sections of the native-born American population only ten years earlier, he declared that the new immigrants "have never been—they are not now—half-hearted Americans. In Americanization classes and at night schools they have burned the midnight oil in order to be worthy of their new allegiance." Roosevelt even indicated his support for a mild form of cultural pluralism. "We take satisfaction in the thought that those who have left their native land to join us may still retain here their affection for some things left behind—old customs, old language, old friends." But Roosevelt quickly added that his acknowledgment of their affection for the old was made possible by their obvious devotion to the new. "Looking to the future," Roosevelt noted, the new immigrants "wisely choose that their children shall live in the new language and in the new customs of this new people. And those children more and more realize their common destiny in America."[15]

FDR's celebration of the immigrants likely owed less to fundamental disagreements with TR than to his perception of the time in which he lived. Because the disciplinary project had accomplished its aims, reducing the number of immigrants and increasing the pressures on those already here to Americanize, there was no longer a need to act tough toward the newcomers. One could embrace them, laud their achievements, and welcome them into the American family. The 1930s called for a kinder and gentler nation builder, able to bring diverse streams of Americans together rather than split them apart. Through such measures, the nation-building plans of TR would not be radically changed. To the contrary, they would be hastened to completion.

RADICALIZING THE CIVIC NATIONALIST CREED

There was something else at work in Roosevelt's demeanor toward immigrants in 1936. He was engaged in a reelection campaign for the presidency, and New York was not only FDR's home state but the nation's largest, bringing the victor the greatest single prize of electoral votes. And within that state, as in most states of the industrialized north, the new immigrants and their descendants had become a sizable voting bloc. Anger at the anti-immigrant legislation of the 1920s had inclined many of them to naturalize and to vote.[16]

And the civic nationalist tradition retained enough of its integrity to allow these new voters to believe that the tradition's potential could be redeemed, and that through it they could fashion a comfortable and secure place within their nation. Roosevelt's mere ascension to the presidency was already a victory for them, for it brought to the White House a veteran of New York state politics, where the new immigrants had become a potent force. And their enthusiasm for him is apparent in the size of the NRA mobilizations in New York City. The largest NRA celebration occurred there, with a massive parade down Fifth Avenue and a patriotic assembly at that temple of Americanization, Yankee Stadium.

But as Roosevelt's economic recovery program went awry, so did the politics of kinder and gentler nation building. The NRA failed to produce economic recovery, and employers rejected NRA rules. In this environment, a popular revolt against corporate power and against a conservative New Deal incubated and then exploded in strikes and radical third-party politics in 1934 and 1935. Interestingly, this was not a revolt against the nation per se but a revolt against the kind of moderate and conflict-free civic nationalism that FDR had advocated. Against it the protesters launched a more radical civic nationalism designed to legitimate far-reaching plans for economic and social reform. In the process, the protesters, including the radicals among them, actually strengthened the bonds of American nationhood.

The NRA had intensified Americanization processes that had been at work since World War I, especially through its propaganda campaign that reached down into virtually every American community and sought to mobilize people around the values of cooperation, hope, and national pride. For workers, the NRA had a more specific meaning. It set guidelines for wages and work hours intended to improve working conditions. Moreover, clause 7 (a) of the NRA's authorizing legislation granted workers the right to join unions and stipulated that employers must recognize unions and bargain with them in good faith. The NRA energized workers demoralized by inadequate work and incomes.

Millions of workers joined labor unions in 1933 and early 1934, encouraged by John L. Lewis, president of the United Mine Workers (UMW), who often declared in his rousing speeches and radio addresses, "The President wants you to join a union." Actually FDR did not then favor the rapid growth of unions. But Lewis reckoned that FDR would not disavow a key clause in his celebrated recovery program. And Lewis also believed that by repeatedly invoking references to "the President" he could transform patriotic affection for FDR into union strength.[17]

Tying this incipient labor movement to FDR and the NRA also meant tying it to nationalist sentiment. Workers came to believe that they were not just joining unions for self-interested reasons; rather they were fulfilling FDR's wishes and thereby aiding the nation. As employers began breaking the wage and hour provisions of the NRA to which they had agreed, workers throughout the country flooded Washington with grievance letters addressed to "Mr. President," "Mrs. Roosevelt," Labor Secretary Frances Perkins, and General Hugh Johnson. In writing Roosevelt and his aides and imploring them to take action, these workers revealed their faith in Roosevelt's leadership, in his compassion, and in his commitment to putting the nation back on its feet.[18]

But Roosevelt did not take action, and workers began to take matters into their own hands. In 1934 they staged 2,000 strikes in virtually every industry and region of the country. Many of the strikes grew out of local disputes and attracted little attention. But a few escalated into armed confrontations between workers and police that shocked the nation. In Toledo in May, 10,000 workers surrounded the Electric Auto-Lite plant, declaring that they would block all exits and entrances until the company agreed to shut down operations and negotiate a union contract. The company asked for police protection and paid for additional deputies. But even a seven-hour pitched battle waged with water hoses, tear gas, and gunfire failed to dislodge the strikers. Ultimately, the National Guard was summoned and two strikers were killed in an exchange of gunfire. In Minneapolis, unionized truck drivers and warehousemen clashed with police, private security forces, and the

National Guard in a series of street battles from May through July that left four dead and hundreds wounded. In San Francisco in July, longshoremen fought employers and police in street skirmishes in which two were killed and scores wounded. Employers there had hoped that the use of force would break the two-month-old strike, but the violence provoked more than 100,000 additional workers in the transportation, construction, and service industries to walk off their jobs in a general strike. From July 5 to July 19, the city of San Francisco was virtually shut down.[19]

The largest and most violent confrontation began on September 1, 1934, with the strike of 400,000 textile workers at mills from Maine to Alabama. Workers who had rarely, if ever, acknowledged a common bond with their fellows—Catholic Euro-Americans in New England and white Protestants in the Southeast—now joined hands. They insisted that they were Americans bound together by class and national loyalties that transcended ethnic and religious differences. In the first two weeks of September, these strikers brought cotton production to a virtual standstill. Employers recruited replacement workers and hired private security forces to protect them. At many of the mills, the arrival of strikebreakers prompted violent confrontations between strikers and police. Riots erupted in Saylesville and Woonsocket, Rhode Island, and in other northern textile cities. Similar confrontations took place in the South, where vigilante bands helped local police and National Guardsmen beat up strikers, kill union organizers or run them out of the state, and incarcerate hundreds of strikers in barbed-wire camps.[20]

By late September, textile union leaders had lost their nerve and called off the strike. But workers took their anger to the polls. In Rhode Island, they elected scores of Democrats to municipal and state offices and broke the Republican Party's thirty-year domination of state politics. In South Carolina's gubernatorial race, working-class voters rejected a conservative Democrat, Coleman Blease, and chose instead Olin T. Johnston, a former millworker and ardent New Dealer. In the country as a whole, Democrats won 70 percent of the contested seats in the Senate and House in what the *New York Times* called the "most overwhelming victory in the history of American politics." No party led by a president had ever done so well in an off-year election.[21] The results were not quite as favorable to Roosevelt as they looked. Many of the new Democrats were radicals ready to challenge FDR's leadership. Radical third parties were rising in Wisconsin, Minnesota, and Washington; workers everywhere were talking about establishing local labor parties. The unrest emboldened Huey Long, senator of Louisiana, and Father Charles Coughlin, the "radio priest," to intensify their criticism of FDR and to offer their populist movements as alternatives to the New Deal. Yet, despite these emerging challenges to FDR and his Democratic Party, workers remained loyal to FDR and to his calls for national renewal.[22]

The loyalty to Roosevelt is apparent in the letters that ordinary workers sent to FDR even as their strikes were failing and they were facing loss of jobs and homes. A Georgia textile worker wrote FDR, "his personal friend," in October 1934 imploring him to "spare the time for a few words from a cotton mill family, out of work and almost out of heart and . . . a house in which to live."[23] An unemployed Rhode Island textile worker who had been writing to Roosevelt for nine months, beseeching him for assistance in regaining a job, could still proclaim: "I believe in the New Deal and the N.R.A. . . . I have traveled in several states in the South . . . and I find that the people especially the laboring class believe and have faith that you Mr. President will pull this country out of the slump. I am a Democrat and proud of it."[24]

This Rhode Island worker lived in an insular and predominately French Canadian city that had long prided itself on its separation from mainstream American culture. That an individual from this community was writing to Roosevelt, traveling in the southern states, and mixing with workers there speaks to the success of FDR and the NRA in penetrating a variety of American subcultures and of strengthening the ties of the people who lived in them to the national community. This was one way in which the New Deal invigorated nationalism in the United States.

The New Deal also popularized the use of civic nationalist rhetoric as a language of protest. Labor protesters and dissenters had begun to wrap themselves in the flag in the 1920s in response to

I. T. U. NEWS

Published Monthly by The Independent Textile Union of America

| Volume 4—No. 10 | Price 50 Cents a Year to Members—Single Copy 10 Cents | APRIL 1940 |

Sowing The Seeds Of Unionism

Spring is the farmer's planting time. However the wise union man sows the seeds of unionism thruout the year. Careful and intelligent planting will result in a bumper crop .... a crop of staunch union men and women who will strengthen American Democracy and place it on an everlasting foundation.

Fig. 13. The Labor Movement Embraces America, 1940. To enhance its legitimacy, the labor movement identified its cause with that of mythic American figures and ideals. In this 1940 issue of a Rhode Island labor periodical, trade unionists are compared with the pioneer farmers who plowed the land. "Sowing the seeds of unionism," the paragraph under the caption suggests, will yield a "bumper crop . . . of staunch union men and women who will strengthen American democracy and place it on an everlasting foundation." (From *ITU News*, 1940)

fierce antiradical and antiunion campaigns to depict them as un-American. In 1925 John L. Lewis, already president of the UMW, made a shrewd attempt to legitimate the labor movement by claiming that it, like other social movements, merely demanded "a return to first principles—a reassertion in practice of the rules laid down by the Fathers of the Republic." Lewis celebrated "the government structure of the Republic" as "broad, sound, and foresighted"; during "most periods of our history," he added, "a revival of those principles or adaptation of them to current conditions has been all that the most ardent champion of popular rights or proponent of public welfare need ask."[25] And a revival of those patriotic principles was "all" that Lewis would demand in the 1930s as he placed himself at the head of the working-class rebellion and created, in 1935, a new labor movement, the CIO, to bring the rebels power. His key phrase was "industrial democracy," by which he meant the extension of democratic principles from electoral politics to the workplace, and the participation of both workers and employers in factory governance. By so extending the reign of democracy, he claimed, he was simply fulfilling the promise of 1776.[26] To those who criticized the un-American character of this demand, Lewis thundered back: "I yield to no man the right to challenge my Americanism or the Americanism of the organizations which at this moment I represent."[27]

A similar use of civic nationalist rhetoric characterized the politics of those, such as Louis Budenz and A. J. Muste, who stood to Lewis's left. Budenz, a radical labor organizer and editor of *Labor Age* from 1921 through the early 1930s, had begun arguing in the 1920s for the need to talk to American farmers and workers in the language of the Founding Fathers.[28] His "American approach" influenced Muste, a pacifist Protestant minister radicalized during a bitter 1919 textile strike in Lawrence, Massachusetts. Muste had been enamored of the American dream, especially as embodied in the life and words of Abraham Lincoln, since his days as an immigrant youth in Michigan. By the late 1920s, Budenz and Muste had joined together to build an "American" radical movement, first in the Conference on Progressive Labor Action (1929), then in a

National Unemployed League (1932), and finally in the American Workers Party (AWP, 1933). A 1932 CPLA Statement of Principles declared: "We hold that the labor movement must grow out of American soil; it must face the realities of American life; it must be built and controlled by the workers of America."[29]

At the founding convention of the National Unemployed League, Muste and his allies put their "American approach" into action. Convention organizers had chosen the July 4 weekend to demonstrate the affinity between the unemployed of 1932 and the revolutionaries of 1776. They modeled their central document, "The Declaration of the Rights of Workers and Farmers," on the Declaration of Independence. After unanimously adopting this document, the 800 delegates burst into "America, the Beautiful." Two years later, Muste's AWP played a key role in the 10,000-worker strike in Toledo. AWP organizers inspired the Toledo workers with banners that proclaimed "1776–1865–1934."[30]

Norman Thomas's Socialist Party tried a similar "American" approach. Throughout 1932, Socialists had been organizing workers, farmers, and the unemployed across the country into "committees of correspondence." In May 1933, 4,000 delegates from these committees convened a Continental Congress in Washington. They, too, wrote a new Declaration, declaring independence from " 'the profit system of business, industry, and finance,' which had 'enthroned economic and financial kings ... more powerful, more irresponsible, and more dangerous to human rights than the political kings whom the fathers overthrew.' "[31]

Even the Communists, the most influential of the 1930s radical groups, took a civic nationalist turn in 1935. In response to directives from the Soviet Union to establish a "Popular Front," the American Communist Party abandoned the ultrarevolutionary politics of the so-called Third Period (1928–34) and allied itself with a broad range of progressive forces, including Lewis's CIO and Roosevelt's New Deal. In rhetorical terms, this turn required Communists to jettison their Marxist-Leninist vocabulary and embrace patriotic language. The Communist leader Earl Browder began declaring that "communism is twentieth-century Americanism"; his followers, in turn, began celebrating him as a descendant of eigh-teenth-century Virginians, and thus as a latter-day Founding Fa-ther.[32]

This campaign had its ludicrous side, as Communists sometimes went to excessive length to demonstrate their patriotic bona fides. And regardless of how much individual Communists truly saw themselves as genuine American patriots, there can be no denying that the Popular Front only flourished here after the order to set one up arrived from Moscow. Even so, the Communists' attempt to fuse radicalism and patriotism was enormously successful in America and in just about every other country where it was tried. In France, the Communist Party gained prestige in the 1940s from its role in *la résistance*, the defense of the French nation against fascist invasion and domination. So, too, Stalin's own popularity in the Soviet Union rested on his defense of the "fatherland" from Nazi attack. Radical anti-imperialist movements in Africa and Asia in the 1940s and beyond embraced the phrase "national libera-tion" to describe the fusion of nation building and social reform that was central to their agenda. And, in the United States, mem-bership in the American Communist Party soared from a few thou-sand in the early 1930s to almost 100,000 during its patriotic de-cade, from 1935 to 1945.[33] Hundreds of thousands more belonged to the American party sometime during that decade, many of whom remained sympathetic to its aims even after they had relin-quished their membership. Communist Party members and sympa-thizers were especially influential in the labor movement, in various agencies of the New Deal, in literary and artistic communities, and in Hollywood.[34]

The radicals' embrace of civic nationalism in the 1930s and 1940s represented a break from the orientation of socialist and Communist movements in the fifty-year period prior to that time. The Second International, a federation of European and American socialist parties and labor unions first assembled in 1889, had repu-diated the language and iconography of patriotism at a time when conservative nationalist parties were constituting socialists as ene-mies of the nation and appropriating patriotism as their exclusive

possession. When war engulfed Europe in 1914, the European socialist parties urged their workers not to succumb to the appeals
of nationalist glory or to enlist in their nation's armies. Everywhere
except Italy their appeals fell on deaf ears.[35] This did not deter
Lenin, once he came to power in Russia in 1917, from denouncing
nationalism, or "social chauvinism," as a reactionary movement
and the working class's enemy. Opposition to nationalism became
a cardinal principle of the Third International, or Communist International, that Lenin established in 1919 to guide revolutionary
movements beyond Russia's borders.[36]

But this hostility to the nation had not been present during the
French Revolution, when modern radicalism was born. Then, as
Eric Hobsbawm has argued, nationalism and radicalism were
joined together in the same movement. The French revolutionaries
who revolted against monarchy and feudal privilege were intent
on creating a new democratic society within the boundaries of the
French nation. Revolution meant not that some abstract or universal "people" would rule but that the French people would exercise
sovereignty over their nation. The revolutionaries did not hesitate
to jettison symbols they associated with the old order: the seven-
day week, the four-week month, saints' days, systems of measure-
ment, names of streets and public institutions that honored the
king, queen, and church. But they never considered getting rid of
the idea or boundaries of France, to which they were devoted.[37]
Their revolution was really an early form of national liberation,
only the oppressors were located not in a distant metropole but in
Paris, their capital. Perhaps nowhere was the legitimacy of nationalist aspiration more apparent than in the adoption by revolutionaries throughout continental Europe of the "Marseillaise" as their
revolutionary anthem. They wanted to make themselves like
France, which meant a civic nation in which the people ruled, and
where there would be no distinctions based on creed, birth, or economic rank. The French revolutionaries bequeathed to the world,
in essence, a radical formulation of the civic nationalist tradition.[38]

Thus the European and American radicals of the 1930s who
were searching for a way to connect their politics to the nation

were reaching back for part of their own history. Reclaiming the nation for the people was really a reiteration of an original radical formulation that had proved enormously successful. There was a natural affinity here, which helps to explain how the sometimes clumsy attempts of 1930s radicals to clothe themselves in nationalist garb yielded such impressive results. The effort to reconcile radicalism and civic nationalism was more difficult to accomplish in the United States than in Europe, for America possessed a civic nationalist tradition that was more conservative than the French variety. The eighteenth-century American revolutionaries had never launched the kind of assault on wealth and economic privilege that their French counterparts had undertaken, and thus their civic nationalism was more respecting of property rights and more hostile to attempts at economic leveling and state building. This divergence was a key reason why American radicals would never achieve the power enjoyed by their European or Third World counterparts. Nevertheless, American revolutionaries found in their own civic nationalist tradition a powerful tool for organizing the "people" against "enthroned economic and financial kings . . . more dangerous to human rights than the political kings whom the fathers overthrew."[39]

Roosevelt understood that the popular mobilization of 1934 and 1935, and the anticorporate interpretation of the civic nationalist tradition that it was employing, threatened his political survival. Thus, as the election of 1936 neared, Roosevelt veered to the left, throwing his support behind strong labor and social welfare legislation. He secured passage of the Social Security Act, the cornerstone of the American welfare state, and the National Labor Relations Act (Wagner Act), which granted workers the federally protected right to organize unions and obligated employers to bargain with them in good faith. FDR also declared war on corporate power and economic privilege by supporting legislation designed to break the hold of a few utility companies on the nation's electric power and to increase tax rates on the wealthiest Americans to 75 percent. In the process of supporting these measures, FDR appropriated the contentious civic nationalist language of his populist and left-wing critics. Addressing Democratic Party delegates who had just re-nominated him for the presidency, Roosevelt couched a sustained rhetorical assault on corporations in terms remarkably similar to those used by the socialists and other radicals only a few years earlier. "In 1776," he declared, "we sought freedom from the tyranny of a political autocracy—from the eighteenth century royalists who held special privileges from the crown." But since that time, "the rush of modern civilization itself has raised for us new difficulties . . . which must be solved if we are to preserve to the United States the political and economic freedom for which Washington and Jefferson planned and fought." The greatest threat lay with the "economic royalists" who "had concentrated into their own hands an almost complete control over other people's property, other people's money, other people's labor—other people's lives. For too many of us life was no longer free; liberty no longer real; men could no longer follow the pursuit of happiness." "The political equality we once had won," Roosevelt intoned, "was meaningless in the face of economic inequality."

Roosevelt did not shirk from the logical course of action called for by such tough talk. "The average man once more confronts the problem that faced the Minute Man"; he must fight a war against the economic royalists, "take away their power," and thereby "save a great and precious form of government [democracy] for ourselves and for the world."[40]

This kind of confrontational talk represented a departure from the soothing character of FDR's nationalist language in 1933. And it contributed to one of the greatest victories ever won by a candidate for the presidency. In 1936 FDR garnered 61 percent of the vote and carried all but two states. Of the 6 million Americans who went to the polls for the first time that year, 5 million voted for Roosevelt. Among the poorest Americans, Roosevelt received 80 percent of the vote; he did especially well, too, among racial and ethnic minorities. New Deal policy makers were euphoric about the mandate they assumed they had been given and they expanded their conception of how the nation's welfare obligated them to increase federal control of the economy. They hatched far-reaching plans to substitute government planning for the chaos and inequities of the market, to contain the economic privilege of the rich, and to shore up the rights and opportunities of the poor. Labor reformers spoke confidently of bringing industrial democracy to the workplace.[41]

Organized labor had been instrumental in FDR's victory and expected to have considerable influence in the second-term administration. Labor's supporters were particularly strong in the Interior Department, the Works Progress Administration, the National Labor Relations Board, the National Resources Planning Board, the Rural Electrification Agency, and the Federal Reserve. Ideologically they were bound together by a belief that chronic "underconsumption" had caused the Depression, by which they meant that consumers did not possess the resources necessary to purchase enough of what American industry could produce. The surest road to recovery was, simply, to increase consumer purchasing power.[42]

Seen in these terms alone, this economic recovery plan seemed to pose little threat to the nation's existing economic structure. But once these New Dealers began discussing how consumer purchasing power was to be increased, their challenge to a capitalist economy came into focus. Not only would extensive unionization be required to wrest wage increases from unwilling employers, but the government would have to adopt policies to redistribute wealth from the richest Americans to the poorest, in order to insure that a higher proportion of the nation's income would flow into consumption channels. Progressive taxation, social welfare spending, and public works investments were all techniques that would accomplish this downward redistribution and thus augment the working class's purchasing power. The deployment of these techniques, of course, could only be done by a strong national government with broad powers to control fiscal policy and to regulate financial and labor markets. The federal government would have to be enlarged, its economic powers enhanced, its role in economic planning legitimated. Ultimately, progressive trade unionists and their New Deal allies hoped to establish a tripartite corporatist system of industrial governance in which the leaders of American labor would meet with those of American industry and government and jointly manage the American economy. In Europe this system came to be known, in the years after World War II, as social democracy. American unionists, worried as always about too close an association with the socialist label, substituted their favorite, and overworked, patriotic phrase, "industrial democracy."[43] Nevertheless, these labor rebels were demonstrating an elasticity in the principles of civic nationalism that others had assumed was not there.

As these plans were being hatched, workers throughout the country drew inspiration from the Wagner Act and from the president's tough rhetoric about battling economic royalists. Union membership grew rapidly, reaching 7 million in 1937, more than double the level of 1933. Union tactics grew bolder, too, nowhere more so than in the strike against General Motors in late 1936. To defeat GM, widely regarded as the most powerful corporation in the world, members of the United Auto Workers (UAW) "occupied" GM plants in Flint, Michigan, refusing to leave until GM management agreed to recognize their union and negotiate a collective bargaining agreement. They stayed for six weeks, aided by Michigan governor Frank Murphy's refusal to send in the National Guard to evict them. GM's capitulation in early 1937 handed workers their greatest victory. The sit-downers emerged from the plants victorious, proudly waving American flags. John Brophy, one of Lewis's top CIO aides, told the jubilant sit-downers that their victory meant "the coming of industrial democracy to the men in these great plants."[44] Both Victor and Roy Reuther, leaders of the UAW who were deeply involved in the Flint sit-downs, likened the ensuing celebration of Flint workers to that of a country achieving independence. Victor Reuther later recalled that "those who doubted the morality of the sit-down in 1937 were fewer than the doubters among the population in 1775, when American independence was won by challenging the tyrannical laws . . . of the British Crown."[45] The favorite song of the strikers, as of CIO unionists everywhere, was "Solidarity Forever," sung to the tune of the "Battle Hymn of the Republic." The fusion of the nation and the working class, of civic nationalism and reform, appeared complete.[46]

Thus, 1936 and 1937 were heady days for those who wished to place the "people" at the center of a patriotic crusade against economic privilege. Many writers and artists depicted labor as America's first and best hope—the voice of the people and the embodiment of the nation's values. Murals sprang up in public buildings featuring portraits of blue-collar Americans at work. Broadway's most celebrated play in 1935 was Clifford Odets's *Waiting for Lefty*, a raw drama about taxi drivers who confront their bosses and organize an honest union. Audiences were so moved by the play that they often spontaneously joined in the final chorus, "Strike, Strike, Strike," the words that ended the play. *Pins and Needles*, a 1937 musical about the hopes and dreams of garment workers that was performed by members of the International Ladies Garment Workers Union, became the longest-running play in Broadway history, until *Oklahoma* broke its record of 1,108 performances in 1943.[47]

Similarly, many of the most popular novels and movies of the 1930s celebrated the decency, honesty, and patriotism of ordinary Americans. In *Mr. Deeds Goes to Town* (1936) and *Mr. Smith Goes to Washington* (1939), Frank Capra delighted movie audiences with fables of simple, small-town heroes vanquishing the evil forces of wealth and decadence. Likewise, in *The Grapes of Wrath* (1939), John Steinbeck told an epic tale of an Oklahoma family's fortitude in surviving eviction from their land, migrating westward, and suffering exploitation in California's "promised land." In 1940 John Ford used Steinbeck's novel as the basis for one of that year's highest-grossing and most acclaimed movies. Moviegoers found special meaning in the declaration of Ma Joad, one of the story's main characters, "We'll go on forever . . . cause we're the people."[48] A people's civic nationalism seemed to have taken deep root.

This was a progressive civic nationalism, first, because it affirmed the social rights of the American people to economic security and opportunity and, second, because it welcomed into the national community a great variety of Americans, including those who had suffered from religious and racial prejudice. The invitation went out most strongly to Jews and Euro-American Catholics, especially those from southern and eastern Europe who had been the target of the 1924 immigration law. Many of them now began to feel, for the first time, that their religion and ethnic background would not be held against them.[49] They saw how FDR had included Catholics and Jews—Thomas "the Cork" Corcoran, James Farley, Steve Early, Samuel Rosenman, and Ben Cohen—in his inner circle of advisers.[50] They heard FDR declare in speeches at Ellis Island and New York in 1936 that he held the new immigrants in high esteem and that he regarded them as better citizens than many Americans who had been here for generations. They applauded FDR's support for labor, because many themselves were working class and involved in the CIO. On the shop floor they were engaged in their own fights against prejudice, directed at discriminatory patterns of hiring that reserved precious jobs for the kin, friends, and *landsleit* of the boss. They readily tied these fights to the nation's civic tradition of equality and fairness, and they conceived of their union struggle as an effort to hold America to its civic promise.[51] In this campaign for fair employment, workers saw FDR as their ally. In word and deed, FDR seemed to be welcoming them into the American nation and encouraging their efforts to secure and extend their rights as citizens.

Actually, opportunities were not as rosy in the 1930s as many eastern and southern Europeans thought they were. As we shall see, prejudice against the new immigrants survived in these years and prompted many Jews and Catholics to hide or erase the visible markers of their ethnic identity and to emulate the Nordic as the quintessential American. And while the New Deal did draw significant support from blacks, Mexicans, and other groups of non-European immigrants, these latter groups rarely heard FDR speak of them with the affection he displayed toward the Europeans.[52] The civic nationalism of the 1930s operated within clear limits.

There were those who wished to break through these limits and who fashioned, in these years, a vision of an American nation that countenanced no racial, religious, or ethnic prejudice of any sort. And they could take heart from the success of economic radicals in 1935 in compelling FDR to launch an assault on economic privilege and to deploy, in the process, a far more combative civic nationalism. Many expected that a full-scale, all-American, assault on racial and religious prejudice was just a matter of time and popular pressure. Indeed, the World War II years seemed to present just such an opportunity.[53]

But there was another, less salubrious, lesson to be learned from the events of 1935 and 1936. As FDR moved left, he clung to the center. He had not become a radical; the content of his legislation attacking economic privilege was less threatening than the rhetoric in which it was couched. Even as he sided with progressive political forces, he continued to cultivate an image of himself as a unifying nation builder, as someone who welcomed all Americans, including racist southerners and corporate elites, into his national family. And in this effort he was enormously successful, as he retained, even increased, his standing as the most revered symbol of American nationhood. At times he even appeared to take on the role of a national sovereign, a monarch, who stood above politics. Prior to 1937, he seemed not to be touched by policies that failed and advisers that erred. He retained a kind of purity, much like the nation he was thought to embody. That many Americans hung a picture of him in their homes, often alongside one of the Madonna, further suggests that he had transcended the realm of the political. Popular affection for him had a racial dimension, too, in that he became a kind of Nordic father whom everyone, Jews and Catholics included, wanted to claim as his or her own as a way of avowing a vicarious Nordic ancestry—a subject we will soon explore. This affection for FDR and a willingness to absolve him for the failures of his policies suggests that there were limits to how far radical plans for political change and civic nationalist reconstruction could go. These limits became starkly clear in 1937 and 1938.

CONSERVATIVE COUNTERATTACK

The fusion of civic nationalism and reform, especially its more radical variants, encountered its first serious opposition in 1937 and 1938. Middle-class Americans grew alarmed at the extent of working-class militancy. They viewed the sit-down strike in particular as too great an assault on the property rights of factory owners. Rumors swirled that Communists were responsible not just for the Flint strike but for the rapid spread of sit-down tactics among workers throughout the country.[54] Opposition to this militancy developed within the ranks of labor itself, as the more conservative American Federation of Labor (AFL) chieftains began denouncing the successful CIO upstarts. The house of labor became formally and bitterly divided in 1937, as the CIO established itself as an alternative and rival labor federation to the AFL. Simultaneously, the CIO undertook a major campaign to organize southern workers, the chief effect of which was to mobilize sentiment in the South against organized labor as a northern and alien force inimical to what was best in American life.[55]

As this backlash against aggressive labor was setting in, FDR embarked on his ill-advised "court-packing" plan. Worried that the Supreme Court was about to invalidate the Wagner Act, the Social Security Act, and other key aspects of the New Deal, Roosevelt asked Congress to allow him to alter the makeup of the Supreme Court. Specifically, he wanted the power to appoint one new Supreme Court justice for every member of the court who was over the age of seventy and who had served for at least ten years. His stated reason was that the current justices were too old and feeble to handle the large volume of cases coming before them. But his real purpose was to prevent the conservative justices on the court—a majority of whom had been appointed by Republican presidents—from dismantling his New Deal.

FDR had reason to be worried that this was exactly what the Supreme Court intended to do, and he believed that his proposal would draw support from a citizenry angered by the judiciary's

apparent eagerness to flout the will of legislative majorities.[56] But
the brazenly deceitful nature of his proposal to compromise the
independence of the judiciary offended many and ignited a storm of
indignation. FDR survived this wave of popular outrage; moreover,
within a month of FDR's announcement of his "court-packing"
scheme, one Supreme Court justice changed from foe to friend of
the New Deal and threw his support behind the Wagner Act and
Social Security Act, both of which were then approved by narrow
5–4 margins. FDR allowed his ill-advised proposal to die in Congress. But the episode wounded him and the New Deal.[57]

Whatever hope FDR may have had for a quick recovery from
this fiasco was dashed by a sharp recession that struck the country
in late 1937 and 1938.[58] The stock market, which was finally ap-
proaching its 1929 levels, plunged downward by 40 percent and
unemployment soared from 14 to 20 percent. To many, this development confirmed their sense that FDR had lost control of events
and that the New Deal was not delivering on its promised economic recovery.[59]

In the 1938 elections, many Americans vented their anger at the
New Deal by electing scores of Republicans to Congress. These
Republicans began raising questions about the New Deal's accu-
mulation of federal power, about labor's size and militancy, and
about Communist influence in the labor movement and the New
Deal. They stalemated further New Deal reform and stymied the
social reform movement that, in 1936 and 1937, had seemed like
a juggernaut.[60]

This moment marked the beginning of a sustained counterattack
on the radical civic nationalism of the mid-1930s. It emerged most
strongly in the South, among middle-class Americans throughout
the country, and in Catholic communities in the Northeast and
Midwest. Its unifying idea was the conviction that dangerous radicals had gotten hold of American ideas, institutions, and people,
and were in the process of destroying the American nation. Conservatives began organizing to identify these radicals (usually labeled
"Communists"), to expose their ideas as "un-American," and to
expel them from power.

No institution symbolized this turn more than the House Special Committee on Un-American Activities, established in 1938 by Martin Dies. Ironically, the committee had been the brainchild of liberal Samuel Dickstein of New York, who intended to use it to pursue Nazi sympathizers. But Congress was not about to allow an immigrant from New York—the son of a rabbi no less—to lead a committee charged with defining the boundaries of American and "un-American" behavior, so they gave it to Dies, a Protestant with a long Texas-American pedigree who was principally worried about the threats of labor militancy and Communist subversion. Dies's committee quickly established itself as the guardian of "America" against its "un-American" enemies. It targeted alleged Communists who had infiltrated government and labor organizations, peace groups, and other civil associations.[61]

To this end, Dies hastily assembled lists of hundreds of organizations that could be connected, in any way, to the Communist Party. He attacked "radical" New Deal cultural agencies, quickly bringing the Federal Theatre Project to an end and numbering the days of the Works Progress Administration. He investigated in highly public fashion labor leaders with Communist ties, such as Harry Bridges, and "left-wing" New Dealers such as Frank Murphy who had demonstrated too great a sympathy for labor. His criticism of the National Labor Relations Board compelled FDR to deny reappointment to two of its more radical members.[62] Dies even raised questions about such high-profile New Dealers as Labor Secretary Frances Perkins and Interior Secretary Harold Ickes, and cast aspersion on Eleanor Roosevelt's willingness to associate with Joseph Lash and others of known Communist affiliation. "The First Lady of the Land," he charged, "has been one of the most valuable assets which the Trojan Horse organizations of the Communist Party have possessed."[63] Dies cultivated relations with right-wing groups, and he received information from J. Edgar Hoover and the FBI. Because his committee could only investigate alleged subversion and not convict, it depended on the media's aid in publicizing its suspicions. For much of 1938 and 1939, the work of the committee was front-page news. Already, the sensational exposure and condemnation by accusation had become the committee's signature tactics. The New Deal, as a result, was suddenly vulnerable.[64]

Although Dies had praised FDR as recently as 1936, he had come to loathe the New Deal. The reason for this did not lie simply in the New Deal's alleged openness to Communist infiltration. It lay as well in Dies's belief that, even apart from the Communists, the New Deal imperiled America. Dies denounced as false the liberal and radical belief that the establishment of a large state able to tame capitalist excess and increase the opportunities—and liberties—of the downtrodden would fulfill the civic nationalist dream. He criticized the "expensive and undemocratic bureaucracy" that the New Deal had brought about and that "usurped . . . the legislative functions of the Congress" and the states.[65] He attacked the New Deal's obsession with "economic security" and with abolishing "all poverty and unemployment," arguing that such an approach would lead inevitably not to greater opportunities and liberties for the poor but to dictatorship and the destruction of the people's liberties.[66] He cried out against the "hundreds of [noncommunist] left-wingers and radicals" who occupied "key positions" in government and who were trying to "substitute bureaucratic state Capitalism for our present political and economic system."[67] Dies counterposed a conservative Americanism of states' rights, congressional supremacy, and individual liberty to the liberal one in an effort to discredit the New Deal. Out of the materials of civic nationalism itself, he sought to construct an "un-American" other that would limit reform ambitions.[68]

Constructing a civic nationalism to discredit alleged radicalism was a venerable tradition that even Theodore Roosevelt had used in his campaign against anarchism and syndicalism. But whereas TR had used his nationalist posturing to defend reform against radicalism, Dies was using it to lump the two together and thus to discredit them both. If he succeeded, the New Deal might lose its legitimacy and its claim on the nationalist imagination.

Many conservatives of the late 1930s also sought to revive the earlier practice of tying the threat that radicalism posed to the nation to the presence of new immigrants and their descendants. The Communist Party and CIO, they alleged, were composed primarily of new immigrants and the New Deal was a "Jew Deal"; all three were alien to America and dangerous to that which "true" Americans valued.[69] Dies, himself, was careful not to be caught speaking in such a prejudiced way (that he left to his trusted ally from Mississippi, Democratic Congressman John Rankin). He liked to declare that he—and his Americanism—stood against "the purveyors of class, religious, and racial hatred."[70] Indeed, he seemed to want to ground his opposition to radicalism and liberalism in the race-neutral terms of civic nationalism. But he was so deeply steeped by background and education in racialized notions of American nationhood that he could not break free of their influence. His father had been a leading restrictionist in Congress twenty years earlier and Martin had fully absorbed his prejudices against the new immigrants. He often blamed the ills of the Depression on the immigrants in America's midst. When the younger Dies entered Congress in 1931, the first bill he introduced called for suspending immigration to the United States for five years. In 1935 he called for waging "relentless war without quarter and without cessation" on the 3.5 million immigrants who Dies claimed had entered the country illegally.[71] That same year he blamed the entire Depression on the foreign-born: "If we had refused admission to the 16,500,000 foreign born who are living in this country today, we would have no unemployment problem to distress and harass us. . . . From any angle of approach it must be evident to every thinking American citizen that the unemployment problem was transferred to American from foreign lands."[72] And these immigrants—who were, of course, predominately eastern and southern European in origin—had brought with them Marxism, fascism, and other foreign ideas that were bedeviling America and threatening to "undermine the principles of Americanism in favor of the totalitarian ideologies of Europe."[73] Equally dangerously, these immigrants were pressuring Congress and the president to enter "into entangling alliances which would involve us in European affairs, at a time when Europe is gathering itself for another suicidal war."[74]

When, in the late 1930s, American Jewish groups and their allies beseeched Congress and the president for a refugee policy that might reduce the barriers to immigration and thus rescue Jews from Hitler's persecution, Dies was a key figure who stood in their way. He mobilized congressional opposition on the grounds that such a policy would make America even more vulnerable to Communist and Nazi subversion. He also turned his files on alleged subversion over to Assistant Secretary of State Breckinridge Long, who was intent on making his own case that increased immigration would threaten national security. Not only would Communists be among the German Jews allowed to enter, but, Long alleged, Hitler would seed that migration with Nazi agents posing as Jewish refugees. So vigilant was Long in guarding American borders and in making it difficult for Jewish refugees to get visas, that only half the German-Austrian immigrant quota was utilized in 1941. It was harder, in 1941, for a German refugee to enter the United States than Britain, which had been at war against Germany for two years.[75]

In these attitudes we can detect the enduring potency of the racialized tradition of American nationalism that had been so influential in the 1920s. This was the tradition that held that full privileges and opportunities were to be granted to particular "racial" groups and not to others. It rooted nationality in race and declared that certain national groups should be barred from the United States because they possessed racial traits that rendered them unassimilable. The racism toward Jews, Italians, and other groups of new immigrants was not as overt as it had been in the 1920s, but it was real nevertheless. That was the message carried by a public opinion poll of 1939, revealing that 42.3 percent of the "general population believed that hostility towards Jews stemmed from unfavorable Jewish characteristics."[76] And in the 1930s and 1940s, many spoke of the Jewish and Italian races as being something other (and lower) than the white race.[77] In a 1939 poll, Americans singled out Jews and Italians as the two nationalities that made the worst American citizens.[78] Racial hostility toward blacks, Hispanics, and Asians also remained strong. The Dies committee tapped into these hostilities, as well as into the anti-Communist ones, as a way of constructing an America faithful to its traditions and equipped to meet and master its future.[79]

This racialized tradition remained an important strain in 1930s politics and culture, its influence extending well beyond the ranks of southern opponents to the New Deal. Historians who celebrate the New Deal and the strength of labor and other popular movements of the 1930s tend to slight its significance. But evidence of its survival can be found not only among right-wing groups but among the progressive forces themselves—the New Deal, the labor movement, the mass media, and even in the cultural practices of the new immigrants. The New Deal was only a few years removed from the immigration restriction movement, not far enough to free itself from the racializing influences of that earlier era.

THE SURVIVAL OF RACIALIZED NATIONALISM

In 1930s America, racialized notions of nationalism were most evident in the South and West. In the South, white supremacy remained a way of life, an integral part of white southerners' American identity. In the West, anti-Asian prejudice had retained its hold on whites, and anti-Mexican bias was gaining strength. Because FDR needed the votes of southern and western Democrats, these prejudices were woven into New Deal legislation and policies. The vast majority of African Americans lived in rural areas of the South where state laws barred most of them from voting. The New Deal did little to challenge their disfranchisement. The New Deal also excluded most rural black southerners from key pieces of New Deal legislation. The Agricultural Adjustment Act bestowed its benefits on farm owners; most rural southern blacks were farm tenants or sharecroppers. At the urging of powerful agricultural interests in the South and West, rural wage laborers, who were disproportionately black, Hispanic, and Filipino, were denied the right to organize unions or to receive Social Security benefits. The Civilian Conservation Corps ran separate camps for black and white youth. The Tennessee Valley Authority hired few blacks.

African Americans, Hispanics, and Asians enrolled in work relief programs frequently received less pay than whites doing the same jobs.[80]

On issues of major concern to the black, Hispanic, and Asian communities, the presence of Roosevelt in the White House seemed to make little difference. Roosevelt consistently refused to support legislation to make lynching a federal crime—a key objective of civil rights activists at the time. The advent of his New Deal failed to halt the campaign among Anglos in the Southwest to repatriate Mexican immigrants. By 1935, this campaign had forced out 500,000 Mexicans. Asian immigrants in the West continued to be denied the right of naturalization and, in many places, the right to own land. Because of their race, they were being denied full membership in the American community.[81]

By invigorating the civic nationalist tradition, the New Deal did inspire movements to challenge these exclusions. Racial minorities began organizing to secure rights that New Deal legislation had extended to whites. CIO unions in the North and West undertook campaigns against racial discrimination. And many radicals from the Socialist and Communist parties gave top priority to the organization of America's most exploited workers, including black sharecroppers in the South and Hispanic and Filipino agricultural laborers in the West. Especially after 1935 they did so with the announced goal of making America live up to its cherished political principles of equality, democracy, and the elimination of all prejudice.[82]

No group did more in this regard than the Communist Party. Not only were Communists tireless and fearless in their advocacy of the workplace and civil rights of blacks and other racial minorities, but they also were determined to achieve full social equality. They made special efforts to recruit blacks to their organizations and to promote them to leadership positions. More than any other group of that era, they also encouraged interracial dating, sex, and marriage, believing that the full extirpation of racial prejudice would only be achieved when love and sex freely crossed the color line.[83] The Dies committee members understood (and despised) this part of the Communist program. One of the witnesses they questioned in 1939 was a Miss Sallie Saunders, a white actress employed by the Federal Theatre Project who had become disgusted with the racial mixing encouraged by radical FTP participants. The white artists, she charged, "hobnob indiscriminately with" blacks all the time, "throwing parties with them right and left." Representative Joe Starnes, presiding in place of Dies, then asked her: "Is that part of the Communist program?" "Yes, sir," Saunders shot back, adding that "social equality and race merging" were Communist aims. Indeed they were.[84] Dies detested anyone who fought for this kind of social equality, and the behavior of Communists in this regard deepened his conviction that they were enemies of America.

The Communist quest for "social equality and race merging" extended well beyond the activities of official New Deal agencies. It was apparent, too, among the musicians, critics, and audiences for swing music, one of the decade's most popular cultural creations. The music itself was a blend of African American and European influences, and it brought together a variety of black and European ethnic musicians who learned from each other, imitated and challenged each other, and, in the process, created something genuinely American. Second- and third-generation European ethnics loved this music and frequently played it at social gatherings of CIO union members.[85]

Few swing musicians were members of the Communist Party, but many identified themselves as left, and they fought to attain in their bands and in the broader society as well what they had achieved in their music—racial mixing, hybridity, and respect. Benny Goodman began participating in interracial recording sessions in 1933 and formally integrated his band in 1936. Artie Shaw's orchestra toured with the black singer Billie Holliday for eight months in 1938, and Charlie Barnet's orchestra did the same with another black singer, Lena Horne, in 1941. These experiments in integration were frequently greeted with racial hostility, and most big bands bowed to the popular demand for racial exclusion and remained all-white. Still, throughout this period Communist Party members and affiliated Popular Front organizations were among swing's most ardent devotees, celebrating both the music's hybrid sound and its promise of interracialism.[86]

But not even the Communists fully escaped the racializing influences of the society in which they lived. Their entrapment is apparent, for example, in their visual representations of the ideal, universal worker, the sort whom they dreamed would lead their revolutionary struggle for socialism. In the 1930s, this worker was most often depicted as male, white, and with a powerful physiognomy that was Anglo-Saxon or Nordic. He rarely looked Jewish, Italian, Greek, or black. These representations were anchored, of course, in a western European tradition, where the match between the idealized and actual European worker was, it might be argued, reasonably close. But why did this image remain so powerful in America where millions of workers were southern and eastern Europeans or nonwhites who bore a scant physical resemblance to the Nordic worker of western European lore?[87]

One answer is that idealized images, once they are established, change only in slow and partial ways; such, certainly, is a conclusion to be drawn from the glacial change in the iconography of Jesus as it was exported over the centuries from western Europe to Latin America, Asia, and Africa. But, in the case of American Communists, it seems clear that their maintenance of the Nordic worker ideal had something to do with the racialized character of the society in which they lived and in which the Nordic type was widely acknowledged to be a superior human specimen. Many seem to have become convinced that they would not succeed at their organizing work as long as they were marked for what they were—ethnic minorities drawn primarily from eastern Europe: from Russia itself, from Finland, and from the Slavic nations along Russia's borders. If they were too easily identified as Jews, Finns, or Slavs, they would be rejected by "American" workers, and rendered ineffective. So they desired to make themselves over into Americans. In undertaking this transformation, they sought to erase, at least in name, their eastern European identities. Communists had long favored name changing, a practice that both protected their families from reprisals and allowed them to acquire a nom de guerre that would arm and strengthen them for the revolution. But the names chosen by the many American Communists who embraced this practice also revealed their hankering for assimilation to a Nordic ideal. Samuel Dardeck became Samuel Adams Darcy, Stjepan Mesaros became Steve Nelson, Itzok Granich became Mike Gold, Saul Regenstreif became Johnny Gates, Avro Halberg became Gus Hall, Joseph Cohen became Joe Clark, Abraham Richman became Al Richmond, and Dorothy Rosenblum became Dorothy Ray Healey.[88] The list could go on for pages.

The label "American" was not a race-neutral one in the 1920s and 1930s, even within the ranks of workers. The postwar turmoil had hardened the division among workers between those labeled "Americans" and those deemed "foreigners." As the labor economist David Saposs wrote in 1919, the terms distinguished not native-born from foreign-born or patriots from traitors but rather "old" from "new" immigrant stock. This distinction was above all a racial one, separating the races capable of assimilating to American life from those that were not. Those races "belonging to old immigrant stock" (or "Nordic" stock, to use the term that would be favored by the framers of the 1924 Immigration Restriction Act), wrote Saposs, "are considered Americans" regardless of where they were born. Anglo-Saxons and "persons of Teutonic descent who speak English are . . . placed in this category." On the other hand, he continued, "those of the 'new immigration' whether born in this country and able to speak English fluently, or recent arrivals[,] are ipso facto termed 'foreigners.' " Saposs continued:

> In this manner races with such divergent temperaments and heritages as Italians, Croates, Serbs, Slavs, Czechs, Russians, Roumanians, Luthuanians [sic], and so on are indiscriminately scorned as "hunkies" and "foreigners." Their children may have been educated in our schools, may know the history and traditions of our institutions, and may speak English without any trace of foreign accent—but they too are despised as "hunkies" and "foreigners." Interviews with persons in all walks of life reveal the prevalence of this distinction.[89]

Saposs offered these observations while covering the great steel strike of 1919. In the discourse on the strike, and in Saposs's own language, race and nationality were indistinguishable. Italians, Czechs, and Russians constituted distinct races. So, too, did the Americans. Thus the eastern European Communists who, in the 1920s and early 1930s, were Americanizing their names were doing so in a racially charged climate. To adopt Anglo-Saxon or Nordic names at that time was an attempt, at least in part, to elevate one's racial status and thereby to gain acceptance as an "American."

On the surface it seems curious that eastern and southern Europeans would have thought assimilation to a Nordic ideal possible. If the Nordic was a racial type, how could a "lower race" rise to its level? The answer lies in the existence in the United States of an alternative racial hierarchy (to the "Nordic-Hunky" one), which divided the world's peoples into only four races: white, black, brown, and yellow. By the terms of this second hierarchy, as we saw in chapter 3, all Europeans were designated "white" with all the privileges that such a superior racial standing entailed. These two racial hierarchies, while analytically distinct, overlapped and caused considerable racial confusion and uncertainty. On the one hand, those from northwest Europe who claimed status as Nordics often looked down upon eastern and southern Europeans as less than white. Indeed they referred to themselves as white or as "Americans" and to the new immigrant groups as Jews, Hunkies, and other designations that conveyed the latter's racial inferiority. On the other hand, these same eastern and southern Europeans, secure in their legal status as whites, sought to rise to the top of the Nordic hierarchy. And why not? If Nordics were white, and the new immigrants were white, why couldn't the new immigrants become Nordic? Racial categories in the United States had long depended for their success on their elasticity, and the Communists who were Anglicizing their names were attempting to turn this elasticity to their advantage.[90]

The Nordic aspiration evident among the Communists is even more apparent among the European ethnics who were not Communist. In the adoration of FDR we can detect a desire on the part of southern and eastern Europeans to gain acceptance in America by claiming for themselves a "Nordic father." The adulation bestowed on the Founding Fathers is also revealing in this regard, for it suggests a yearning not only for the principles of freedom and equality but also for "Nordic" ancestors. And the figures of Washington, Jefferson, and Lincoln were not remote to 1930s Americans: their names and deeds were constantly invoked, their visual images endlessly reproduced. Carl Sandburg published the second volume of his populist Lincoln biography in this decade, while FDR dedicated the Jefferson Memorial in 1943.[91]

In certain sections of the CIO labor movement, we can detect a tendency among ethnic workers to push to the fore—or at least to defer to—the most Nordic or Americanized among them, who were, in rank-and-file eyes, the best equipped to lead. The CIO leader, John L. Lewis, was a man of Welsh descent. In the UAW, Walter Reuther, a thoroughly assimilated son of German immigrants, and Homer Martin, a white southerner, vied for leadership. Philip Murray, a Scotsman, headed up organizing efforts in steel. "Americans" such as Irwin, Mullen, Maloy, and Patterson also took the lead in local organizing efforts in the steel towns of western Pennsylvania and northeastern Ohio and among work forces predominately made up of Slavic and Italian workers.[92] In Woonsocket, Rhode Island, an assimilated Jew whose ancestors had come from Austria (making him more of an "old" than a "new" immigrant) took charge of a powerful textile union movement that was overwhelmingly French Canadian.[93]

Sometimes these "Americans" simply assumed leadership in these unions, thinking of themselves as fit for the role. But in many instances they were aided by the deference shown them by the less assimilated rank and file who saw in these "Americans" qualities that they could not find in themselves. This deference is captured by Thomas Bell, né Adalbert Thomas Belejcak, in *Out of This Furnace*, his semiautobiographical 1941 novel about three generations of a Slovak steelworking family in Braddock, Pennsylvania. The last third of the novel focuses on Dobie Dobrejak, a third-generation Slovak who, through his commitment to trade unionism and Americanism, becomes the novel's hero. In one scene, Bell offers this reflection on Dobie's reaction to the "CIO men" who had come to town to lead a steelworkers' organizing campaign. "Working with them, listening to them . . . he [Dobie] was conscious of this something about them that he couldn't place. It puzzled him until he realized why." Bell continues: "They were all sorts of men, Scotch and Irish and Polish and Italian and Slovak and German and Jew, but they didn't talk and act the way the steel towns expected men who were Scotch and Irish and Polish and Italian and Slovak and German and Jew to talk and act." These CIO men were confident and fearless, "obviously convinced that they were individually as good as any man alive, from Mill Superintendents up or down, as the case might be, and probably better. . . . And nobody in the steel towns," the narrator muses, "had ever been heard to talk the way they talked—without stumbling over words, uttering them as though they meant something real right there in Braddock—about liberty and justice and freedom of speech."[94]

This is a key moment in the novel, as Dobie realizes for the first time that he, too, can stand tall, claim his rights as an American, and bring himself and his fellow steelworkers a better deal. Here, Bell celebrates the country's civic nationalist tradition that allows a "foreigner," even a poor one, to be treated with as much respect as a steel baron or a tenth-generation Yankee. But the quoted passages communicate two other messages as well. First, no blacks or other racial minorities seem to be part of this Americanizing and unionizing process; they are conspicuously absent from the list of nationalities whom Bell depicts as contributors to the ranks of "CIO men." Second, the CIO men who have so impressed Dobie are all outsiders to Braddock. They have left their ethnic communities and seem to be shedding their ethnic pasts. It is precisely this break with their communities and with the way in which they were expected to "talk and act" that becomes the source of their power and provides them with a claim on leadership. In Bell's saga, the ghetto-bound ethnic is simply not as able an American as the one who has cut his ties.

Of course, it need not have been the case that the "CIO men," or other Americanizing ethnics who were leaving their homes, were simultaneously emulating the Nordic ideal. Indeed, it can be argued—as Werner Sollors and others have—that there were many avenues of Americanization and that this country's greatness lies precisely in the freedom it gives its citizens to choose the content of their Americanness.[95] But, in the 1930s, the allure of Nordic Americanization (or what some scholars have called "Anglo-conformity") was difficult to escape or resist. We have already seen how much it influenced the Communists, the most radical of 1930s workers and immigrants. And it was deeply ingrained in the movies and other aspects of mass culture from which millions of Americans took their cues about how to dress, act, and talk American.

The movies are particularly important in this regard, not only because of their popularity (an estimated 75 million Americans went to the movies every week) but also because new immigrants and their descendants—Jews and Italians especially—played such a large role in their creation, production, and distribution. The famed "Jewish moguls"—Louis B. Mayer, Samuel Goldwyn, the Warner Brothers, Carl Laemmle, Harry Cohn, and Adolph Zukor—ran five of the major movie studios in the 1930s: MGM, Warner Brothers, Universal Studios, Columbia Pictures, and Paramount. They were all tough businessmen bent on making it in America. They were also terribly anxious about being accepted in an America where hostility toward immigrants and Jews was strong. Many conceived of acceptance as depending on their ability to shed their Jewish pasts, which they did through a variety of techniques, including Anglicizing their names, marrying Gentile women, and even hiding their Jewish identity from their children. But they also sought to do so on screen, by creating images of America in which Nordic types loomed large and Jewish and other new immigrant types disappeared from view.[96]

One of the outstanding examples of the cinematic erasure of the new immigrant occurred in the work of the Italian American Frank Capra, arguably the most successful director in 1930s Hollywood. With *It Happened One Night* (1934), produced by Columbia Pictures (Harry Cohn's studio), Capra established himself as the master of the social comedy and, simultaneously, as an incisive critic of the pretensions and corruption of America's social, professional, and political elites. In that film and in two that followed, *Mr. Deeds Goes to Town* (1936) and *Mr. Smith Goes to Washington* (1939), Capra took his stand with the "common man," who, armed with nothing more than personal integrity, "common sense," and a beautiful woman, convulsed the world of power and privilege and struck a blow for democracy and equality.[97]

Although Capra liked to think of himself as a Republican, he was in awe of Roosevelt.[98] His films both drew on and contributed to the reform civic nationalism that was so crucial to the success of Roosevelt and his New Deal.[99] But there are never any new immigrants in the ranks of Capra's ordinary Americans. The heroic ordinary American in *Mr. Deeds Goes to Town* is a Yankee, Longfellow Deeds (played by Gary Cooper) from Mandrake Falls, Vermont, who goes to New York City to claim a fortune that a deceased uncle has left him. Deciding to give the fortune away, he becomes the laughingstock of slick city lawyers, hardboiled newspapermen, cynical literati, and self-styled aristocrats. But he also becomes a hero to the unemployed and downtrodden to whom he wishes to give the money. Here was a perfect opportunity for Capra to depict Italian, Jewish, and other groups who formed the vast majority of New York City's working class and unemployed. But no workers appear on screen, only farmers who have been dispossessed and who come to Deeds for money to purchase new land and implements. The only immigrants in their ranks are Scandinavian farmers from the Midwest, members of the racially distinguished old immigrant stream.[100] The movie never pauses to ponder the incongruity of midwestern farmers appearing on relief lines in New York City. Except for brief appearances by a pompous Italian opera star and a scheming and pushy New York (Jewish) lawyer, the new immigrants are utterly absent from Capra's 1936 representation of America's great polyglot metropolis.[101]

Capra was a Sicilian immigrant who came to America in 1903 when he was six. His screenwriter, Robert Riskin, was an eastern

European Jew, as was Harry Cohn, the movie's sponsor. The same new immigrant team produced *Mr. Smith Goes to Washington*, except that Riskin's place had been taken by Sidney Buchman, another eastern European Jew who was also a member of the Communist Party (and who would be blacklisted in 1953).[102] Buchman's radicalism is discernible in the sharper political focus of this second film: the enemies are not New York City's social elite but venal senators who are beholden to Jim Taylor, a powerful and ruthless boss. But, in other respects, the plot of this film follows the same lines as the one in *Mr. Deeds*: a young, naive man, Jefferson Smith (Jimmy Stewart), arrives from a rural area, this time in the West, to take his seat in the U.S. Senate. His experienced colleagues regard him as a hayseed and laugh at his innocence and ignorance; they also plan to use him to push through Jim Taylor's land swindle. But his good heart wins him allies (including Jean Arthur, playing the same tough-gal-with-a-heart-of-gold role that she pioneered in *Mr. Deeds*), who reveal to him Taylor's plot. Relying on his patriotic faith and common sense, Smith undertakes a herculean filibuster and thwarts Taylor's ambition.

In this film, there is no need to undertake the deliberate kind of social erasure of new immigrants required of a film on the unemployed set in New York City. There were few, if any, descendants of new immigrants in the Senate, so their identities did not need to be hidden. But the adulation of the Nordic runs through this picture just the same. The hero is another lanky Yankee whose integrity and common sense have been nurtured not in cities but in the small, rural towns of the West. There he led the Boy Rangers, an organization seeking to develop strong bodies and minds through rigorous outdoor activity. Capra depicted these boys as well-scrubbed, all-American youngsters living in homes surrounded by white picket fences,[103] and imagined Smith himself as a "young Abe Lincoln, tailored to the rail-splitter's simplicity, compassion, ideals, humor, and unswerving moral courage under pressure."[104] At a moment of crisis, Jefferson Smith visits the Lincoln Memorial and draws inspiration from the words of the Gettysburg Address that he reads there.

It may well be that Capra and Buchman come closest to revealing their immigrant identities in the sheer intensity of their identification with patriotic imagery and heroes. Capra once admitted that he "was a silly goose about things patriotic" and recalled that, during his first meeting with Roosevelt, he had been overwhelmed by the announcement, "The President of the United States." Foreign-born Americans, he mused, "more fully appreciate the awesome aura" of that title.[105] But the embrace of Lincoln and FDR, as we have seen, was also a way for immigrants to distance themselves from their cultural roots.

Capra never hesitated to declare that he wished to get as far away from his roots as possible. He opens his autobiography with words of contempt for his origins: "I hated being poor. Hated being a peasant. Hated being a scrounging newskid trapped in the sleazy Sicilian ghetto of Los Angeles. My family couldn't read or write. I wanted out. A quick out. I looked for a device, a handle, a pole to catapult myself across the tracks from my scurvy habitat of nobodies to the affluent world of somebodies."[106] Film became that device.

The autobiography then becomes the story of how film allowed Capra to reinvent himself and to become, in the 1930s, the preeminent cinematic interpreter of traditional American myths. Capra celebrates the freedom that America gave him to pursue his dreams, and he joins a large chorus of immigrant Americans who have sung praises to their adopted land for placing no limits on the ambitions of hardworking and imaginative individuals. Capra's story, as he told it, was a narrative of civic nationalist triumph as it chronicled his successful journey from outsider to insider, from lowly immigrant to honored American.

But many immigrants who came to America experienced roadblocks to economic mobility and cultural inclusion that no amount of effort could overcome. Capra's own parents may not have been sufficiently imaginative, but they were honorable and hardworking, neither of which seemed to have been enough to free them from the "sleazy Sicilian ghetto" and the "scurvy habitat of nobodies." And then there was the threat that Sicilians in America might actually become black. Capra reveals this threat in the first few pages of his autobiography, when he recounts the moment in 1902 when a letter from his big brother Ben arrived in the Capra household in Sicily. Ben had disappeared from Sicily five years earlier and had not been heard from since. In the letter he announced that he was alive and well in California, but that his journey had been harrowing. Ben left Italy on a Greek trading steamer bound for America and had tried to jump ship at Boston, only to be caught and returned to the ship. He escaped in New Orleans, and quickly found himself laboring in the Louisiana sugarcane fields alongside Italian and black workers. When he fell ill and almost died of miasma, he was cared for by a Negro woman who nursed him back to health and took him into her family. For two years, he lived contentedly with his adopted black family. This episode ended unexpectedly when Ben and a fellow Italian were beaten senseless in New Orleans, put on a tramp steamer full of other kidnapped Negroes, Italians, and Cubans, and transported to a distant Pacific island where Japanese bosses ran huge sugarcane plantations. There he labored in servitude until he and his Italian buddy escaped in a small rowboat and, miraculously, were spotted and picked up by an Australian passenger liner heading for San Francisco. A rescued Ben had settled in southern California and was writing now to implore his family to join him.[107]

Ben's journey was remarkable and one that Frank Capra might have celebrated in his autobiography or in his films, especially because Ben's adventurousness, pluck, and good luck made possible Frank's arrival and triumph in America. But Frank never touched the subject of his brother in his films. And in his autobiography he says nothing more about his brother until the penultimate page, when Frank, in 1969, recalls learning about Ben's death by reading his obituary in the paper. Apparently, the two brothers had completely lost touch.[108]

It may have been that Frank's flight from Ben was merely part of his desire to get as far from his "scurvy habitat of nobodies" as he possibly could. But one wonders whether Frank also felt threatened by Ben's initial Americanization experience, which entailed joining a black family in Louisiana and, presumably, becoming a Negro. For Italian Americans, this was not a wildly improbable outcome of their arrival in America. In the eyes of native-born Americans, southern Italians were seen as a group that, of all the European immigrants, most closely resembled blacks. In some areas, and especially in Louisiana, the two populations mixed extensively at work, at leisure, and in families. An Italian government official who arrived in Louisiana in 1906 to investigate the conditions of Italian sharecroppers there reported that a " 'majority of plantation owners cannot comprehend that . . . Italians are white,' and instead considered the Sicilian migrant 'a white-skinned negro who is a better worker than the black-skinned negro.' " The official was distressed by this descent of the Italian to the level of the Negro, and he conceded that the only way for Italians to lift themselves up was to abandon their Italianness and " 'identify completely with the Americans.' "[109] Here, again, we see the use of "Americans" as a racially charged term, synonymous in this instance with white.

Was Capra himself distressed by his brother's descent to the level of the Negro, and did he seek to escape a similar fate by cutting his ties with California's Sicilian community, including with his brother, and identifying completely with the "Americans?" We cannot be sure. But it certainly seems significant that Capra uses the story of his brother's racial descent as a framework within which to understand his own desperate quest for ascent.[110] And the threat of racial descent also underscores the racialized nature of the impulse to leave the ethnic ghetto and to "talk and act" like Americans, like Gary Cooper, Jimmy Stewart, and other Nordic stars of Capra's movies.[111]

We can find many other instances of the ethnic impulse to "talk and act" like Americans within the reform discourse in 1930s America. In 1938, the *Superman* comic strip debuted, capturing the imagination of millions and sustaining it through comics, television, and movies for fifty years. Superman's creators, Jerry Siegel and Joe Shuster, two Jewish American artists from Cleveland, located him within the civic nationalist discourse of the New Deal.

In fighting for "truth, justice, and the American way," Superman saved workers from coal mine explosions, urban residents from slum housing, and consumers from shoddily produced automobiles. In Siegel and Shuster's telling, greedy, negligent, even villainous capitalists were depicted as the source of these social problems.[112]

Unlike Capra, Siegel and Shuster were willing to contemplate the contributions that immigrants could make to America, for Superman was himself an alien who, at birth, had no knowledge of or love for America or its traditions. Siegel and Shuster play in fascinating ways with the benefits and costs of alienage. On the one hand, Superman's extraterrestrial birth endows him with extraordinary powers; on the other, it subjects him to a marginal status, unable to marry, to raise a family, or even fully to disclose his true identity and thus to enjoy real intimacy. But the connection between this mythological immigrant and the real immigrants in Cleveland, New York, and elsewhere is deeply submerged, for Superman bears no physical resemblance to eastern and southern Europeans. Further, his assimilation into America occurs in the countryside under the loving care of the Kents, a rural farm couple who, like Longfellow Deeds and Jefferson Smith, are steeped in "true" American values. Through this Nordic (Yankee) upbringing, Superman comes to understand the "American way." He also gains a new identity that is "authentically" American. Clark Kent can "pass" anywhere, his alienage tightly concealed even as it remains a source (literally) of great strength. Exposure is a constant worry, however, because it will increase his vulnerability to his enemies, who have learned that Kryptonite strips him of his superhuman powers. Superman's immigrant story is, in short, a triumphant saga of a Nordic Americanization, although it carries a harsh warning about the consequences of having one's real alien identity uncovered.[113]

A particular kind of gender politics accompanied Capra's and Siegel and Shuster's quest for Nordic Americanization. In *Mr. Deeds* and *Mr. Smith*, the protagonist's triumph depends on his ability to win a cynical and hardhearted working woman, played in both films by Jean Arthur, to his side. In each film, the Jean Arthur character, Babe Bennett in the first and Clarissa Saunders in the second, almost destroys the hero by exposing his vulnerabilities and naiveté and encouraging his enemies to use those weaknesses to manipulate him for their own advantage. Her meanness is seen as masculine and is associated with her abandonment of the natural female realm of hearth and home for the rough-and-tumble male realm of work. In order for the populist hero of these films to have his way, he must first convince this woman, with whom he falls in love, to see how her transgressive work among men has damaged her sweet, womanly soul and contributed to personal anguish and social misery. Thus, by both films' ends, Jean Arthur has fallen hard for her Nordic man, come to see the error of her ways, and is prepared to quit work for a blissful future built around marriage, family, and domesticity.

Superman's story also warns its readers about the dangers inhering in women who work. The greatest threat to Superman, other than the enemies who discovered his Kryptonite secret, is the newspaperwoman, Lois Lane. Lois resembles the Jean Arthur character in the two Capra films: independent, sexy, aggressive, and manipulative. She does not share Arthur's cynicism; to the contrary, a love for Superman—and a desire to find out who he really is—motivates her desire to expose him. Still, a working woman is once again represented as a threat to a would-be savior of the nation, and Superman must resist her wiles if he is to carry out his mission. In this make-believe Nordic nation, women had to know their place.

The notion that women ought to occupy a separate and subordinate sphere had long been a cardinal principle of Theodore Roosevelt's civic nationalism, and thus its popularity in the 1930s, a period in which TR's vision of the American nation was nearing fulfillment, should not come as a surprise. But the Depression had actually strengthened this component of nationalist thought among men, many of whom felt emasculated by the economic hardships inflicted upon them. They regarded hard work and the ability to provide economic security for their families as critically important measures of their manhood. The loss of their jobs and the seeming impossibility of earning adequate income unleashed feelings of inadequacy in them. That the unemployment rates of men—most of whom labored in blue-collar occupations—tended to be higher than those of women, more of whom worked in white-collar occupations less affected by job cutbacks, exacerbated male vulnerability. Many fathers and husbands resented wives and daughters who had intruded upon their breadwinner roles. The Jean Arthur character, in other words, had real-life counterparts.[114]

This male anxiety triggered social policies and proposals designed to restore men to their former status. Several states passed laws outlawing the hiring of married women. New Deal relief agencies were reluctant to authorize aid for unemployed women. The Social Security pension system did not cover waitresses, domestic servants, and other largely female occupations. Some commentators proposed ludicrous gender remedies to the problem of unemployment. Norman Cousins of the *Saturday Evening Post*, for example, suggested that the Depression could be ended simply by firing 10 million working women and giving their jobs to men. "Presto!" he declared. "No unemployment, no relief roles. No Depression." Countless artists, meanwhile introduced a strident masculinism into their paintings, sculptures, and illustrations, as if powerful male figures with muscle-bulging physiques would somehow compensate men visually for what they lacked in fact. The labor movement made the celebration and the protection of the male wage earner its principal goal. Thus, in Thomas Bell's labor novel, Dobie, the protagonist, conceives of his fight for unionization in terms of his ability to keep his spouse, Julie, in a domestic sphere where she can focus exclusively on being a wife and mother. The prospect of her going to work is so remote that neither the characters nor the narrator ever bring it up.[115]

The gendered character of American nationalism was a different phenomenon than were its race-based notions of belonging. The latter aimed to exclude inferior groups from the national community or, as in the case of Capra, to erase any marker of their presence. Women were to be excluded from work and other key nation-

Fig. 14. Men at Work, Women at Home, 1930s. This picture is one section of a large mural painted on the walls of a federal building in Camden, New Jersey, by an artist (Greenwood) employed on a New Deal arts project. Its depiction of strongly muscled, industrious, and efficient men at work is characteristic of much New Deal art. So, too, is its refusal to represent the ethnic and racial diversity that was so integral a feature of the American working class at this time. Many New Dealers and radicals also shared the view of gender relations expressed in this image—men belonged at work, women belonged with their children at home. (Courtesy Library of Congress)

building activities, but not from the nationalist community itself, whose very future depended on women's procreative and mothering abilities. The mere presence of women, then, posed no problem akin to that presented by unwanted immigrants or native-born racial minorities. Problems only arose when women wandered off the female reservation, as Jean Arthur and Lois Lane had done, entered territory designed for men, and joined in activities meant to enhance male fellowship, the sinew of nationhood.

In Bell's fiction, in the films of Frank Capra, and in the Superman comic strip we see how widespread were the urges to assimilate in ways that erased markers of one's alien and racially inferior past and to demarcate proper male and female spheres. We can also detect these twin urges in the official political culture of the New Deal. Despite its dependence on the votes of urban immigrants and their descendants, New Dealers turned repeatedly to images of suffering among white, rural, native-born Americans. The Depression era's most celebrated photograph was Dorothea Lange's searing 1936 portrait of the worn but proud, simple but virtuous "Migrant Mother" in transit from Oklahoma to California. It mattered both that this woman was native-born white and that her primary female identity was that of a mother rather than of a worker; she had not violated female nature, as Jean Arthur's characters had. The popularity of Lange's visual image was matched in print by John Steinbeck's *Grapes of Wrath* (1939), an epic tale of the flight of the gallant Joad family (sustained by the matriarch, Ma Joad) after machines had entered and ravaged their rural Eden. In cultural terms, the New Deal privileged the suffering of these Americans. Their ubiquity in New Deal culture underscored the belief that they were the best and truest Americans. Their suffering hurt the most. No photograph of an eastern European immigrant, black, or working woman during the decade came close to evoking a similar kind of response to that elicited by the Migrant Mother. She was the universal American; she was a mother; she was also a Nordic.[116]

Scholars such as Linda Gordon, Alice Kessler-Harris, and Robyn Muncy have incisively studied the gender conservatism inherent in

Fig. 15. "Migrant Mother," 1936. This photograph by Dorothea Lange, the most celebrated documentary image of the 1930s, powerfully evokes both the pain and fortitude of this American woman and of the nation of which she was a part. Part of the photograph's appeal lay in the sheer brilliance of its composition, but part depended, too, on its choice of a "Nordic" woman. Her suffering could be thought to represent the nation in ways that the distress of a black, Hispanic, Italian, or Jewish woman never could. (Courtesy Library of Congress)

the New Deal.[117] But the role of racial nationalism in this period of liberal reform has remained more obscure. The point of documenting the contributions made by European ethnics and New Dealers to the tradition of racialized nationalism is not to put them in the same camp as a Martin Dies or John Rankin. They saw themselves as civic nationalists who wished to remake the nation in ways that opened it up to marginalized groups of Americans and widened opportunities for the downtrodden. Most opposed white supremacy in the South and, in the abstract, favored a society that did not discriminate against blacks or other racial minorities. The Communist Party, as we have noted, was a leading force for workers' rights and racial equality. Liberal intellectuals, meanwhile, were organizing a revolt against racialist interpretations of history and society. And Frank Capra would, in the 1940s, supplement his celebration of ordinary Americans with *The Negro Soldier*, an influential film honoring the contributions of blacks to the American military. Martin Dies would never have been capable of making such a statement in any medium. If Capra and Dies shared portions of the tradition of racialized nationalism, they did not share all of it; or, to put it another way, the civic tradition of American nationalism occupied a larger place in the thinking of Frank Capra than it did in the thinking of Martin Dies. Altering the mix of the two traditions yielded significantly different kinds of nationalist politics.

But it is also the case that the tradition of racialized nationalism was a more important force in liberal politics of the 1930s than has generally been recognized. Immigration restriction in the 1920s had increased the strength and influence of America's racial hierarchy by legitimating a discourse that treated the world's nationalities as races unevenly endowed with intelligence and the capacity to be citizens. The immigration laws not only stigmatized certain foreign nationalities as racially inferior; they did the same to members of those nationalities already present in the United States. In parts of the country this stigma did not abate much in the 1930s. Where the Nazis and other right-wing groups were strong, it revived.[118] Eastern and southern Europeans, in particular, felt the sting of racial prejudice and sought to escape it. One way was to devote oneself to America's civic nationalist tradition and to fight for an end to all forms of racial discrimination. Another way was to hide one's lowly ethnic origins and to emulate "the Nordic" in the hopes that somehow one could join the loftiest American race. In the 1930s, these two responses coexisted side by side, sometimes in the minds of the same individuals. Thus we need to see the decade both as a time when the civic nationalist tradition gained strength and when the Nordic ideal was reaffirmed.[119]

It is easy to criticize those who embraced the Nordic ideal or became complicit in its promulgation, for they were reaffirming the nation's racializing tendencies. But it is important to remember what happened to those in the public eye who made little effort to hide their new immigrant origins. Samuel Dickstein, who wore his Jewishness on his sleeve, was denied the chairmanship of his creation, the Dies committee, because, as one of his House colleagues put it, "many members of Congress felt that an investigation of this kind should not be headed by a foreign-born citizen."[120] As Sidney Hillman, the Russian Jewish immigrant and CIO leader, ascended to the inner circles of New Deal policy making in the early 1940s, he became the target of vicious anti-Semitic attacks. In terms of political orientation, Hillman was a "CIO man" of the sort who impressed Dobie in 1930s Braddock. But Hillman had never fully learned how to "talk and act" American, for he had grown up in insular Jewish urban ghettos and then spent his early trade-union career in the equally insular Jewish needle trades unions. Thus, in the 1944 presidential election, Republicans delightfully schemed to discredit him and, by extension, Roosevelt, by luring Hillman "into speaking on a nation-wide hookup to get his foreign-Jewish accent on the air."[121]

And then there is the chilling response of Roosevelt, his Jewish advisers, and Jewish congressmen to the 400 Orthodox rabbis who had come to Washington three days before Yom Kippur in 1943 to plead for FDR's assistance in rescuing their European coreligionists trapped in Hitler's death machine. A Jewish congressman from New York, Sol Bloom, had tried to abort the mission, arguing "that it would be undignified for such an un-American looking group to

Fig. 16. Rabbis March on Washington, 1943. These Orthodox rabbis pleaded with President Roosevelt to do something to stop the destruction of European Jewry. Roosevelt refused to meet with them. Congressman Sol Bloom regarded this "un-American looking group" as too "undignified . . . to appear in Washington." Here they pose on the steps of the Lincoln Memorial, seeking to identify their cause with the emancipator's vision of what America could be. (Courtesy UCLA Film and Television Archive)

appear in Washington." Bloom was apparently referring to their untrimmed beards and long black coats, both of which endowed these men with a strong "Old World" demeanor. Sam Rosenman, too, had attempted, in the words of FDR secretary William D. Hassett, "to keep the horde from storming Washington." An irritated Roosevelt refused to see them, even though his light schedule that day afforded him plenty of time. Instead, he accepted Rosenman's counsel that the rabbis were "not representative of the most thoughtful elements in Jewry."[122]

Over the years, Rosenman no doubt had learned to respect the limits of his boss's tolerance for Jews. Those limits—to Jews and

Catholics—had been starkly revealed to the Catholic economist and New Deal official Leo T. Crowley during a 1942 lunch with Roosevelt. "Leo," Roosevelt had remarked, "you know this is a Protestant country, and the Catholics and Jews are here under sufferance. It is up to you [Crowley and Henry Morgenthau] to go along with anything I want."[123]

So, it turns out, Roosevelt was something of a Nordic father, with an emphasis on both the words in that phrase: Nordic, in the sense that power in the country should continue to reside with those who had been here the longest and had the highest ranking as Americans; and father, in the sense that he was willing to put his "uppity" Jewish and Catholic children in their proper place.

By 1940 Roosevelt and the New Deal had done a great deal to nationalize American life. FDR had strengthened the notion that all Americans belonged to a single national community. He accomplished this through the force of his own personality; through pushing through reform policies that made real differences in the lives of many Americans, especially among those who had been considered outsiders; and through the New Deal's role in transforming and implanting itself on the American landscape. In reinforcing the bonds of nationhood, Roosevelt was aided by a national media, the movies in particular, that enhanced the national imaginary.

The dominant form nationalism assumed in the 1930s was civic. It insisted on equal rights for all Americans and it took major steps to insure that discrimination against ethnic and racial minorities would be reduced. It encouraged campaigns against prejudice and for civil rights. It inspired a massive labor movement—certainly the most significant of the decade's mass movements—that gave this civic nationalism social democratic meaning. The upheaval generated by labor impelled Roosevelt to secure for Americans important social rights—to welfare, to unemployment insurance, to retirement pensions, to savings insurance, to homeowner loans, and to agricultural subsidies. These social provisions were meant to insure that Americans would not suffer discrimination because they were poor and that they would be able to attain the kind of economic security they needed to fulfill their personal and civic obligations. The task of insuring that all Americans had access to social rights was hardly complete by 1940, but although New Dealers had suffered reversals, the progress had been impressive. This would be the most enduring triumph of New Deal civic nationalism.

But shadowing this triumph were two threats: first, the coalescing of a conservative patriotism around Dies and his congressional supporters that depicted communism, rather than unregulated capitalism, as the nation's worst enemy and that identified the New Deal as an emergent dictatorship every bit as dangerous to America as Marxism or fascism; and, second, the survival of a racialized nationalism that continued to define America as a society in which some races were better than others. In some individuals, the two threats merged into one, as they did in Dies. But racialized nationalism survived not only among conservatives but among liberals and radicals, too, sometimes in ways that were barely acknowledged or understood. In the name-changing practices of Communists, in the leadership tendencies of the CIO, in Frank Capra's movies and in the Superman comic, and even in official New Deal culture, we have detected a tendency to erase markers of one's inferior immigrant origins and to emulate the Nordic. The emulation of the Nordic put checks on the behavior of newcomers who, otherwise, might be too inclined to disrupt American customs. It revealed a complicity in racialized notions of Americanness that carried consequences not just for the new immigrants themselves but for nonwhite groups of Americans who had been stigmatized as the most dangerous of the racial others. In such ways did the tradition of defining Americanness in racialized terms live on, even as the push for civic nationalism reached new heights. And it would live on through World War II, even as civic nationalism achieved the greatest power and influence in its history.

CHAPTER 5

Good War,

Race War,

1941–1945

In the 1940s America became the most powerful nation on earth. Its civic nationalist creed, moreover, was in full flower. Forced to fight a "good war" against enemies that virtually everyone regarded as both reprehensible and dangerous, a large majority of Americans became convinced of their nation's essential goodness and benevolence. During this time, Euro-Americans achieved a unity and a sense of common Americanness greater than what they had previously known. Full acceptance into American life finally seemed within the grasp of Catholics and Jews, especially once the government invigorated the civic nationalist tradition and made the elimination of racial and religious prejudice central to its war aims. African American and other minorities, meanwhile, seemed to be making significant strides of their own, at least in terms of pushing civil rights issues higher on the nation's agenda. Faith in America among all these groups was buoyed by the belief that the state had taken on the role of patrolling the economy, insuring that no center of capitalist power would become too great and that no deserving individuals, irrespective of their ethnic or racial background, would be denied economic opportunity or assistance should they become indigent for reasons beyond their control. The New Nationalist state, envisioned by Theodore Roosevelt and implemented by Franklin Roosevelt, had become a pillar of American political economy.

But if World War II was a "good war,"[1] it was also a "race war." In the Pacific, racial hatred between American and Japanese troops fueled a combat savagery far exceeding that engaged in by American and German troops. At home, this hatred prompted the American government to incarcerate the entire West Coast Japanese American population, a policy without precedent or parallel in American immigrant history. Of equal, and perhaps greater, significance, was the government's decision to maintain race as an organizing principle of the American military. The 12-million-person military of World War II was arguably the most important institution of nationalist mobilization in the twentieth century, and it was almost entirely segregated. Black troops trained, served, and fought separately from their white counterparts. While the military maintained the black-white division, it lowered others: whites from every region and every ethnic group were thrown together in circumstances that demanded cooperation and comradeship, if only for the sake of survival. The military became, in effect, an enormously important site for melting the many streams of Euro-Americans into one white race. This crucible of racialized assimilation did not go unchallenged. African American civilians and servicemen in particular, inspired by the government's promotion of civic nationalist ideals, fought with words, fists, and guns to integrate the armed forces. The pressure they brought to bear frightened American military planners and accelerated the pace of change. But they did not succeed in integrating the armed forces during these years, and the 15 million Euro-Americans who served in it learned an important lesson about the continued centrality of whiteness to the American nation.

THE GOOD WAR

"Never before in its history," John P. Diggins has written, "and never again in its immediate future, would America enjoy such unity in time of war."[2] From almost any perspective, the evidence bears out Diggins's claim. Only one-half of 1 percent of the millions drafted into the military either refused to report for induction or deserted training camp shortly after their arrival; the comparable figures for World War I and the Vietnam War were 12 and 20 percent, respectively.[3] Outside the military, resistance was equally slight. Political radicals, Protestant ministers, and women's reform groups, all important antiwar constituencies during World War I, now lined up behind their government. So did African Americans, who had particularly good reasons to stay on the sidelines. In World War I, at the behest of W.E.B. Du Bois and other leaders, they had put their demands for equality on hold, believing that if they served America loyally and well they would be rewarded in the war's aftermath. Bitter disillusionment overtook the black community when no such rewards were forthcoming. A black nationalist might have made a compelling case in 1941 or 1942—as Marcus Garvey had done in 1919—that African Americans should not fight until America granted them full citizenship rights. They could have drawn on North American precedents for an aggrieved minority group refusing to fight for its country: thousands of French Canadians, for example, not wanting to strengthen Anglo ascendancy either in Canada or Europe, had refused to serve in the Canadian army in World War I.[4] While black leaders declined to mute their criticism of American racism, very few advocated outright resistance to the war itself.

There were, of course, small groups of conscientious objectors and other kinds of resisters. Pacifists such as A. J. Muste and Bayard Rustin remained true to their principles and served time in jail as a result.[5] African American and Mexican American zoot-suitors adopted a style of dress and behavior that some historians have interpreted as a protest against the war and against military regimentation in particular.[6] In pockets here and there, other African Americans cultivated an affection for the Japanese, a nonwhite people that had struck hard and successfully at white imperial supremacy.[7] "I don't want them [the Japanese] to quite win," admitted one black man to William Pickens, NAACP field secretary and Treasury Department supervisor of war bond sales in African American communities. But, this man added, he did want the Japanese "to dish out to these white people all they can dish out to them."[8] Meanwhile, some German Americans and Italian Americans openly subscribed to Hitler's and Mussolini's fascist dreams. The U.S. government kept these people under surveillance and placed some in jail. But the numbers in all these groups were small; politically they were inconsequential. Even among the tens of thousands of Japanese Americans, ripped from their homes and forcibly resettled in barren and isolated camps, patriotic sentiment remained strong.[9]

This prowar consensus was really a remarkable development, for most wars in U.S. history that lasted longer than a month or two have given rise to large and voluble oppositions. An estimated third of the colonials living in the thirteen colonies on the eve of the Revolution sided with the Tories and subsequently fled to Canada. World War I and Vietnam both deeply divided the American people. And, as late as 1939, opposition to war was one of the most popular sentiments in American society, as the country's traditional isolationism had been inflamed by the belief that American intervention in World War I had been a colossal mistake, benefiting no one but the munitions makers who had garnered obscene profits. Responding to this sentiment, Congress had tied Franklin Roosevelt's hands, passing neutrality legislation that made it impossible for him to use trade with Britain as a lever with which to push the country into war, as Woodrow Wilson allegedly had been able to do in 1917.[10]

The Japanese attack on Pearl Harbor, however, changed everything. December 7, 1941, was one of those days, like John F. Kennedy's 1963 assassination, where everyone ten years of age and older would always be able to recall exactly where they were and what they were doing when they received the shattering news of the Japanese raid. Since the War of 1812, no foreign power had carried out so devastating an attack on American soil, and virtually all Americans reacted to this one with shock, disbelief, and outrage. That this act had been executed, with brilliance, by a nonwhite people deepened the outrage, for it struck at Americans' belief in the racially superior and unassailable character of their civilization. Of course, some white Americans, especially in the West, had admitted long ago that the Japanese were the one nonwhite people capable of defeating America in any competition, including battle. For them, the Pearl Harbor attack was the realization of their worst nightmare, for it exposed what they had hoped to hide—American vulnerability to Japanese cunning. Hysteria quickly swept the West Coast, as tens of thousands of white residents became convinced that Japanese ships and airplanes were already within striking distance of their homes. Americans there and everywhere had to rally together and to seek, at all costs, to protect their nation. Opposition to war collapsed overnight and would never be revived. Hitler's quick decision to support his Asian Axis ally by declaring war on the United States squelched whatever American opposition there might have been to fighting the Nazis.[11]

If the Japanese attack was one reason for the virtual unanimity on the need to go to war, the evil embodied by Adolf Hitler was another. Hitler's brutal aggressiveness toward Germany's neighbors and the savagery of his verbal and, increasingly, physical attacks on Jews shocked American intellectuals. Here was a new barbarism, emanating not from some peripheral land populated by an ignorant, premodern people but from the very heart of European civilization. Hitler threatened to plunge all of Europe into darkness. American liberal and radical intellectuals became obsessed

with Nazism and, through their involvement with government propaganda organizations, were eventually able to convince most
Americans that this evil creed threatened most of what Americans
held dear.

A basic reorientation in liberal thought, however, had to precede
the efforts of liberal and left intellectuals to reach out to a broader
public. These intellectuals believed deeply in progress; in their
minds, industrial progress implied moral progress. Since the 1920s,
many had argued that economic advances and capitalist regulation
would make people more secure and sophisticated and less prone
to "crude" forms of race hatred and religious prejudice. Thus, for
example, they expected that the South's ugly race relations would
disappear as soon as the region's economic and cultural backward-
ness could be overcome.[12]

But Hitler had shown that the technological prowess and economic abundance associated with industrial progress could be
harnessed to immoral and barbaric rather than moral and civilized
ends. As intellectuals reckoned with the virulence of racism in Germany, they began to confront racism in the United States. It became
impossible any longer to turn one's eyes away from legislation,
such as the Immigration Restriction Act of 1924, built on racist
principles. It became impossible to support or tolerate science constructed on eugenic principles. It became much harder, too, to take
the position that Jane Addams had taken in 1912: that tackling
racism should be put off until a vigorous movement for social and
economic justice was well under way. Reinhold Niebuhr, the German American Protestant theologian who would exert a large influence on post–World War II liberalism, excoriated his fellow liberals in 1942 for thinking that the distribution of property was a
more fundamental cause of social division and conflict than were
racial and ethnic differences. Scholars such as Franz Boas and Ruth
Benedict, who had been doggedly attacking racialized science for
years, suddenly became celebrated figures. Ashley Montagu's
Man's Most Dangerous Myth: The Fallacy of Race and Ruth Benedict's *The Races of Mankind* were best-sellers in 1942 and 1943.[13]

That this attack on racism occurred in a war setting helped to insure that the assault would be framed in patriotic terms. Eliminating racism would help Americans realize their most deeply cherished ideals—equality, freedom, democracy. The most eloquent and influential statement of this position appeared in a book by the Swedish economist Gunnar Myrdal, *An American Dilemma* (1944), an exhaustive study of racist practices in the American South. Myrdal celebrated what he called the "American Creed," a belief allegedly shared by all Americans in "the fundamental equality of all men, and . . . inalienable rights to freedom, justice, and fair opportunity." Myrdal called on Americans to use these creedal principles to criticize and dismantle racist institutions, confident that reform of this sort would then proceed quickly and smoothly. Myrdal's definition of the American Creed was flawed, for it presumed that racialist thought was extraneous to the creed's core civic principles and thus that such thought could be repudiated without calling into question fundamental notions of American identity. But this misconception did little to halt the popularity of Myrdal's analysis and the rallying of liberals around the American Creed as a way to confront racist practices and extirpate them from American society. The battle to implement the American Creed at home merged seamlessly with a battle to defeat Nazi tyranny abroad. Causes that had languished on the liberal agenda—civil rights and immigration law reform, to take the most obvious examples—were now embraced.[14]

In the process of denouncing racist beliefs and practices, American liberals and intellectuals cast the war against Hitler as a great crusade. They depicted America, with all its flaws, as the last bastion of civilization against Nazi barbarism. They celebrated America's civic nationalism—which they variously referred to as the "American creed," the "American dream," or the "American way of life"—as the antithesis of Hitler's racial nationalism. And they gave themselves entirely to the war, believing that humanity's very future depended on an Allied victory. A new liberal journal, *Common Ground*, founded in 1940, expressed the urgency gripping liberal intellectuals: "Never has it been more important," wrote the editors, "that we become intelligently aware of the ground Americans of various strains have in common; that we sink our tap roots deep into its rich and varied cultural past and attain rational stability in place of emotional hysteria; that we reawaken the old American Dream, a dream which, in its powerful emphasis on the fundamental worth and dignity of every human being, can be a bond of unity no totalitarian attack can break."[15] These sorts of heartfelt declarations, which became commonplace during the 1940s, helped to make the fight against the Nazis the "good war."

African Americans, of course, did not have to be shocked out of their complacency concerning racism, but many were newly energized by the perception that racial equality might now be within their grasp. They understood how much they stood to gain from supporting America's war against the Nazis and, through their eagerness to fight and their willingness to purchase war bonds, they demonstrated as much patriotic ardor as any other group in the population. They were energized, too, in ways only dimly perceived by whites, by Japan's swift destruction of citadel after citadel of colonial power in Asia: Hawaii, Singapore, Burma, the Philippines, the Dutch East Indies, French Indochina, and so on. In the 450 years of Western colonial domination, beginning with Columbus's arrival in the New World in 1492, there had been no shortage of rebellions against European control; but virtually all had failed because the native populations could not match the military prowess of the West. Japan had finally demonstrated that a people of color could defeat, even rout, the Western imperialists. The vast majority of African Americans did not wish that Japan, itself, would triumph over America; and the peoples of color in Asia who hailed the arrival of the Japanese armies quickly learned that the Japanese were more brutal and just as racist as the Western imperialists they had displaced.[16]

Nevertheless, the boost that the initial Japanese conquests gave nonwhite peoples in America and elsewhere remained substantial, for now they could dare to imagine a world in which all imperial powers were sent home and rule based on racial subjugation would be banished from the earth. For colored people everywhere, World War II became a fight not only against the Axis powers but against racialized systems of imperial rule. Many African Americans linked themselves to this struggle and participated in an emergent anticolonial movement that was international in scope. This movement contained antinationalist tendencies, as it looked forward to an internationalist anti-imperial uprising that would bring together all peoples of color. But, within the United States, the antinationalist tendencies remained weak, and most African Americans saw the American civic nationalist tradition as something that could be deployed against racial domination, both in the United States and abroad. Thus, the organization that benefited most from this black awakening was not a new one organized primarily around anticolonial politics, but the venerable NAACP, which mushroomed in size in the war years from 50,000 to 400,000 members.[17]

White and black intellectuals were eager to serve in government war agencies charged with publicizing American war aims. They helped FDR craft an image of the United States as a democracy in which people of all races, creeds, and religions coexisted and prospered. They hailed FDR's elaboration of the Four Freedoms— of speech and religion, from want and fear—as the core American identity. And they helped to engineer a government-endorsed celebration of America's ethnic and racial diversity without precedent in the country's history. This initiative was a frank effort to underscore the vast gulf separating America from Germany, where only one race was honored. It also signaled a departure in how Americans constructed their own civic nationalist tradition. Theodore Roosevelt had abhorred diversity, believing that the maintenance of Old World traditions would diminish immigrants' devotion to America. Immigrants were welcome in his America only if they agreed to rapid and wholesale assimilation. This approach had maintained its potency through the 1930s, deeply influencing New Deal culture (as we have seen). But by the 1940s its appeal had dimmed, and the respect for ethnic difference had grown. This new respect did not represent a radical development, however, for it rested on an unstated belief that European ethnicity no longer threatened America as it had done in the century's early decades; assimilation was thought to have eroded ethnic differences. Diversity had become tolerable as a result of the growth of a common Americanness. Still, even such a modest recognition of the value of group distinctiveness significantly altered (Theodore) Rooseveltian civic nationalism.[18]

It would be a mistake, of course, simply to assume that all Americans shared in this modest celebration of their society's diversity and tolerance. Segregation remained entrenched in the South and religious prejudice was still an integral feature of American life. In 1942, 40 percent of Americans believed that Jews had too much power.[19] And, if Hitler inspired Americans to fight racism, the Japanese impelled white Americans to reassert their racial superiority. We will attend to the survival and, in some circumstances, the intensification of the racial nationalist tradition, in due course. But it is equally important to reckon with the broad reach of the official liberal, and civic nationalist, culture. Few Americans could escape its influence. Government propaganda efforts were more sophisticated than they had been in World War I, less centralized and overbearing, more subtle and attentive to the varying tastes of the many constituencies (regional, ethnic, class, racial) that composed the consuming public. Communities of ethnic workers and blacks, for example, received a disproportionate share of government propaganda missives advertising and celebrating America as a land of many peoples, races, and nationalities. Many in these communities interpreted this propaganda to mean that they were being fully accepted as Americans, and their devotion to their nation increased accordingly.[20]

Government efforts to mobilize the people for war benefited too from the fact that so many Americans, irrespective of their ethnic, class, or racial background, had a profound personal stake in the war. A total of 16.3 million young men and women, representing about 12 percent of the total population, served in the wartime military.[21] If we add to this total the parents and siblings of the servicemen and servicewomen, as well as grandparents and other relatives, we can see that kinship ties alone involved half of the

American population of 132 million in the war effort. In most towns and cities, enthusiasm for home-front war-related activities, as measured by war bond purchases, blood donations, participation in civil defense organizations, and attendance at USO dances, ran high.[22]

Not all the participants, of course, cared as much about the nation's official war aims as they did about getting a loved one home alive. Many, we know, grew perturbed at the endless appeals to patriotism that always seemed to conclude with a request for money or sacrifice. Still, the average American's personal investment in the war, measured in terms of family members or kin serving in the military and risking death, made a skeptical, detached attitude toward the country's war aims difficult to maintain. Mary Bednarchuk, an aging Polish textile worker in Rhode Island eagerly awaiting retirement, declared that loyalty to her son, a much decorated aerial gunner, rather than to her country, made her determined to "keep going until the war is over." Yet she lavished great attention on her son's medals and diligently collected newspaper and magazine clippings describing his heroic acts. In such ways did loyalty to kin merge imperceptibly with patriotic feeling. Similarly, a Lowell, Massachusetts, mother with five sons in the service, her daughter later recalled, followed the war "every which way she could, because of [her] . . . boys being here and there." She "had put a big map in the dining room and, oh, she just followed everything that was going on during the war." In these circumstances, distinctions between personal involvement with the war and ideological commitment to it proved difficult to sustain.[23]

War bond purchases illuminate the depth and character of the average American's involvement in the war effort. Americans bought a staggering total of 85 million bonds, virtually one for every adult American. The resulting revenue of $185.7 billion represents, according to the historian Lawrence R. Samuel, the greatest amount "ever raised for a war" through voluntary subscription.[24] War bond purchasers came from every racial, ethnic, economic, and regional group. Corporations and small businessmen subscribed; so, too, did trade unionists, 90 percent of whom bought bonds. In one three-year period, unionists purchased a full third of all the Treasury bonds sold.[25] Virtually every ethnic and racial group, including Jews, Poles, Germans, Italians, Chinese, Japanese, Native Americans, Mexicans, Slovaks, Serbs, Lithuanians, Lebanese, and African Americans, bought large number of bonds. Impressionistic evidence suggests that groups with the greatest stake in the war's outcome—Jews, Poles, and African Americans, for example—purchased the most bonds. But precise figures on the contributions of these different groups are not available; the Treasury refused to track purchases according to race and ethnic affiliation.[26]

We do know that in different locales, bonds were sold in different ways, appealing to different instincts. Treasury Department advertisements variously called on Americans to support the boys overseas, to sacrifice something of their own for the war effort, and to defend the Four Freedoms. In ethnic and racial communities, bond posters and drives celebrated America's ethnic and racial diversity as a source of strength and called on individuals to do everything they could to insure that American democracy prevailed over Hitler's racial dictatorship.[27]

The Treasury Department advertisers also appealed to the purchasers' financial self-interest. In loaning money to their nation in its hour of need, bond purchasers were told, they were also helping themselves, making investments that would earn a fine rate of interest and that would increase their economic well-being over the long term. Bond-buying Americans would thus profit from their patriotism.[28] Some scholars have discerned in such appeals the true engine of wartime unity. They have argued that privatism and individualism underlay the nationalism of the war years and that Americans, throughout the conflict, remained far more committed to themselves and their families than to a civic creed or the commonweal.[29] There can be no doubt that individual and familial well-being loomed large in the minds of many Americans. But it seems wrong to divorce the personal from the national in so mechanical a way, as though individuals make a clear-cut decision to embrace one or the other. In America, in particular, the promise of prosperity was integral to the civic nationalist ideal. In unveiling the New Nationalist program in 1910, Theodore Roosevelt had explicitly sought to expand economic opportunity for ordinary Americans. Civic nationalist fulfillment, he had argued, depended on the ability of a large state to restrain capitalist power and to improve the economic condition of the disadvantaged. Thus the Treasury Department's appeal to financial self-interest should not be examined in isolation but in relation to the government's overall effort to create a society of greater economic well-being and fairness.

From this perspective, we can see how the war propelled forward the economic aspects of the Roosevelts' civic nationalist agenda. As government war orders poured into the private sector, unemployment—still 14 percent in 1940—vanished. A tight labor market pushed wages up. In manufacturing, the average weekly earnings grew 65 percent between 1941 and 1944; adjusting for inflation and higher income taxes still leaves a net gain of 27 percent. Fifteen million workers—a full third of the prewar work force—moved up the occupational ladder during the war. Largely as a result of government policies, the poorest-paid enjoyed the greatest wage hikes. Conditions did not improve as rapidly for minorities as for whites, but, by 1944, black men and women in war production areas had gained access to jobs and were enjoying wages that five years earlier had been beyond their reach. The government added additional value to jobs by requiring employers to offer their workers nonwage benefit packages that included paid vacations and hospitalization insurance. Bank accounts began to fill (especially since the opportunities for consumption were limited by war-induced scarcities), and feelings of plenty began to replace the insecurity of joblessness or insufficient income. These were especially important developments, following as they did twelve long years of depression and lost opportunity.[30]

Wartime economic gains did not mean that inequities, injustices, and inconveniences in the workplace went unnoticed. On the contrary, the reclassification of factory workers and the wages assigned particular jobs caused conflict between workers and bosses and among different groups of workers who were jockeying for labor market advantage. The influx of new workers to war production centers, meanwhile, everywhere overwhelmed local transportation systems and housing supplies, adding further frustrations to daily life.[31] The resentments and discomforts of wartime living, however, must be set against the growing remuneration and security of wartime employment. By itself this economic experience would not have been enough to bring about inclusion of workers who had keenly felt their marginality, but in conjunction with the wartime celebration of the nation's multicultural character it allowed many heretofore marginal groups (and especially the European American ethnics) to believe that the American dream was finally within their grasp. In such ways did many Americans tie personal advancement to national fulfillment.

Few would deny, moreover, that the state played a central role in economic improvement. The government inundated America's private economy, newly christened the "arsenal of democracy," with orders for food, tanks, uniforms, guns, airplanes, ships, and munitions, and thereby restored its vigor. In the process it made Keynesianism—the government's use of its fiscal and monetary powers to stimulate the economy—a popular faith. The government also intervened in economic matters to protect corporate profits, to grant workers the right to organize and bargain collectively with their employers, and to insure farmers a profitable return on their production. It set up institutions to control prices and to defuse disputes between capital and labor. All these activities were oriented to achieving the highest levels of production possible while maintaining social harmony. High and progressive rates of taxation triggered a modest, but significant, redistribution of income from the rich to the broad middle. Finally, the government sustained the welfare state that had been established in the 1930s and, in certain areas, expanded its services. The GI Bill of Rights, passed in 1944, was the single most important piece of wartime welfare legislation. In the postwar, millions would use its educational and home mortgage benefits to lift themselves into the middle class.[32]

In the eyes of the most ardent liberals and of the non-Communist left, the state did not do nearly enough. Too much production remained in private hands. The largest corporations continued to grow in power at the expense of small businesses. Labor leaders like Walter Reuther were particularly disappointed in the rejection of corporatism, a system of public industrial governance in which labor, capital, and the state would jointly manage the economy. The government, moreover, steadily narrowed the scope of collective bargaining, sealing off investment and pricing decisions from union purview. Franklin Roosevelt's ambitious Economic Bill of Rights, calling for the government to guarantee every American breadwinner a job, home, and health care, made little headway in Congress. And Congress also scuttled plans generated by the National Resources Planning Board to involve the government in extensive public works projects.[33]

Still, the state established and maintained by the government in the 1940s was far larger than conservatives in America had wanted it to be, and they tolerated it only in the interest of national security, first for World War II and then for the Cold War. As a result, something resembling the New Nationalist state that Theodore Roosevelt had envisioned in 1912 did establish itself, curbing the power of the largest corporations to some extent, building up labor and agriculture as countervailing powers to big business, and improving economic opportunity for the disadvantaged. As a consequence of such regulation, American capitalism became somewhat more humane and responsive to the needs of the nation.

RACE WAR

As the civic nationalist ideal was triumphing in politics and economics, the racial nationalist ideal was being reinvigorated. Japan's attack on the United States, as we have seen, inflamed ingrained prejudices against Japanese among white Americans, leading to the incarceration of the West Coast Japanese American population.

The American-Japanese war in the Pacific, meanwhile, took on the coloration of a "race war" (to use John Dower's apt phrase), in which the two opposing sides engaged in savage struggle, of which Theodore Roosevelt would have approved, to determine which race would triumph.[34] Battles between the Japanese and the Americans were, on the whole, more vicious than those between the Americans and Germans and Italians in Europe, with both sides committed to fighting until death. The ratio of killed to wounded servicemen in the Pacific soared well beyond that of the western European theater. Japanese soldiers often decapitated and disemboweled American corpses, while many Marines collected the ears and gold teeth of Japanese warriors they had killed.

Both sides were guilty of slaughtering combatants whom they had captured: sometimes these acts emerged from the fury of battle, other times they were the result of direct orders. "Kill Japs, Kill Japs, Kill more Japs" was the slogan Admiral William Halsey used to rally his troops in the South Pacific Force.[35] Even the end of the war did not slake America's thirst for dead Japanese. A December 1945 poll found that almost a quarter of Americans surveyed wished that the United States had had the opportunity to drop more atomic bombs on Japan before it had surrendered.[36] Long before that, the two sides had lost the ability to recognize each other's humanity. To the Americans, the Japanese were vermin who had to be exterminated. To the Japanese, the Americans were devils.[37]

Historians disagree on responsibility for this savagery, with some, such as John Dower, attributing it to both sides and others, such as Gerald Linderman, placing blame squarely on Japanese battle practices in the Pacific, practices that the American troops then felt compelled to imitate. The Japanese do seem to have established patterns of torture and savagery in their initial attacks of the war, as Linderman argues. But Linderman also ignores the long history of white Americans' constructing racial stereotypes to demean and dehumanize the Japanese. These stereotypes arose in reaction to encounters with Japanese immigrants and other nonwhite groups in American society, not with Japanese soldiers on a field of battle. Their existence made it relatively easy for American servicemen to work themselves into a savage mentality in the Pacific war.[38]

Samuel Eliot Morison explicitly linked the savage fighting against the Japanese to America's earlier experience with Indian warfare on the frontier: "This may shock you, reader," Morison declared in his official naval history of the assault on Guadalcanal, "but it is exactly how we felt. We were fighting no civilized, knightly war. . . . We cheered when the Japanese were dying. We were back to the primitive days of fighting Indians on the American frontier; no holds barred and no quarter. The Japs wanted it that way, thought they could thus terrify an 'effete democracy': and that is what they got, with all the additional horrors of war that modern science can produce."[39] In his narrative, Morison both blamed the Japanese for the savagery and acknowledged that Americans had a long tradition of savage warfare of their own, which they were ready, if not eager, to deploy.

World War II was also a race war in the degree to which race remained the organizing principle of the U.S. military. Throughout the war, all branches of the military remained largely segregated. Black and white GIs trained, served, and socialized separately from each other. Proportionately far fewer black servicemen than whites, whether in the infantry, tank corps, air corps, navy, or Marines, were allowed to engage in combat; when they did, they almost always fought in all-black units commanded by white officers. The military segregated its blood supply to make sure that a white serviceman would never receive an infusion of black blood. This thorough separation of the races was a reality of enormous importance that went a long way toward fulfilling Theodore Roosevelt's prescription for forging a racialized American nation: through war and conditions of controlled, racialized assimilation.[40] Indeed, the mobilization and deployment of the World War II military can be viewed as the reenactment of the Rough Riders script on a massive scale. The military brought together millions of white American boys from every region of the country; the mixing exceeded that of previous wars because, for the first time, geographic residence did not serve as a basis for regimental organization. Relatively few local or state units fought in the World War II army. Most regiments drew on servicemen from every region of the country and from every religion and European nationality. Sometimes together for as long as four years, these units became extraordinary vehicles for melding the many streams of Euro-Americans into one. The simple act of removing all these young men from their native surroundings—southern towns, western farms, eastern cities—for an extended period of time heightened the possibilities of assimilation. And this assimilatory process was racialized from its inception because no blacks and few Asians were permitted to take part, in the sense that they were excluded from regiments defined as white.[41] Theodore Roosevelt himself could not have hoped for a better opportunity to fashion a united and racialized American nation.

The key image of this racialized army was that of the multicultural platoon, a unit made up of Protestants, Catholics, Jews, southerners, westerners, and easterners, all of whom were white. This image was not new, for Theodore Roosevelt and other nationalists had used similar images to describe earlier armies, including those raised for the Spanish-American and First World Wars. But, in World War II, this image became ubiquitous in official and popular culture, which it had not been in earlier wars. And the image makers had become more comfortable acknowledging the legitimacy of ethnic and regional difference. The creators of earlier platoon images had been quick to demonstrate the rapid transformation of servicemen of different backgrounds into one mold, that of the "all American fightin' man."[42] But the invigorated and altered civic nationalist tradition of the 1940s made it possible to recognize that GIs could preserve their ethnic, religious, and regional background while dedicating themselves to America and its fight. Because these mythic platoons usually excluded blacks, they reaffirmed the racial boundaries of the American nation.

More than any single institution, Hollywood was responsible for the spread of this image. During the war years, it structured numerous combat films around the exploits of multicultural platoons. A partial roster of such films would include *Guadalcanal*

Diary (1943), *Bataan* (1943), *Sahara* (1943), *Gung-Ho* (1943), *Action in the North Atlantic* (1943), *Air Force* (1943), *Destination Tokyo* (1943), *Purple Heart* (1944), *The Fighting Seabees* (1944), *Objective Burma* (1945).[43] An early scene in each of these movies is used to establish the diverse backgrounds of platoon or crew members. The diversity roster varied from one film to another, but the stock characters were the Anglo-Protestant, the Irish Catholic, and the eastern European Jew. This trinity harked back to the older divisions separating the native-born (the Anglo-Saxons) from the foreign-born, and the old immigrants (the Irish) from the new (the Jews). It also, however, looked forward to newer divisions grounded in religious affiliation—Protestant, Catholic, Jew—that were superseding ethnic groups as the preferred way for distinguishing among European Americans. This religious trinity could be easily modified to absorb other groups of European Americans, with the Catholic category, in accommodating Italians, Poles, Slovakians, and others, demonstrating itself to be the most elastic.[44]

In introducing us to these servicemen, the films also emphasize that they are peace-loving civilians at heart: in moments of relaxation on ships, planes, or at debarkation centers in the States, they talk about baseball and sweethearts, they strum on guitars and sing tunes from popular songs. They are innocent boys, not experienced warriors, and they have little notion of what battle has in store. Only the platoon leader, customarily portrayed as a battle-hardened sergeant or a professionally trained lieutenant (he is usually a Protestant, sometimes an Irish Catholic, never an Italian or a Jew), knows what lies ahead. Thus battle itself—often in jungles against the "Japs," the most savage and cunning of foes—is the crucible that transforms them from civilians into warriors, and from many individuals into a single fighting force.[45] Their success in these harrowing circumstances depends not simply on their courage as individuals but in their willingness to give themselves entirely to the group, in the process erasing whatever prejudice they may have harbored toward the Jew, the Dago, or the Mick in their bunch. Often this unity can only be achieved through sacrifice, through one or more platoon members giving their lives so that others may live.[46]

Unity is thus sanctified by blood, and savage combat is justified in terms of avenging a buddy's cruel death. These moments of sacrifice and retribution mitigate regional and class, as well as ethnic, difference. The survivors possess a bond that no force can break, and this will carry them—and the nation—to victory.

As Hollywood was popularizing these images and stories of racialized assimilation on tens of thousands of movie screens, it was also struggling with the issue of discrimination against African Americans. Below the level of the movie moguls, who tended to be Republicans, the Hollywood industry was liberal-left in political orientation. Numerous actors, directors, writers, and animators supported the New Deal, and a significant minority were, at one time or another, close to or members of the Communist Party.[47] In the context of World War II, the liberal-left proclivities of this industry meant that a large portion of those who worked within it embraced the revitalized civic nationalist tradition and sought to eradicate prejudice not simply against Jews and Catholics but against blacks and other racial minorities as well. Several of the screenwriters assigned to work on the "platoon" movies, men such as Dalton Trumbo, Alvah Bessie, and John Howard Lawson, had ties to the Communist Party through its Popular Front institutions, and they shared the party's dedication to the cause of racial equality. The Communist Party had allied itself with the Roosevelt administration in 1941, making itself one of the most enthusiastic supporters of American war aims in general and of the strengthening of America's civic nationalist tradition in particular. Thus, Trumbo's, Lawson's, and Bessie's leftist ties were considered a boon rather than a liability, and figured into studio decisions to select them for prowar pictures.[48]

A deep commitment to racial equality inclined these radical screenwriters to look for ways to include blacks in their cinematic representations of the multicultural platoon. They received support from the Office of War Information (OWI), charged by the government with overseeing Hollywood movies to make sure they conformed to American war aims and presented American society in a positive light. The OWI, too, was a bastion of liberal partisanship that saw the invigoration of the country's civic nationalist tradition as the surest way to victory. With regard to the situation of American blacks, however, they were motivated by conflicting aims. On the one hand they wished to include blacks in celebrations of American equality and diversity; on the other, they were intent on censoring any movie that depicted blacks, or race relations, in a bad light. They thus made some curious, but telling, censorship decisions.[49]

Slotting blacks into representations of the multicultural platoon was not an easy act to accomplish, because rarely, in real life, did black and white GIs fight alongside each other. Racial mixing occasionally happened among troops in the European theater, especially in chaotic battles in which regimental authority had broken down, and elements of black and white units were, willy-nilly, thrown together. But these events were infrequent and happened late in the war—too late, in fact, to convert most of them into movie material while the war was still going on. The opportunities for racial mixing were even scarcer in the Pacific theater; there, the major fighting force, and the one most venerated on screen, was the Marines, which as late as 1941 had yet to accept its first black recruit. The navy did sign up blacks, but, for most of the war, only in the most menial of roles—as cooks and cleaners aboard ships.[50]

But "reality" has rarely stymied Hollywood for long, and the film colony's screenwriters who were looking to include blacks in multicultural platoons found a variety of ways to do so. In *Sahara*, for example, Lawson and his cowriters hit on the idea of fashioning a "platoon" out of stragglers from several nations' armies, all of whom had become isolated in the vast North African desert during the Allied counteroffensive against the Germans there. The North African location made it plausible to include a black Sudanese corporal, Tamdul (played by Rex Ingram), in this multinational platoon, in addition to several Americans, a British doctor, and a Frenchman active in the resistance. The plot involves this group's effort to escape a pursuing German army and reach British lines before the Germans or thirst kills them. In a climactic scene, Tamdul catches a German prisoner who has escaped from the platoon and is dashing for enemy lines. Against the backdrop of the white desert, Tamdul kills the blond Aryan with his bare, black hands.[51] German fire cuts him down as he struggles to return to his own lines, making him a martyr. His death enables the platoon to live, sealing the unity of this pan-racial and pan-national fighting force.

Sahara was perhaps the most radical of the war films that included blacks, for Tamdul is depicted as every bit the equal of white Europeans and Americans. He, as much as the American platoon leader, Sergeant Joe Gunn (played by Humphrey Bogart), saves the platoon from destruction.[52] The OWI censors had worked hard to make sure the Sudanese soldier would be portrayed as a man of independence and bravery, and they applauded the result.[53] But their intervention in other platoon films led to significantly different, and worse, results.

The OWI's approval of *Sahara's* racial radicalism rested, at least in part, on the international character of the film's multiracial platoon. Moviegoers could root for Tamdul without directly confronting the issue of racial segregation in the American military. But in reviewing movies in which the proposed multiracial platoon was an American military unit, the OWI applied different standards. It objected to both excessively submissive and overly strong African American characters, for either might generate racial anger among audiences: the former would disturb blacks, the latter would offend many whites. Thus, the OWI determined, it was often better to exclude black characters altogether.

This is what the OWI forced Lawson and other screenwriters to do in *Action in the North Atlantic* (1943), a film about the heroics of a multiethnic Merchant Marine crew in convoying supplies across the Atlantic to Britain and the Soviet Union. In the original screenplay, Lawson had created a part for a black pantryman. This was a realistic touch, for the menial tasks of food preparation and cleaning were the only ones usually given to blacks in the U.S. Navy and Merchant Marine. Lawson had wanted to underscore this subservience and to challenge it: at one point in the original script, Lawson has the pantryman ask why he should fight for the Allies, implying that racial subordination diminished African Americans' patriotic ardor. Lawson was not interested in sowing the seeds of racial division; to the contrary, he saw the raising of this question as a mechanism for getting the white crew members— and white movie viewers more generally—to reevaluate their opinions of blacks and to treat them as equals. This episode makes possible a later one in the original screenplay, in which a white crew member gives up his life so that the black pantryman may live. Lawson clearly wanted moviegoers to contemplate the benefits that would accrue from such displays of interracial brotherhood. But the OWI regarded this message as entirely too dangerous. Its censors objected both to the portrayal of a black as subservient and to the screenwriters' determination to have this black character challenge his subservience. The only option, then, was to excise the black character from the script, which Lawson and his team agreed to do.[54] OWI oversight of other scripts resulted in similar excisions.[55]

The OWI might have responded differently to the initial script of *Action in the North Atlantic*. It might, for example, have encouraged Lawson in his efforts to ask some tough questions about why blacks were confined to menial roles in the U.S. Merchant Marine and Navy. It might also have demanded of other filmmakers that they craft African American fighting men—as opposed to African Sudanese ones—whose strong characters and personalities would challenge the legitimacy of segregation in the U.S. military. But to do so was to risk opening a general debate about the place of blacks in the American military and in American society more generally, and this, the OWI judged, would be too dangerous to American unity and resolve. Thus the OWI limited what it would do to express its commitment to racial equality. All too often its actions backfired. By removing "offensive" black characters from *Action in the North Atlantic* and other films without pushing the filmmakers to substitute for them other characters who were more equal to whites, the OWI was helping to whiten visual representations of the multicultural platoon and thus to deepen the exclusion of blacks from this critical image of national membership and belonging.

Guadalcanal Diary, a movie about the Marines taking Guadalcanal, giving American forces their first great land victory in the

Pacific, exemplifies how little the OWI was able to accomplish its goal of encouraging racial equality. The movie follows the Hollywood formula, in that it narrates the exploits of a multicultural Marine platoon in island fighting. There is, of course, no black in this platoon. One black serviceman is allowed to appear in the film, however. A sailor, he materializes on screen while the Marines are still on their troopships and is asked by them to identify the battleships and destroyers that have just joined the invasion force. The scene conveys a surprising degree of interracial affection as the black sailor is surrounded, even nuzzled, by a chummy group of white Marines. Expressed in this moment is the possibility of interracial comradeship. But the scene lasts all of ten seconds, during which the black seaman calls out the names of a half-dozen ships. He appears in no other scene; he has no role in the film's main action—the landing on the island and the assault on the Japanese. He takes no part in the ordeal by fire that forges the motley Marine crew into true Americans. The interracial possibilities entertained in that early cinematic moment are not realized and, by the film's climax, entirely forgotten. The OWI celebrated this film as the "most realistic and outstanding picture" of the Pacific theater yet made.[56] Through such judgments the OWI helped to insure that the color line in Hollywood war movies, though stretched in places, would remain intact.

"SOMETHING DRASTIC SHOULD BE DONE": THE MILITARY'S HIDDEN RACE WAR

The OWI's struggle with racial representations reveals, however, that racial exclusion had become a problem, both in the military and civilian life, that the government could not ignore. The greatest pressure was emanating from the black community itself, where both leaders and members were doing everything they could to end exclusion and segregation. Early in the war, black newspaper editors announced their commitment to a "Double V"—victory over the Axis abroad and over racial inequality at home—and made clear their determination to pursue both with equal intensity. They filled their newspapers with stories of racial injustices both in civilian and military life. Their agitation over the exclusion of blacks from production work, in combination with the labor leader A. Philip Randolph's threatened March on Washington to protest discriminatory employment patterns, compelled the government, in 1941, to establish the Fair Employment Practices Commission. The black press also covered blacks' experience with military service in detail, documenting not only the extent of segregation but also patterns of exclusion, subordination, and harassment. The African American population, as a result, kept abreast of countless stories of black GIs being concentrated in service rather than combat divisions, passed over for military positions deemed to require intelligence, and harassed by white servicemen and white military police intent on their humiliation.[57]

What made these stories particularly galling to blacks was how they stood in sharp contradiction to America's professed aim of fighting a war against racial prejudice and inequality. Letters written by young African American men to Roosevelt, Secretary of War Stimson, and other government officials pleading for the opportunity to serve their country repeatedly pointed this out; they also reveal how deeply many African American youth felt their Americanness and how committed they were to making their country's civic nationalist tradition the dominant one in social and political life. The immediate occasion for these letters was the army's refusal to allow them to enlist. Blacks had responded to the Selective Service Act of 1940 and the initial calls for soldiers with much greater enthusiasm than the army had anticipated, and the proportion of black recruits quickly rose far higher than the desired 9 to 10 percent.[58] Because the army did not have a sufficient number of segregated training centers and because it felt too great a proportion of black GIs would demoralize the white majority, it began turning blacks away from enlistment centers. After experiencing such a rejection in Dallas, W. E. Mahon wrote to Roosevelt: "I am one of the Negro citizens who is awfully proud that I am an American, and am ready to contribute my share whatever it is for the defence

of my country. . . . I speak the sentiment of a number of my race
. . . [who] certainly want an opportunity for training that we may
be better able to Defend America with you."[59]

He certainly spoke for four young men from New York City who
sent their letter to Eleanor Roosevelt, believing that she would be
more sympathetic to their complaints than her husband. Wanting
to be part of the Colored Tenth Cavalry, whose proud history they
knew well, these men showed up at the Tenth's New York City
enlistment office, only to be turned away. They then learned that
the other existing Negro divisions were also "already over their
quotas" and that there was, as a result, no opportunity at all for
them to enlist. Their letter communicated more anger than did Mahon's: "The very fact that there should be separate divisions for
white and colored in such a democratic nation as this at all is bad
enough. But to deprive those who really wish to serve their country
of the opportunity to do so because of their race is intolerable and
something drastic should be done to eliminate the situation."[60]

After Pearl Harbor, the complaints intensified and expanded in
scope. In a December 15, 1941, letter, William C. Wyatt of Rolla,
Missouri, pleaded with Franklin Roosevelt to "please give thousands of young American Negroes the chance to serve in the *actual*
combat units of the U.S. Army. Let *our* country live up to the
Democratic Concepts that it is now fighting for."[61] And Harry A.
Hamilton of Philadelphia, after a lengthy summary of the many
"humiliating setbacks" that Negroes suffered in the military, in defense work, and in education, queried the president: "Where does
the Democracy or the principles of the very essence of the fight
we are staging come in? Is there a Democracy for only the white
American?"

Hamilton might have answered his question in the affirmative
and, in thus recognizing the influence of the racial nationalist tradition on American life, withdrawn or temporized his support for
the war. But he did nothing of the sort. "My dear Mr. President,"
he intoned, "I am as proud and am as loyal and faithfull to my
country as any white man ever dared to be and I want my children

to feel the same as I do." He worried, however, that his children would feel differently because they "never see or hear of any thing that the Negro Soldier is doing," except that he is being excluded from the armed forces. "Does this tend to make the best citizens of my children," Hamilton wondered, does it make them "feel that it is an honor to die and to fight for democracy?" Hamilton believed that it would not, that it would incline them instead to think that democracy, freedom, and equality are "just for the white man." He urged the president to "say something in answer to my questions on your next fireside chat," to give young blacks in particular a reason to believe in America.[62]

In the minds of Hamilton and other African Americans, the civic nationalist tradition continued to inspire, even as they feared that it might soon lose its grip. Indeed, in these letters, one can detect a rising impatience, especially among the young, with Jim Crow and other indignities to which blacks were subjected. This impatience would find expression in urban race riots in 1943 and 1944, and it would find another among those young people who most fully experienced the contradictions between the civic and racial traditions of American nationalism—the black GIs in the U.S. military who were being asked to die for freedom and democracy while being told on a daily basis that those ideals were not theirs to enjoy.

By 1942 and 1943 the government had relinquished its efforts to limit the number of blacks in the armed forces. The military's immense need for men in combination with the pressure brought to bear by the black community made the costs of that policy too high to sustain. By September 1944 the army alone included more than 700,000 African Americans in its ranks.[63] But many African Americans quickly discovered that simply getting into the military did not give them the opportunities that regularly went to white servicemen. Jim Crow was practiced as intensely inside the military as it was in civilian life. Blacks were trained separately from whites, often by white officers convinced of their troops' innate inferiority. Most military brass, from the lowest second lieutenants to the highest generals, believed that blacks lacked the character and intelligence for combat. Some were hardened southern racists who despised blacks. Others who thought of themselves as above prejudice nevertheless indulged in damaging racial stereotypes. A memo sent in July 1943 to commanding officers of black troops in the European theater described black soldiers as "well-meaning but irresponsible children" who "cannot be trusted to tell the truth, to execute complicated orders or to act on their own initiative."[64] The memo went on to note that "the colored individual likes to 'doll up,' strut, brag and show off. He likes to be distinctive and stand out from the others." Rather than cure black soldiers of these unfortunate tendencies, officers were told, they were to do "everything possible" to encourage them. "For example," the memo advised, "know their names and occasionally call a man 'Corporal John' in place of 'Corporal Smith.' "[65] A related memo argued that because blacks had been "fathered for generations," the army "can't make completely independent individuals out of them in a brief year."[66]

Given the low estimation of black capability and the apparent decision to treat black soldiers as children rather than as men, it is hardly surprising that the U.S. military refused to assign many blacks to combat units and relegated overwhelming numbers to labor and service battalions. Of the more than 700,000 serving in the army in 1944, only about 86,000, or 12 percent, were serving in infantry, artillery, and armored force divisions. The rest labored in construction, transportation, and supply units.[67] In 1945 African American soldiers accounted for 20 percent of the corps of engineers, 33 percent of the transportation corps, and a staggering 44 percent of the quartermaster corps.[68] Of the hundreds of thousands of black servicemen stationed in Great Britain in 1944 and 1945, virtually all were building and maintaining airports, unloading supplies from ships, and transporting them from camp to camp. Very few landed on the Normandy beaches on D-Day. As one African American soldier told NAACP director Walter White during the latter's 1944 tour of U.S. bases in England, "It is hard to identify one's self with fighting a war when all one does is dig ditches and lay concrete."[69]

Fig. 17. African American Soldiers, 1941-43. Private Clarence E. Muse of Philadelphia, Pennsylvania, plays the guitar for fellow African American soldiers at
the reception center at Fort Meade, Maryland. These soldiers, still in training,
were preparing to depart for Fort Huachuca, Arizona. They assembled in the
"Colored Cantonment" area, the recreational area set up for black soldiers.
The white recreational area at this base, as in most U.S. military facilities,
was off limits to African Americans. (Courtesy Library of Congress)

   Black servicemen were also routinely denied basic liberties accorded their white counterparts. Until 1943, they were barred from
using military base clubs, snack bars, and other recreational facilities frequented by white GIs. In the South, where most army training bases were located, black servicemen were regularly hassled
when they left bases to go into town for recreation. They were
often kicked off civilian buses to accommodate white passen-
gers who needed their seats. In town, they were harassed by white

sheriffs and white MPs, looking for any hint of misbehavior—including visiting bars—that could be construed as a violation of Jim Crow. White officers even tried to transpose Jim Crow from the American South to England. Alarmed by the willingness of English women to associate with Negro soldiers, and interpreting all such liaisons as sexual in nature, some white officers confined to base all the Negro soldiers under their command.[70] Others announced that they would order their white soldiers to boycott English hotels and pubs that served black GIs.[71] Some actually took it upon themselves to identify certain pubs around their bases as "exclusively for colored troops."[72]

For many black GIs, especially for those from the North, this experience of discrimination and daily humiliation became intolerable. Relations between black and white GIs in training camps in the United States and in staging areas in England became so tense that they verged on civil war. And because the young men on both sides had been trained in the use of firearms and had access to weapons, armed confrontations were a distinct, and frightening, possibility. Between 1941 and 1945, hundreds of brawls broke out between off-duty black servicemen who had gone to the towns adjacent to their camps, and white MPs and civilian police who were patrolling, often aggressively, black districts. Many of these brawls produced injury, some resulted in death. In addition, those same years produced numerous confrontations between white and black units inside military camps, usually triggered by a fight over access to camp recreation facilities or military buses.[73] Here was the hidden race war, carefully kept out of newsreels and white newspapers during the war. Only the black press covered it in detail.[74]

In Britain, on June 24, 1943, long-simmering resentments exploded in violence outside a Lancashire pub frequented by African American troops. A report of a disturbance brought white MPs, who began arresting black servicemen, only to be intimidated by the combined resistance of the black soldiers and English civilians. The MPs returned with reinforcements; when black soldiers resisted arrest with bricks and bottles, the MPs opened fire, wounding two. The uninjured blacks then returned to base and persuaded their fellow soldiers to take up arms and fortify their camp against white troops. One black soldier who observed the gathering riot wrote, "I saw some two or three hundered [black] soldiers standing around and saying what a damn shame it was to have come all the way over here to be treated like dogs, and shot and kicked around at will."[75] Both white and black officers tried to quell the revolt, but with only partial success. Some black soldiers went off base, setting up roadblocks; others drove around, looking for the "enemy." By the time military authorities restored order the next day, five soldiers had been injured by gunfire and two had been beaten. Remarkably, no one had been killed.[76]

This episode and similar ones in the States awakened military authorities to the threat posed by interracial hostility to the morale and battle readiness of U.S. troops. They took extraordinary measures to keep racial peace and made some concessions to blacks. Before America even entered the war, Secretary of War Stimson had appointed the African American William O. Hastie, dean of Howard Law School and an NAACP leader, to the post of civilian aide on Negro affairs in the expectation that race relations in the military would require close monitoring and regular intervention. Stimson also established a separate (and largely white) advisory body on racial matters and made Assistant Secretary of War John J. McCloy its chairman. Widespread racial unrest in the military quickly gave these two men and their operations as much as—and probably more than—they could handle, and they became extremely active in monitoring problematic situations, responding quickly to racial crises, and proposing reforms to military policy. Their activity made a difference. Aided by extensive undercover operations, the army began reacting swiftly and firmly to outbreaks of racial disorder and disciplining all servicemen, black or white, who violated martial law.[77]

The army also began assigning more African Americans to combat divisions than it had wanted to, and by war's end some black infantry units, tank battalions, and air squadrons had seen significant action. The military hired Frank Capra to make a movie that would document the long and honored history of African American military service; after its release in 1944, *The Negro Soldier* became required viewing for every American soldier, black and white. Troop surveys reported that most troops reacted positively to what they saw on the screen. None of this happened quick enough to satisfy Hastie, who quit in disgust in 1943, his place taken by his assistant, Truman K. Gibson Jr.[78]

The various services, too, began experimenting with integration. In 1943 the army ordered that all soldiers, irrespective of their race, were to have equal access to training camp recreational facilities. In 1944 the navy integrated the crews of twenty-five noncombat ships by including in the crews one black for every ten whites. Also in 1944 the army began integrating a few of its European divisions. At first this meant simply that black regiments fought alongside white ones. In early 1945, however, as a result of unexpectedly large casualties among white troops, the First Army in Europe integrated some of its regiments, battalions, and companies, allowing black platoons to fight alongside white ones.[79]

Although each of these changes carried symbolic importance, their cumulative effect on the overall experience of segregation was rather small. The twenty-five ships whose crews the navy integrated represented only 1.6 percent of its 1,600-ship fleet. All were noncombat "auxiliary" ships, whose crews enjoyed lower status than the crews of battleships, destroyers, cruisers, and aircraft carriers. Throughout the war, blacks' proportional representation in army combat units remained far smaller than that of whites; the same can be said of their representation in officer ranks. In the Marines, no black "leathernecks" were assigned to combat battalions and none of the 20,000 who served became an officer until the war had ended. And as promising as the First Army experiment with mixed companies was, it stopped short of integrating platoons. Even the most farsighted and liberally minded white generals could not conceive of white and black soldiers sharing the same barracks and foxholes.[80]

Thus, wartime agitation on the part of black servicemen and civilians shook up segregationist practices in the military but failed to upend them. It did not help that most U.S. bases were located

Fig. 18. Japanese American Soldiers, 1943. Even as the U.S. government rounded up West Coast Japanese Americans and sent them to internment camps, it was willing to take young men from these camps into the U.S. military. Like African American soldiers, Japanese American ones were given their own units, for no mixing with whites could be tolerated. The soldiers depicted at this dance at Camp Shelby, Alabama, in June 1943 were part of the newly formed 442nd regiment. The women pictured here were bussed to the dance from their "relocation center" in Arkansas, where they were imprisoned on account of their race. The 442nd was preparing to depart for the European theater, where its bravery in battle would make it the most decorated unit in United States military history. (Courtesy Library of Congress)

in the South, that a disproportionate number of officers were south-erners, or that a large number of southern black inductees scored poorly on the IQ tests administered by the military. These facts deepened the military's belief that the war was no time for social experimentation on so large a scale. Generals did not think that they could train their troops to fight effectively while undermining long-standing and deep-seated racial practices. Thus the critical racial line held, and virtually all the 16 million men and women who served in the military experienced it in terms of racial separation. For all its attention to race relations and its concern for the morale of black troops, the military nevertheless did what it had done before: create a racialized melting pot. This one was far larger than the ones created for the Spanish-American War or World War I, and its effects on American society would last well into the 1950s and 1960s.

COMBAT AND WHITE MALE COMRADESHIP

Combat intensified the social consequences of the military's decision to segregate black troops. As blacks looked on from the rear lines, whites thrown into battle often bonded with each other, as much out of necessity as of goodwill. On the one hand, the omnipresence of death made the individual GI acutely conscious of the value and fragility of his life; only his fellow servicemen could appreciate that fragility and give him the kind of support he needed. Everyone else, including loved ones at home, was too far away or too removed from combat situations to understand what was going on and to give the troops the sustenance they required. On the other hand, a serviceman's survival depended entirely on the actions of his fellow GIs. They were responsible for preserving his life, and he for theirs. These circumstances of mutual dependence were extreme, and they often contributed to the development among platoon mates of particularly intense affective ties. An infantry private wounded in the North African campaign could reminisce that "[t]he men in my squad were my special friends. . . . We bunked together, slept together, fought together, told each other where our money was pinned in our shirts. If one man gets a letter from home over there, the whole company reads it. Whatever belongs to me belongs to the whole outfit."[81] These were conditions that encouraged servicemen to put aside personal prejudice and to develop friendships with individuals from religious, ethnic, and regional groups whom, in civilian life, they had not known or had disdained.

Studying the process through which interethnic and interreligious friendships unfolded in combat units is difficult to do, especially since the military chose not to keep records on white servicemen who were Catholics, Protestants, and Jews or to track Protestant-Catholic and Jewish-Gentile conflicts as they did racial ones. Even the civilian authors of the exhaustive and authoritative *The American Soldier* series paid no attention to ethnic or religious differences among white U.S. troops.[82] But the memoir literature written after the war by former servicemen is illuminating in this regard, and William Manchester's memoir of his Marine years, *Goodbye, Darkness*, is especially instructive.[83]

Manchester was a sergeant in charge of an intelligence section of the Twenty-ninth Marines, a regiment that saw extensive combat in the Pacific—at Guadalcanal and Guam, but especially at Okinawa, where 2,812 of the 3,512 men in the regiment fell. Manchester's squad was unusual in that it comprised mostly college students who possessed the education and intelligence to perform the map-reading and reconnaissance tasks demanded of their unit. Quite a few were "eggheads"—intellectuals, physicists, medical students, and chess players—who saw themselves as misfits in civilian life, an attitude they carried over into the Marines, where they styled themselves "Raggedy Asses" who disdained neat uniforms, officers' pretensions, and chests full of medals. Yet, they did volunteer for the Marines, revealing a patriotism that they shared with more mainstream American male youth, black and white; and for all their contempt for military regalia and ritual, they loved being leathernecks.[84]

Their unit was also a melting pot, bringing together northerners and southerners, Jews and Gentiles, and privileged Ivy League Protestants with working- and middle-class Catholic kids from Fordham and Holy Cross. In its geographical, religious, and ethnic diversity, Manchester's group was fairly typical.[85] The story that Manchester tells is how these men from varied backgrounds came to love each other as family and to trust each other absolutely. This is not a simple or easy story for Manchester to tell, in part because he has first to unearth the story's fragments in himself; there they had lain buried for thirty-five years, like the real pieces of shrapnel too dangerous to extricate that Manchester had carried in his body since 1945. But a 1970s trip to the South Pacific, and to the islands where Manchester had first gone as a Marine rifleman, becomes his mechanism for remembering and for telling his tale.

The story begins in boot camp, which Manchester loathed but considered "a useful shakedown cruise. Like couples in forced marriages, we were compelled to explore one another's traits. On the whole we liked what we found."[86] It continues with the death of the first unit member, Lefty Zepp, a pre-med, Jewish Harvard man, whose penchant for fancy dress made him the target of a Japanese sniper on Guadalcanal. Lefty is laid out under a tree, and each of the Raggedy Asses, in tears or near tears, "went over one by one to say goodbye." The last is Manchester, himself, who cites a few lines from a poem and then "leaned over and kissed him full on the lips."[87]

For Manchester, such a physical display of emotion to a fellow man would have been inconceivable in peacetime. When recounting the battle of Okinawa, Manchester reveals that he committed another physical act that was equally unthinkable in any circumstances other than that of the security and fraternity he felt among his Marines: he defecated in public. While riding on a truck to the front, he was overcome by the need to relieve himself. When a fallen tree halted the line of trucks, Manchester popped out of his vehicle and "squatted in full view" of his buddies. Unfortunately, the trucks started moving before he was finished, forcing him to complete "the job with one convulsion" and spring back to his vehicle, "pulling my pants as all hands cheered." Manchester seemed as amazed that he had hurried "so personal an errand" as that he had carried "it out in the full view of strangers." But he had no alternative, for he could not "be left behind by the Raggedy Ass Marines. I had to be with my own people."[88]

This humorous episode prompts Manchester to offer one of the deepest moments of self-reflection of the entire memoir: "I had been, and after the war I would again be, a man who usually prefers his own company, finding contentment in solitude. But for the present I had taken others into my heart and given of myself to theirs. . . . I had no inkling then of how vincible that made me, how terrible was the price I might have to pay."[89] That price would be paid in the battle for Okinawa, and especially for Sugar Loaf Hill, where most of Manchester's squad was wiped out in some of the most vicious fighting of the war. This was the moment where his precious world of comradeship was torn apart, where he ceased being himself, becoming psychotic in his urge to kill, hating "Japs," and hating the Marines, too: the "Corps' swagger" and "ruthless exploitation of loyalty," Manchester now believed, had contributed to the "mass butchery on the islands."[90] But in the midst of this nightmare, his love of his fellow Marines sustains him and then nearly kills him. Upon learning that the few Raggedy Asses who had survived Sugar Loaf were to take part in yet another battle on Okinawa, Manchester sneaks out of a field hospital where a minor wound had landed him and rejoins his men. "It was an act of love," Manchester writes. "Those men were my family, my home. They were closer to me than I can say, closer than any friends had been or ever would be. . . . I had to be with them."[91] In this last battle, Manchester is so badly wounded that he is given up for dead. But a corpsman from his own regiment finds him, determines he is still alive, and saves his life, along with teams of surgeons in Hawaii and San Diego hospitals. Months after the war has ended, Manchester's ordeal finally ends.

Manchester's story reveals that combat in World War II created settings in which men could develop ties to each other stronger than any they had experienced in civilian life.[92] In Manchester's unit, moreover, these bonds respected few religious, regional, ethnic, or class lines. Manchester felt as close to Bubba Yates from Alabama as to Lefty Zepp from Harvard, to blue blood Shiloh Davidson III from Princeton as to Catholic Rip Thorpe from

Fordham.[93] Manchester notes that homosexuality marked one critical boundary for all these relationships that was not to be crossed; yet, his unit tolerated a sergeant major who, when drunk, regularly bragged about his male sexual conquests during his long and much decorated Marine career. What got him tossed out of the unit was not his homosexuality but combat fatigue that caused him to crack under a concentrated Japanese artillery barrage.[94]

It could be argued, of course, that the cohesion of Manchester's unit benefited from the college experience that so many of its members had shared, an experience that may have worked to narrow sizable differentials in their families' class origins. But even if a prewar college experience did serve as a homogenizing and cohesive force, its success likely depended on the military's own efforts, intentional and unintentional, to weaken extant class divisions among the enlisted men by superimposing on them a harsh system of officers' rule. Many enlisted men became disgusted with privileges of rank that allowed officers to ignore, abuse, and humiliate the soldiers under their command. Officers' actions of this sort— "chicken shit" was the term of opprobrium favored by enlisted men—were rooted in a training philosophy that called upon drill instructors to assault the dignity and personhood of new recruits as a way of toughening them up for the battles that lay ahead. And there can be no doubt that the Marines were tough, in some cases sustaining themselves in Pacific battles even as the casualty totals of their units reached 70 and 80 percent, far exceeding the 40 percent customarily used by the military to determine the point at which a unit loses its combat effectiveness. These Marines would not have continued to fight had they lost all respect for their officers. To the contrary, many Marine Corps officers achieved legendary status because of their courage, smarts, and willingness to share the perils of their men.[95]

But, sometimes, the perceived misbehavior of officers extended to the war theaters themselves and was thought to put the lives of individual soldiers at risk. In World War II memoir literature, one can discern a steady stream of criticism directed at officers' abuse of their authority and at the sadistic undercurrent that was often

associated with it. Occasionally these abuses provoked near or outright rebellion. Manchester himself refused a particularly offensive
direct order while in officers' training and was hauled before a
court-martial, where he told the presiding officer that he had
"joined the Marines to fight, not to kiss asses and wade through the
very sort of chickenshit we were supposed to be warring against."[96]
Expelled from the officer corps, he was remanded to the Twenty-
ninth Marines, and assigned to the intelligence unit that became
the officer-hating Raggedy Asses. Later, in the assault on Tarawa,
Manchester and his men refused to follow a newly arrived second
lieutenant over a seawall, because they considered the task a suicide
mission and regarded the officer who had ordered it a pompous
fool. When the lieutenant decided to mount the wall himself, as a
way of rallying his troops, he was immediately destroyed by machine gun fire.[97]

The very abuses of authority that some officers displayed, however, often brought the rank-and-filers closer together, much the
way in which a tough foreman or factory owner creates common
bonds among the diverse elements of his work force. And there
were clear signs that a "class consciousness" of this sort emerged
among enlisted men. Many middle-class soldiers tossed off their
gentility and other markers of class status and adopted distinctive
(and often coarser) patterns of male working-class language and
physicality that gave them an identity that stood in opposition to
that of the "bourgeois" officer corps. This "class struggle" usually
did not escalate to the point where the enlisted men revolted
against their officers or questioned the country's mission (as it
would in Vietnam). But it certainly contributed to the intense ties
that formed among members of the "subordinate" class.[98]

The power of these ties did not mean that the enlisted ranks
had purged themselves of all prejudice. In Manchester's unit, Lefty
Zepp hid his Jewishness from all his platoon mates, except for Izzy
Levy from Chicago, the only other Jew in the unit. When Bubba,
the Alabama boy, challenged Lefty on what Manchester calls
"the race question," Lefty flatly denied his Jewishness, insisting
that his Semitic looks reflected Armenian, rather than Jewish,

roots.[99] Manchester, himself, only learned of Lefty's Jewish identity from Levy thirty years after the war had ended.

It may not have been necessary for Lefty to have kept his Jewishness a secret in order to win the approval of the Raggedy Asses. From Manchester's telling, the openly Jewish Izzy Levy seems to have been accepted by the Gentiles in his squad.[100] Yet Manchester's opinion may not have been the most reliable one in this instance, for, as a descendant of an old-line Yankee family, he may not have sufficiently appreciated the social pressures and prejudices experienced by Jews and other ethnic minorities. Evidence drawn from sources other than Manchester's memoir suggests that relations between Jewish and Gentile enlisted men generated significantly greater tension than those between white Protestant and Catholic ones. This is the view of Leon Uris, a Jewish youth from Baltimore and future novelist who joined the Marines as a seventeen-year-old in 1941. Although his thinly fictionalized first novel, *Battle Cry*, published in 1953, characterizes the assimilative work of a Marine unit in the Pacific in ways very similar to those of Manchester's memoir, it treats anti-Semitism as a far more serious issue than Manchester understood it to have been. Many years later, Uris told a newspaper writer that when he was in the Marines, he "was quiet about being a Jew. It was hard for Jews in the Marines."[101] Many Gentile servicemen still regarded Jews as a race apart and believed that they could not be assimilated into their own white race. Some groups among them also asserted that Jews were inferior in combat, or that they shirked combat duty by using their brains and alleged slyness to garner for themselves a disproportionate number of service and desk jobs in the rear.[102] Retired Marine Lieutenant General Bernard E. Trainor recalls a ditty that he learned during his wartime youth in the Bronx, set to the tune of the Marine Corps Hymn, in which Jews are depicted as singing, "Let those Christian saps go fight the Japs while we make the un-i-forms."[103]

Gerald Linderman has made a different kind of argument about the limitations of wartime comradeship. In his view, these bonds were not so much limited by ethnic or religious difference as by the brutality and terror of war itself. Frequently, comradeship did not extend to soldiers beyond the platoon level, and even the bonds of the small unit frayed when it suffered excessive casualties and too many replacements were being rotated in. The love of buddies was sometimes matched by a loathing of servicemen regarded as outsiders. Those who had seen too many buddies snatched away sometimes concluded that the price of comradely love of any sort was simply too high.[104] This may explain why it took Manchester thirty years to return to the scenes of his battles and to rediscover how much he had valued those who had fought alongside him. Others were able to recover from the trauma of war more quickly, especially as they saw how much noncombatant Americans celebrated their courage, devotion, and sacrifice, bestowed privileges on them to start new lives, and thus helped them to forget, or repress, combat's terror.[105]

If the war sustained no lasting revolution in male comradeship, it did expose men to a much greater range of individuals and groups than most had ever known, and did so in circumstances of extreme vulnerability where they had no choice but, if they wished to survive, to trust each other. In the process, individuals' conceptions of who belonged in their American community expanded enormously. Jews, Catholics, southerners, and others who were suspect gained a status they had not previously enjoyed. This may be one reason why the authors of a 1950 study on the dynamics of prejudice among northern, white Gentile veterans found that anti-Semitism, while certainly present among them, was not nearly as virulent as "anti-Negro feeling."[106] Comradeship had taught enduring lessons about tolerance and the ability to respect difference.

And would "anti-Negro feeling" have likewise diminished had African Americans fought alongside white Americans in the same squads and crews? One could make the argument, and the military made it, that whites and blacks were simply too different, and that the fighting effectiveness of American troops would have been ruined had these two groups been thrown together in the same units and asked to become each other's buddies. But one can make a different argument, too, namely that an integrated military would have diminished the gulf separating white from black Americans and, especially under military discipline and the pressures of war, allowed these two races to find common ground. This is certainly what happened on at least one integrated navy ship in 1943 and 1944. In January 1944 a white officer on this ship wrote his father about how "very interesting" he found his "mixed white and Negro crew." He was especially impressed that "[w]hite and Negro boys live together in the crew's quarters and eat together and get along with no difficulty." The black sailors, he noted, were from "both sides of the Mason-Dixon line" while the whites were all southerners; but this strong southern presence seemed to pose no problems. All the "boys [black and white] were well indoctrinated with a feeling of loyalty for the Navy and a sense of pride in the job they were trained in, and above all, a feeling of confidence and self assurance that they can do the job and they are doing it."[107] Another interesting, if curious, example of military loyalty super-seding race loyalty occurred on Guam in the midst of a race riot involving black sailors who had been harassed by white Marines. Despite the blatant nature of the abuse directed against the black sailors, the black Marines on Guam refused to support them. They sided instead with their "fellow" white leathernecks.[108]

The most compelling report on the salutary effects of integration on black-white bonding came from Walter White, NAACP chairman, during a 1944 tour of the Mediterranean and European war theaters sponsored by the War Department. White was particularly impressed by race relations among troops in southern Italy, where white and black soldiers were both engaged in combat, as opposed to England, where the overwhelming number of troops, black and white, were not fighting. "As men approach actual combat and the dangers of death," White wrote in a memorandum to the War Department, "the tendency becomes more manifest to ignore or drop off pettinesses such as racial prejudice." At Anzio, Italy, he noted, "men eat, sleep, and associate together with apparent complete ignoring of race or color of their neighbors. When German shells and bombs are raining about them, they do not worry as much about the race or creed of the man next to them." Such

Fig. 19. First Graduating Class of African American Pilots, Army Airs Corps, 1942. These pilots, pictured at the Advanced Flying School, Tuskegee, Alabama, would soon be heading for Italy. Benjamin O. Davis, pictured second from left, was to become the first African American general in the U.S. military. (Courtesy Library of Congress)

experiences continued to make a difference, too, once the fighting had ended or moved to another theater, as memories "of dangers shared appear to leave a greater tolerance."[109]

Integration, in White's view, had advanced the furthest among the fliers and ground crews of the Air Corps' Seventy-ninth Pursuit Group, comprising one black (the Ninety-ninth) and three white squadrons. Almost half the personnel in the three white squadrons came from the South. "But one would never know that," White wrote, simply by observing relations between white and black airmen:

In the Operations Building, I saw a colored sergeant marking out the bombing runs for both white and colored pilots for that day. In another part of the room, a white sergeant and a Negro sergeant were working together on another phase of the impending operation. Inside the building and outside, pilots, both white and colored, stood talking and smoking together with apparent complete forgetfulness of race.[110]

Their socializing sometimes continued after-hours. At a dinner dance to mark the Seventy-ninth's completion of a year of combat, "the white members of the group over-rode objections to a so-called 'mixed' occasion by saying that they had fought and faced death together and saw no impropriety in their celebrating together." White discerned in this "spirit of friendship and cooperative effort" an enormous step forward, not just for the war but for the postwar years as well.[111]

Here was an example of the positive outcome that could result from black and white soldiers fighting alongside each other, just as the fighting on San Juan Hill had provided an earlier example. The results were all the more impressive because they followed upon a period of rocky race relations within the Seventy-ninth: a shaky combat debut by the black pilots had initially confirmed for many white airmen the low opinions they held regarding black intelligence and character. Once the performance of the black pilots had improved with experience, their white counterparts, to their credit, had tossed the stereotypes aside.[112] But just as racial mixing in Cuba was deemed to be too dangerous a precedent for an 1898 America still deeply invested in racialized images of itself, so, too, the mixed character of the Seventy-ninth Pursuit Group was judged too risky a proposition. Later in 1944, the Ninety-ninth squadron was removed from the Seventy-ninth and made part of the all-Negro 332nd Fighter Group. The formation of the 332nd reflected the increasingly positive evaluation of black combat capabilities, because it required the army to throw three additional black squadrons into battle.[113] But White deplored the unit's creation, for it once again upheld the principle of segregation. White had wanted to see the black Ninety-ninth left in the Seventy-ninth, and a white squadron added to the black 332nd "as an experiment, which I am confident will be highly successful if good judgment is shown in the selection" of pilots.[114] The military ignored White's advice.

The results of World War II, in the long term, were different than those of the Spanish-American War and World War I, in that the pressure brought to bear by black servicemen and the black population more generally would compel President Truman, in 1948, to desegregate the military. But this postwar victory, as important as it was, could not alter what had transpired in World War II. In the largest, and arguably the most important, institution of nationalist mobilization of the twentieth century, millions of young men had learned how deeply racial separation mattered to their country. Millions of white boys from different ethnic, religious, regional, and class backgrounds were thrown together in the harsh circumstances of military discipline and war. Many found common ground, sometimes as much out of necessity as of goodwill; in the process, they deepened their ties to their nation and to the white community that, as war taught them, formed its core. A war that, rhetorically, strengthened the civic nationalist tradition, gave new life to its ideological opposite, the idea that America was, first and foremost, a white nation.

The links tying together army comradeship, nationalist feeling, and whiteness have not always been obvious either to the participants in World War II or to the scholars writing about them. Thus, for example, a long line of scholars, from Samuel Stouffer and the other authors of *The American Soldier* through Paul Fussell and beyond have challenged the notion that American GIs cared deeply about any high ideals, including nationalist ones. They have depicted the soldiers as men who, in contrast to the soldiers of World War I and the Civil War, were skeptical of big ideas and emotions. GIs, in this view, looked upon war as a disagreeable obligation; they disliked the military and often loathed their officers. They pledged themselves to get the job done mainly so that they could get home and resume their normal lives. If they cared deeply about anything having to do with the war itself, it was only about keeping themselves and their buddies alive.[115]

These sentiments emerge strongly in Manchester's memoir. The Raggedy Asses were wise guys, skeptics, with no patience for anyone lecturing them on honor, valor, and devotion. And whatever passion Manchester harbored for the Marine Corps died "somewhere on the slopes of that hill [Sugar Loaf]" on Okinawa. In reflecting on why, after Sugar Loaf, he left the hospital to rejoin his unit, Manchester writes that he did it only for his mates. "Men, I now knew, do not fight for flag or country, for the Marine Corps or glory or any other abstraction. They fight for one another."[116]

But Manchester's renunciation of flag, country, and corps barely hits the page when he does an about face. Love of buddies, it turns out, was not enough to sustain him and others. "You had to know that your whole generation, unlike the Vietnam generation, was in this together, that no strings were being pulled for anybody." And you "needed nationalism, the absolute conviction that the United States was the envy of all other nations, a country which had never done anything infamous, in which nothing was insuperable, whose ingenuity could solve anything by inventing something. You felt sure that all lands, given our democracy and our know-how, could shine as radiantly as we did." That this nationalist peroration erupts immediately after a disavowal of flag and country suggests that Manchester did not fully understand or feel comfortable with his nationalist inclinations; but their power is undeniable. Manchester is a man who loved his buddies and his country. Indeed, the love of one seems to have enhanced the other and vice versa.[117]

One would never call Manchester a racist. He harbored no prejudice to anyone in his unit. He was as upset about the deaths of Lefty Zepp and Chet Prayastawaki as of Shiloh Davidson III. He did not even hate the "Japs," and he probably supported integration of the military when it happened in 1948. Had African Americans been in his unit, he would have treated them as equals and sought comradeship with them. Yet his entire memoir is told without reference to blacks. This narrative exclusion is made necessary, of course, by the physical exclusion of blacks from his unit: he cannot know or love a black man as he does a Jew or a Pole, because there are no blacks in his Marine section with whom he can become friends. But it also reflects something deeper. In an evocation of those elements of American history and culture that stimulated his sense of national devotion, Manchester mentions the Argonne, Memorial Day, scouting, Stonewall Jackson, Lionel Barrymore as Scrooge, and Gary Cooper as Sergeant York. Manchester barely ever acknowledges an African American presence, let alone a contribution.[118]

Indeed, only once in the entire memoir does Manchester even take note of a black presence in American culture. When his unit bivouacks in a captured Japanese officers' pagoda on Guadalcanal, a few of his men discover and then play a Louis Armstrong record that the fleeing Japanese had left behind (along with a working Victrola). It seems entirely fitting that only the capture of Japanese possessions on an island thousands of miles from home makes possible this encounter between African American music and Euro-American troops. Everyone, even Bubba from Alabama, "was enchanted with Armstrong," and the music, along with some "liberated" Japanese beer, becomes the occasion for a nightlong bull session that functions to solidify the fraternity of the Euro-American fighting men. But, in Manchester's telling, Armstrong's music serves only as an exotic mood setter for this moment of white male bonding. Blacks remain excluded from Manchester's imagined community, even as their music helps to facilitate its formation.[119]

It is precisely in the realm of imagination that segregation of the military in World War II may have had its longest-lasting effects. The exclusion of blacks from combat platoons in the Marines and in other military branches denied servicemen like Manchester the opportunity to challenge and to reconstitute their racially inflected conception of American community. Because of African Americans' absence, Manchester could not learn to include them in his sacred circle as he learned to include Jews, Catholics, and white southerners. In such a way did World War II reinvigorate traditional, racialized notions of America even among those, such as

Fig. 20. War and Euro-American Male Fraternity, 1944. Taking advantage of a lull in a battle somewhere in the Marshall Islands, six American soldiers gather for small talk and to imbibe captured Japanese beer. Such moments strengthened the bonds among fighting men, just as a similar moment did for William Manchester's Marine unit, the night it bivouacked in a captured Japanese officers' pagoda on Guadalcanal. The soldiers depicted here are all white, of course, fashioning from their experience a powerful sense of Euro-American male fraternity. (Courtesy Library of Congress)

Manchester, who rejected overtly racist patterns of thought and behavior.

Another argument could be made, of course, about the effects of ethnic mixing on the white GIs who served in the World War II platoons. The ability of these whites to overcome prejudices toward Jews, Catholics, and other groups whom they had feared or despised may also have allowed them to question the validity of prejudice applied to any group, blacks included, in ways they had not been able to before. The historian Anthony Badger has uncovered evidence for precisely such a response among a group of white ex-GIs who, in 1948, won election to the Mississippi State Senate. One of their members, Frank Smith, characterized the entire group as idealists who, as a result of their wartime experience, "hoped to have a part in making a better day." These reformers were determined to improve Mississippi society, which meant extending the New Deal and improving the condition of the Negro. One of their allies was liberal newspaperman Hodding Carter, himself a veteran army journalist. In 1946 Carter implored his Greenville, Mississippi, readers to "shoot the works in a fight for tolerance."[120] If the civic nationalist tradition was working a change of consciousness among some white southern veterans, it was undoubtedly doing so among white northern ones as well.

But Badger also reveals the limits of such a change. To the aforementioned Mississippi liberals, racial progress did not mean integration; it meant instead "the maintenance of segregation, with the provision of genuinely equal facilities."[121] Apparently even the Hodding Carters could not yet imagine living alongside blacks, sharing schools and other local facilities with them. Nor could many northern whites, who often greeted black efforts to move into their neighborhoods with anger and violence. In the North, black veterans often led struggles for residential integration, both because they believed that military service had entitled them to such improvements and because local public-housing authorities often gave preference to veterans (black and white). But black veterans fared no better at the hands of segregationist whites than those who had not served. Thus, in Chicago, in 1947, thousands of furious whites attacked the Fernwood Park Homes project, where a few black veterans and their families had moved in. The white mob stoned the army of police assembled to protect residents and pummeled unsuspecting blacks whom they pulled from cars and streetcars.[122]

The Fernwood riot, as the work of Arnold Hirsch and Thomas Sugrue demonstrates, was not an isolated incident. In what Hirsch aptly called the "era of hidden violence," whites throughout the

North often greeted black attempts to move into their neighborhoods with rage and violence.[123] In these struggles, the civic nationalist tradition, allegedly so powerful after the war, did make a difference, for it had mobilized support among northern white liberals
for the very integration efforts that were being met with such virulent opposition. But this tradition was by no means a dominant,
or consensual, American creed.[124] One is therefore impelled to ask
whether civic nationalism would have enjoyed somewhat more
sway in the immediate postwar period had black and white men
learned to fight alongside each other in the military, to experience
each other as friends and buddies, and to begin the delicate process
of imagining each other as neighbors. It is impossible to know the
answer to that question with any certainty; but it is difficult to
avoid the conclusion that an opportunity had here been lost.

World War II's stature as the "good war," a stature that would
only increase with time as Americans grew resentful of Korea and
Vietnam, magnified the costs of the government's decision to fight
the Axis powers with a segregated military. Positive images of
World War II appeared everywhere in postwar popular culture: in
novels such as Leon Uris's *Battle Cry* (1953); in movies such as
Sands of Iwo Jima (1949), *The Longest Day* (1962), and *PT-109*
(1963); and in television series such as *Combat* (1963–67). Central
to virtually all these dramas are images of Euro-American male
fraternities acting with courage and resolve. Such representations
were not self-consciously racist. Indeed, some evidence suggests
that black as well as white youth of the 1950s and 1960s sought
to emulate the models of male heroism and sacrifice they saw projected on the screen.[125] But these images did communicate a racialized image of America, of young white men, often led by John
Wayne, doing the job that had to be done to save the nation. And
the endless recycling, reconstitution, and reenactment of these images, not just on the written page, silver screen, or picture tube, but
also in the imaginative play of a new generation of boys enthralled
by war stories, helped to invigorate a tacit assumption that whites
were better than blacks, especially when the nation's survival hung
in the balance.[126]

Ron Kovic, born in Massapequa, Long Island, on July 4, 1946, has written about the many Saturday afternoons of his youth when, after seeing a war movie at the local cinema, "all the guys would go down to Sally's Woods . . . with plastic-operated machine guns, cap pistols and sticks. We turned the woods into a battlefield. We set ambushes, led gallant attacks, storming over the top, bayoneting and shooting anyone who got in our way. Then we'd walk out of the woods like the heroes we knew we would become when we were men."[127] In recalling these episodes, Kovic made no mention of the racial identity of John Wayne or of his other military heroes; that was not something that he consciously thought about. Yet the Marines and soldiers he saw in these movies were always white. They, and not their colored counterparts, were the men who had saved the nation in a moment of extreme crisis. A belief in the valor of the Euro-American fighting man was as much a legacy of World War II as was the more evident conviction that notions of racial superiority no longer had a place in America.

The subtle reinvigoration of racial nationalism did not come at the expense of the civic nationalist tradition, for that too gained strength during the war years. That both traditions emerged from the war fortified guaranteed only one thing: that there would be a violent collision, and that prevailing notions of American nationalism, and perhaps even the foundational notion that Americans ought to compose a single, national community, would not emerge unscathed. The early years of the Cold War delayed the showdown, but it would come, with fury, in the 1960s.

CHAPTER 6

The Cold War,

Anticommunism,

and a Nation in Flux,

1946–1960

The Cold War that broke out in 1946 insured that key nationalist institutions of the 1930s and early 1940s would survive into the 1950s and beyond. Because the "virtual" war against the Soviet Union followed so closely on the war against the Axis, it was deemed too reckless, by Republicans as well as Democrats, to return to a quarter-of-a-million-man military or to undertake the kind of rapid dismantling of regulatory and welfare institutions that had occurred after World War I. Thus the opportunity state erected by the New Dealers in the 1930s and 1940s remained largely in place under Presidents Harry S. Truman and Dwight D.

Eisenhower. And the challenge posed by the Soviets and by international communism put a premium on national security and national cohesion, and thus further contributed to a keen sense of American nationhood.

The Cold War also continued, even intensified, fears of American vulnerability that the Japanese attack on Pearl Harbor had unleashed in 1941. The focus of those fears, of course, shifted from Japan and Germany to the Soviet Union and its allies in Europe and the Third World. Policy makers were obsessed with "national security," and constantly invoked the phrase to justify large government expenditures on a variety of projects including the maintenance of a huge military establishment, the reconstruction of western Europe's and Japan's economies, the expansion of America's institutions of higher education, and the building of a high-speed, nationally integrated interstate highway system. National security, too, meant going to war in Korea, Vietnam, and other countries in which Communist subversion threatened; at home, it meant identifying and ostracizing those individuals and groups who seemed sympathetic to communism and thus treasonous to the United States. In pursuit of this latter goal, the government imprisoned Communist Party leaders, eliminated real and suspected Communists from government employment, and sought to expose, harass, and punish alleged Communists in media, education, the labor movement, and other social sectors deemed vital to the nation's well-being. This fear of Communists developed into a more generalized "Red Scare" that prompted Americans to shun not only communism but other traditions of dissent that could be construed as imperiling their nation. Thus the premium placed on political and social conformity increased during these years while the parameters of legitimate political debate narrowed.

For many individuals and groups in American society, the repression unleashed by the anti-Communist crusade was catastrophic. But from the perspective of those who thought of themselves primarily as nation builders in the Rooseveltian mold, this crusade could be construed as an advance. Theodore Roosevelt had always stressed how disciplinary campaigns would invigorate the nation, strengthening devotion to national ideals among the large majority of citizens while silencing those whose politics and culture threatened national cohesion and purpose. Arguably, the postwar campaign against the Communists served this dual purpose, and it did so while maintaining crucial New Deal institutions in place. In such ways did the Cold War prolong the heyday of the Rooseveltian nation.

But beneath a rigid surface of national consensus, the civic and racial traditions on which the nation's vigor had long depended were undergoing complex change. Racial nationalism lost some of its virulence in these years; not only did a civil rights movement gather steam at this time but anti-Semitic sentiment plummeted. Indeed, in a startling departure from the first Red Scare of 1919–20, anti-Communist crusaders of the 1950s targeted high-born Anglo-Saxons far more than lowly Jews or Italians. Moreover, a key immigration reform measure passed in 1952 removed long-standing bans on Asian immigration and naturalization that, only a decade earlier, had seemed immutable. As the racial nationalist tradition declined, its civic nationalist counterpart added strength. In this changing political environment, many Jews, Italians, Japanese, and members of other formerly despised European and Asian groups enjoyed improved opportunities for cultural acceptance and economic advancement. As long as they were not themselves Communists, they found many reasons to celebrate America and to rejoice in its defense of the free world.

Arguments for the opening of American society to religious and racial minorities should not be pushed too far, however. If racial nationalism was losing some of its grip on the American imagination, its adherents were not yet ready to see it die. In the South, white southerners were mobilizing to resist civil rights. The same immigration reform measure that opened America up to Asian immigrants kept the odious racial quota system of the 1924 law in place, its supporters still fearful of seeing America overrun by unruly eastern and southern European immigrants. Meanwhile, the gains made by the civic nationalist tradition during these years seemed to come at the cost of its earlier flexibility. Specifically, it became much harder in the 1950s than it had been in the previous half century to fashion from this tradition a radical economic critique or even to attack corporations as injurious to the commonweal (as both Roosevelts had done). Those who attempted such a critique in the 1950s could be discredited as Communists or as Communist dupes and denied respect and political influence.

In sum, then, these Cold War years were marked by a good deal of uncertainty about the character and relative strength of the civic and racial nationalist traditions. This uncertainty was a mark of a nation in flux; few understood how much was changing, for the threat of communism prompted American leaders to depict the American nation as strong, unified, and steadfast in its devotion to timeless ideals. The nation was strong, but the imperatives of Cold War readiness had unsettled racial and civic conceptions of nationhood in portentous ways.

WAR, REPRESSION, AND NATION BUILDING

Theodore Roosevelt probably would have judged the Cold War a good thing for the American nation. By keeping the United States either at war, or perpetually ready for war, the Cold War insurec that a preoccupation with the nation and its virtue would remain strong. The enemy was communism, an ideological descendant of the anarchism that Roosevelt had so loathed and against which, he had often implied, one had to fight until death. That America had to maintain a large military would have pleased Roosevelt, as would have the large quantities of public funds that the government injected into the private economy to maintain war readiness. He would have understood how the Cold War dampened conservative opposition to big government and thus made possible the maintenance of Social Security, the National Labor Relations Act, farm subsidies, and other core reform programs of the New Deal state.[1]

The Cold War also became the occasion for achieving another element of nationhood that Theodore Roosevelt had always considered vital but that had remained elusive: the establishment of a powerful disciplinary state authorized to place large numbers of Americans under surveillance and to punish those engaged in forms of "un-American" dissent. On the eve of the American entry into World War II, Congress had made such a state possible by passing laws that gave the government the power to prosecute individuals who advocated overthrowing the government by force and violence, and to deport those among them who had been born abroad. The executive branch of the government used these powers during the war itself; but, with the exception of the Japanese American internment, there were no violations of civil liberties on the scale that had occurred in World War I. The broad consensus supporting the war made the government's job relatively easy.

All this changed, of course, once the war ended, and the United States and the Soviet Union found themselves locked in a worldwide struggle for economic and ideological supremacy. As in the aftermath of World War I, communism emerged as a threat not only to American interests abroad but to American security at home. The House Un-American Activities Committee (HUAC), established in 1945 to succeed the Dies committee, worked to expose Communists in Hollywood and spies in government; so did the FBI, President Truman's Justice Department, Senator Pat McCarran's Internal Security Subcommittee, set up in 1950, and Senator Joseph McCarthy's Government Operations Subcommittee. The threat of nuclear war, and then the reality of a large, conventional land war in Korea, permitted the institutions of national security to carry on longer and with greater powers than otherwise would have been the case. New institutions, such as the Central Intelligence Agency and the National Security Council, sprang up to counter foreign threats to American security.[2]

Domestic threats were largely handled by existing institutions, especially the FBI. A series of executive orders, stretching from the dawn of World War II to the twilight of the Korean War, allowed

J. Edgar Hoover to investigate virtually any form of political dissent without having to worry about congressional or presidential oversight. During this time (1939 to 1953), Hoover increased the number of FBI agents more than sevenfold, from 851 to 7,029, and established a network of 109,119 informants across 11,000 defense plants, research centers, bridges, and telephone exchanges. By 1954 the FBI had placed 26,000 Communist Party members and functionaries on its Security Index, a list of people who were to be rounded up in a time of national emergency. Another 430,000 people and organizations appeared on a list of "slightly less dangerous individuals." To implement the federal government's loyalty security program authorized by Truman in 1947, the FBI reviewed the files of 2 million federal employees and conducted full-scale investigations of 20,000 of them. In addition to supplying information on suspicious individuals to relevant agencies in the executive branch, Hoover sent his findings to HUAC, to the Senate's Internal Security Subcommittee, and to Senator McCarthy. And he cultivated contacts with a large number of employers, journalists, American Legion officials, Catholic trade unionists, and professional anti-Communists to whom he leaked information on "suspicious" individuals.[3]

All this occurred, of course, in a climate of mounting hysteria that American greatness, indeed the very existence of the American nation, had been imperilled by the presence of Communist traitors in the American midst. The Communists, Hoover repeatedly alleged, "poison and pollute the very atmosphere of freedom with venomous attacks upon everything which we hold dear—our flag, our country, our churches, our homes, our institutions and our traditions." They were waging "a relentless campaign to pervert our thinking and undermine our freedoms," and Hoover was convinced that they had penetrated every key American institution.[4] In his eyes, they had infiltrated the State Department, where they were undermining the formulation of American foreign policy; Hollywood, where they were perverting American filmmaking; the labor movement, where they had led masses of American workers

Figs. 21 and 22. The Two Faces of Communism, 1961. These two images illustrate the danger of communism as understood by Dr. Fred C. Schwarz's Christian Anti-Communism Crusade in Houston, which published them as part of two comic books distributed for free in 1961. The Communists, the "Two Faces" image on top suggests, like to present themselves as ingenuous, well-meaning neighbors doing their best to create a better world. But the "Double Talk" image on the bottom reveals the terrible truth about this neighbor and his murderous, godless Communist ideology. Although communicated in a humorous way, these images of the evil Communist and of the vulnerabilities of naive, good-natured Americans to his deceptions appear to justify an extreme anti-Communist crusade, one that would not relax its vigilance until the last Communist infiltrators were eliminated from American life. (Courtesy Michael Barson/ Past Perfect)

astray; universities and public schools, where they were corrupting the minds of American youth; defense industries, where they had leaked critical technological secrets to the Soviets.[5]

Individuals and groups within each of these sectors felt the heavy hand of repression. The State Department dismissed its best Asian experts because they had allegedly formulated a policy that turned China Communist. The movie moguls assembled a blacklist of known and suspected Communists that prevented hundreds of screenwriters, actors, and other film professionals (including Sidney Buchman, Dalton Trumbo, John Howard Lawson, and Alvah Bessie) from getting work. The CIO, desperate to resist criminalization charges, ousted eleven Communist-led unions and almost a million unionists from its federation; it would never again wield the power it had achieved in the 1930s and 1940s. Universities fired subversive professors while school boards fired Communist teachers. J. Robert Oppenheimer, head of the Manhattan Project, was deprived of his security clearance for his alleged Communist sympathies, and Julius and Ethel Rosenberg were executed for atomic espionage. With a great shudder, American institutions were ridding themselves of alleged subversives, and a big chill enveloped American society, freezing most radical dissenters, Communist or not, in their tracks.[6]

In most respects, this second Red Scare followed the lines of the first, except that it was worse. The conditions of war or near war gave the former a longer and more successful life. The peacetime espionage law that Hoover had attempted but failed to get in the early 1920s he possessed in the early 1950s. The first Red Scare hobbled the left; the second eliminated it as a political force. The damage extended well beyond the Communist Party, which became a shell of its former self, for the Red Scare rendered suspect anyone who dared to challenge American capitalism or to insist that class inequality disfigured American life. In this climate of fear, non-Communist socialists and anticorporate liberals found it increasingly difficult to win support for their views. As recently as 1942, an Elmo Roper poll had revealed that 25 percent of Americans favored socialism and another 35 percent had an open mind

about it; by 1949, only 15 percent wanted to move toward socialism while a decisive 61 percent opposed it. By the mid-1950s, even
that 15 percent had shrunk to imperceptible levels. Theodore Roosevelt had himself attacked corporations as a danger to the nation,
as had Franklin Roosevelt and many other New Deal liberals. But
even this moderate anticorporate orientation disappeared from liberal discourse in the late 1940s and 1950s. The reasons, as a number of historians such as Alan Brinkley have elucidated, are complex; but the chilling effect of the Cold War on political groups that
dared to challenge American capitalism or the equation of "free
enterprise" with the "American way" has to figure prominently
in any explanation. In economic terms, the meaning of freedom
narrowed during the Cold War years, making civic nationalism a
less flexible, and less capacious, creed.[7]

THE RED SCARE AND THE DECLINE OF
RACIAL NATIONALISM

In one important respect, however, the second Red Scare followed
a different, and less damaging, course than the first. From the first
Red Scare through the late 1930s, the threat of communism had
been conflated with the threat of unwanted immigrant or racial
groups. This conflation began to break apart in the Cold War, and
the "radical other" began to lose the ethnic or racial connotations
to which it had long been tied. Now it was being constructed almost entirely from the tradition of civic nationalism itself, a development that revealed how much this tradition, too, relied on exclusion—of individuals deemed un-American because of their
behavior and ideas, rather than because of their race or ethnicity.
Julius and Ethel Rosenberg, the spies executed for espionage, were
Jewish; but so were the judge, Irving R. Kaufman, and prosecutor,
Irving Saypol, who sent them to their death. The black radicals Paul Robeson and W.E.B. Du Bois were persecuted for their
Communist sympathies, but other black activists, ranging from
World War II veterans to southern preachers such as Martin Luther

King Jr., found in the 1950s a more favorable climate for civil rights agitation. The Supreme Court delivered its momentous *Brown v. Board of Education* decision outlawing school segregation in 1954, a moment of acute Cold War tension. These developments revealed an incipient shift in criteria determining how the nation would draw its boundaries and define who could or could not belong to the American nation. Large majorities of Jews, Catholics, blacks, and other minorities would benefit from this shift, for, as long as they agreed to stay away from communism and ideas associated with it, they found their opportunities for inclusion in American society enhanced. The racial nationalist tradition was losing some of its potency, setting the stage for the civil rights revolution of the 1960s and its declaration that the civic tradition was the only true tradition of American nationalism.

This weakening of the racial tradition is easier for us to see in hindsight than it was for many of the participants to discern at the time, for it unfolded unevenly and uncertainly. Catholic groups were perhaps quickest to grasp it; since the 1930s, anticommunism had been one of the strongest elements of their faith, and to see America embrace it encouraged many among them to think that America was embracing them as well. From Senator Joseph McCarthy, himself, to Francis Cardinal Spellman of New York, from the labor priest and Richard Nixon advisor Father John Cronin to Senator Pat McCarran of Nevada, from ex-Communist-turned-informer Louis Budenz to the brilliant Yale graduate William F. Buckley, Catholics were among the lions of the anti-Communist crusade. As the names on this list suggest, Irish Catholics seized the lead and showed other groups of ethnic Catholics the way.[8]

Jewish and black groups were slower to believe that they might benefit from the 1950s political climate, and with good reason. The percentage of Jews who became Communists, while small in relation to the overall Jewish population, was probably higher than that of any other group. In the 1920s, immigration restrictionists used this kind of evidence to charge that sympathy for the Communists revealed the Jewish "race's" inferiority and unfitness for membership in the American nation. In the 1930s and 1940s, Hitler

embraced this way of thinking to justify his exterminationist campaign against European Jewry, the carriers of the "Judeo-Bolshe-
vist" virus.[9] In the late 1940s and early 1950s, some developments
suggested that this vicious conflation of Judaism and Bolshevism
was appearing in America. Jews were disproportionately represented on the Hollywood blacklist. The Jewish Rosenbergs were
the only atomic spies to be executed. In the 1950 California race
for the U.S. Senate, the Republican challenger Richard Nixon and
his supporters in the Christian right made sure that everyone knew
that the "Pink Lady" who opposed him, Helen Gahagan Douglas,
was married to a Jew. And in 1949, in what looked disturbingly
like a pogrom, Gentiles in Peekskill, New York, rioted against the
town's Jewish summer residents (many of whom were Communists
or Communist sympathizers) who, in their eyes, were responsible
for bringing the black Communist Paul Robeson to town for a
concert.[10]

As this last episode suggests, blacks had reason to believe that
the anti-Communist crusade would undermine their struggle for
racial equality. While communism appealed to proportionately
fewer blacks than Jews, it had, in the 1930s and 1940s, attracted
a steady stream of high profile African American intellectuals and
artists including Richard Wright, Langston Hughes, Ralph Ellison,
Robeson, and Du Bois.[11] More to the point, the Communists' devotion to racial equality encouraged many white supremacists, especially in the South, to attack the entire civil rights movement as
Communist-inspired. Operation Dixie, a 1946 CIO campaign to
organize southern workers, foundered on charges that it was a
Communist plot to put black workers on the same footing as white.
Not only would blacks and whites share the same unions, white
southern critics charged; they would soon become each other's
friends and lovers, thereby rending the South's social fabric. Blacks
who insisted on remaining Communists through the Cold War
years were subjected to unrelenting persecution. Beginning in
1950, government agents put Paul Robeson under constant surveillance, bugged his phone, intercepted his mail, and seized his passport to bar him from traveling and speaking abroad. Increasingly

vilified by mainstream groups and media within the United States, he had suffered, by 1956, a physical and emotional collapse.[12]

And yet the years of the anti-Communist crusade were a time when non-Communist blacks and Jews saw opportunities for inclusion that had not been there before. In the case of blacks, optimism arose from a variety of factors, including migration north (and the improved job and political prospects that awaited them there), an altered ideological climate less tolerant of racial subordination, and the success of Indians and other colonized peoples of Africa and Asia in overturning imperial, and white, rule. Equally important, however, were international, Cold War considerations that impelled those branches of the federal government most concerned with foreign affairs, the presidency and the State Department, to support the black struggle for racial equality in America. Once the "Iron Curtain" had descended on Europe in the late 1940s, forcing virtually every one of that continent's nations into the Soviet or American camp, Cold War strategists on both sides increasingly shifted their attention to the emerging nations of Asia and Africa, whose ideological tendencies had yet to harden. The Soviet Union believed it could win many of these peoples, who were overwhelmingly nonwhite, to its side by championing racial equality and anticolonialism, while baring the truth about the poverty, discrimination, and insecurity of black life in the United States. The Soviet Union delighted in spreading stories about black children in the American South being denied adequate schooling, about black accident victims dying because a white hospital refused to give them medical care, and about the humiliation of African diplomats who had been refused access to white restaurants and washrooms.[13]

Already in the late 1940s, the American State Department had geared up its own propaganda mill to counter the negative press that the Soviets were disseminating in Africa and Asia, but its top officials quickly came to understand that their propaganda counted for little as long as the American South remained segregated and as long as whites there committed acts of wanton violence against blacks without any apparent fear of punishment. The United

States, they concluded, had to demonstrate through deeds a commitment to dismantling segregation and to achieving racial equality. This realization was an important factor impelling the U.S. Justice Department, first under Truman and then Eisenhower, to file amicus curiae briefs in support of NAACP lawsuits challenging the legality of school segregation. In these briefs, the government repeatedly stressed the embarrassment that race discrimination was causing America abroad and the damage it was doing to national security. Thus, in the amicus brief filed in *Brown v. Board of Education*, the Justice Department reproduced a statement from former secretary of state Dean Acheson declaring that "hostile reaction [to American racial practices] among normally friendly peoples . . . is growing in alarming proportions" and jeopardizing "the effective maintenance of our moral leadership of the free and democratic nations of the world." A similar kind of worry weighed upon Secretary of State John Foster Dulles and President Eisenhower in 1957 and influenced their decision to send federal troops to Little Rock, Arkansas, to enforce a school desegregation decree that whites there had greeted with angry and violent protests. In such ways did geopolitical exigencies impel several reluctant presidential administrations to advance the cause of racial equality and to enhance the success of civil rights struggles.[14]

Black activists, in turn, seized the opportunities opened up by this favorable Cold War atmosphere to widen and amplify their protests. It was vital, of course, that these protests be couched in the language of civic nationalism, so that no one could impugn the patriotism of the protesters. But young preachers such as Martin Luther King Jr. began to demonstrate how much could be gained from a militant deployment of civic nationalist language during a time of intense popular devotion to the principles of freedom and democracy. In a 1955 speech to a Montgomery, Alabama, group that had organized a boycott of the city's bus lines, the event that first brought him national attention, King declared: "We are here in a general sense because first and foremost we are American citizens, and we are determined to apply our citizenship to the fullness of its meaning."[15]

Cold War factors did not benefit American Jews to the same extent as they did blacks. The legacy of World War II mattered more, in particular the rhetorical assault on racial and religious prejudice and the attempt to define America in terms antithetical to Hitler's Germany. The campaign against prejudice continued after the war; among some groups of intellectuals and reformers it even deepened as they attempted to come to terms with Hitler's racist evil and the catastrophe it had visited upon European Jewry. That countless Gentile servicemen had lived and fought alongside Jewish soldiers made a difference, too, for it allowed them to imagine a national community in which Jews were full-fledged members. And it was not just the wartime experience that altered attitudes, but the postwar celebration of that experience in print, film, and other forms of nationalist mythmaking. That celebration also inscribed itself in social policy, in the GI Bill in particular, legislation that made World War II soldiers the most lavishly rewarded group of veterans in American history. In addition to ratifying the importance of the war experience, this legislation also gave veterans opportunities to rise in American society. In 1945 American Jews, in economic terms, were already one of the best positioned minority groups, and the GI Bill gave many of the remaining poor among them an opportunity to secure their middle-class standing. By the mid-1950s, most Jews had moved away from the working-class, immigrant milieux in which Communist and other radical sympathies had flourished.[16]

As a result of these converging factors, anti-Semitism, as measured by opinion polls, plunged downward in the late 1940s and early 1950s, just as the Cold War was reaching its apogee. In 1940, more than 60 percent of Americans believed that Jews had objectionable traits; by 1962, that figure had shrunk to 22 percent. In that same year, less than 10 percent of those surveyed believed that Jews were unscrupulous and had too much power in business. The percentage objecting to having Jewish co-workers and neighbors or supporting limitations on Jewish enrollment at colleges was equally inconsequential. This collapse in anti-Jewish sentiment may explain why none of the anti-Communist episodes that targeted Jews in disproportionate numbers or in highly visible ways—the Hollywood blacklist, the Nixon senatorial campaign, the Rosenberg trial and execution, the Peekskill riot—gave rise to a generalized anti-Semitic crusade.[17]

And it is also significant in this regard that the most important anti-Communist crusader, Senator McCarthy from Wisconsin (Republican), seemed to have little interest in persecuting Jews. In a symbolic act, he chose a young Jewish lawyer from New York, Roy Cohn, as his chief counsel. In the 1950 Wheeling, West Virginia, speech that brought him to national prominence, McCarthy explicitly relieved Jews and other minorities of responsibility for the Cold War crisis: "It has not been the less fortunate or members of minority groups who have been selling this Nation out," McCarthy declared. Rather it was "the young men who were born with silver spoons in their mouths," "those who have had all the benefits that the wealthiest nation on earth has to offer—the finest homes, the finest college education, the finest jobs in government we can give."[18]

With that salvo, McCarthy made clear that America's main enemies were not the Jews, Italians, or blacks, but a dessicated Protestant elite. One member of this elite, Alger Hiss, had already been exposed. President of the prestigious Carnegie Endowment for International Peace, Hiss was a graduate of the Johns Hopkins University and Harvard Law School and a member of Washington's Social Register. His talent, charm, and "Anglo-Saxon" background had opened doors for him in the Roosevelt State Department. In February 1945 he accompanied Roosevelt to the Yalta Conference; in April he organized the founding conference of the United Nations in San Francisco. In the 1930s heyday of the New Deal, Hiss's reforming zeal had prompted him to join a Communist network of government employees and to engage in espionage. Evidence suggests that his Communist affiliation persisted into the 1940s. Nevertheless, when charges of his Communist involvement surfaced in the late 1940s, he desperately denied them. A federal jury convicted him of perjury for lying about his past affiliations and activities and sent him to jail.[19]

McCarthy, like other anti-Communists, believed that Hiss's presence in government was not a fluke. The State Department, in particular, McCarthy alleged, was full of subversives, all of them, like Hiss, privileged, weak-willed Americans who had sold their country out. McCarthy's mission, as he defined it, was to identify these traitors, remove them from government, and, if possible, send them to jail. His crusade focused mostly on the State Department's China hands, men such as John Stewart Service, John Carter Vincent, and John Paton Davies Jr., who had allegedly engineered American policy in order to weaken the anti-Communist Chinese nationalist, Jiang Jieshi (formerly spelled Chiang Kai-shek), and to insure the victory of his Communist opponent, Mao Zedong. But McCarthy was convinced that this pro-Communist conspiracy had been authorized at higher levels, by Secretary of State Dean Acheson and his predecessor, Secretary of State (and former secretary of war) George C. Marshall. McCarthy loathed Acheson the most, perhaps because the latter, in McCarthy's eyes, looked the part of an aristocratic traitor. Acheson's elegant clothing, groomed moustache, and manner, which emulated the style of the British upper class, reflected in part the influence of his English mother and in part the Anglophiliac grooming he received at Groton, Harvard College, and Harvard Law School. McCarthy regarded Acheson's demeanor as an act and hated every bit of it; Acheson, he charged, was nothing but "a pompous diplomat in striped pants, with a phony British accent."[20]

In depicting Acheson in such terms, McCarthy was embracing an old, and still powerful, American tradition of lambasting the rich who put on airs. Aristocratic pretension could not be tolerated in the American republic, any more than could men who, in their quest for refinement and delicacy, betrayed feminine inclinations. Theodore Roosevelt, himself, of course, had despised such aristocratic, effeminate men, and had constructed his image of the manly, backwoods, and democratic warrior in opposition to it. McCarthy constructed a similar image of manhood, signaling through his unkempt appearance, hard drinking, and bruising style of interrogation something of the persona of the Kentucky backwoodsman.

Through his roughness, McCarthy wished to declare that he was forthright and without pretension, qualities that would enable him to preserve the republic.

McCarthy's exaggerated and unruly masculinity, and the heterosexual vigor that it implied, were widely admired in anti-Communist circles, where fear of the homosexual bordered on the obsessive. Indeed, several of McCarthy's Republican colleagues were, by 1950, charging that the government was full not only of Communists but of "sexual perverts" and "sexual offenders" who threatened to corrupt the young and, because of their moral debasement, sell out their country to the Soviet Union. So deep ran this fear and so concerted was the attack on suspected homosexuals that many more homosexuals than Communists lost their government jobs in the early 1950s. The roots of this obsession were complex. As noted, some were old, stretching back to Theodore Roosevelt and to his conceptions about the indispensability of heterosexual manliness to strong nations. At least two were new: one was the reemergence during World War II, after years of invisibility, of a public gay subculture, mostly among single-sex groups of servicemen and -women, and the fear that it generated among straight men and women; another expressed political opposition to the New Deal by portraying it as the work of Roosevelt and an elite band of Protestant men who had allegedly forced collectivism on America and thus corroded the individualism that stood at the heart of American manhood. But the level of anxiety aroused by homosexuality at this time seems inconceivable apart from the pressures of the Cold War itself and the conviction that America could lose this fight and its national soul because well-educated and intelligent men such as Acheson, entrusted with positions of extraordinary responsibility, had betrayed their manly natures and gone soft.[21]

McCarthy never accused Acheson of homosexuality. The charge was the more diffuse, but almost as damning, one of effeminacy. Acheson had forfeited his place among men, which meant that he had no right to lead the nation. Indeed, McCarthy even challenged Acheson's right to membership in the American nation by referring to him as an alien, "Russian as to heart, British as to manner."[22] In the process he underscored his point that "Anglo-Saxons" had taken the place of immigrants as the "outsiders" working to destroy America from within. The inability of these "aliens" to understand American values and traditions arose not from foreign birth or racial inferiority, but from a life of privilege that had dulled their democratic instincts, masculinity, and moral sense. In the hands of McCarthy and his fellow crusaders, "un-American activities" became a matter of class and sexual behavior rather than of ethnicity or race. Exclusion from the American national community thus lost a good deal of its historic affinity with alleged racial and ethnic inferiority.

But not all. What made the actions of "Anglo-Saxons" Hiss and Acheson so despicable in the eyes of many anti-Communists was that these were the people whom the country had relied upon to keep the true aliens—the southern and eastern European immigrants and their progeny—in line. Another glance at popular culture in the 1930s and 1940s reveals how much it was generally assumed, even by the eastern and southern European movie moguls and directors, that Protestants—sometimes assisted by Irish Catholics—would provide leadership to the millions of eastern and southern European Catholics, Christian Orthodox, and Jews who were filling the ranks of the New Deal and the World War II citizen army. Frank Capra's 1930s films invariably chose upright Protestants Gary Cooper and Jimmy Stewart as populist heroes. In the 1940s war movies, leadership of the multiethnic platoons almost always fell into the hands of such capable Nordics as Humphrey Bogart or Robert Taylor, never into those of an Italian, a Greek, or a Jew. Irish Catholics occasionally assumed control of platoons, especially when a Protestant lieutenant was killed; but the Irish role was virtually always defined as that of an adjunct—someone capable of taking over temporarily until a Protestant replacement could be found.[23] Of course, no Protestant leader was more important in this regard than Franklin Roosevelt, himself, whose job it was to include eastern and southern European ethnics in the American national community while guiding the country through the trauma of depression and war. McCarthy and other 1950s anti-

Communists rarely targeted Roosevelt explicitly, but the relentless attack on Hiss, Marshall, and others of FDR's top associates suggests that he was never far from their minds.

As much as McCarthy played the role of the outsider, he also represented an ascendant Irish and German Catholic power bloc that, in the 1930s and 1940s, had begun to see itself as both an ally and rival to the ruling Protestants. In the process of asserting its influence and leadership claims, this bloc often sought to increase the distance separating it from eastern and southern Europeans and their descendants, including the many Catholics in the latter's ranks. Sometimes this effort at distinction expressed itself in outright antagonism between the two European ethnic communities, other times in the efforts of Irish and German Americans to join Protestants in determining the pace and character of the eastern and southern Europeans' assimilation. It is thus possible to discern in McCarthy's obsession with the betrayals of the Roosevelt elite a continuing, if submerged, anxiety regarding the southern and eastern European "newcomers." Someone had to direct the assimilation and absorption of these newcomers into America. Because Roosevelt, Marshall, Hiss, and other members of this liberal elite had failed in this duty, McCarthy and his supporters were determined to take their place. In doing so, they would restore cultural and political order and prevent future Rosenbergs and other lowly descendants of the new immigrants from getting out of hand and committing treason.

RACIAL NATIONALISM REDUX: THE CASE OF IMMIGRATION REFORM

Some of the most intriguing evidence for this line of interpretation comes not from the dramatic investigations and interrogations of alleged Communists that formed the core of the anti-Communist crusade, but from a concurrent movement to reform and rationalize immigration law. As McCarthy was reaching the apogee of his power and influence in 1952, a close associate of his and a fellow Irish Catholic, Senator Pat McCarran of Nevada (Demo-crat), was bringing a five-year effort at immigration reform to a successful conclusion. The resulting bill, the McCarran-Walter Act of 1952, was the first major piece of immigration legislation since the Johnson-Reed Act of 1924.[24]

In political terms, McCarran was an indefatigable anti-Commu-nist crusader. The "loss of China" in 1949 had turned him against the Truman administration. From his powerful post as head of the Senate Judiciary Committee, he secured the passage of the Internal Security Act in 1950, a law that required all Communist and Com-munist-front organizations to register with the federal government. And as much as, even more than, McCarthy, he led the attack on the alleged Communist sympathizers in the State Department.[25] He was intimately involved, in other words, with the campaign to rid government of a "traitorous" Protestant elite and to put the coun-try in the hands of Irish Catholics and others who could be trusted.

The immigration act that bore his name was an omnibus mea-sure that addressed numerous immigration issues. Not surprisingly, it strengthened the measures that the government could take to bar or deport immigrants who were found to have Communist affilia-tions. It sought to make American immigration policy more coher-ent and the administration of the law more efficient. It removed sexual discriminations that had put American-born women and resident women aliens with alien husbands at a distinct and unfair disadvantage. Additionally, it changed in fundamental ways the legal status of Asian immigrants. First, it removed the ban on immi-gration from Asia and granted each country in a designated "Asia-Pacific" triangle a quota of 100 immigrants a year. Equally im-portant, the act mandated that Asian immigrants, both those al-ready present in the United States and those who wished to come, were now eligible for naturalization. For the first time in American history, in other words, the federal government granted Asian im-migrants an opportunity to become U.S. citizens.[26]

That one of the country's longest-standing principles of racial exclusion was eliminated in a stroke—and only seven years after Americans had fought a savage race war against the Japanese in the Pacific—testifies to the enormous change in political climate brought about by the 1940s campaigns against racial prejudice and the consequent invigoration of the civic nationalist tradition. The 1952 act struck as hard at the tradition of racial exclusion as the 1954 Supreme Court decision outlawing segregation. Cold War considerations contributed to this change as they did to *Brown v. Board of Education*, for Congress was worried about giving the Japanese, the Indians, the Filipinos, and other groups of Asians reasons to resent America and thus to gravitate toward the Soviet orbit. As Congressman Walter H. Judd of Minnesota (Republican) declared, "the struggle between the Free World and the Slave World will be decided in Asia, and we will lose that struggle if Asians perceive us as labelling them 'inferior and unworthy human beings.' "[27]

Overwhelming numbers of senators and congressmen, both Democrats and Republicans, endorsed this new, egalitarian approach to Asian immigration. Indeed, the only significant opposition to this portion of the bill came from liberals who felt that 100-person-per-year quotas did not go far enough in granting Asian immigrants equal rights and access to America.[28] In congressional debates on the bill, few senators or congressmen indulged in the kind of racialist- or eugenics-inflected talk that had characterized the 1924 discussions, although an elderly Senator Walter George from Georgia (Democrat) did declare, almost plaintively, that he "hoped the time has not come when one must apologize for being a hateful Anglo-Saxon."[29] Virtually every senator and congressman who spoke out on the bill wanted to position himself or herself as a supporter of racial equality.

But in one important respect, immigration law did not change: if racialist discourse had all but disappeared, the racist-inspired quota system of 1924 remained in place, despite furious liberal opposition. The Democrat Emanuel Celler, a young turk-turned-congressional-veteran who had led the fight against the Johnson-Reed Act in 1924, had lost none of his fire on this issue. His pleas for a civic nationalism were as eloquent as ever, and no longer sullied by his earlier willingness to endorse Japanese exclusion. In the Senate, Hubert Humphrey of Minnesota and Herbert Lehman of New York (both Democrats) took up the cause. But despite having the support of the White House, the liberals could not prevail and once again went down to defeat in the House and Senate by wide margins. Truman even vetoed the bill and, in the process, expressed liberal outrage at the maintenance of the 1924 quota system:

> The idea behind this discriminatory policy was, to put it baldly, that Americans with English or Irish names were better citizens than Americans with Italian or Greek or Polish names. . . . Such a concept is utterly unworthy of our traditions and our ideals. It violates the great political doctrine of the Declaration of Independence, that "all men are created equal." It denies the humanitarian creed inscribed beneath the Statue of Liberty proclaiming to all nations, "Give me your tired, your poor, your huddled masses yearning to breathe free." It repudiates our basic religious concepts, our belief in the brotherhood of man. . . . It is incredible to me that, in this year of 1952, we should again be enacting into law such a slur on the patriotism, the capacity, and the decency of such a large part of our citizenry.[30]

Truman's moving evocation of the country's civic nationalist tradition was to no avail. The Senate overrode the veto, and the McCarran-Walter bill became law. Jewish and Italian groups reacted bitterly to its passage.[31]

Defending the quota system even as they posed as defenders of racial equality created some awkward moments for McCarran and his supporters. Sometimes they resorted to demagoguery, suggesting that the liberals' desire to defeat the bill reflected their indifference to the Asian immigrants' quest for racial equality. Congressman Judd took this approach when he accused Truman, who had just vetoed the bill, of effectively telling the Japanese that each of them, "no matter how gifted or cultured," was unfit to "come to the United States as an immigrant because he is not of the white, the black, or the red race." McCarran, himself, in a statement that would have been unimaginable coming from the mouth of a western senator ten years earlier, declared that the veto, if upheld, would "dash the hopes of 86,000 orientals within our borders who have been our friends and neighbors for a quarter of a century, and who have hoped to realize their ambitions to become American citizens."[32]

Other times, McCarran's forces took a different tack, admitting that there might be something wrong about perpetuating the racist quota system, but arguing that the international situation was simply too unstable to consider jettisoning it at that time.[33] But liberals had a retort for this claim, declaring that abolition of the quota system would actually improve America's image overseas, especially in eastern Europe, where Communist rulers would no longer be able to tell their people that America regarded them as undesirable human specimens.[34] And so, McCarran and his allies were forced, on occasion, to reveal their true reasons for maintaining the quota system. If America were to scrap the system, McCarran argued, "we will, in the course of a generation or so, change the ethnic and cultural composition of this Nation. The times, Mr. President, are too perilous for us to tinker blindly with our national institutions."[35]

For McCarran, changing the "ethnic and cultural composition" of the nation meant ending the dominance of northwest Europeans—of the Anglo-Saxons and their Irish, German, and Scandinavian allies. This move was not one that McCarran was prepared to make. Unlike the restrictionists of 1924, McCarran did not think that eastern and southern Europeans were so inferior so as to prevent altogether their assimilation of American values and customs. He did not indulge in racial stereotypes or in inflammatory racialist discourse. "I would be the last one," McCarran told the president, "to deny that the immigrants who have come to this country have made a great contribution to our Nation."[36] But he still shared the views of the 1924 restrictionists that the arrival of too many eastern and southern Europeans would undermine the assimilation process and change America for the worse. The "cold hard truth," McCarran averred, "is that in the United States today there are [still] hard-core, indigestible blocs who have not become integrated into the American way of life." If the immigrant gates were to be

reopened and if America, the "oasis of the world[,] shall be overrun, perverted, contaminated, or destroyed [by immigrants], then
the last flickering light of humanity will be extinguished."[37] Thus,
McCarran concluded, "I am firmly convinced that the flow of immigrants must be strictly controlled so that we will not receive
more aliens than *we* can assimilate."[38]

With these words, McCarran revealed his two key beliefs: first,
that only careful regulation of the numbers and national origins of
immigrants would allow assimilation to proceed; and, second, that
assimilation would only work if "we" Americans, by which
McCarran meant "old-stock" Protestants and Catholics, controlled it. McCarran and his supporters were prepared to celebrate
the contributions that eastern and southern Europeans had made
to American society. Thus McCarran colleague and fellow Democrat Senator Willis Smith hailed "the people of Greek ancestry"
who had come to North Carolina and "conducted themselves in a
businesslike way." Smith was sure that there were "no better citizens" of his state. But, of course, their successful absorption reflected the fact that "the percentage of foreign born in my State is
the smallest of any State in the Union."[39] Eastern and southern
Europeans were welcome in America as long as they came in small
numbers, agreed to behave themselves, and left the tasks of governing and shaping America to Protestants and their Irish and German
Catholic allies. In such circumstances, McCarran asserted,
America, "the last hope of western civilization," would remain
"strong and free . . . and lead the world in a way dedicated to the
worth and dignity of the human soul."[40]

McCarran's satisfaction with the national origins system explains the manner in which he and his supporters chose to end
Asian exclusion. By agreeing to admit 100 immigrants per year
from each Asian country and by removing the ban against Asian
naturalization, the McCarran camp was essentially bringing Asians
into the national quota system. Like eastern and southern Europeans, the numbers of Asian immigrants would be kept pitifully low;
and this would allow the American crucible to work its magic.[41]

If opening America's immigrant gates to large numbers of eastern and southern Europeans and Asians threatened America from
one direction, the moral weakness of the traditional Protestant elite
threatened it from another. Thus, for McCarran, there were no
contradictions between pursuing State Department Communists
on the one hand and maintaining sharp limits on immigration from
eastern and southern Europe on the other. They were part of the
same task of protecting the nation from its potential enemies.

The McCarran-Walter Act was not the tragedy that advocates
of the new immigrant groups made it out to be. It did not recreate
the rabidly anti-immigrant climate of the 1920s or legitimate the
frank racism that had underpinned it. The termination of the specifically anti-Asian immigration and naturalization laws, moreover,
marked an important triumph for the civic nationalist tradition.
But the act did function as a warning, as did the anti-Communist
crusade, that minorities had better behave, that they should do everything possible to play by America's rules. Playing by the rules
meant, most obviously, distancing themselves from the stigma of
communism; this entailed, first and foremost, an explicit repudiation of the Communist Party and of individual Communists who
shared their ethnic or racial background. This imperative explains
why most mainstream Jewish groups, such as the Anti-Defamation
League and the American Jewish Committee, went to great lengths
to dissociate themselves from the Jewish Communists Julius and
Ethel Rosenberg, and to insist that the Rosenbergs' arrest and execution could in no way be construed as evidence of anti-Semitism.
Few expressions of sympathy for the Rosenbergs arose from within
these Jewish organizations, and relatively few calls for mercy
gained support. Any time such sentiments began to emerge, Jewish
anti-Communist committees were quick to identify and discredit
them as part of a Communist plot to allow the convicted spies to
escape their deserved fate.[42]

Distancing one's group from the stigma of communism also
meant, more subtly, jettisoning views that could be linked to Communist influence. The aforementioned Jewish groups, along with
the American Jewish Congress, had played a pivotal role in the

civic nationalist campaign against religious and racial prejudice in the late 1940s and early 1950s, sponsoring numerous studies of social problems linked to such prejudice and disseminating reams of publicity on the virtues of religious and racial tolerance. Before the ideological contours of the Cold War era had hardened, these groups had looked favorably upon studies that examined the socio-economic roots of prejudice and advocated solutions entailing structural changes in the distribution of economic wealth and power in American society. But by the 1950s, they had retreated from this economic approach, at least in part because they feared it too easily opened up their organizations to the charge of being soft on communism.[43]

A similar evolution characterized the black struggle for civil rights, whose advocates, in the 1940s, had often mounted critiques of an economic system that kept blacks impoverished. In those years, unionized groups of black workers, North and South, had thrust themselves into the leadership of the struggle for racial equality in many locales, insisting that black advances depended on checking corporate power and on asserting the economic rights of blacks to good jobs, decent pay, and some voice in the determination of the conditions of their labor. Impressed by the dynamism of this union effort, many middle-class black institutions, such as the NAACP, the Urban League, and the black press, became significantly more prolabor in their politics.

But, by the early 1950s, this prolabor civil rights initiative had vanished, another victim of the Cold War. Communists had often been in the forefront of black unionization struggles, making the unions that emerged from those struggles easy targets for anti-Communist crusaders. Worried that any perceived association between communism and the civil rights movement would make progress for blacks impossible to attain, many mainstream institutions within the black community were quick to dissociate themselves from black organizations that harbored Communists, criticized American foreign policy, or challenged the emerging Cold War ideological consensus. Thus, in 1948, the *Pittsburgh Courier* castigated A. Philip Randolph, an anti-Communist socialist, for calling on blacks to refuse induction into the military as long as it remained segregated. "It would be extremely dangerous, and perhaps catastrophic," the *Courier* editors warned, "if the idea became widespread that there was any intention on the part of even a small segment of the colored population to hamper national defense in any way."[44] Mainstream black institutions and leaders saw similar dangers in advocating policies, including several others advocated by Randolph, that could be attacked as "socialistic." The fear of being labeled traitors did not deter blacks intent on achieving racial equality, but it did lead many to winnow their discourse of prolabor and anticorporate themes. By the mid-1950s, when Martin Luther King Jr. emerged as the charismatic leader of the black struggle, churches had replaced unions as the key institution of protest, and demands focused largely on "civil" as opposed to "economic" rights.[45]

Sometimes, too, it became apparent that "playing by America's rules" meant more than simply steering clear of communism or jettisoning anticorporate reform proposals. The government conducted investigations of organized crime throughout the decade, often targeting Italians, not just because the Mafia had achieved notoriety but also because of a lingering racialist suspicion that Italians were "naturally" prone to lawlessness, corruption, and flamboyance. Italian American groups fought hard against such stereotyping and labored to create a social space that allowed a range of Italian "types" to thrive.[46] Italians also felt pressured, however, both from within their own communities and from the outside, to exchange their less attractive "Italian" traits for respectable "American" ones. Such pressure helps to explain the celebrity of Joe DiMaggio, the New York Yankees star centerfielder from the mid-1930s to the early 1950s. In public, the courteous and gentlemanly DiMaggio, the son of Italian immigrants, was never heard to utter a mean word or to issue a threat; nor was he usually seen in the company of disreputable, mob-related figures. He was the model American ethnic: hardworking, respectful, and reserved, someone who played baseball brilliantly, but in a quiet, unprepossessing, even Anglo-Saxon, way. For his skills, speed, and his

Figs. 23 and 24. Contrasting Images of European Ethnics in the 1950s. The first of these two images shows Ethel and Julius Rosenberg under guard after being convicted of espionage in 1951; they "broke the rules" and suffered a terrible fate. The second image depicts the joyous newlyweds, Marilyn Monroe and Joe DiMaggio, in 1954 as they prepare to extend their honeymoon with a trip to Tokyo. That Monroe, the Anglo-Saxon sex goddess, was available to DiMaggio, the Italian American slugger, is one measure of the opportunities that were opening up in the 1950s for model ethnics. (Courtesy AP/Wide World Photos)

serene, graceful approach to the game, he was dubbed the "Yankee Clipper" and given the status of a national icon. He even won the heart, if briefly, of the Anglo-Saxon sexual goddess, Marilyn Monroe, demonstrating that nothing was out of reach of an Italian American, or any other southern or eastern European, who worked hard and lived by the rules. But even as he achieved the acclaim accorded almost no other Italian American of the middle decades of the twentieth century, his constrained public demeanor conveyed a potent message about how ethnic Americans should comport themselves if they wished to get ahead.[47]

As the experience of Jews and Italians in the 1950s suggests, the permutations in the racial and civic nationalist traditions during the Cold War years were complex. The racial nationalist tradition lost some of its potency, in part due to ideological changes set in motion by World War II and in part owing to the political exigencies of fighting the Cold War. Anti-Communist crusaders did not target "inferior" immigrants as the principal source of subversion, as the proponents of the Red Scare had done in 1919 and 1920. Both *Brown v. Board of Education* and the ending of the ban on Asian immigration and naturalization struck blows at the legal edifice that had sustained racial nationalism. In taking a forthright stand against Asian exclusion, liberal groups in Congress demonstrated that they had freed themselves from the racist attitudes that had informed their attitudes toward the Japanese in the 1920s. The executive branch of the federal government, too, emerged from the Cold War's first decade more willing to challenge the most egregious displays of white supremacy. These changes enlarged the constituency looking to overturn racial nationalism and energized rank-and-file groups seeking to make social equality an American reality. But the racial tradition did not entirely disappear from American politics or culture. White southerners were mobilizing to resist the Supreme Court's integration decree, and the descendants of southern and eastern Europeans remained vulnerable to coded warnings that they had better behave and conform to expectations set by white Protestants and their Irish Catholic allies. The power of the racial nationalist tradition, in other words, was diminished but not broken; a full-scale confrontation with it had yet to come.

As the racial nationalist tradition lost some of its power, the civic nationalist tradition gained in prestige. Truman's message vetoing the McCarran-Walter Act was one of the most stirring affirmations of that tradition ever to emerge from the Oval Office. Many ethnics and blacks sensed in the 1950s that American society was opening up to them in ways it had not before. Anti-Semitic sentiment plunged during the 1950s, while black activists intensified their insistence that the practice of American democracy conform to the nation's civic ideals. That so many Americans, during these Cold War years, harbored a keen sense of national identity and believed in America's mission to lead the "free world" further strengthened hopes that civic ideals could be deployed against racist realities. As the civic tradition gained in power, however, it lost capaciousness. In the hands of anti-Communist crusaders, it became a tool for narrowing the political and ideological boundaries of the American nation. Communists were excluded from this nation, and their ideas condemned as un-American; fear of exposure and censure spread beyond Communist circles to those individuals and groups who sought extensive changes in the economic organization of American society. By the mid-1950s, the opportunity to use the language of civic nationalism to advance a radical economic program—so prominent a feature of Progressive and New Deal reform—had largely vanished.

Throughout the 1950s, America maintained its Rooseveltian character. Conditions of near war intensified nationalist consciousness and impelled large majorities of Americans to express loyalty to their nation. The civic tradition of American nationalism was strong, the racial tradition weaker but still potent. A powerful state stood as the guarantor of economic opportunity, national security, and anti-Communist consensus. But the changes in the power and character of the two nationalist traditions were signs of a nation in flux, and precursors of political and social upheaval.

CHAPTER 7

Civil Rights,

White Resistance, and

Black Nationalism,

1960–1968

In the 1950s the boundaries of the Rooseveltian nation
were stretched, allowing ethnic and racial minorities a good deal
of room for maneuver and integration. In the 1960s they ruptured
altogether. A civil rights revolution arose during those years and,
before it had run its course, overturned the legal foundation on
which the American tradition of racial nationalism rested. The
Civil Rights Act of 1964 outlawed segregation in civil society while
the Immigration Act of 1965 dismantled the national origins system that had been in place since 1924. In 1965 Congress passed
the Voting Rights Act to insure that white southerners could no

longer manipulate state laws to keep blacks from going to the polls. And in 1967, the Supreme Court threw out the 1924 Virginia law prohibiting marriage between the races, signaling that the imposing edifice of state antimiscegenation law would have to be torn down. Only in the 1860s and 1870s could a precedent be found for so rapid and sweeping a period of legislative and legal reform in matters of race, a connection that has prompted some to refer to the 1960s as the "Second Reconstruction."[1]

Despite the speed of this revolution, none of it was accomplished easily or without bitter struggle. The revolution depended on a resolute civil rights movement, composed mostly of southern blacks and led by Martin Luther King Jr. King believed fervently in the American dream, and he insisted that the revolution could be accomplished peacefully and through appeals to Americans' civic nationalist ideals. But King's own dream was not to be realized. By forcing a showdown with the racial nationalist tradition, King and his black supporters triggered furious resistance from white Americans who could not accept the elimination of race as a defining characteristic of American nationhood. White liberals, led by President Lyndon B. Johnson, attempted to carve a middle way between black civil rights activists and white resisters, endorsing civil rights while placating white southern Democrats whose support was deemed critical to the party's continued electoral success. In pursuing this strategy, white liberals actually went much further than their progressive and New Deal forebears had done in committing themselves to an America in which race would have no place. But, as Johnson and his supporters discovered at the 1964 Democratic Party Convention, a civil rights strategy resting on any degree of equivocation no longer worked. Black civil rights militants associated with the Student Nonviolent Coordinating Committee (SNCC), the university arm of the civil rights movement, had risked their lives to register blacks to vote and to desegregate bus stations, restaurants, and other public institutions in the South. They came to the 1964 convention in no mood to compromise. When a compromise was forced upon them, they not only quit the convention but repudiated their faith in the civic nationalist tradition. Turning from Martin Luther King Jr. to Malcolm X, and from civic nationalism to black nationalism, their words and actions spawned a nationalist crisis, the most serious since World War I. In the process, they triggered the unraveling of the Rooseveltian nation.

CIVIL RIGHTS AND CIVIC NATIONALISM

The civil rights revolution depended on a mass movement that was every bit as significant a social force as the labor movement of the 1930s had been. The NAACP, membership in which had soared to almost half a million in the 1940s, led the way, especially in terms of formulating a strategy to upend the legal basis of segregation. But as in the 1930s, when the CIO eclipsed the AFL, the NAACP was soon judged by many African Americans to be too conservative and timid a vehicle for their ambitions. Southern black ministers founded the Southern Christian Leadership Conference (SCLC) in 1957, hoping to use it to link together the millions of southern black churchgoers and to encourage them to confront segregation with marches and boycotts. University students at southern black universities, such as Fisk in Nashville and North Carolina A&T in Greensboro, formed SNCC in 1960, using such tactics as the "sit-in" at segregated lunch counters and "freedom rides" on segregated interstate buses to force nonviolent confrontations over issues of segregation. Surrounding these three principal organizations were many others, some, such as Congress of Racial Equality (CORE), dating back to the 1940s and others springing forth in 1961 and 1962 from the imaginations of small groups of activists determined to advance the cause of racial equality in their locale. In 1963, as this movement was reaching a climax, an estimated 1 million activists participated in civil rights protests in numerous American cities, such as Birmingham, Washington, New York, Los Angeles, San Francisco, Cleveland, Detroit, and Chicago, and across small towns in the South.[2]

Many factors contributed to the rise of this movement, most of them rooted in 1940s developments. Black World War II veterans returning to their southern homes after the war proved unwilling to tolerate any longer the indignities of Jim Crow. They infused militancy to the long-standing NAACP campaign to undermine the legal basis of segregation. Millions of southern blacks, meanwhile, had migrated to industrial centers in the North and West in the 1940s, their expectations rising as their economic and political circumstances improved. These migrants quickly made African Americans a force in the labor movement and in northern urban politics, compelling Democratic Party politicians there to support their quest for racial equality. Many of these politicians were eager to do so, not just for practical reasons but because they were looking for some way to redeem the world in the wake of the racial holocaust Hitler had unleashed on European Jewry.

But one factor outweighed every other in triggering the civil rights movement, and that was the collapse of the European empires in Africa and Asia as a result of the Second World War. Germany had either conquered the metropoles of these empires (Paris, Amsterdam) or brought them to their knees (London) while Japan had swept through prized imperial colonies in southeast Asia. British Singapore, the Dutch East Indies, French Indochina, and the American Philippines all fell quickly before the Japanese advance. In the 450-year period of the West's world hegemony, no nonwhite people had ever executed so devastating a strike on European mastery and might, and Europe's role in the world would never again be the same. Colonized peoples everywhere now dared to dream that they could be not only free of, but also equal to, their Western masters; during the war and postwar years, they intensified their movements for independence. India become a sovereign nation in 1947, Ghana in 1957, and Nigeria in 1960. By 1963, a total of thirty-three new nations had emerged from former European colonies in Africa alone.[3]

Had it not been for the Cold War, western European countries, with the assistance of the United States, might have slowed or even stopped this imperial disintegration. But where Western countries tried to restore imperial rule, as the French and Americans attempted to do in Indochina, they confronted liberation movements supported by the Soviet Union and China. The Soviets saw decolonization as a way to weaken the West, and they did everything they could not only to speed it along but to bring the newly emerging nations into the Soviet orbit. Some nations, such as Gamal Abdul Nasser's Egypt and Ho Chi Minh's North Vietnam, did just that, but others, such as India, saw greater advantage in maintaining a neutrality and thus in being able to play the Cold War rivals off against each other. Such nonalignment had the desired effect of causing the United States and the Soviet Union to intensify their efforts to win the support of these nations, which could only happen by recognizing their desire to be independent and offering them military and economic assistance. In such ways did the newly independent nations gain power and prestige that might have eluded them in a less polarized world.

The American civil rights movement was part of this worldwide revolt against "Western" domination and its associated ideologies of white supremacy. Civil rights activists in the United States studied the techniques of nonviolent resistance pioneered by Mohandas Gandhi in India's struggle for independence. Later, as angry American activists turned away from nonviolence, they read with similar intensity the writings of the radical French ex-colonial Frantz Fanon. They also followed closely the various Third World movements for independence and monitored developments within those nations that had won their independence. To visit one of these nations, and to meet with its leaders, as Martin Luther King Jr. did in 1957 and 1959, when he traveled to Ghana and India and met with Nkrumah and Nehru, was a thrilling experience. King was present in Ghana at midnight, March 5, 1957, at the ceremonies marking that country's formal establishment as a sovereign nation. As the Union Jack was lowered for the last time over the British Gold Coast colony and the Ghanaian flag raised in its place, King recalled that he "could hear people shouting all over that vast audience, 'Freedom! Freedom! Freedom!' " King "started weeping . . . and crying for joy," not only for what the Ghanaians had achieved for themselves but also for the impetus that the "birth of this new nation ... would give ... to oppressed peoples all over the world"—in Africa, Asia, and the United States.[4]

King's elation over these events did not mean, however, that he wanted African Americans to return to Africa or to establish a black nation within American territory. In response to an individual imploring him to sponsor a back-to-Africa movement, King declared: "To have a mass return to Africa would merely be running from the problem and not facing it courageously. ... We are American citizens, and we deserve our rights in this nation."[5] With these words, King signaled his belief in America's civic nationalist tradition; African Americans could use that tradition, King believed, to achieve full equality in the United States and thus to make America their nation.

As early as 1944, when he was only fifteen, King expressed his belief in the ideals of American freedom, which he identified as "the spirit of Lincoln," in an oration that won him a statewide prize sponsored by Georgia's Black Elks. While acknowledging the chains that still shackled blacks, King argued that America "experiences a new birth of freedom in her sons and daughters," and that they would renew the work that the martyred Lincoln "left unfinished." "My heart throbs anew," King declared, "in the hope that" these American sons and daughters "will cast down the last barrier to perfect freedom."[6]

As King rose to prominence in the civil rights movement in the mid-1950s, he increasingly identified "the stride toward freedom" as its central goal. As noted in the preceding chapter, King, in 1955, began his first speech to the Montgomery bus boycotters with a declaration that the protesters were demanding their rights as American citizens.[7] In 1961 he praised the university student militants sitting in at segregated lunch counters for "seeking to save the soul of America." The students, King avowed, were "taking our whole nation back to those great wells of democracy which were dug deep by the Founding Fathers in the formulation of the Constitution and the Declaration of Independence. In sitting down at the lunch counters, they are in reality standing up for the American dream."[8]

The notion of an American dream, as "yet unfulfilled" but still alluring, appears increasingly frequently in King's speeches and writings from 1960 on, culminating, of course, in his famous 1963 oration before the hundreds of thousands gathered at the Lincoln Memorial during the March on Washington. "I still have a dream," he declared on that day, "a dream rooted in the American dream that one day this nation will rise up and live out the true meaning of its creed—we hold these truths to be self-evident, that all men are created equal." A few moments later he shared with his audience his vision of "the day when all of God's children will be able to sing with new meaning—'my country 'tis of thee; sweet land of liberty; of thee I sing; land where my fathers died, land of the pilgrim's pride.' "[9]

King's American dream, of course, drew on more than reverence for the Pilgrims, the Founding Fathers, and Abraham Lincoln. King was a deeply religious man who had culled from the ethics of the New Testament a dream of universal brotherhood that would unite not only Americans but all the world's peoples, all of whom were "God's children." His theological studies at Crozer Theological Seminary and then at Boston University in the late 1940s and early 1950s had also impelled him to critique America as a society too preoccupied with money, materialism, and economic power. He disliked capitalism both for what it did to the souls of the rich and for its indifference to the fate of the poor. Because the American civic nationalist tradition was, as we have seen, a capacious creed, capable of accommodating a variety of ideological positions, King had little difficulty weaving into it his religiously based universalism and anticapitalism. In a 1961 commencement address at Lincoln University, King asked his listeners to use the "amazing universalism" residing in the American dream to "develop a world perspective" and to work for a "world of brotherhood and peace and goodwill."[10] To a National Urban League gathering in 1960, by contrast, he stressed the importance of economic equality and mutuality "to bring into full realization the dream of our American

Fig. 25. Martin Luther King Jr., Birmingham, Alabama, 1963. (Courtesy Library of Congress)

democracy." He spoke then of a "dream of equality of opportunity, of privilege and property widely distributed; a dream of a land where men will not take necessities from the man to give luxuries to the few; . . . a dream of a place where all our gifts and resources are held not for ourselves alone but as instruments of service for the rest of humanity."[11] King believed that the 1930s labor movement had brought this kind of democracy to America, and he held it up as something that civil rights activists ought to emulate.[12]

King did not shy away from acknowledging the dark side of America, especially the strength of its racial nationalist tradition. "Our nation was born in genocide," he noted in 1964, referring to America's decision to "wipe out its indigenous [Indian] population." The fight to exterminate the Indian yielded a "massive base of prejudice" upon which "prejudice toward the nonwhite was readily built and found rapid growth."[13] For that reason, King explained, America had always "been something of a schizophrenic personality, tragically divided against itself," its principles of democracy forever warring against its commitment to white supremacy. But King shared with Gunnar Myrdal the belief that the noble principles of freedom and democracy, what Myrdal called the American Creed, could be used to eliminate the ugly practices of racial domination. "Our hard-won heritage of freedom," King argued in 1964, "is ultimately more powerful than our traditions of cruelty and injustice."[14]

Some scholars have located the sources of King's optimism in the security and intimacy of his family upbringing and in the strength of his religious faith. Others have questioned whether King believed as deeply in the American dream as he professed, discerning in King's words a strategy on King's part to appeal to white liberals and win their support for the civil rights movement. There can be no doubt that King considered such white support essential, and his optimism soared in 1963 and 1964 as whites seemed to be coming around. Even the militant actions undertaken by blacks in the summer of 1963, King believed, "far from alienating America's white citizens, brought them closer into harmony with its Negro citizens than ever before."[15]

Determining the depths of King's private belief in the American dream is not required, however, to understand how perfectly suited his public profession of it was to America's ideological climate in the 1950s and early 1960s. This was the heyday of the Rooseveltian nation, a time when most Americans believed in their country's virtue and saw their nation as a force for freedom, at home and abroad. Such national confidence had been born of the World War II experience, in which American economic might and military resolve had brought the country and the world a great victory while restoring faith in the capacity of the American economy to create opportunity and abundance. The Cold War, while generating an undercurrent of fear and uncertainty and sowing the seeds for political instability over the long term, kept nationalist consciousness razor-sharp and, if anything, intensified popular devotion to principles of freedom and democracy. This climate affected blacks as well as whites and made them receptive to King's declarations that American ideals were of the utmost importance, critical weapons in worldwide struggle for freedom and against tyranny. The times appeared to demand that America's civic nationalist tradition triumph over its domestic and foreign adversaries. This was the spirit that impelled a majority of Americans to endorse the civil rights revolution that began with the passage of the Civil Rights Act of 1964 and that, during the next four years, dismantled the legal basis for minority segregation, disfranchisement, and subjugation. It seemed as though the country finally had confronted the racist burden of its past and elected to push ahead into a new, colorblind future in which every American would be judged by "the content of his character" and not the color of his skin. King's presence in the pantheon of American heroes rests on his contribution to this breakthrough.[16]

But King paid a price for his ascent, discernible in his reluctance to incorporate his critique of capitalism into his most public expositions on the American dream. King did not hesitate to discuss the anticapitalist dimensions of his thought with the predominately black Urban League audience in 1961, but he dared not do this during his March on Washington oration in 1963, when the national media was broadcasting his words to the White House, to the Congress, and to millions of white and black Americans throughout the country. That he declined to do so is especially significant given that the march's two principal organizers, A. Philip Randolph and Bayard Rustin, were Old Left socialists who would have welcomed such a critique. Randolph and Rustin had officially titled the Washington protest a "March for Jobs and Freedom" in order to impress upon Americans their belief that economic reform was an essential element of racial progress. Moreover, numerous placards at the march itself carried the message "Jobs and Freedom." Randolph and Rustin were not out of step with political realities. They had powerful allies in Walter Reuther, the president of the United Autoworkers of America (UAW), and his key congressional lobbyist, Joseph Rauh Jr.; in Arthur Goldberg, former legal counsel to the United Steelworkers of America who had recently been elevated to the Supreme Court; in Willard Wirtz, secretary of labor and several of his key staffers, including a youthful Daniel Patrick Moynihan; and even, to a certain extent, in Robert F. Kennedy's Department of Justice. Most of these individuals were not radicals, but they did harbor a New Deal conviction that the successful reform of race relations required that more jobs and better wages be made available to black men and women. They wanted the government to create jobs programs and, through them, to regulate private labor and capital markets. In other words, they still clung to the New Deal goal of a government able and willing to direct the private economy in the public's interest.[17]

But this kind of politics had become an extremely hard sell in Cold War America, when any perceived censure of capitalism risked being condemned as Communist.[18] Many Americans, moreover, had lost the ability, which they had possessed in the 1930s, to imagine how a civic nationalist emphasis on "freedom" and "democracy" might be used to criticize an economic system based on "free enterprise." This perhaps accounts for the lack of commentary during the March on Washington about the numerous placards calling not just for freedom but for jobs. In this regard, King's muteness on the subject takes on added significance. Had he been willing to challenge his listeners with his dream of a society in which "privilege and property is widely distributed" and "where men will not take necessities from the man to give luxuries to the few," the efforts of Randolph and Rustin to imbue the march with

Fig. 26. "Jobs and Freedom" at the March on Washington, 1963. Participants in the March on Washington, August 1963. In a line moving right to left at the center of the photograph are a number of march organizers and civil rights leaders, including Walter Reuther, president of the UAW (his face partially obscured by a sign); A. Philip Randolph, co-organizer of the march; Roy Wilkins, executive secretary of the NAACP; Whitney Young, executive director of the National Urban League; Joseph Rauh Jr., liberal activist and lobbyist; and Joachim Prinz of the American Jewish Congress. Note the many signs calling for "jobs and freedom" and "jobs for all," an economic demand of the marchers that slipped the notice of observers at the time and of many who have written about the march's history. (Courtesy Library of Congress)

social democratic meaning might have succeeded. But such an initiative might also have backfired, by delegitimating King's more elementary quest for a national consensus on the imperatives of granting African Americans in the South their civil rights. It is well to remember that King lost considerable white support in later years as he became more willing to voice his reservations about capitalism.[19] Those who wished to mount radical critiques, as we shall see, increasingly felt compelled to abandon the language of civic nationalism altogether.

King's reticence at the march also reflected his desire not to jeopardize the support that President Kennedy had recently given the civil rights movement. In June 1963, after Kennedy, along with millions of other Americans, had seen dogs and power hoses unleashed on civil rights protesters, many of them children, in Birmingham, Alabama, he abandoned the caution that had marked his relationship with King and embraced the cause of civil rights. "One hundred years of delay have passed since President Lincoln freed the slaves," Kennedy declared to a national television audience on June 11; "yet their heirs, their grandsons, are not fully free. They are not yet freed from the bonds of injustice. They are not yet freed from social and economic oppression." It was time, Kennedy insisted, for "this Nation to fulfill its promise," and to carry through a peaceful revolution in race relations. To fulfill his responsibility, Kennedy announced that he would call on Congress "to act, to make a commitment it has not fully made in this century to the proposition that race has no place in American life or law."[20] In the next week, he requested Congress to take up a civil rights bill that would bar discrimination in public places, insure that black Americans could exercise their right to vote, and give the federal government the powers it needed to enforce this new racially egalitarian regime.[21] Kennedy's willingness to speak about the "economic oppression" of blacks was an intriguing initiative on his part but also a limited one: he was not contemplating jobs programs to alleviate the structural roots of black poverty but a federal commission empowered to prosecute private employers who refused to hire blacks on account of race.

To many civil rights workers in the South, a discussion about the economic dimensions of the civic nationalist tradition may have seemed academic, for they were beginning to believe that civic nationalism, in whatever form, was irrelevant to their struggle. White southerners had done everything in their power to resist the dismantling of Jim Crow and the repudiation of white supremacy. They formed organizations throughout the South to resist integration, declaring that this policy rested on federal laws and judicial decisions that illegally infringed on states' rights. They reinvigorated the tradition of racial nationalism, arguing that blacks would never achieve the worth of whites and thus did not deserve first-class citizenship. John P. Brady, an intellectual leader of the Citizens Councils, a movement of southern whites organized to resist integration, echoed Theodore Roosevelt's declarations a half century earlier that African Americans deserved nothing more than a subordinate place in the American nation. For what, Brady wanted to know, had African Americans contributed to the building of the American nation? In reviewing the American Revolution, the War of 1812, westward expansion, and the Civil War, Brady repeatedly declared that "it is ridiculous to assume that the American negro played any part" in these struggles. On what basis, then, Brady wanted to know, could these "negroes" claim the same rights as whites?[22]

The illegality and immorality of the Supreme Court's 1954 *Brown v. Board of Education* decision was so great, Brady declared, that every "patriotic American" had a duty to resist.[23] Already in 1955, a movement of "massive resistance" had sprung up in the South to stop the civil rights crusade. In places like Little Rock, Arkansas, white southerners refused to go along with federal integration decrees. Local sheriffs threw civil rights protesters in jail and kept them there as long as possible. White vigilantes organized by a resuscitated Ku Klux Klan and other reactionary groups threatened civil rights activists with physical abuse and death. King himself suffered severely for his insistence that blacks ought to have access to the American dream. He was thrown in jail on numerous occasions, endlessly vilified in the southern press, repeatedly threatened with physical harm, and verbally abused by countless obscene and hate-filled phone calls, sometimes reaching twenty-five a day. His home and other places where he resided were bombed, and in New York in 1958, an attacker plunged a knife into his chest and came within an inch of severing his aorta.[24] The FBI, under J. Edgar Hoover, saw him as a troublemaker and joined the campaign to vilify him.[25]

The suffering experienced by other civil rights activists may actually have been worse. As early as late 1961 and early 1962, SNCC volunteers had gone to Greenwood, Mississippi, to register blacks to vote in a county that was 80 percent black but had only one black registered voter. These SNCC members, such as Lawrence Guyot, Diane Nash, James Bevel, Robert Moses, John Lewis, and Marion Barry, were talented but anonymous young men and women, most of them having come from Fisk, Howard, Tougaloo, and other black colleges to advance the civil rights struggle. Even though their goals of voter registration were modest (they did not dare to integrate restaurants for example), they alarmed local white authorities who feared them as the advance guard of a social revolution. For merely talking to local blacks and walking with them to the courthouse to register them to vote, these volunteers were harassed and assaulted by the local police and their vigilante allies. The volunteers, armed with their ideology of nonviolence, refused to fight back, but this did little to lessen the incidence of beatings or the use of psychological terror against them.[26]

Lawrence Guyot recalled for Howell Raines how he had been both terrorized and beaten in Mississippi. "You would be taking someone down to register, and you would simply be trailed by two cars of whites. Maybe they would do something, but you would never know. Maybe they would get and whip you. Maybe they wouldn't." Guyot knew what it was like to be beaten within an inch of his life. When he arrived in the town of Winona, trying to locate a group of his colleagues who had been arrested, he was greeted by nine policemen, "who took turns punching me with the butts of guns . . . forced me to take all my clothes off, then . . . threatened burning my genitals with fire and a sharp stick." Doing all he could do not to lapse into unconsciousness, Guyot endured this assault for four hours, until a doctor warned his attackers that he might soon die. Only then did the beating stop, but Guyot was thrown into jail and, incredibly, charged with attempted murder.[27]

Every civil rights worker in the South had to be prepared to undergo this kind of ordeal. But, aided by a transcendent belief in the transformative power of nonviolent resistance, each believed that he or she could endure it. SNCC activists, moreover, developed elaborate survival techniques, monitoring the whereabouts of all their members, flooding local sheriffs' offices with calls of inquiry if one of their group had been arrested, informing other civil rights organizations of dangerous situations, and hoping, in general, to generate enough bad publicity to compel local authorities to desist from injuring or killing their colleagues. And they also harbored the hope that, if a situation deteriorated and lives were at stake, the federal government would rescue them and restore some semblance of law and order. The government had done this during the Freedom Rides of 1961 and 1962, when Attorney General Robert F. Kennedy ordered federal marshals to disperse the furious white mobs that were assaulting freedom riders and their supporters in Birmingham and Montgomery, Alabama. In Montgomery, the mob had surrounded and seemed intent on killing hundreds of civil rights activists, including King, who had assembled in a black church. Without the intervention of the federal government, many of these individuals may well have died. But SNCC was less successful in provoking this kind of intervention in Greenwood and other more isolated areas of the South, especially when neither King nor some other high-profile civil rights leader was involved. Protecting the lives of ordinary blacks did not seem to rank high enough on the federal government's list of priorities; and even if federal authorities showed up, they might vacillate, unable or unwilling to put their authority firmly behind those who had put their lives at risk. By 1964, an estimated sixty-three civil rights volunteers had died as a result of their involvement in voter registration, and hundreds more had been beaten or tortured.[28]

Many of these volunteers had originally conceived of themselves as American patriots, standing tall for the American dream. But their experience in the South made believing in this dream increasingly difficult. By 1963 they had begun implicitly to question whether the tradition of civic nationalism could ever become the dominant one in America and whether nonviolent appeals to brotherhood would ever turn racial hate into love. Their brewing disillusionment became apparent in the March on Washington, when their representative, SNCC leader John Lewis, prepared to deliver an angry and threatening speech to the crowd gathered before the Lincoln Memorial. Lewis had no intention of dwelling on the possibilities of universal brotherhood or of arousing nationalist ardor by invoking, as King would soon do, the words of a patriotic poem. He resolved instead to speak of the suffering of civil rights workers in the South, of how the federal government had simply not done enough, and of how the faith of the civil rights activists in nonviolence and in civic ideals was faltering. At his colleague James Forman's suggestion, he included an incendiary passage in the draft of his speech, warning America of impending war. "We shall march through the South, through the heart of Dixie, the way Sherman did," Lewis planned to announce. "We shall pursue our own 'scorched earth' policy and burn Jim Crow to the ground, nonviolently. We shall crack the South into a thousand pieces and put them back together in the image of a democracy."[29]

The power of this passage derived from the allusions to battle— to Sherman's march, and to the scorching, burning, and cracking of the South—unlikely phrases for someone steeped in nonviolence. Lewis never spoke many of these words, however. The Kennedy administration and more moderate civil rights leaders pressured him to excise the entire Sherman section as well as other "offensive" passages. Lewis and his SNCC colleagues attempted to resist this censorship, holding firm until minutes before his scheduled time to speak, capitulating only when the strain proved too great. The veneer of unity at the march was preserved, allowing King, who spoke after Lewis, to define this moment as one of great advance for America's civic creed and for dreams of colorblind brotherhood. In the months following the march, the fissures in the civil rights movement only widened. By the following summer, at the 1964 Democratic Party Convention held in August in Atlantic City, New Jersey, the virtual collapse of the alliance was at hand.

The nation had been shocked the previous November—only three months after the March on Washington—by President Kennedy's assassination. His successor, Lyndon B. Johnson, had moved into the White House with an aggressive legislative agenda, partly reflecting his long-term desire to complete Roosevelt's New Deal and partly expressing his determination to do something to redeem the nation in the wake of Kennedy's murder. At the center of this agenda was the powerful civil rights act that Kennedy had initially proposed. As a southerner, as a veteran congressman and senator with superb legislative skills, and as the man to whom countless Americans had turned for guidance, Johnson possessed the abilities and the mandate to get such an act through Congress. This he did in July 1964, an accomplishment that, he believed, would be recognized and celebrated at the convention, paving the way for his nomination as the Democratic presidential nominee.[30]

But John Lewis and his SNCC comrades came to this convention with no intention of coronating Johnson, even congratulating him, for pushing through the civil rights law. Since the March on Washington, they had continued with their voter registration campaign in Greenwood, Mississippi, and the surrounding counties, suffering through another year of terror at the hands of southern Klansmen and local police authorities. For the summer of 1964, they had accepted 300 volunteers from the North, most of them young, white university students who wanted to join their struggle. Shortly before these students arrived in Mississippi in June, Klansmen abducted three civil rights workers, two northern whites and one southern black, and secretly killed all three, disposing of their bodies in the soil of a newly made dam. The abduction and disappearance of civil rights workers was a distressingly familiar event in the South, but the presence of northern whites among the ranks of southern terror victims was a new development. It attracted national attention and a vigorous FBI investigation that uncovered the crime and the bodies of the victims, and led to the arrest of twenty-one alleged perpetrators, including the sheriff and deputy sheriff of Neshoba County. The FBI's swift action might have been taken as a hopeful sign of the federal government's determination to punish segregationists who broke the law. But many blacks believed that only the presence of whites among the victims had triggered this rapid response.[31]

These and related events deepened the anger of civil rights workers in Mississippi. Still they plunged ahead, registering blacks to vote. When these new voters were barred from participating in the lily-white Mississippi Democratic Party primary, they formed a new, avowedly interracial party, the Mississippi Freedom Democratic Party (MFDP). Sixty-eight delegates from the MFDP appeared at the Democratic Party Convention in Atlantic City in August 1964, demanding to be recognized by the credentials committee as the true representatives of Mississippi voters and to be seated in place of the state's official delegation.

Even as the civil rights workers were losing their faith in civic nationalism, they still allowed themselves to hope—such was the power of the American Creed during the Cold War era—that American democracy would work for them. But, by summer 1964, they had been through too much to participate in the normal political game of give-and-take and of compromise. They needed to be affirmed, to have their simple request validated in full. Their disposition set the stage for a convention crisis.

"I QUESTION AMERICA": THE CRISIS IN ATLANTIC CITY

President Johnson was prepared to welcome the MFDP delegates as "honored guests" of the convention, even at the risk of offending Mississippi's regular (white) delegates. But the MFDP delegates rejected Johnson's offer out of hand. They had prepared a detailed and emotional case for why the convention should seat them rather than the Mississippi regulars, and they were determined to present their case to the convention's credentials committee. Their goal was either to sway the committee to their side or, at least, to gain the support of enough committee members to force the issue out of the committee and onto the convention floor.[32]

Johnson was counting on David Lawrence—chairman of the credentials committee, former Pennsylvania governor, trusted and experienced ally—to contain the MFDP challenge in the committee. But the MFDP had powerful allies, including eleven northern and western delegations that had passed resolutions of support for it.[33]

Fig. 27. Fannie Lou Hamer, 1964. The Mississippi Freedom Democratic Party delegate appears before the credentials committee at the Democratic National Convention. (Courtesy Library of Congress)

The MFDP delegates turned to Joseph Rauh Jr., the dependable liberal with strong connections to the union base of the Democratic Party, to help them make their case. And the MFDP also put before the credentials committee one of their own, Fannie Lou Hamer, a forty-six-year-old Mississippi sharecropper, to describe what happened to southern blacks who attempted to register to vote. In riveting testimony that television cameras broadcast to the entire country, Hamer recounted how she had been carried off to the county jail and assaulted. Her words still retain their power:

> I was carried to the county jail. . . . And it wasn't too long before three white men came to my cell. . . . I was carried out of the cell into another cell where they had two Negro prisoners. The state highway patrolman ordered the first Negro to take the blackjack. The first Negro prisoner ordered me, by orders from the state patrolman, for

me to lay down on the bunk bed on my face, and I laid on my face. The first Negro began to beat, and I was beat until he was exhausted . . . the state highway patrolman ordered the second Negro to take the blackjack. The second Negro began to beat and I began to work my feet, and the state highway patrolman ordered the first Negro who had beat to set on my feet and keep me from working my feet. I began to scream, and one white man got up and began to beat me on my head and tell me to "hush." One white man—my dress had worked up high—he walked over and pulled my dress down and he pulled my dress back, back up. All of this is on account we want to register, to become first-class citizens, and if the Freedom Democratic Party is not seated now, I question America.

In her speech, Hamer claimed that she wanted to be an American patriot, to embrace America's democratic ideals. But, she wondered, "is this America, the land of the free and the home of the brave . . . where we are threatened daily because we want to live as decent human beings?"[34]

Johnson was distraught that Hamer's tale was becoming the story of his convention. If a solution to the MFDP challenge was not found, and found quickly, he expected it to trigger a walkout by the white delegations of fifteen southern states, a development from which he did not think his presidential campaign or the Democratic Party could recover. Even prior to the MFDP challenge, several of the southern delegations had openly revolted against Johnson and the national party as a result of the latter's sponsorship of the Civil Rights Act. The Mississippi delegation had approved a resolution in July condemning the legislation. "We believe," the resolution declared, "that the separation of the races is necessary for the peace and tranquility of all the people of Mississippi."[35] These Mississippi Democrats saw segregation, not integration, as the American way, and they regarded a federal decree ordering southerners to integrate their institutions as unpatriotic and unconstitutional. Following the lead of George C. Wallace, Democratic governor of Alabama, who had campaigned for the Democratic presidential nomination on a segregationist platform, the

Mississippians and other southern Democrats were prepared to commit what, in other circumstances, they would have regarded as a treasonous act: voting for the Republican Barry Goldwater rather than the Democrat Johnson in the November 1964 elections. In the Senate, Goldwater had opposed the Civil Rights Act on the grounds that it interfered with states' rights and individual freedom. On August 15, 1964, as the Democrats were preparing to gather in Atlantic City, Governors Wallace, Paul B. Johnson Jr. of Mississippi, and Orval E. Faubus of Arkansas plunged a dagger into the Democrats' back by publicly announcing their support for Goldwater. Most members of their state delegations, they made clear, were ready to follow their lead.[36] It would not take much in the way of an MFDP rebellion to prompt white southern Democrats to quit the convention altogether. If that were to happen, Johnson did not think he could prevail over Goldwater in the general election.

Johnson was so dejected about this possibility that he privately contemplated withdrawing from the race. At the same time, he ordered Lawrence and Hubert Humphrey, the Minnesota Senator and likely vice-presidential nominee, to manufacture some kind of compromise that would stop the Democratic Party from disintegrating. He even hauled Walter Reuther away from important UAW contract negotiations in Detroit to assist Lawrence and Humphrey in their task. These power brokers crafted a compromise in the form of a new plan that made what they regarded as two major concessions to the MFDP. First, the convention would seat only those Mississippi regulars who promised that they would vote Democratic in the presidential election, and, second, beginning in 1968 the Democratic Party would refuse to seat any state delegation that had discriminated against registered voters on account of race. Humphrey, Reuther, and presidential aides believed that these concessions handed the MFDP a major victory.

But the Freedom Democrats did not agree. They did not trust promises made about 1968. They could not tolerate what the compromise implied: that their delegates would be completely excluded from participation in 1964. They were angered by the willingness of the national party to bow to the demands of white southerners, most of whom had already declared their intention of abandoning the Democrats in the fall. The Freedom Democrats, moreover, indicated a willingness to accept a different form of compromise, namely, that the convention agree to seat all those delegates from the ranks of the Mississippi regulars and the MFDP who pledged loyalty to the Democratic Party ticket. But this compromise, which would have resulted in a delegation dominated by the MFDP, was anathema to Johnson. He did not want to see the Mississippi delegation controlled by a group that, however impressive its moral legitimacy, had not fully complied with Democratic Party rules governing the selection of delegates. More important, the sight of a largely black convention delegation, Johnson believed, would conjure up negative images of the post–Civil War First Reconstruction when, according to a version of that era's history still popular in the white South and white North, uneducated and immoral blacks aided by venal white northerners had gained control of southern legislatures and thrown southern politics and society into turmoil. In an emotional phone discussion with Walter Reuther two nights after Hamer's televised testimony, Johnson declared that the "Northerners are [even] more upset about this [the MFDP's demands]. They call me and wire me, Walter . . . that the Negroes have taken over the country. They're running the White House. They're running the Democratic party." What blacks "don't understand," Johnson continued, is "that nearly every white man in this country would be frightened if he thought that the Negroes were gonna take him over."[37]

Johnson was hardly a reactionary white supremacist. Beginning in the 1950s with his refusal to sign the Southern Manifesto (a 1956 document condemning *Brown v. Board of Education*, signed by 100 members of the U.S. House and Senate) and climaxing in his sponsorship of the Civil Rights Act of 1964, he risked his political career to advance the cause of racial equality. The Democratic Party platform of 1964, which his supporters engineered, hailed the Civil Rights Act of that year as "the greatest civil rights measure in the history of the American people."[38] In taking such a forthright stand on civil rights and, in the process, bucking the powerful southern wing of his own party, Johnson seemed to have moved far beyond the position Theodore Roosevelt occupied in 1912. Then, the Republican Roosevelt, though troubled by his decision to exclude southern blacks from the Progressive Party convention, had done nothing either in the party platform or legislatively to promote the cause of racial equality. Measuring Johnson's behavior against Roosevelt's, it is possible to see substantial progress in the willingness of liberals to fight racism. Many commentators, at the time, saw one of the most hopeful moments in the history of American race relations in the developments of 1964. And Johnson, as we know, was hardly finished with his campaign for racial equality, for he had yet to unveil many of the antipoverty measures that would be at the heart of his "Great Society" crusade.[39]

It is possible, therefore, to understand Johnson's desire that the MFDP exhibit a little patience and to comprehend his concern that if the Democrats moved too quickly or radically on race reform, they might weaken the party's support in congressional and presidential elections for a generation or more. Indeed, as blacks lost their forbearance and escalated their militancy after 1964, the white South did abandon the Democratic Party, making it impossible for Democrats to win the White House. With the exception of Jimmy Carter, a Democrat propelled into office largely as a consequence of Nixon's Watergate follies, Johnson would be the last Democrat to win the presidency for twenty-eight years.[40]

But we can also understand MFDP impatience and anger. The Freedom Democrats had risked their lives to establish the MFDP, and they had suffered greatly simply to affirm their most basic American rights—the freedom of speech and assembly, the right to vote. They could no longer respect Americans who continued to argue that blacks should accept a subordinate position in American life, even for temporary or strategic reasons. Although they knew nothing of Johnson's outburst to Reuther on the night of August 24, they had begun to detect the limits of his and his aides' egalitarian vision. In the early—and more hopeful—stage of negotiations with the MFDP, Johnson had instructed Humphrey to impress on "the Negroes [of the MFDP] . . . that they've got the President, they'll have the Vice President [Humphrey], they've got the law, they'll have the government for four years."[41] In other words, Humphrey was to tell the MFDP militants to calm down, for Johnson and his white Democrats, if successful in the November 1964 elections, would take care of their needs.

It matters little whether Johnson's paternalism was heartfelt or strategic, meant to assist his pursuit of racial egalitarianism. In either case, we can see here his belief that most white Americans were not yet ready to accept blacks as their equals. They were not yet ready, in other words, to grant blacks the same scope of self-activity they reserved for themselves. Here was the heart of the problem that had no easy solution. Johnson had committed the Democratic Party to a political course that would undermine the legal bases of white supremacy and punish whites who continued to engage in racially prejudicial behavior. But because this program struck hard at a racial superiority that many whites, South and North, still cherished, it was politically risky and potentially suicidal. It would succeed, LBJ believed, only if its pace and strategy were managed by whites themselves. This was a condition that the MFDP could not accept, for it looked upon any effort to limit the role that blacks could play in the pursuit of racial equality as nothing more than an insidious attempt by white liberals to reinscribe, yet again, notions of black inferiority into their professed egalitarianism.

By the standards of the late 1960s, the Johnson liberals and Freedom Democrats were rather close in their views. Both groups believed in integration and in the virtue of an orderly, democratic process of political change. Both thought that America could be reformed and redeemed, and purged of its racial nationalism. Both still held that civic nationalism could triumph and, in the process, bind all Americans to a common set of egalitarian ideals. But the MFDP fight also revealed how difficult it was going to be to achieve these changes peacefully, through compromise, coalitions, and civility. The process of eliminating racism demanded of participants a degree of sacrifice, foresight, trust, and equanimity that was simply beyond the capacity of most Americans to summon up, either because they still clung to the benefits of racial privilege or because they had experienced too much racial hatred.

Thus, the "solution" to the MFDP-generated crisis was really no solution at all. When the president's men offered one more concession to the MFDP—seating two Freedom Democrats as "at-large" delegates—and threatened reprisals against those who still refused to accept the administration's compromise, virtually all members of the credentials' committee concluded that the MFDP had received its due.[42] The committee endorsed the compromise nearly unanimously, without further consultation with the MFDP. The MFDP only learned of the settlement when it was publicly announced; at the time, its leaders were closeted with Walter Reuther and Hubert Humphrey, both of whom were acting as though the assent of the MFDP still mattered. Outraged by this apparent duplicity, the Freedom Democrats were further enraged upon learning that the credentials committee had already determined which of the MFDP members would be seated as the two at-large delegates, Aaron Henry (a black) and Rev. Edwin King (a white). Many in the MFDP regarded these men as the titular heads of their organization, not their true leaders. Governor John Connally of Texas, a close associate of Johnson's, had preferred them because he saw them as relatively moderate, respectable, and therefore safe. He and Johnson worried that the MFDP would choose the "emotional" and "illiterate" Hamer as one of its delegates, giving this "lowly" sharecropper yet another opportunity to grab the convention spotlight. White paternalism was once again showing its ugly face. MFDP leader Robert Moses, known and loved among civil rights workers for his mild mannered way and moral integrity, exploded when Humphrey told him about the ban on Hamer, dashing whatever hope that Joseph Rauh and other mediators retained of winning the MFDP's consent to the deal.[43]

After the convention formally approved the compromise, about twenty MFDP members entered the convention hall and occupied seats in the Mississippi section. A scuffle broke out with convention security guards, leading to the ejection of one demonstrator. The rest were allowed to stay at the convention, but only as guests and not as official delegates.[44] Two days later, six MFDP members gained access to the convention floor, blocked an aisle and formed a circle, hands clasped, both in tribute to the murdered John F. Kennedy and in protest against not being seated.[45] But by this time the convention had moved on. Reuther rushed back to his contract negotiations in Detroit, convinced that he had put his bargaining skills to good use in Atlantic City. Shortly thereafter Johnson was acclaimed as the Democrats' presidential nominee and Humphrey as his running mate. Their easy victory over Goldwater in the November election would allow many Democrats to forget, at least for a time, the MFDP drama that had come close to derailing the entire convention.

Members of the MFDP, however, did not forget what had happened. The gulf separating them from the Democratic Party leadership was wider than ever. The party leadership looked upon the MFDP compromise as a victory for the forces of racial equality, and they congratulated themselves on how well they had handled a difficult, and potentially destructive, situation.[46] The MFDP saw things differently. "The national Democratic party's rejection of the MFDP at the 1964 convention," MFDP activist Cleveland Sellers would recall in his memoir, "was to the civil rights movement what the Civil War was to American history: afterward, things could never be the same."[47] If Sellers's rhetoric was overblown, it does accurately capture the sense of rupture felt by many MFDP stalwarts. Atlantic City was the blow that shattered the Freedom Democrats' fragile faith in the redemptive power of the American political system, in the American ideals of equality and fair play, in what activists Lawrence Guyot and Mike Thelwell called the "ultimate morality of our national political institutions and practices." Jack Minnis, director of research for SNCC and a member of the MFDP, argued that the compromise forced on the Freedom Democrats at Atlantic City revealed liberalism's "ultimate bankruptcy."[48] Not even liberals, he and others had concluded, could detach American democratic ideals from the equally powerful

American instinct to arrange peoples in a system of racial hierarchy. "Never again," declared Sellers, would SNCC activists be "lulled into believing that our task was exposing injustices so that the 'good' people of America could eliminate them."[49] Some civil rights workers, most notably Robert Moses, were so disheartened by the Atlantic City experience that they fled to Africa, hoping to find there the dignity denied blacks in America. Among those who stayed to fight, most saw no alternative but to abandon coalitions with white liberals and to reject the American Creed.

Jack Minnis chose the grim words of Frederick Douglass to communicate the new mood among SNCC militants: "What, asked Douglass," in an 1853 speech to a white audience in Rochester, New York, "is July 4th to the black American?" Douglass had answered his question in this way: "To him, your celebration is a sham: your boasted liberty, an unholy license; your national greatness, swelling vanity . . . your prayers and hymns, your sermons and thanksgivings . . . mere bombast, fraud, deception, impiety, and hypocrisy—a thin veil to cover up crimes which would disgrace a nation of savages. There is not a nation on earth guilty of practices more shocking and bloody than are the people of the United States, at this very hour." Out of the disappointment of Atlantic City black power was born.[50]

"SPEAKING AS A VICTIM OF THIS AMERICAN SYSTEM"

Black power was a political ideology calling on African Americans to free their communities and consciousness from white control. Although the term "black power" was new, the ideology itself belonged to a much older tradition of black nationalism that had emerged in the nineteenth century and that had periodically attracted large numbers of adherents since then, especially in moments of deep anger among black Americans toward whites. The conviction that America was too beholden to its racialized tradition ever to welcome blacks into the national community on terms equal to whites was the driving force behind all expressions of black nationalism. African American progress, black nationalists argued, would come not from integration into white society but from the thorough separation of the black and white races culminating in the establishment of an independent black nation. Those who embraced this project differed on the form that a black nation should take. Some had in mind a metaphorical nation, defined by culture and ethnicity; others, such as Communists in the early 1930s and the Nation of Islam and the Black Panthers of the 1960s, wanted to create a physical black nation in America, with its own territory, borders, economy, government, and army. Still others, such as the followers of Marcus Garvey, dreamed about creating a black nation in Africa that would bring together all the African peoples of the world.[51]

Support for each of these forms of black nationalism developed in the 1960s. The various streams never became a majority movement within black America, but their influence on African Americans and, indeed, on all Americans, was nevertheless immense. Between 1964 and 1968, black nationalist sentiment broke with a fury upon America, the most significant assault on the claims and integrity of the American nation since the Garvey movement of the late 1910s and early 1920s. And unlike this earlier movement, which attracted almost no support from nonblack groups before it declined in the mid-1920s, the black nationalist movement of the 1960s appealed to other racial minorities and to substantial groups of whites. Its ideological influence, as a result, was far broader than Garveyism had been and much more enduring.

The first black nationalist to achieve national prominence in the 1960s was Malcolm X. Born Malcolm Little in 1924, Malcolm had become attracted to the Nation of Islam, a religious black nationalist group, while incarcerated for burglary in the late 1940s and early 1950s. The Nation of Islam, under the leadership of Elijah Muhammad, had combined traditional Islamic teachings with some homegrown theology to produce a faith designed to meet the needs of poor urban African Americans. Muhammad preached that whites were literally devils, the descendants of an evil scientist, a Mr. Yacub, who had genetically engineered a weak but wicked white race to take revenge on the original, good, and black people of Mecca, who had cast Yacub out of their peaceful community. Over thousands of years, whites were able to assert their control over blacks and, in the process, to spread evil throughout the world. The Nation of Islam demanded that blacks do everything possible to free themselves from this evil influence. The arduousness of this struggle demanded not only the creation of autonomous black institutions and paramilitary training for defense against white violence, but living by a strict moral code (no drugs, coffee, cigarettes, alcohol, pork, sexual promiscuity, gambling, or movies; a dedication to hard and honest labor) that would instill in all Nation of Islam members discipline, dignity, and strength. The group developed a small but dedicated following among poorer, inner-city blacks who wanted to escape a once glamorous life of hustling that had lost its appeal. Few Americans knew anything about this group before the late 1950s and early 1960s. But Malcolm X possessed a razor-sharp intellect, a fearlessness among whites, and a mesmerizing speaking style. Those qualities, combined with the rising national interest in the conditions of black Americans, brought him and his movement to national attention. By the fall of 1963, one *New York Times* poll reported, Malcolm X was the second most popular speaker at American colleges and universities.[52]

What gripped and alarmed Americans who heard Malcolm X speak was the directness with which he expressed his anger at America for what it had done to his people. America had enslaved blacks, bringing them to the United States "in chains, like a horse, or a cow, or a chicken." Neither emancipation nor twentieth-century liberalism, Malcolm asserted, had changed American attitudes toward blacks. From the very beginning America had constituted itself as a white nation—the American Revolution was "white nationalism," Malcolm once asserted—and would always remain so.[53] So alien were blacks to the American idea that they would never be accepted as Americans; unlike European immigrants, the African American claim on the civic nationalist tradition would never be recognized. At a CORE-sponsored symposium in Cleveland in April 1964, Malcolm declared to his largely black audience: "Those Hunkies that just got off the boat, they're already American. Polacks are already Americans; the Italian refugees are already Americans. Everything that came out of Europe, every blue-eyed thing is already American. And as long as you and I have been over here, we aren't Americans yet." He continued:

> No, I'm not an American. I'm one of the 22 million black people who are the victims of Americanism. One of the 22 million black people who are the victims of democracy, nothing but disguised hypocrisy. So, I'm not standing here speaking to you as an American, or a patriot, or a flag-saluter, or a flag-waver—no, not I. I'm speaking as a victim of this American system. And I see America through the eyes of the victim. I don't see any American dream. I see an American nightmare.[54]

The reference to the American dream was a thinly veiled attack on the patriotic politics of Martin Luther King and other civil rights leaders. Malcolm delighted in skewering sacred nationalist myths and moments. He called the March on Washington "nothing but a circus, with clowns and all." The whole event, he claimed, had been staged by "Uncle Toms" who were only serving their white masters.[55] He mocked any dream of universal brotherhood rooted in Christianity, for the gospel of Christ was just one more manifestation of "white nationalism." He scoffed at the notion that black Americans could find any positive meaning, as King had, in the Pilgrims' story: "We didn't land on Plymouth Rock, my brothers and sisters—Plymouth Rock landed on us!"[56] And he thought absurd the idea that blacks might appeal through nonviolence, love, and good faith to some national conscience, where the Myrdalian creed allegedly resided. "America's conscience is bankrupt," he declared. "She lost all conscience a long time ago."[57]

As Malcolm X saw it, America understood only one language, the language of power and force. At a rally in Harlem to raise money for the MFDP in December 1964, Malcolm challenged his listeners to learn the language of the southern law officer who ordered Fannie Lou Hamer's beating. "If his language is with a shotgun, get a shotgun. Yes, . . . if he only understands the language of a rifle, get a rifle. If he only understands the language of a rope, get a rope. But don't waste time talking the wrong language to a man if you want to really communicate with him."[58] In the same and other speeches, Malcolm praised the Mau Mau in Kenya for being fearless "freedom fighters," willing to fight anyone, including any of their African brothers and sisters who stood in the way of Kenya's independence. No revolution, Malcolm declared, ever succeeded without bloodshed. By its very nature, he argued, "revolution is hostile, revolution knows no compromise." The Negro revolution would never succeed in America as long as it remained nonviolent.[59]

As his appearances with Fannie Lou Hamer suggest, Malcolm's itinerary increasingly intersected with that of civil rights workers in SNCC and CORE. And the willingness of these civil rights activists to listen to Malcolm and to share a podium with him reflected their readiness to jettison the commitment to nonviolence, integration, and civic nationalism that had been the hallmark of their movement. Malcolm X was gunned down in February 1965 by Nation of Islam assassins, instructed by Elijah Muhammad to eliminate a man whose popularity and discomfort with elements of Nation of Islam theology had rendered him too dangerous a rival. But those who no longer had an opportunity to hear Malcolm speak could now read his autobiography, written with the assistance of Alex Haley for a mass market and published shortly after his death, a gripping narrative that told of his revolt against America, Christianity, whites, and meek, "Uncle Tom" blacks. As the historian William L. Van Deburg has written, "following his death, Malcolm's influence expanded in dramatic, almost logarithmic, fashion. He came to be far more than a martyr for the militant, separatist faith. He became a Black Power paradigm—the archetype, reference point, and spiritual adviser in absentia for a generation of Afro-American activists."[60]

The year 1966 marked the moment in which large numbers of African American civil rights workers officially broke with their civic nationalist and nonviolent pasts. In the midst of a civil rights

march from Memphis, Tennessee, to Jackson, Mississippi, to protest the shooting of civil rights hero James Meredith—the last time
that the leaders of SCLC, SNCC, and CORE would march together—an angry Stokely Carmichael, newly elected as chairman
of SNCC, declared that the "only way we gonna stop them white
men from whuppin' us is to take over. We been saying freedom for
six years and we ain't got nothin'. What we gonna start saying now
is black power!" The audience of 600 immediately responded with
a black power roar of its own.[61] By late 1966 SNCC formally voted
to expel the remaining white members from its organization.
CORE would soon follow suit. Carmichael had chosen an image
of the black panther to represent SNCC's new militancy. Huey P.
Newton, Bobby Seale, and other young black nationalists in Oakland, California, followed his cue and formed the Black Panther
Party in 1966. With their decision to brandish guns, to guard the
streets of Oakland against incursions by threatening whites, to seek
verbal and physical confrontations with white police, whom they
disparaged as "pigs," and to adopt a dashing, militarist, and intim-
idating style of black dress, the Black Panthers quickly grabbed the
attention of the media and of a disbelieving nation. By 1969 the
Panthers boasted thirty chapters in urban areas throughout the
North and West.[62]

The number of blacks who belonged to the Black Panthers,
SNCC, CORE, Nation of Islam, and other black nationalist organizations was not that large, probably never exceeding 50,000. But
they formed an articulate vanguard, their stature enhanced by a
national television media corps that could not resist showcasing
them in news broadcasts and documentaries. Even more important, these organizations possessed indirect but powerful links
to tens and perhaps hundreds of thousands of poor and restive
blacks living in impoverished and isolated ghettos in northern and
western cities. Already in 1962 and 1963, Malcolm X, who probably understood the circumstances of poor black life in the North
as well as any other black leader of the time, was predicting that
the urban ghettos were on the verge of explosion. The civil rights
movement had raised black expectations without delivering mean-

ingful change. Young blacks in particular, who, according to Malcolm, had seen "the hell caught by their parents" who were unable to get anywhere in "the prejudiced, intolerant white man's world," began to burn with anger and impatience. Influenced by the ghetto hustler, whose sharp dress, street smarts, easy money, access to women and guns, amorality, and utter fearlessness represented an alluring alternative path to success, young urban blacks, Malcolm believed, were not likely to stage protests demonstrating the patience, nonviolence, and moral scrupulousness of their southern counterparts.[63] Malcolm was right, in his predictions both that the ghettos would erupt and that the eruptions would be violent. The urban black revolt that began in New York in 1964 and Los Angeles in 1965 spread by 1968 to Detroit, Newark, Washington, D.C., Chicago, and many other American cities. These uprisings featured violent confrontations between blacks and the police, the torching of buildings and the looting of stores, and assaults on countless innocent individuals, black and white. By the time the revolt had ended, hundreds of Americans had died, thousands had been wounded, hundreds of millions of dollars in property had been destroyed, and large stretches of urban America had become wasteland.[64]

This massive urban rebellion became an important factor in further radicalizing civil rights activists, inclining them to dispense with their remaining pieties about nonviolence, to embrace a fiery language of protest and confrontation, and to arm themselves for revolution. Increasingly, they imagined themselves to be Third World revolutionaries, fighting to free the ghettos, which they now labeled "internal colonies," much as Africans and Asians were fighting to liberate their peoples from imperial rule. They attacked America as an empire built on the exploitation of nonwhite labor, and they saw the revolt of the black poor as similar to the uprising of the Viet Cong in Vietnam: both groups were straining to throw off the imperialist American yoke and to declare themselves free. They discarded the civic nationalist pantheon, featuring Lincoln, the Pilgrims, Washington, and others who had fired the imagination of Martin Luther King Jr., and constructed a new one from the figures of Mao Zedong, Ho Chi Minh, Che Guevara, the Mau Mau of Kenya, and like-minded Third World leaders who had led armed struggles against imperial or capitalist tyrants. They turned their back on the nonviolence of Gandhi, finding a more relevant inspiration in the fervent antiwhite writings of Frantz Fanon, an anticolonial psychiatrist from Martinique who found his vocation in the struggle of Algerian revolutionaries against France. Fanon's 1961 book, *The Wretched of the Earth*, which focused on the psychological damage done by imperial rulers to colonized peoples and on the imperatives of militant struggles for national and personal liberation, was translated into English in 1965. By 1970 it had sold a remarkable 750,000 copies.[65] Concerning the United States, Fanon had written: "Two centuries ago, a former European colony decided to catch up with Europe. It succeeded so well that the United States of America became a monster, in which the taints, the sickness and the inhumanity of Europe have grown to appalling dimensions." These words were quoted in Stokely Carmichael and Charles Hamilton's 1967 manifesto, *Black Power*, revealing how deeply Fanon's anti-Americanism had already sunk its roots into American soil.[66]

Urban black youths, in turn, recognized an identity between themselves and organizations in the black nationalist vanguard. While relatively few joined the latter, many admired the Panthers and other groups for their declarations that there could be no easy coexistence between whites and blacks, for their determination to confront the police (the most visible and despised symbol of the white power structure in poor black communities), and for their willingness to use virtually any tactic to protect black lives, autonomy, and power. The Panthers, too, exploited black youth's fascination with the hustler, demonstrating audacity, a contempt for rules governing civic order, an eagerness for action, and a hip language drawn from "the street." Meanwhile, much of white America looked on in horror.[67]

The combination of black nationalist agitation and ghetto unrest gave rise to a variety of black power–sponsored initiatives that unsettled race relations in virtually every major institution in American society. On university campuses across the country, groups of black students, increasingly organized in black student unions, began demanding that administrations admit more black students, appoint more black faculty, inaugurate black studies programs, and establish separate black dormitories and eating facilities. Administration resistance often led to sit-ins, takeover of university facilities, and, sometimes, as in the cases of San Francisco State College, University of Wisconsin at Oshkosh, and Cornell University, violent confrontations. In northern and western urban school districts, groups of black parents armed with the slogan "community control" sought to wrest command of their children's schools away from a "white power structure" consisting of the central school administration and white-dominated teachers' unions that, they alleged, were doing more to oppress than to educate their children. In New York City in 1968, one such group took over the Ocean Hill–Brownsville district in Brooklyn and ousted nineteen white teachers without due process. This act, in turn, prompted an infuriated United Federation of Teachers to call out more than 50,000 teachers in three strikes that shut down the city's schools for more than two months and set the city on racial edge.[68]

In union strongholds such as Detroit, meanwhile, black militants formed "revolutionary union movements" to fight battles against white bosses and white unions. Black nationalist groups appeared both in the military and in jails in the late 1960s, determined to address the grievances of black soldiers and prisoners and to expose the racism on which the white power system rested.[69] Black nationalism even invaded sports, where black athletes were becoming a steadily more important part of baseball, basketball, football, and track-and-field teams at a time when the industry was becoming one of America's biggest businesses. A stunning black power protest materialized at the 1968 summer Olympics in Mexico City, when two victorious African American sprinters, Tommie Smith and John Carlos, mounted the awards platform wearing black, knee-length stockings in place of shoes and a black glove on one hand. Their shoelessness, they later explained, was meant to express their solidarity with America's black poor, abandoned in the ghettos. When the band struck up the national anthem, Smith and Carlos bowed their heads and raised their black gloved fists in a black power salute. Television cameras beamed this angry rejection of America by two of its own to a world audience of millions.[70]

Millions of white Americans were shocked by this blasphemous act, even though they had already been staggered the same year by repeated blows to their nation's prestige and morale. The year began with the surprise Tet Offensive, during which Vietcong and North Vietnamese troops fought their way into the heart of Saigon and other American redoubts before being turned back. It continued with Lyndon Johnson's pained announcement that he would not run for reelection because his administration had so seriously mismanaged the war. In April, Martin Luther King Jr. was assassinated in Memphis, sparking days of furious black protest and violence in America's major urban centers. In June, Robert F. Kennedy, the man to whom many Americans had turned in the wake of King's death as offering the best hope for racial reconciliation, was himself gunned down after winning the California Democratic primary. In August, thousands of antiwar protesters gathered in Chicago to disrupt the Democratic National Convention; their nighttime battles with phalanxes of Chicago cops were broadcast on network television, upstaging the Democrats gathered in convention to nominate Hubert Humphrey for president. In September, the Ocean Hill–Brownsville confrontation had erupted in New York City. To many Americans it seemed as though their nation was unraveling strand by strand.[71]

The Olympic protests deepened their anger and gloom. Since 1936, when Hitler had used "The Games" to such brilliant propagandistic effect, nations had seized upon the Olympics to showcase national prowess, power, and unity. The Cold War had only intensified this tendency, as the United States and the Soviet Union used the Olympic contests to square off against each other in a metaphorical war, giving their populations nightly tallies of battles won and lost, as though the medals race were just another version of the arms race. American victory in the summer games depended on the success of its predominately black track-and-field team, for

Fig. 28. Black Power Protest at the Olympics, 1968. Gold-medalist Tommie Smith (center) and bronze-medalist John Carlos (right) issue their black power protest during the playing of the "Star Spangled Banner" at the Olympic Games in Mexico City. Their heads are bowed, the black-clenched fists raised, their feet clothed only in black socks. The silver medalist, Australian Peter Norman, is at left. (Courtesy AP/Wide World Photos)

no other country, not even the Soviet Union, could match the swiftness of the American runners; in no other area of competition, with
the possible exception of swimming, could the Americans ring up
such an abundance of victories and medals. All members of the
Olympic team were expected to battle hard for their country and to
honor their flag. Thus America was shocked when its finest athletes
dissociated their personal victories from the nation's triumph and,
in the process, seemed to repudiate the American nation.

In addition to their radical political challenge, black nationalists
put forward a radically new attitude toward black culture and history. Mobilizing behind the magnetic phrase "black is beautiful,"
black nationalists undertook a systematic campaign to eliminate
the shame that, they alleged, had long shaped blacks' attitudes toward their physical appearance, culture, and heritage. Black nationalists viewed this shame as a product of black subservience to
white society and culture, arguing that blacks had to bend every
muscle to free themselves and their psyches from white control.
Freedom involved eliminating every aspect of white influence. It
meant rejecting the name "Negro," a word selected for them by
whites, and substituting for it ones—"black," "Afro-American"—
of their own choosing. It meant dispensing with the "conk" and
other hairstyles meant to emulate those of whites and proudly dis-
playing their natural, "nappy," hair; by the end of the 1960s, many
blacks measured their radical status by the radius of their "Afros."
Other blacks began shaving their heads in emulation of particular
African tribes, such as the Masai. For many, too, freedom entailed
repudiating their Christian names, which, in their eyes, were a constant reminder of how their ancestors had been ripped from their
African roots and forced to submit to slavemaster customs, mores,
and language. In an interesting reversal of 1930s naming practices,
when radicals had been eager to hide their ethnic identities by
adopting Anglo-Saxon names, one black militant after another
sought to celebrate his or her "foreignness" by choosing African
and Islamic appellations. Thus, the boxer Cassius Clay became
Muhammad Ali and the basketball player Lew Alcindor became
Kareem Abdul Jabbar; the writer LeRoi Jones became Amiri

Fig. 29. Angela Davis, c. 1970. A leading black power militant of the late 1960s and 1970s. Place and date of the rally at which Davis is speaking are not known. Note her Afro hairstyle (and its size), a measure of the cultural radicalization of black activists that had been occurring since the 1964 Democratic Party convention. Compare Davis's hair with that of Fannie Lou Hamer on p. 287. (Courtesy Library of Congress)

Baraka, while Stokely Carmichael took the name Kwame Toure, after the names of his two African mentors, Kwame Nkrumah of Ghana and Ahmed Sekou Toure of Guinea. A few groups, too, rejected Christianity altogether for its complicity in black enslavement and then of white supremacy. This was most obvious among the members of the Nation of Islam, but by the mid-1960s, it also became a defining characteristic of a new black nationalist organization, United Slaves (US), based in southern California and headed by Maulana Ron Karenga. Karenga's followers were the first to wear dashikis in place of American or African American clothing; and they invented a new holiday, Kwanzaa, modeled on harvest-time festivals of African agriculturalists, to be celebrated from December 26 to January 1 each year in place of the newly despised Christmas. Members of Karenga's group, like other black nationalist ones, became ardent students of African history, searching for an authentic and proud past on which Afro-Americans might build a new future. In place of the civic nationalist consciousness that had so dominated the early stages of the civil rights movement, they substituted an Afrocentric and diasporic one.[72]

This celebration of Africa and, more generally, of blackness, carried within it the danger of imputing to blacks a "natural," even "racial," superiority over whites. This tendency had congealed in Nation of Islam theology, in which whites were depicted as evil and blacks as gentle and kind. It sometimes manifested itself, too, in secular efforts to impute to African Americans or Africans more generally a unique and inborn culture ("soul") that was quintessentially black and inaccessible to whites. In these ways, black nationalism had very little to do with Africa itself; instead, it was very much the offspring of America's own tradition of white racial nationalism, unwittingly mimicking that tradition's insistence on judging individuals by the characteristics of their "race." The cultural radicalism of the black nationalists further widened the chasm separating them from mainstream white America and deepened the fear they inspired.

As much as we might wish that the outcome of the 1960s civil rights struggles had been more peaceful and optimistic, it is hard to know how that could have happened. The fight over the MFDP at the 1964 Democratic Party Convention revealed how difficult it was, even for two well-intentioned groups, Lyndon Johnson's liberals and Fannie Hamer's Freedom Democrats, to find common ground. Achieving racial equality meant destroying the racialized tradition of American nationalism in law and in consciousness. It meant punishing the white South, a large population that had long (and legally) lived by its precepts. It entailed forcing whites throughout the country to relinquish their own, often unrecognized, adherence to aspects of the racial nationalist tradition. President Johnson had unintentionally revealed his belief in the prevalence of this tradition when he told Walter Reuther how dangerous it would be if, as a result of civil rights struggles, the white man began to feel "that the Negroes were gonna take him over." Many whites, North and South, could not imagine an America in which blacks were truly their equals, in which they granted blacks the same aspirations and opportunities that they reserved for themselves. The tradition of racial nationalism simply ran too deep. That was the central conviction that impelled many blacks and their white sympathizers to denounce the American nation and to jettison their patriotic sentiments.

By the late 1960s, law enforcement authorities in the United States were doing everything in their power to defeat or undermine black power organizations. Urban police forces monitored Black Panther chapters in their areas, looking for opportunities to provoke armed conflicts with them. By the early 1970s, a sizable number of Black Panthers had been killed or jailed, and their movement broken up. In 1967, FBI head J. Edgar Hoover ordered COINTELPRO, a federal counterintelligence program, to intensify efforts to monitor, disrupt, and neutralize activities of all "black nationalist, hate-type organizations and groupings," including SNCC, CORE, and the Nation of Islam.[73] Federal agents infiltrated these organizations, reporting to their superiors on group members and activities, fomenting internal discord, and in other ways seeking to undermine these organizations from within. Meanwhile, more and more white Americans turned to politicians, mostly Republican, running campaigns to restore "law and order" to America's streets and to rehabilitate American national pride. The promise of "law and order" was a crucial element in Richard Nixon's triumph in the 1968 election. By the spring of 1969, black nationalist organizations were on the defensive and in decline.[74]

But, as we shall see, these organizations had lasted long enough and aroused enough support beyond the black community itself to open fatal fissures in the Rooseveltian nation. Any reckoning with their influence on American politics and culture, however, must first take into account the damage done to the Rooseveltian nation by another set of events—a war in Vietnam and a movement that arose to oppose it.

CHAPTER 8

Vietnam, Cultural Revolt,
and the Collapse of the
Rooseveltian Nation,
1968–1975

From Theodore Roosevelt's charge up San Juan Hill to the celebration of the multiethnic World War II platoon, war figured centrally in the rise and triumph of the Rooseveltian nation. Wars gave the nation opportunities to rally its people against external enemies and internal threats. They were occasions for drawing firm boundaries around the national community and for intensifying popular devotion to its most cherished ideals. They spawned campaigns to turn immigrants into Americans and political radicals into outcasts. They legitimated the idea of a strong state authorized to dispense social justice and to discipline those who were perceived to be its enemies. The Rooseveltian nation is scarcely imaginable apart from them. But in Vietnam, this nation encountered a war it couldn't master. As military victory proved elusive, and explanations for America's failure proved evasive, questions about why we were there fueled a huge antiwar movement. By 1968 and 1969 partisans of this antiwar movement were challenging not only the rationale for the war but the moral integrity of the American state and the American nation. The antiwar movement, as a result, speeded the collapse of the Rooseveltian nation.

The antiwar movement incubated among groups, black and white, whose disillusionment with civil rights inclined them to view America's Vietnam policy with suspicion. These protesters tended to see the persistence of racial inequality at home and the war against Vietnamese Communists abroad as two faces of the same problem—the corruption of American ideals and the repressive character of the American state. In truth, the crises in race relations and in Vietnam arose from quite distinct sources, for the first turned on race and the second on the geopolitics of the Cold War. But there can be no doubt that their convergence magnified the import of the black nationalist turn in American politics and culture, spreading anti-American attitudes to far larger segments of the population. If by 1968 and 1969 black power sympathizers numbered in the hundreds of thousands, antiwar supporters numbered in the millions. And many among these millions had come to view America as an oppressive society that systematically undercut the civic nationalist ideals to which it was ostensibly dedicated.

The spread of black nationalist influence can also be discerned in a gathering revolt against the cultural practices of the American mainstream. This revolt took many forms, but one of its most important was the declaration that one's particularist culture—black, Hispanic, Native American, Jewish, Italian—was a more authentic and satisfying identity than "American culture," usually defined as white, Anglo-Saxon, and middle class. This is what black nationalists were asserting when they declared that "black is beautiful." Their example was quickly emulated by a variety of other groups, including those, such as white ethnics, usually regarded as black nationalism's diehard foes. Some of the individuals in these groups shared the black nationalists' radical political views while others did not; but all hastened the decline of the Rooseveltian nation by insisting that Americans had to respect the competing, even superior, claims of ethnicity and race. Under the strain of racial antagonism, antiwar protest, and cultural revolt, the prestige and authority of the nation that Theodore Roosevelt had labored so hard to create collapsed.

A CATASTROPHIC WAR

America's involvement in Vietnam began as an effort, in the late 1940s and early 1950s, to restore France's crumbling Indochinese empire. That empire had been overrun by Japanese forces in World War II. As France sought to reestablish imperial rule after the war, its forces encountered stiff resistance from independence movements that had arisen among the region's colonized peoples. In Vietnam, the struggle for independence was led by the Vietminh, an indigenous and pro-Communist nationalist movement. As fighting between the Vietminh and French forces escalated, the United States bolstered the latter with matériel, money, and advice. When a key French garrison was overrun in 1954, prompting France to give up the fight, the United States expanded its role in Vietnam, hoping to prevent the victorious Vietminh from extending Communist control throughout the country. The United States helped to establish a non-Communist government in South Vietnam in 1954 and endorsed its refusal to participate in 1956 free elections that, by the terms of the treaty signed by the French and the Vietminh in 1954, would have reunified South and North Vietnam under one government. Whether that government was to be Communist or not was to be determined by the votes of the Vietnamese people themselves. By violating the treaty, South Vietnam opened itself to military attacks from Communists living within the South (who would become known as the Vietcong) and their supporters in the North. The United States, meanwhile, undertook to insure the survival of the non-Communist South Vietnamese regime and country.[1]

The U.S. commitment to Vietnam cannot be understood by reference to Vietnam alone, for it was a country of too little economic and geopolitical consequence to occupy a large place in the thinking of American policy makers. What did worry policy makers was the "domino theory," which held that if one country in East Asia fell to the Communists, the rest would fall as well. Ultimately, of course, this would entail the loss of Japan, on which the United States pinned its hopes of building a "free" Asia, full of market societies ruled by democratic governments open to Western influence. Credibility mattered to policy makers, too, in the sense that the Soviet Union, viewed as the mastermind of an international Communist conspiracy, had to be convinced that America would fight anywhere to protect the freedoms it cherished. Vietnam, in this scenario, became a test of America's anti-Communist resolve. And anticommunism, of course, undergirded American national identity. To be an American in the 1950s and 1960s meant to be against communism. Thus a war against the communists strengthened the values and purposes Americans were thought to cherish most deeply.[2]

America's slowly escalating presence in Vietnam in the late 1950s and early 1960s drew little public criticism or comment, in part because the threat of communism was thought to be so great and deserving of a tough American response, and in part because few Americans doubted that their country, with its economic and military power, would prevail as long as its resolve remained strong. Thus America allowed itself to be drawn into a war against the Vietcong and North Vietnamese without ever formally declaring war on them and without a frank, public discussion of their skills and resources, the likelihood of victory, and the costs of waging war. American policy makers, moreover, never adequately grappled with the inadequacy of their South Vietnamese allies: none of the South Vietnamese governments of the 1950s and 1960s enjoyed broad support from the Vietnamese people, demonstrated a commitment to democratic rule, or showed themselves capable of building an effective army.[3]

The toughest decisions about the war fell to Lyndon Johnson soon after he assumed office in 1963, as the Vietcong were turning the countryside against the South Vietnamese government in Saigon. Johnson tried to manage the war on the side, so to speak, keeping American costs in lives and money low enough so as not to arouse public ire or sidetrack him from his favored Great Society programs. When the situation in Vietnam deteriorated further in 1965, and Johnson rushed tens of thousands of American troops to South Vietnam while launching an all-out bombing campaign against the North, his administration began to dissemble in order to obscure the extent of American involvement and the uncertainty of the results. The hope was that American military forces would somehow right the situation before too much had gone awry. These strategies turned out to be the worst miscalculations of Johnson's distinguished political career, and they would cost him the presidency, a position he had striven his whole life to attain.[4]

Questions about the war had arisen first among small groups of pacifists, who, on principle, opposed all military engagements. But the questioning became far more politically threatening once it spread to angry, disillusioned veterans of the civil rights struggles. Conditioned by their bitter experience in voter registration and desegregation campaigns to challenge America's claims to stand for freedom and democracy, they began to dispute the notion that America was striving to achieve those ideals in Vietnam. Already in 1965, SNCC voiced its opposition to American involvement in Vietnam, declaring that it represented another instance of imperial, white America seeking to impose its will on a colored race, in this case the Vietnamese.[5]

By 1965 white Americans, too, were opposing the war. These individuals tended to be university students from the North, some of them the children of Old Leftists, who, in 1963 and 1964, had joined the civil rights movement. Freedom Summer had been a turning point for them, as it had been for SNCC, and the intransigent racism they learned about from those who had gone to Mississippi pushed them toward harsher critiques of American society and more radical programs of change. Focused on the gap separating American political ideals from actual practices, and influenced by SNCC, whose members they admired, these white students began to scrutinize U.S. policy in Vietnam. When encounters with representatives of the U.S. government in university settings and other forums failed to give these students convincing explanations for American involvement in this war, they turned harshly against them. At the same time, the students began ferreting out and publicizing facts about the war that the government had attempted to hide: high levels of corruption in the South Vietnamese government and military; extensive support enjoyed by the Vietcong among the Vietnamese peasantry; the inability of the American military to flush out Vietcong soldiers from the jungles and civilian populations that gave them cover, and the consequent turn to ever more desperate and damaging military techniques—napalming of foliage, destruction of villages, killing of civilians, bombing of civilian targets in North Vietnam, torture.[6]

Coalescing in a self-styled New Left, white university students made a crusade out of their opposition to Vietnam and helped to build a massive antiwar movement. By 1968 and 1969 the numbers of Americans who counted themselves part of this movement had reached the hundreds of thousands, even millions. Not all who became involved in this movement were radical. Many were more simply self-interested, not wanting to fight, and perhaps sacrifice their lives, for a war whose purpose and legitimacy seemed increasingly obscure. But they wanted America out of Vietnam. A military draft that made all young American males vulnerable to conscription and service in Vietnam dramatically increased the urgency and scale of the protests.[7]

The United States had not witnessed an antiwar protest of this magnitude since World War I. By 1968 and 1969, this protest had gone beyond attacks on bad leaders and their ill-conceived policies. It critiqued, too, the reflexive anticommunism of American politics that had produced such a deep involvement in so unthinking a way, and raised questions about the virtue of a nation that had invested so much of its "self" in the fight against communism. If that fight was flawed, then, so too was the nation that stood behind it. In rapidly increasing numbers, antiwar protesters turned with fury on the proposition that "America" was a special nation, destined to spread civic ideals throughout the world. Many of these protesters had themselves been great believers in the American dream, the children of the intensely nationalistic Cold War era. Now some were burning draft cards and American flags. In the ferocity of their denunciations of America, we can discern their pained conviction that they had been betrayed.[8]

The attack on American ambitions in Vietnam was, at every turn, informed by the attack on treatment of African Americans at home. The antiwar radicals viewed the efforts of the American military to prevent the "yellow" Vietcong and other Vietnamese from determining their own future as an extension of American efforts at home to deny African Americans their freedom. In the United States and abroad, New Leftists argued, America was a brutish empire built on white racial domination. Like the black nationalists, they became enamored of Third World revolutionaries and armed struggle. In the process of turning against America, antiwar protesters transformed many universities, designed in post–World War II America to train a technocratic cadre that would preserve America's Cold War and international supremacy, into institutions of nationalist "demobilization." They demanded that universities sever ties to all projects, public and private, that contributed to the Cold War and other imperial projects. They fought as well, with considerable success, to control the intellectual content of their curriculum and to imbue it with their radical perspectives on matters of war, race, and oppression. When university administrations resisted, radical students at a number of universities, such as Columbia, Harvard, and the University of Wisconsin, occupied university buildings, vowing to stay until their demands were met. University administrators, in turn, called in the police, triggering physical confrontations with the protesters and hardening their radical resolve. More and more students were beginning to graduate from these institutions, if they graduated at all, less patriotic and less willing to serve their country than they had been when they arrived.[9]

The implications of this university transformation were far-reaching, for it occurred in institutions of enormous intellectual and strategic importance. The New Left was strongest in elite universities; its members were disproportionately drawn from the ranks of the more affluent sectors of American society, giving them a shared class experience with their principal antagonists, the university administrators and other sectors of the liberal establishment.[10] Thus, it is not entirely surprising that by the late 1960s and early 1970s, the New Left had won over a portion of the liberal establishment to its point of view. A liberal antiwar movement emerged in 1968, led by Eugene McCarthy, Democratic senator from Minnesota, who stunned the Democratic Party establishment by almost defeating Lyndon Johnson in the Democratic primary in New Hampshire. Less than two months later, Johnson announced he would not run again for president. On October 15, 1969, an estimated 1 million people, not only students but also liberal Democrats, trade unionists, clergy, and even veterans, took part in a day of protest against the Vietnam War. A month later, a half million protesters converged on Washington to press their antiwar demands on the government, making it the largest demonstration ever to assemble in the nation's capital.[11]

As the war effort was losing support at home, it was also disintegrating within the ranks of the military itself. By the late 1960s, millions sought to evade military service through the procurement of draft deferments, draft dodging, or desertion. A staggering 20 percent refused induction or deserted soon after reaching training camps.[12] A total of 65,643 soldiers—the equivalent of four infantry divisions—deserted the army in 1970 alone.[13] Legal forms of escaping military service proved far easier for well-connected groups of affluent Americans to attain, meaning that working-class Americans, black and white, bore the brunt of the fighting and dying. Within military ranks, tensions between enlisted men and their officers ran high. Morale was especially problematic among army infantrymen whose job it was to fight an enemy that they often

Fig. 30. Protesting the Vietnam War, 1969. This antiwar march on Washington, the largest demonstration ever to assemble in the nation's capital, brought together student radicals with mainstream groups, such as unions and religious organizations. That some marchers still considered themselves patriots is evident in the American flag unfurled on the left. But the flag of the National Liberation Front (Vietcong) dominates the foreground of this photo, revealing the anti-Americanism of the more radical marchers. (Courtesy Corbis)

Fig. 31. Vietnam Vets against the War, 1971. The long hair, headbands, and counter-cultural dress of many of these veterans constitute one measure of their disaffection with the military. (Courtesy Library of Congress)

could not see or distinguish from ordinary, noncombatant Vietnamese. Frequently their missions lacked clear objectives, such as when "grunts," or infantrymen, "humped the boonies," patrolling territory aimlessly in the hope that they could draw enemy fire and thus expose concentrations of enemy troops. As tactics such as this failed to deliver positive results and the war's unpopularity at home increased, soldiers lost the vital assurance that, however difficult or confusing their task, the American people stood behind them.[14] This deteriorating situation prompted one military historian to declare in 1971 that the "morale, discipline and battleworthiness of the U.S. Armed Forces are . . . lower and worse than at any time in this century and possibly in the history of the United States."[15]

Military policies compounded the problems caused by the nature of this guerrilla war. The cohesion of platoons and companies, still regarded as the primary combat groups, was hurt by the military's policy of removing from combat units every soldier who had served twelve months. As a result, the units that depended most for their success on a sense of solidarity and personal attachment were constantly losing their veterans and having to assimilate new men.[16] Even more problematic may have been the policy of having officers serve only six months in combat units, a rule that only deepened the anger of enlisted men toward an officer corps they regarded as bloated, pampered and unwilling to share the dangers that they endured daily. The rate at which enlisted men killed their officers in the field, acts usually referred to as "fraggings," soared well beyond that experienced by American forces in any previous war, as did reports of men refusing to fight. Approximately 100 fraggings occurred in 1969 and more than double that number in 1970.[17] One underground newspaper circulating on a military base in the United States told its readers that in "Vietnam, the Lifers, the Brass, are the true Enemy, not the [Vietcong]."[18] Given these attitudes, it is not surprising that increasing numbers of GIs refused to follow their officers into battle. As one American soldier from Cu Chi told a reporter in 1970: "It is no big thing to refuse to go [into the field]. If a man is ordered to go . . . he no longer goes through the hassle of refusing; he just packs his shirt and goes to visit some buddies at another base camp." Sometimes entire units would refuse to fight or to follow their officers down a dangerous jungle path; more subtly, GIs altered numerous "search and destroy [the enemy]" missions into "search and evade" ones.[19]

A 1972 congressional investigation revealed yet another dimension of the collapse in discipline: a majority of GIs in Vietnam were smoking marijuana and more than a quarter had used a hard narcotic, such as heroin, in the previous twelve months. Eliminating the drug problem, moreover, seemed impossible, given that high officials in the South Vietnamese government as well as various groups in the CIA were thought to be deeply involved in the drug trafficking.[20] The discovery, in 1970, that an Air Force major who served as a pilot for the American ambassador to Vietnam had concealed $8 million of heroin in his aircraft revealed how deeply the drug trade had penetrated military ranks.[21]

Not all the news from the military was bad. In conventional battles between U.S. troops and North Vietnamese regulars, American
troops performed well. This became especially apparent in the
1968 Tet offensive when, after the Communists' shocking initial
advances into a variety of South Vietnamese cities, American
troops had pushed them back while inflicting devastating losses
upon them. Good news arose, too, from the success of the military,
and the army and the Marines in particular, in integrating African
Americans into combat units. By 1972, the percentage of blacks in
the army and the Marines exceeded their proportion of the U.S.
population. Moreover, a greater percentage of black military personnel than white served in combat units, reversing what had been
a seventy-five-year-long pattern of excluding blacks from actual
fighting roles. Of course, these developments occurred in a context
of the white middle class's determination to avoid military service
of any sort, and in the context of an increasingly white-collar military, in which technical, noncombat roles were proliferating and
being filled disproportionately by whites. Still, within the military's
upper command echelons, combat service maintained its prestige
and blacks' ability to secure their "right to fight" constituted an
important step forward.[22]

That some blacks saw the situation in this way is evident in the
large numbers who rose into the noncommissioned officer (NCO)
ranks. In the army, by 1972, nearly one out of every four staff
sergeants was black. Elevation to these ranks usually required more
than one term of service; that blacks were disproportionately represented in them suggests that many were serving longer than whites.
Indeed, they were, as reenlistment rates for blacks consistently exceeded those of whites. A large presence in NCO ranks meant, of
course, that some blacks were commanding white troops, a development that indicated another important advance. It seems significant, too, that very few of the military's morale problems seem to
have been associated with white troops refusing to obey their black
sergeants. More generally, black and white grunts seem to have
gotten along quite well in the field. "You couldn't think just white
or just black," wrote the black veteran Stan Goff in 1982; "you

Fig. 32. Beyond the Euro-American Platoon, c. 1970. In Vietnam, whites and blacks fought alongside each other in integrated platoons, destroying for all time Theodore Roosevelt's dream of war as the crucible for forging a superior, white race. The break with the military's rigid policy of segregation had begun in the Korean War but was thoroughly implemented in Vietnam. (Courtesy Library of Congress)

had to think for everybody. That was one of the things the war did for me." His buddy Bob Sanders, though more receptive to a black nationalist perspective, likewise declared that black and white soldiers, when "out in the field . . . were just a force of unity and harmony. We became just one person. When I first got to Nam, I saw a lot of prejudice and shit like that. But Charlie the enemy had a tendency to make you unify in a hurry."[23]

But these advances in race relations were difficult to celebrate in the late 1960s and early 1970s, a time when the failures of the military, in regard to both the enemy and to self-discipline, reached such alarming proportions. Black enlisted men themselves, during this period, lost confidence in the aims of the war. Between 1966 and 1970, first-term reenlistment rates among them plummeted from 40 to 13 percent in the army and from 16 to 5 percent in the

Marines.[24] Many black GIs became no more willing than their white counterparts to risk their lives for a war that seemed to have no purpose. Increasingly, too, they interpreted any evidence that black troops were being exposed to combat at a rate greater than that of whites as a sign of racial discrimination rather than of egalitarian advance. Many also believed that they were promoted at a slower rate and awarded fewer medals than whites. They reacted with anger to southern white troops who flew confederate flags over their encampments and who occasionally terrorized black troops with Ku Klux Klan–style "cross burnings."[25]

Amid this growing atmosphere of racial hostility, black power attitudes spread like wildfire through the ranks of African American troops. Off duty, black enlisted men rigidly separated themselves from whites; they developed black power styles of dress (Afros, black berets, the wearing of "slave" bracelets), flags, handshakes, language, and salutes. One 1970 survey found that almost two-thirds of black GIs and a sizable proportion of black officers regularly used the clenched-fist black power salute—rather than an approved military salute—in greeting and recognizing each other. That same survey found that black GIs in Vietnam gave the most radical black leaders at home—Eldridge Cleaver, Malcolm X, and Muhammad Ali—approval ratings reaching and exceeding 70 percent. Black enlisted men, too, became increasingly defiant of military authority, sometimes spectacularly so, as when one small group attempted to assassinate a black Marine sergeant whom they despised and, on another occasion, when 200 black military prisoners in Vietnam, in white kerchiefs and African-styled robes, demolished the Long Binh stockade in which they were kept, killing one inmate and injuring scores of others. More common were more mundane and less lethal challenges to military authority—violating military dress and salute protocols, disobeying orders, and skirmishing with white troops—which, nevertheless, landed a far greater proportion of blacks than whites in stockades awaiting military trial. Such behaviors revealed the disdain with which large numbers of black GIs regarded the American military and the cause for which America was fighting in Vietnam. Several astute observers had come, by the early 1970s, to regard racial division and the spread of black power consciousness in the ranks as the military's gravest problem.[26]

Precisely how much black power consciousness among African American troops was generated by the deterioration of the war effort in Vietnam itself and how much by the embittered turn of race relations in the United States is difficult to determine. But rather than try to pin down the share contributed by each development, it may make more sense to emphasize the degree to which the front lines and the rear lines were interpenetrating each other, and how easily ideas traveled back and forth between them. The military's rotation policies, if anything, accelerated this interpenetration. Fresh soldiers from the States were constantly arriving with news about racial tensions in the ghettos and on domestic military bases, while returning black veterans brought home tales of declining morale, discipline, and combat efficacy in Vietnam. Many returning veterans also brought with them a far greater familiarity with drugs and violence than they had known before they had left. Several observers of the time observed that a large number of Black Panthers were ex-GIs.

This constant circulation of servicemen between the home front and the battlefront made the Vietnam War radically different from World War II, World War I, and even the Spanish-American War. Then, most of the fighters who went overseas stayed there until the war had ended—unless, of course, they were killed or wounded. Communication between the troops and their friends and family at home was hampered in earlier wars not only by physical separation but also by the military's strict censorship policies, which limited what enlisted men could reveal in their letters and what journalists could write in their newspapers. In Vietnam, the military's control of the media broke down, while the constant return of servicemen to the United States made mail censorship futile.[27]

The military, as a result, could not wall itself off from the society from which it drew its troops. This interpenetration, in combination with the worsening military situation in Vietnam and the increasingly fractious relations between black and white troops and

Fig. 33. Black Soldiers, Black Power, c. 1970. How much this black soldier on patrol in Vietnam sympathized with black power ideology cannot be known, but his pose suggests how much he had internalized the black power style: the clenched fist, the swaggering celebration of weaponry and ammunition for the power it bestowed on its operator, and the use of a fearsome submachine gun to enhance one's manliness. (Courtesy Library of Congress)

between enlisted men and their officers, meant the military could no longer serve as an agent of nation building. By the early 1970s, the military could no longer pose as a proud representative of the American nation or function as a crucible in which groups of diverse origins were melded together in a single, patriotic mold. A pillar of the Rooseveltian nation had crumbled to the ground. The inability of the university, gripped by its own turmoil, to supplant the military as an institution of nation building magnified the consequences of the military's collapse.

THE SPREAD OF ANTI-AMERICANISM AND THE REVOLT AGAINST ASSIMILATION

The antiwar protests both in the United States and within the American military in Vietnam did not claim the allegiance of all Americans. Moreover, radicals in the ranks of the protesters who insisted on the bankruptcy of the civic nationalist tradition never amounted to more than a minority of both blacks and whites. But the protesters did shatter a broad consensus on the virtue of the American nation, the beneficence of its civic ideals, and the imperative of fighting communism wherever it reared its head. In the process, the Vietnam protesters enlarged the space, first opened by black nationalists, to construct a politics and culture antagonistic or indifferent to American nationalism.

The construction of this new politics and culture proceeded from two premises. The first argued that America was a repressive society in which civic ideals counted for little. Change could not come from appeals to conscience or to some vacuous American creed. If America had any hope at all, it would depend on institutional, economic, and political change of the most fundamental sort. This conviction spread beyond the ranks of black nationalists to other nonwhites—Hispanics, Native Americans, and Asians—who began to document their own sufferings in an oppressive America and to chart programs for change.[28] It shaped the politics of the white New Left whose 1960s radicalization, as we have seen, paralleled the political trajectory of SNCC. By the late 1960s, it had reached significant portions of the liberal establishment, many of whose members began sympathizing with a black nationalist perspective. This last development became strikingly apparent in the Ocean Hill–Brownsville school controversy that tore New York City apart in 1968. Mayor John Lindsay, a liberal Republican, sided with the black parents and black nationalists who had established an independent, community-controlled school district in Brooklyn and against the white teachers and their unions; so did the *New York Times*, the *New York Review of Books*, and other important organs of the city's liberal news media. Meanwhile, McGeorge Bundy, former Harvard University dean of faculty, national security advisor to Presidents Kennedy and Johnson, and a key architect of America's Vietnam policy, swung the considerable prestige and resources of his Ford Foundation behind the Ocean Hill–Brownsville militants.[29]

These white liberals had in no sense become revolutionaries. To the contrary, they saw themselves as reformers seeking to achieve social justice and, in the process, restore civil order. But the achievement of these goals, in their eyes, required supporting black nationalist demands for autonomy, community control, empowerment, and black and Third World studies. These beliefs would unite liberals behind a program of minority rights for the next twenty years. And while most of these white liberals were not virulently anti-American, many nevertheless felt chagrined by America's racial inequalities and its imperial foreign policy. They opposed the war in Vietnam. They had difficulty expressing love for or pride in their nation. Many had even lost Martin Luther King's conviction that America's "hard won heritage of freedom is ultimately more powerful than . . . [its] traditions of cruelty and injustice." Such sentiments would incline them, in the 1970s and 1980s, to advocate a dovish foreign policy and to seek out alternatives to American nationalist myths of belonging.[30]

The second premise shaping the new, anti-American politics and culture treated assimilation to mainstream America—variously defined as Anglo-Saxon, white, middle class, Protestant, and anti-

Communist—as stultifying and soul-denying. Here, too, black nationalists, with their "black is beautiful" campaign, were the pioneers. Without the disillusionment spread by the Vietnam War, however, it is unlikely that so many whites would have followed the black nationalist lead. To be sure, there were other factors implicated in the revolt against assimilation, including an old grudge among European ethnics against the pressure brought on them to jettison their traditional ways, and new frustrations at how Cold War imperatives had constricted the "American way of life" to a too narrow band of suburban, middle-class options. But black nationalists were the ones who demonstrated how American culture might be radically transformed, while the Vietnam experience persuaded many that the old values and lifestyles were no longer worth preserving.

Thus, by the late 1960s and early 1970s, the cultural style of black nationalism had spread well beyond the boundaries of black America. It shaped the struggles of other nonwhite groups—Hispanics, Native Americans, Asian Americans—to establish proud identities grounded in a reconnection to their native cultures and traditions. It transfixed the New Left, which found an authenticity in this new black culture lacking in its own. It powerfully informed the struggle for women's liberation, especially among radical feminists who sought to throw off a male culture that had insinuated itself, as had a white supremacist one, into virtually every aspect of social and human relations and had suffocated women's efforts to achieve independence, self-knowledge, and pride. It even influenced white ethnics—Jews, Italians, Poles, and others. This was a particularly interesting case of cultural diffusion precisely because these ethnic groups, by the early 1970s, are often depicted by scholars (and by themselves) as the defenders of the American nation against black nationalist assault. Too great a focus on the antagonism between blacks and white ethnics, however, obscures the degree to which these antagonists were watching and imitating each other in the 1960s and beyond.[31]

In the early stages of their efforts to lay the cultural foundation for a black nation, black militants had sometimes thought that they were simply modeling themselves on white ethnic groups, who appeared to possess proud cultural traditions and strong ties to a homeland that blacks lacked.[32] But many white ethnics had never really broken with the notions that "Anglo-Saxons" stood at the apex of American society and that it was the obligation of all groups to assimilate to Anglo-Saxon ideals. Implicit in these notions was another, namely that Jews and Catholics ought to leave behind their more offensive traditions and habits, or at least keep them out of the public eye, for the sake of fitting in. Assimilation into the national culture took precedence over the maintenance of cultural or religious particularity. This had always been a cardinal principle of the Rooseveltian nation. Although softened in the 1940s and 1950s, it survived intact into the 1960s.

The black nationalist challenge and Vietnam blew apart that principle. Much of what white ethnics saw in black nationalism appalled them—the frightful denunciations of America; the loose, and to their minds, irresponsible, celebration of violence and revolution; the contempt for everything American. But there can be no doubt that the cultural style of black nationalism, and especially the defiant declaration that "black is beautiful," allowed them to glimpse a new imaginative landscape on which to build their own individual and group identities. And the disorder spread by the antiwar movement, as well as the disillusionment experienced by their sons who had gone to fight, impelled white ethnics to rethink their relationship to American society. Many began to dream about an America in which "Anglo-Saxons," or "White Anglo-Saxon Protestants" (WASPs) as they were now called, were not regarded as the best Americans and in which Anglo-Saxon styles of beauty, dress, and comportment were not to be emulated. Following the lead of Michael Novak, a then obscure college professor whose 1971 book, *The Rise of the Unmeltable Ethnics*, became an unexpected publishing sensation, they began to question the virtue of assimilation and to assert the pride and wonder of their own particularist identities as Jews, Italians, Poles, and Greeks.[33]

Novak had little sympathy for the New Left or for the university-based antiwar protesters, but he nevertheless was appalled by

America's presence in Vietnam. He blamed it on a repressed, hyper-rational, and soulless WASP elite that was seeking "to modernize and to Americanize a faraway land" much as it had attempted, in the United States itself, to impose Anglo-Saxon cultural tyranny on communities of immigrants desperate to retain their own traditions. Novak refused to renounce his belief in the American dream, but he argued that its realization required a new patriotism built on the cultivation, rather than the denial, of ethnic identities. Those who shared Novak's view, and there were many, began withdrawing some of the energy they poured into establishing their bona fides as Americans, investing it instead in the search for cultural roots. Given the political climate of the late 1960s and early 1970s, a time when the nation's prestige was falling, this move further contributed to the sense of national drift.[34]

Consider the case of American Jews. In the 1960s, Jews still felt the insecurity of living in a Christian America, still eager to demonstrate their ability to fit in. Many Jews had strongly identified with and participated in the early phases of the civil rights movement, seeing it as a chance to hold America accountable to its civic nationalist dream. A vocal minority had become leaders in the New Left and were quick to follow black nationalist calls for breaking with prevailing patterns in American culture. But, by the late 1960s, the black-Jewish alliance was under strain, especially as black nationalists increasingly depicted Jews not as fellow sufferers but as the enemy—as "slumlords," as Zionist imperialists suppressing Arab liberationist movements, and as white supremacists. Here, again, New York City's Ocean Hill–Brownsville crisis was pivotal, as the black nationalist school board and its supporters indulged those who were declaring that the source of black oppression lay in the Jewish character of the teachers' union. Many Jewish unionists and their supporters in New York reacted with outrage to this toleration of anti-Semitic slurs, condemning black nationalism and breaking their affective and organizational ties to the struggle for black equality.[35]

But many Jews in New York and elsewhere also found much to like in black power—the self-assertiveness, the public declarations of love for their race and culture, the rejection of demands that minority groups concentrate on assimilating to the national culture. In the fifteen years following the 1968–69 peak of black power, Jewish cultural life in the United States became more public and assertive than it had ever been. Many Jews abandoned their own hair-straightening efforts and began celebrating their curls, or "Isros." Orthodox Jewish men became more willing to display their religiosity in public, especially through the wearing of yarmulkes, or head coverings. Young Jewish parents began giving their newborns biblical names rather than Christian or "American" names that their parents had given them. In Brooklyn, a Rabbi Meir Kahane formed the Jewish Defense League, an organization of Jewish vigilantes pledged to an aggressive and, if necessary, violent defense of Jewish communities. Though Kahane and his supporters despised black nationalists, they had clearly been inspired by the swagger, defiance, and violent tactics of the Black Panthers.[36]

And then there was the filmmaker and actor Woody Allen. Allen was the antithesis of Kahane—secular, not religious; nerdy, not armed; eager to escape, rather than embrace, his Jewish roots. But the screen persona he displayed in his movies, beginning with his breakthrough film, *Annie Hall* (1977), was that of a stereotypical Jew—brainy, neurotic, obsessive, urban, alienated. Most remarkable about Allen's performances was his willingness to showcase, probe, mock, and subvert this stereotype to a national, and largely Gentile, audience. The Jewish movie moguls of the 1930s and 1940s, who had tried so hard to keep such images of Jews off the silver screen, would have been shocked by Allen's antics.

It is, of course, important to note the role of the Arab-Israeli Wars of 1967 and 1973 in provoking these changes in the American Jewish community. From the 1967 war came a deep sense of pride in being Jewish, as the Israeli Army, in destroying, in a matter of days, several large Arab armies arrayed against it, seemed to lay to rest the haunting Holocaust image of a people going sheepishly to their deaths. The 1973 war, by contrast, revealed the continued vulnerability of Israel and, by extension, world Jewry to enemies intent upon its destruction, and many Jews responded to this threat by rededicating themselves to Jewish survival. This potent combination of pride and vulnerability clearly influenced American Jews but cannot, by itself, explain the deep alterations in their relationship to the nation of which they were a part.[37]

The influence of black nationalism and Vietnam on ethnic self-perceptions comes into sharper focus if we shift our attention to another group, Italian Americans, far less affected than Jews by events in their homeland. By the late 1960s, tensions between urban Italians and urban blacks were running high; in some ways they were worse than Jewish-black relations, for the Italian community had never developed the same commitment to the civil rights movement that had emerged among Jews. At the same time, Italians who, as a group, were poorer than Jews, tended to live in closer proximity to blacks and see them as rivals for a shrinking base of urban jobs, housing, and government patronage. During the great urban rebellions of the 1960s, Italian communities, because they frequently abutted black ones, were often the white areas most vulnerable to black rioting, arson, and personal assaults.

But even Italians found a good deal to emulate in the cultural style of black nationalism. The Italian American priest Geno Baroni offers one example. Born to working-class Italian parents in Acosta, Pennsylvania, in 1930, Baroni was ordained in 1956 and assigned to a series of parishes in western Pennsylvania steel towns. He failed in each of these parishes, unable to adjust to Irish American parishioner expectations, conservative priests, and what he took to be the spiritual banality of white, suburban, middle-class parish life. A 1960 assignment to St. Augustine, a black parish in Washington, D.C., saved him, as he found his vocation in working with the black poor, Catholic and non-Catholic alike. Stokely Carmichael, then a Howard University student, was an occasional visitor to Baroni's community service center. Through him, Baroni learned about the religiously based spirit of nonviolence that was propelling Carmichael and other black university activists toward SNCC. In SNCC's profoundly Christian commitment to nonviolent change and to achieving a "beloved community," Baroni glimpsed the spirituality that had eluded him in western Pennsylva-

nia; he deepened his involvement in civil rights as a result. When
SNCC's turn toward black power cut him adrift yet again, Baroni
refocused his attention on poor and lower-middle-class whites. Baroni knew these groups well, for they were his people—the working-class Italians, Slavs, and Irish among whom he had grown up
in western Pennsylvania.[38]

Like Richard Nixon and George Wallace, Baroni had begun to
think of these people as the "forgotten Americans," those ignored
by policy makers in their rush to solve the problems of the ghetto.
But unlike Nixon and Wallace, he had no interest merely in ex-
ploiting their resentments to oust the liberals from power or, as in
the case of Wallace, to restore white supremacy. Instead, he hoped
to launch a new populist movement that would bring the white
and black poor together around common economic concerns and
grievances. He hoped, as well, to encourage whites to follow the
example of blacks and recover their group heritage and pride. Baroni celebrated the role of blacks in challenging the "melting pot
myth and the Americanization process that dictates everyone is to
be 'the same,' " and he called for a new "urban ethnic pluralism"
that would encourage all sorts of groups to rediscover their particularist identities. In this pluralist movement, Baroni expected his
people, a group he had begun to call "white ethnics," to play "a
most important part." In 1972, he praised white ethnics in Detroit
for refusing to "accept any [public school] teacher . . . who was
not trained and oriented to the cultural, racial, labor and ethnic
heritage of their community." No longer would these parents tolerate teachers who insisted on instructing their children about how
"America was the great 'melting pot' of the world," and how the
lives of "Rockefellers, J. P. Morgan, Thomas Edison" offered important lessons in " 'how to make it in America.' "[39]

For a brief moment in the early 1970s, it seemed as though Baroni's multiracial populism might make headway. It attracted
Michael Novak, the labor leader George Meany, the Democratic
Senator Edmund Muskie (Maine), and the populist insurgent Barbara Mikulski, a Democratic Baltimore councilwoman.[40] But the

failure of this group to draw black support doomed its efforts. Baroni's "new pluralism" did catch on, however, and white ethnics began asserting their group identities in ways they had not done since prior to World War I. The celebration of Italianness or Polishness, moreover, did not require an alliance with blacks, or even a recognition that this new white ethnic consciousness depended on the cultural space that black nationalist agitation had created. Indeed, for many it would become a vehicle to sharpen their consciousness of the chasm separating them from blacks.

The new appeal of white ethnicity and of changing conceptions of nationhood became startlingly apparent in the popularity of *The Godfather*, the blockbuster 1972 film directed by Francis Ford Coppola, a third-generation Italian American. Its sequel, *Godfather, Part II*, released in 1974 and also directed by Coppola, was also a box office smash. By 1975 an estimated 132 million people had seen the two movies, either in theaters or in a specially released TV drama that integrated the two movies into one.[41] Coppola's third major film of the decade, *Apocalypse Now* (1979), was not as cinematically successful or as popular among audiences, but its relentless attack on America for what it was doing in Vietnam deepened Coppola's exploration of themes that he had developed in the *Godfather* epic. A consideration of these films allows us to see how radically the forces unleashed by black nationalism and Vietnam had transformed popular attitudes toward ethnicity, American identity, and the American nation.

Based on a novel by the Italian American writer, Mario Puzo, that itself had sold 10 million copies, *The Godfather* and *Godfather, Part II* told the epic story of the rise and fall of the Corleones, a Mafia family, from the arrival of the penniless and orphaned Vito Corleone in New York in the early years of the twentieth century through the desperate efforts of his youngest son, Michael, to maintain the family's empire in Nevada after World War II.[42] The family and its minions routinely broke the law and committed acts of ruthless and terrifying violence in the pursuit of economic wealth and political control. These practices, we learn, were rooted in old Sicilian customs imported and adapted to America. Before *The Godfather*'s 1972 release, Italian American groups worried that the movie would generate a cascade of anti-Italian sentiment, as Americans would once again, as they had done on so many other occasions, generalize on the basis of the characters they saw on the screen and come to see all Italians as the product of a vicious and amoral immigrant culture.[43] But nothing of the sort happened; on the contrary, moviegoers adored the Corleone family for its large size, its obvious warmth, its love of food, ritual, and celebration, and the absolute commitment members displayed toward each other. *The Godfather* offered viewers vicarious participation in a spectacular Italian wedding. Other key scenes in it revolve around the fondness and love coursing between fathers and sons, between grandfathers and grandsons, and among brothers. Michael Novak applauded the movie for revealing "aspects of American life never before glimpsed by the public," especially "a thick and dense family life, so different from the Anglo-Saxon cult of the individual."[44] All this was quite deliberate on the part of Coppola, who admitted in a 1972 interview that he "made a very conscious decision" to celebrate Italian American ethnicity, as he knew it, on screen. "I've almost never seen a movie that gave any real sense of what it was like to be an Italian-American." This movie, with the weddings, decorations, baptisms, "were all exactly as I remembered them. My father [an accomplished musician] wrote all that [wedding] music."[45]

There was a dangerous romanticism at work here, for Coppola (and his fellow screenwriter, Mario Puzo) seemed to be representing a hardened crime family as simply the average Italian American family, not that very different from his own. Indeed, in an effort to humanize the Corleones, Coppola deliberately softens the hard facts of illegal trade, extortion, and murder that were integral to their business. In the first *Godfather*, we never see Vito commit, or even authorize, a murder. He declines an offer to partake of heroin trafficking because he deems that business, unlike liquor and gambling, too dirty. That refusal leads to an explosion of violence, beginning with the attempt by rival gangs to assassinate Vito. His sons rally to save his life and restore the power of the Corleone family. But their own violent acts are portrayed as defensive, made necessary not simply by some ancient code of Sicilian honor and revenge but by the inability of properly constituted American government authorities to do their job and keep the peace.

Ultimately, Coppola, however, is not a romantic, for the ethnic family that he has lovingly recreated and that survives the initial attacks on its patriarch is itself, over the course of the two Godfather movies, consumed by its own violence. In telling this story, Coppola actually reveals a proximity to a black nationalist–New Left point of view—not just in his declaration that "Italian is beautiful," but also in his insistence that the wickedness of American society was the force that undermined the Corleones.

The key figure in this story is Michael Corleone, Vito's youngest son. When we first meet Michael in the early scenes of *The Godfather*, he is wearing an army uniform, having just returned from combat in World War II where he had become a much-decorated soldier. He is university educated, refined, even soft. He has no intention of joining the "family business" and, in choosing WASP Kay Adams as his fiancée, he is signaling his intention to move in circles larger than those of his Sicilian Catholic tribe. He appears to be the model ethnic, cut from the Joe DiMaggio mold. But everything goes wrong with Michael's plan, and the story of Michael being sucked back into the family business is what gives the two Godfather movies their drama and horror. Michael's initial, and fateful, return to the mob is motivated solely by his love for his father and a determination to save his life. But the pressures of replacing his father as don transform Michael from a bright and attractive young man into a brooding, cold, and ruthless power broker. He assembles an empire that dwarfs the one his father had built but he is so apprehensive about betrayal that he comes to suspect everyone, even those closest to him—his sister, his brother, his most trusted adviser, his wife. At the end of *Godfather, Part II*, after cold-bloodedly ordering the execution of brother Fredo who, despite an earlier betrayal, presents no threat at all, Michael is depicted as utterly alone, without a family and drained of all humanity. In that way, Michael is much worse off, and a much more terrifying figure, than his father ever was. America, it turns out, is a graveyard for dreams.

Michael's fall, in one sense, was simply the price exacted from him for striving to become the dominant figure in a savage business. How could he succeed in this ambition without becoming savage himself? But Coppola was not content to blame Michael's transformation on the evils of the Mafia. Coppola instead suggests that America made the Mafia worse, ensnaring it in a ruthless, hyperrationalized world of capitalist profit-making that allowed its participants none of the compassion that had marked the reign of Vito Corleone and other first-generation dons. Coppola makes this point in *Godfather, Part II* by dressing up Michael Corleone as a corporate executive, and showing his extensive involvement with "legitimate" corporate and government figures, most of whom seem to regard Michael as one of their own. But Michael has not corrupted big business; big business and big government already share his and the mob's values. As Pauline Kael wrote in 1972, "In *The Godfather* we see organized crime as an obscene symbolic extension of free enterprise and government policy, an extension of the worst in America—its feudal ruthlessness."[46] Coppola acknowledged in an interview shortly after the movie came out that he "always wanted to use the Mafia as a metaphor for America."[47] And just as the Mafia worsened over the fifty-year period covered by the two Godfather movies, as it moved from an "urban frontier" to a "corporate" phase, so too, Coppola implies, did America.

The anti-Americanism of Coppola's Godfather movies is thrown into even sharper relief if we compare them to those made by his Italian American predecessor, Frank Capra. Capra's movies erased ethnicity and celebrated America, implying that immigrants would do well as long as they pushed their questionable ethnic backgrounds to the side, declared their loyalty to America, and pursued the American dream. Coppola's movies, by contrast, celebrated ethnicity, condemned America as an immoral and cold land, and warned moviegoers of the disastrous effects of Americanization. For many moviegoers, Coppola's films deepened the sense of nationalist gloom. Vincent Canby observed of *The Godfather*, it "is as dark and ominous a reflection of certain aspects of American life as has ever been presented in a movie designed as sheer entertainment."[48]

Coppola's celebration of ethnicity and his condemnation of America as a society so compromised by evil that it could not be reformed or redeemed suggest that he was drawn to black power and New Left perspectives. In this sense, Coppola's politics were more radical than Baroni's, Novak's, and those of many other white ethnics, who never lost faith in America. Coppola's radicalism deepens in *Godfather, Part II*, for here he adopts a Third World perspective and portrays the Cuban Revolution of the late 1950s in a sympathetic light. For Coppola, the revolution mostly serves as the backdrop to a Cuba-based section of the movie that highlights the greed, immorality, betrayal, and murderousness of American mobsters, American corporations, and their cronies in the Cuban government. But Coppola uses the depravity of this main story to make the revolution seem inevitable, even appropriate. In Coppola's eyes, the mob's activities have become an expression of an ugly, decadent, and rapacious form of American imperialism.

Coppola's anger about American imperialism had, of course, become common in the early 1970s, a time when antiwar protesters were furious over their perceived inability to force their nation to withdraw from a war that, in their view, was destroying both Vietnam and America. Coppola had wanted to be the first to reveal the evil of America's involvement in Vietnam on the big screen. He would not succeed in this, largely because his ambitions became so grandiose and his mismanagement of production so severe that it took him four years to make his movie. By that time, *Coming Home* (1978) and *The Deer Hunter* (1978) had already made heralded debuts.[49] When Coppola's movie *Apocalypse Now* finally appeared in 1979, it came too laden with allegory, metaphor, pretentiousness, and sheer confusion to be acclaimed as the definitive Vietnam movie. Conceptualized as an adaptation of Joseph Conrad's novel, *Heart of Darkness*, the movie focuses on a journey up a Vietnamese river by a Captain Willard and his small navy crew in search of Colonel Kurtz, a former Green Beret who has deserted the Special Forces and set himself up as the godlike leader of a murderous Montagnard kingdom.[50]

In divorcing himself from "civilization" and going over to barbarism, Kurtz symbolizes the ultimate, if mysterious, madness of the Vietnam War. Coppola's filming of the crew's actual encounter with Kurtz is bizarre, perplexing, and anticlimactic, obscuring rather than clarifying the source of Kurtz's madness. But if the film fails in this important way, it nevertheless grippingly recreates the terror, chaos, surrealism, and death that envelop Willard's crew during its river journey in search of Kurtz. Coppola constructs Willard's four-person crew as a multiracial platoon—two blacks, the boat skipper and a seventeen-year-old youth from Harlem, and two whites, a former chef from New Orleans and a drugged-out surfer from Los Angeles. He presents all of them as fundamentally decent. But the war is so bizarre and terrifying that solidarity means little. Not even the ethnic fraternity that served the Corleones so well advances any purpose here. Instead, Coppola shows us all four crew members being killed or driven mad. This section of the movie, on its own, was compelling enough to maintain Coppola's reputation as an anti-American mythmaker and gain for *Apocalypse Now* a prominent place in the genre of films castigating America for its involvement in Vietnam and for the devastating effects of its policies on Americans and Vietnamese alike. One could hardly imagine more negative images of war and nationhood than those which Coppola chose to emphasize in his 1979 movie.

A focus on Vietnam had pulled Coppola away from his interest in and preoccupation with white ethnicity. But the Godfather movies and *Apocalypse* were intimately related to each other. Above all, they brutally criticized America, depicting it as a nation driven by power and greed and in which such virtues as honesty, fairness, and compassion had little meaning. Coppola treated the notion that America aspired to some higher civic nationalist destiny as a murderous illusion. Truly democratic government did not exist; rhetoric about the beneficence of American power overseas was nothing but a cruel deception.

Coppola's films spoke to an extraordinarily large cross section of America. Those on the left responded positively to his insistence that America was a repressive, even evil, society. Those in the center and on the right focused less on Coppola's preoccupation with American evil than on his celebration of the Corleones, depicted as an honorable ethnic family attempting to survive in an immoral world. These conservative viewers ignored Coppola's notion that America was irredeemably flawed. To the contrary, Coppola's Corleone characters inspired them to think that powerful white men armed with a strong moral sense and a determination to use whatever means at their disposal would find a way to protect their families and, in the process, restore American greatness. This would become the theme of a raft of Godfather-inspired films, especially the enormously popular *Rocky* and *Rambo* movies starring another Italian American, Sylvester Stallone, that began appearing in the 1970s and continued well into the 1980s.[51] But conservative viewers shared Coppola's sense that America was in trouble. They were angered by America's defeat in Vietnam, by the black urban rebels and their supporters who had done so much, in conservatives' eyes, to generate lawlessness in American society, and by the failure of the federal government to set things right. They shared, in other words, Coppola's belief that America was in crisis.[52]

Indeed, it was. On the heels of the shattering struggle for racial equality and the Vietnam debacle came the Watergate fiasco, in which President Richard Nixon's efforts to cover up a burglary committed by his underlings forced him from office in 1974. That made him the third consecutive chief executive whose presidential career had been cut short: Kennedy's by assassination, Johnson's by the unpopularity of his Vietnam policies, Nixon's by crime. By 1974, the American economy, strained from years of high military expenditures, shocked by the organization of Third World oil producers into a powerful cartel, and increasingly bested in international competition by resurgent Germany and Japan, slipped into a long recession characterized by high and unmanageable rates of inflation and unemployment. Having lost a war, America now lost its international economic supremacy and the capacity to deliver affluence to its people. Jimmy Carter, the Democratic president elected in 1976, looking for a way to overcome the profound malaise that had settled over America, called on Americans to turn inward and to learn to live within limits. Not much seemed to remain of the fabled Rooseveltian nation.

THE COLLAPSE OF THE ROOSEVELTIAN NATION

The 1970s crisis in American nationalism, of which Coppola's movies were an expression, arose from multiple roots in domestic politics, foreign policy, and economics. Two issues more than any other, however, triggered it: the struggle for racial equality and the war in Vietnam. A civil rights movement that had begun in such optimism, buoyed by equal doses of faith in the American nation and in a religiously anchored dream in the possibilities of true interracial brotherhood, had been overtaken by black nationalist anger, violence, and pessimism. Among the leaders of the black struggle, and among such important white constituencies as university students and urban liberals, a hatred of America quickly replaced an older love. It was the disillusionment with the possibilities of true racial equality and the growing belief in the fraudulence of American democratic ideals that conditioned key black and white groups to respond with skepticism and then fury to American policies in Vietnam. The sheer size and militancy of the antiwar movement, and the anger it unleashed on the American state and culture, then became critical factors in their own right, impelling Americans to challenge the nationalist premises of their politics and the assimilationist premises of their culture.

The crisis sparked by the civil rights revolution and Vietnam marked the end of the Rooseveltian nation. Neither the racial nor the civic traditions of American nationalism, both essential props of the Rooseveltian nation, could any longer bind a large majority of Americans together or give them reason to make common cause. The civil rights and black nationalist movements had failed fully to destroy the racial nationalist tradition, but they had eroded its legitimacy. After the 1960s, few Americans dared to celebrate white supremacy as a foundational principle of the American nation or to reinscribe it in laws regulating immigration, marriage, employment, or public accommodations. The proponents of civic nationalism might have claimed this outcome as a victory for the American Creed, and indeed some did; but many had been so disillusioned by the arduousness of the struggle against American racism and the war in Vietnam that they had lost their faith in the transformative power of American civic ideals. The civic nationalist tradition, like its racial nationalist counterpart, emerged from the 1960s in a considerably atrophied state.

The techniques of Rooseveltian nation building had suffered along with the ideals. Theodore Roosevelt had stressed the role of a large and powerful state in propagating a nationalist faith, in disciplining those who, for political or cultural reasons, chose to remain outside the nationalist consensus, and in extending economic opportunity to the poor. Sixties liberals had tried to remain true to this inheritance, attempting to use the federal government to push through a Second Reconstruction. Indeed, through congressional legislation and Supreme Court decisions the power of the federal state to intervene in schools, universities, businesses, and public accommodations to eradicate racial and sexual discrimination was vastly augmented. In the process the state institutionalized the civil rights revolution, insuring that the fundamental changes in racial and gender relations that this revolution had initiated would live on. But the state failed in its efforts to eliminate poverty and, in a remarkable turnaround, began relinquishing its power to discipline political and cultural dissenters. By the mid-1970s, congressional committees were limiting the broad surveillance powers of the CIA and FBI, allowing ordinary American citizens to view and to contest incriminating or defamatory information that those agencies had assembled on them.[53]

Meanwhile, the government's affirmative action policies, unveiled in 1968 and widely implemented by the early 1970s, revealed that the state was willing to relinquish its earlier role in promoting assimilation and to champion minority group rights instead. This was so not only for blacks but also for Hispanic, Asian, and Pacific Islander immigrants—all of whom, as a result of the 1965 immigration law, were coming to the United States in increased numbers. The liberal state had not expected its affirmative action policies to retard assimilation; to the contrary, it had hoped that increasing economic opportunities for those Americans who had suffered the most from racial discrimination would give them reason to believe in the American dream and to dedicate themselves to the American nation. But the very process of identifying certain groups as deserving of assistance and of tying substantial benefits to membership in those groups strengthened the corporate identity of those groups.[54] And, within those groups arose influential leaders, deeply influenced by black power, who insisted on cultivating an ethnic or racial identity at the expense of a national one. That so many new immigrants with deep ties to their homelands swelled the ranks of the affirmative action population further intensified the reluctance among them to identify with America. The government might have counteracted these tendencies with a vigorous Americanization effort, reminiscent of the 1910s crusades, or with a disciplinary project making affirmative action benefits conditional upon naturalization (in the case of immigrants) or a pledge of allegiance (in the case of the American-born). Theodore Roosevelt would have demanded nothing less. But few, in the 1970s, possessed the will or saw a way to mount these kinds of efforts.

An additional factor was the decline of the U.S. military, the institution that Roosevelt had seen as indispensable to building national and masculine prowess, to integrating the diverse ethnic streams of Americans into one nationality, and to impressing American superiority upon the world. Vietnam marked the first time in American history, with the possible exception of the War of 1812, that the U.S. military had failed to win a war. The military's prestige had plummeted long before the war had ended. Already in the late 1960s, millions sought to evade serving in its ranks. Those who did serve, meanwhile, increasingly encountered a military bereft

of morale, discipline, or purpose, a state of affairs that Theodore
Roosevelt would have regarded as calamitous.

The 1970s crisis in American nationalism did not trigger, of
course, a literal fragmentation or unraveling of the American nation. No state, region, or ethnoracial group seceded, and no foreign
army pushed through U.S. borders and seized a portion of American territory for itself. Although lawlessness in American society
increased significantly in the 1960s and 1970s, state authority
never collapsed, as it would in parts of Africa, Asia, and eastern
Europe in the 1980s and 1990s. The nationalist crisis occurred primarily in the realm of ideology, culture, and institutions. Many
people who resided in America no longer imagined that they belonged to the same national community or that they shared a common set of ideals. The bonds of nationhood had weakened, and
the Rooseveltian program of nation building that had created those
bonds in the first place had been repudiated. A nationalist era that
had begun in the early decades of the twentieth century had come
to a stunning end.

EPILOGUE

Beyond the Rooseveltian
Nation, 1975–2000

The collapse of the Rooseveltian nation demoralized many Americans and dampened their patriotism. The 1970s and early 1980s, in particular, were a time of drift, anxiety, and uncertainty, and of proliferating pronouncements from a variety of quarters that America's greatness—economic, cultural, and political—was finished. Many were unsure about whether the American nation could ever regain its former glory or whether it should even try.

From this period of crisis, two bold but radically different programs for renewing American society emerged. The first, coming from the left, sought to reestablish a sense of community on a basis of ethnicity, race, or gender. This program, which would become known in the 1980s as multiculturalism, emerged from the ranks of black nationalists and spread to a large number of groups and institutions, especially those involved in education, media, and social services. It emphatically rejected "melting pot" metaphors and policies of assimilation in favor of celebrating the diverse cultures of America's many racial and ethnic groups. A significant minority in its ranks went beyond such celebrations to denunciations of the American nation, which it viewed as inescapably exclusionary and repressive. It also saw in racial, ethnic, and sexual identities preferable modes of social and political organization.

The second program, located on the right, sought to restore American national pride and power through a military buildup; through confrontations with America's enemies in the world; through an antifeminist stance and a corresponding celebration of strong men in charge of their families, communities, and nation; and, finally, through a coded rehabilitation of the racial nationalist tradition. This was a nation-building program that, in the 1980s, would find its champions in Ronald Reagan and the Christian right. In its glorification of the nation, its abhorrence of communism, and its veiled hostility to African Americans, it resurrected features of the Rooseveltian nation. But in its embrace of religion as the source of moral obligation and in its opposition to big government, it veered in a sharply different direction. Its adherents furiously contested the claims and programs of the multiculturalists, and, from the mid-1980s to the mid-1990s, fought a series of political battles and "culture wars" with them that left Americans bitterly divided.

By the mid-1990s, however, it was not clear which, or whether either, would carry the day. For, by this time, a third program of renewal associated with Bill Clinton had emerged. This one drew on both multiculturalism and Reaganism. From the former it took a commitment to racial equality and a toleration of cultural difference. From the latter it drew an eagerness to celebrate the nation and a determination to define citizenship in terms of obligations as well as rights. As some liberals tied the receipt of social benefits to declarations of national loyalty and demonstrations of responsible living, they began to advocate policy measures that recalled the disciplinary campaign of Theodore Roosevelt's era. It does seem, indeed, that the liberal nation is reviving, though it is likely to assume a shape significantly different from that of its Rooseveltian predecessor.

VARIETIES OF MULTICULTURALISM

It is useful to distinguish, as Gordon Wood did in 1994, between a "hard" and "soft" multiculturalism.[1] "Soft" multiculturalists believe in diversity but also continue to value the nation, as long as that nation allows for a wide range of ethnic and racial difference. Among its most eloquent champions today are Lawrence Fuchs and Michael Walzer. Theirs is not really a new position. This multiculturalism had appeared as early as the 1910s in the work of Horace Kallen, who called it cultural pluralism, and resurfaced periodically after that in a wide range of pronouncements and writings, including the government's World War II propaganda campaigns, the post–World War II scholarship of Oscar Handlin, Will Herberg, Nathan Glazer, and Daniel Patrick Moynihan, and even the curricular initiatives of some urban school districts in the early 1960s. These multiculturalists argued that cultural diversity and national pride were compatible with each other—indeed, that ethnic diversity and a respect for ethnic and racial differences strengthened America.[2]

This multiculturalism bloomed in the 1970s, its popularity secured by the increasing support shown it by white ethnics such as Geno Baroni, the Washington priest, and Roman C. Pucinski, a Polish American congressman from Chicago who led the fight in Congress to establish Ethnic Heritage Studies Centers. Pucinski, like Baroni, believed that European ethnics had suffered from coercive Americanization and from a determination to deny the legitimacy, even the necessity, of ethnic and racial difference. This denial was at the heart of the turmoil of the 1960s and the key to under-

standing why the country, in Pucinski's words, was "falling apart."
But Pucinski also affirmed that the country could be put back together again, with ethnics marching alongside racial minorities in
a patriotic rainbow coalition. This kind of sensibility achieved popularity in large stretches of Euro-America and found eloquent expression in many bicentennial celebrations, such as the Smithsonian's "Nation of Nations" exhibit, which located the greatness of
America in the diversity of its people.[3] Its popularity seems to be
surging again today. But this is not the multiculturalism that, in
recent years, has aroused so much controversy.

The proponents of that multiculturalism, the "hard" version,
hold that racism, conquest, and empire have so compromised the
American nation that its virtue or goodness cannot be salvaged.
Thus, not only have these multiculturalists denounced assimilationist strategies as simply covers for programs of racial, male,
bourgeois, or heterosexist domination, but they have refused to
acknowledge that an alternative strategy of belonging would redeem the nation and its civic nationalist promise. They do not
believe that their aspirations can be realized as long as they are
bound by ties of affection or coercion to the American nation. They
want instead to see the American nation exposed, weakened, even
broken up.

These hard multiculturalists actually harbor two distinct camps
in their ranks. One group believes that some minority cultures possess the purity, authenticity, and goodness that mainstream American culture lacks, and that these cultures can serve as the basis of
social renewal. Those who celebrate the greatness of ancient African civilization and argue that its timeless virtues should guide the
rehabilitation of black America, individuals usually referred to as
Afrocentrists, are the most visible example of this tendency. Prominent in their ranks are Leonard Jeffries, professor of African-American Studies at the City University of New York; Molefi Kete
Asante, professor of African-American Studies at Temple University; and Asa Hilliard, a Georgia State educational psychologist
and designer of an Afrocentric public school curriculum, "The African-American Baseline Essays." Their counterparts can be found,

too, among Hispanics, feminists, gays, and Native Americans who locate in Chicano, women's, homosexual, or Indian culture innate strength, value, and truth. In addition to criticizing American national culture as exploitative, these multiculturalists treat it as too thin and inauthentic to give people the emotional sustenance they need. Such sustenance is to be found instead in a particularistic cultural identity. As Asante wrote about Afrocentric culture in 1988, with black readers in mind, Afrocentricity "captivates the cautious by the force of its truth. You are its ultimate test. . . . At the apex of your consciousness, it becomes your life because everything you do, it is. As I write this paper with black ink on white paper, I recognize the ordering power, the civilizing ability, and the intelligence of our [African] ancestors." Afrocentricity, he concluded, "supersedes any other ideology because it is the proper sanctification" of African American history.[4]

The second group of hard multiculturalists sympathizes with the revolts of minority cultures against the mainstream but does not want to see any of them harden into an Afrocentric-like form. Its members repudiate the notion that any culture possesses an unchanging essence that imparts to its adherents a higher humanity. They argue that new myths of cultural purity, superiority, and domination will inevitably arise among those who follow this path. They value cultural hybridity rather than purity or homogeneity, and celebrate the construction of identities that are cosmopolitan, contingent, and fluid. Some scholars focus their search for hybridity on "borderlands," physical regions located on the margins of nations, where the conformist pull of national loyalties is often weakest and the process of cultural syncretization most advanced. Others have turned their attention to diasporas, which they celebrate as "places," unlike nations, where cultural flows and interpenetrations are unusually vigorous. This "hybridic" version of hard multiculturalism is strongest among literary scholars, historians, and anthropologists associated with the "cultural studies" movement, now dominant in the American Studies Association and the Modern Language Association, among others. Despite their profound divergence from Afrocentric-style multiculturalists, these hybridic multiculturalists often join the former in denouncing the oppressive and restrictive effects of American nationalism. Thus, the literary scholar Janice Radway, in her 1998 presidential address to the American Studies Association, celebrated scholars who had made the hybridity and contingency of cultures the hallmark of their work. At the same time, she called for putting the study of American imperialism "at the heart of the field's agenda," a move that would facilitate analyzing American national identity as "a material and social entity . . . brought into being through relations of dominance and oppression." She also mused about changing the name of her field from American Studies to U.S. Studies, Inter-American Studies, or Intercultural Studies as a way of distancing herself and her constituents from the imperial perspective embedded in a preoccupation with "America" and its culture.[5]

This emphasis on the dominance, oppression, and imperialism of American culture reveals the roots of hard multiculturalism (both varieties) in the black power and New Left movements of the 1960s. This multiculturalism did not dominate in the 1970s, when it had had to compete with a vigorous soft multiculturalism promoted by Baroni, Pucinski, and others. In the 1980s, however, several factors converged to widen its appeal. First, a severe economic recession damaged working-class communities, especially African American ones, and, in combination with Reagan's conservative social policies, embittered relations between blacks and whites and deepened pessimism about the possibilities of racial equality. Second, a variety of liberal state policies dating from the 1960s but persisting through the years of Reaganite conservatism unintentionally hardened minority group consciousness. Third, a global reorientation of American business in the 1980s and 1990s eroded the nation's boundaries and generated intense interest in creating communities no longer constrained by the nationalist imaginary.

An economic crisis marked by slow growth, rising unemployment, and spiraling inflation overtook America in the late 1970s and early 1980s. Unfolding in a more gradual and uncertain way than had the Great Depression forty years earlier, its effects were nevertheless profound. Sparked by soaring energy costs and intensified international competition, this crisis impelled manufacturers in the North and West to cut millions of jobs from their payrolls, either shifting them to newer productive facilities in the South (or overseas) or simply relinquishing them altogether. Despair and desperation coursed their way through countless white and black working-class communities, but matters were worse in urban black districts, in the "ghetto," where unemployment rates among male youth reached rates of 50 percent. In such circumstances, significant numbers of young blacks turned to an illegal, underground economy built on drugs and firearms, and, in doing so generated an atmosphere of lawlessness and fear in many American cities. Many whites reacted with trepidation and anger to these developments. This was especially true of working-class and lower-middle-class white ethnics, who often lived in urban neighborhoods that abutted black districts. Their anger was stoked on the one hand by the belief that blacks received benefits from the government, in the form of welfare and affirmative action, that they did not, and on the other by a tendency to see poor blacks as forming an underclass of hardened criminals who lived beyond the pale of customary civility and morality. They were encouraged to do this by an intellectual and popular discourse on the "underclass" that insistently represented urban blacks as less than human, incapable of uplift, and unfit for inclusion in any normal community of men and women. In such circumstances, the hope of generating a populist and soft-multiculturalist alliance among working-class whites and blacks, slim to begin with, faded altogether.[6]

Blacks, meanwhile, regarded the effort to depict them as subhuman as a racist renaissance. This only confirmed the anger toward America that many blacks already felt, and impelled them to renew their efforts to denounce "American" culture and ideals and to celebrate defiantly their own peoplehood. These initiatives became especially apparent in educational venues, as black militants and their Hispanic, Asian American, and white allies sought to curtail or eliminate the celebration of the American nation from history, social studies, and literature curricula and to substitute for it stories of minority oppression and accomplishment. These new curricula did not all call for condemnations of the nation, although the evils that Euro-Americans had unleashed on Indians and Africans were to be laid bare. Virtually all were silent on those issues long thought to have imparted a special quality to America—its freedom of religion and speech, its commitment to equality, liberty, and opportunity, its technological prowess and economic abundance, its beneficent role in world affairs. The civic nationalist tradition was at best irrelevant, at worst a fraud.

This educational transformation made its most rapid progress at colleges and universities, where the decentralized nature of teaching allowed individual professors with a hard multiculturalist agenda to push rapidly ahead. Thus, the 1980s were the years in which Asante published his seminal books on Afrocentricity and made Temple University a center of Afrocentric studies. By the late 1980s, this educational transformation had spread to public school curricula of the nation's cities and states. A variety of school districts adopted Asa Hilliard's Afrocentric curriculum. And, in 1987, the two most populous and ethnically diverse states, New York and California, instituted multiculturalist curricula for grades K through 12. The agenda of multicultural militants in New York, led by Leonard Jeffries, is evident in the first sentence of the minority task force report submitted by Jeffries and others to the New York State superintendent of schools in 1989 as part of an effort to harden further the multiculturalist character of the state's curriculum: "African-Americans, Asian-Americans, Puerto Ricans/ Latinos and Native Americans," the report began, "have all been the victims of an intellectual and educational oppression that has characterized the culture and the institutions of the United States and the European American world for centuries."[7] The report went on to propose reforms that would rescue New York's minority schoolchildren from this oppression. Although ultimately rejected, the minority report revealed how far hard multiculturalism had advanced.[8]

Government policies that inadvertently hardened minority group consciousness constituted a second factor invigorating hard multiculturalism. In the late 1960s, the federal government had begun to sort Americans into four ethnoracial groups—white, black, Native American, and Asian or Pacific Islanders. Hispanics became, in effect, a fifth ethnoracial group. Although classified as white, they were counted and categorized independently of non-Hispanic whites. The Bureau of the Census used this classificatory scheme, as did other public and private institutions, to track—and eventually to promote—the three nonwhite groups and Hispanics in schools, universities, integrated neighborhoods, and public and private employment. Yet the very decision to classify millions of Americans in these terms, and to do it in so public a way, encouraged Americans to think that their status in the United States depended first and foremost on the welfare of their assigned group. By focusing attention on minority group life in this way, the government gave multiculturalism a powerful boost.[9]

It also strengthened multiculturalism through programs of minority and female patronage, most of them tied in one way or another to affirmative action. By the late 1970s, the government was hiring minorities and women as civil servants, as teachers, and as policemen and firemen. It was also demanding that private employers, ranging from multinational corporations to construction firms to universities and professional schools, do the same. The architects of affirmative action had not intended to encourage hard multiculturalist, and anti-American, views among minorities. To the contrary, they had sought to advance the traditional goals of assimilation and integration. But in the process of pursuing these goals, the government often helped to secure jobs and influence for adherents of hard multiculturalist agendas. This phenomenon manifested itself the most among university professors and public school teachers, as well as among social workers, social psychologists, and other members of the so-called helping professions. By helping hard multiculturalists to secure positions from which they could broadcast their views, the government implicated itself in ideological attacks on the nation that it was obligated by law to protect. Hard multiculturalists were themselves little troubled by this contradiction, defending their government-sponsored attacks on the nation in terms of the right of free speech, a venerated revolutionary strategy of "boring-from-within," or simply in terms of service to a higher, and uncompromisable, cause. Moreover, many of these individuals had not been hard multiculturalists when first hired. But their experience as affirmative action beneficiaries radicalized them, for they came to believe that they functioned as tokens, their presence in predominately white and male workplaces fulfilling the letter of the law without achieving for minorities and women true equality. This latter experience helps to explain a curious phenomenon that political scientists such as Jennifer Hochschild have noticed: that educated and relatively well remunerated blacks have tended to be far more disenchanted with the American dream than those without university education or a middle-class level of resources.[10]

Changes in the hiring and marketing practices and global orientation of big businesses formed the third key spur to hard multiculturalism. As industries began diversifying their work forces in response to affirmative action pressures, some large employers came to appreciate the revenues that diversity could bring, especially as the global marketplace began to eclipse the national one in their long-range plans. In a literal way, business revenues and prosperity began depending more and more on corporations' ability to handle culturally divergent groups of buyers and sellers. For these purposes, having a culturally and racially varied work force began to make good business sense.[11] Within certain corporations deeply involved in global finance and commerce, the commitment to diversity signified more than a banal celebration of the American mosaic. It signified, too, a growing indifference to the physical and ideological borders of the American nation. Robert Reich and Eric Hobsbawm have both argued that corporations have outgrown the national economies that once suited them so well and that, as a result, they have been shedding their economic and cultural loyalties to them. Fewer and fewer corporations headquartered in the United States show any inclination to put the name "national" or "American" in their names, as so many were eager to do in the late nineteenth and early twentieth centuries. Declarations such as that made by General Motors president and Secretary of Defense Charles Erwin Wilson in the 1950s, that "what was good for our country was good for General Motors and vice versa," no longer inspire corporate leaders. Large corporations do not, of course, partake of the Afrocentricity of a Molefi Asante or the anti-imperialism of a Janice Radway; but in their dollars-and-cents indifference to the fate of the American nation, they have diminished the authority and prestige of the nation-state and helped to generate intense interest in postnational forms of associations. They have done this, too, by generating labor demands within the United States that can only be satisfied through high-volume streams of immigration. The country, as a result, harbors millions of recent immigrants who are living actively transnational lives. In ways that Karl Marx would have well understood, the practices of multinational capital constitute the materialist underpinnings of multiculturalist forms of imagining.[12]

"A SPRINGTIME OF HOPE": RONALD REAGAN AND THE NATIONALIST RENAISSANCE

The attack on hard multiculturalism has been furious, led by a conservative movement that arose to roll back the liberal and radical advances of the 1960s. Its defining figure was Ronald Reagan, a politician who turned further and further to the right as a result of his confrontations, as governor of California, with the advance guard of black nationalism and the New Left—the Black Panthers in Oakland and student radicals in Berkeley. Nothing enraged him as much as 1960s radicals and their liberal supporters. Reagan was furious at their denunciations of America, outraged that they had dared to declare the American dream a nightmare. He regarded their protests as criminal and was determined to punish them, as he did when he called out the National Guard in 1969 to "take back" the University of California's Berkeley campus from student radicals.[13]

Sharing a party affiliation with Theodore Roosevelt and cultivating a lifelong admiration for Franklin Roosevelt, Reagan adhered to several of the Roosevelts' key beliefs. In Reagan's eyes, as in those of the Roosevelts, the nation came first. Those Americans who refused to declare their patriotism and to honor their nation were traitors. Second, America's freedom depended on its military strength, for America had enemies abroad against whom it had to be prepared to fight. Reagan's anticommunism was as fervent as TR's antianarchism had been. As president, Reagan orchestrated a vast ideological and military buildup against the Soviet Union that would play a significant role in that archenemy's 1989 collapse. Like Theodore, too, Reagan tried to turn a small conflagration in the Caribbean—in this case occurring in the small tourist island of Grenada, where U.S. Marines easily deposed a defenseless Marxist regime—into a test of national resolve and an opportunity for national glory. Finally, he shared TR's discomfort with the presence of African Americans in his nation. He could not describe that discomfort in the same terms that TR had used, for the civil rights revolution had banished them from public discourse. But he intended to rid the government of the remedies it had embraced to uproot racism. He wanted to end affirmative action and court-ordered school busing, eliminate bilingual programs in the nation's schools, weaken the Voting Rights Act, affirm the right of whites to live in segregated neighborhoods, and allow private universities that excluded blacks and other minorities to maintain federal tax-exempt status.[14]

In their election campaigns, Reagan and his successor, George Bush, usually resisted explicit appeals to white racial solidarity. But their campaign committees understood how much could be gained by portraying blacks as the lawless, violent, and lazy "other" who threatened the values that "true" Americans held dear. This initiative reached its peak in Bush's 1988 campaign when the Republicans ran television commercials and printed literature with stories featuring Willie Horton, a black man convicted of murder who, while on furlough from a Massachusetts prison, had brutally beaten a Maryland man and raped his wife. The Republicans were able to pin the blame for Horton's release on the Democratic presidential nominee, Michael Dukakis, who, as governor of Massachusetts in 1976, had vetoed a bill that would have excluded first-degree murderers like Horton from the furlough program. One particularly notorious television advertisement, produced by a Republican group ostensibly independent of the Bush campaign, drew special attention to race, emphasizing that Horton was black and his rape victim white. Dukakis's campaign manager, Susan Estrich, denounced the ad, declaring that "there is no stronger metaphor for racial hatred in our country than the black man raping white women." Even Bush felt compelled to criticize the ad's message, but this did not stop him from referring frequently to Horton in his stump speeches. These references, in turn, gave the media reason to run countless pictures of the "black rapist" in newspapers and television news programs. Such publicity pleased Bush's campaign manager, Lee Atwater, who had told reporters in the summer of 1988 that the Horton case was "one of those gut issues that are values issues, particularly in the South, and if we hammer at these over and over, we are going to win." Merle Black, a liberal professor of political science at Emory University, made a similar argument from a critical point of view. The Horton case is "the kind of issue George Wallace would have used," he told reporters in 1988. "This is updated George Wallace style politics." The Republicans were, in effect, resurrecting the tradition of racialized nationalism, which had long made the alleged sexual aggression of black men grounds for excluding them from the American community. Bush, Atwater, and their party rode this strategy to victory in 1988.[15]

To see only racism in the nationalism of Reagan and Bush would be a mistake, however, for to do so overlooks the message of faith in the American dream—articulated by both men, and especially by Reagan. In 1980 Reagan declared that "it is impossible to capture in words the splendor of this vast continent which God has granted as our portion of His creation. There are no words to express the extraordinary strength and character of this breed of people we call Americans."[16] In his 1981 Inaugural Address, Reagan upbraided Americans for allowing themselves to become dejected over their own and their nation's future. "We're too great a nation to limit ourselves to small dreams. We're not, as some would have us believe, doomed to inevitable decline. . . . We have a right to dream heroic dreams."[17] And four years later, in a voice-over to a 1984 campaign commercial, Reagan spoke of how his presidency had taken "people who were losing faith in the American dream" and given them hope. He celebrated the jobs that his administration had created and the decline in inflation that the Republicans had brought about. Thus, "Americans are working again. So is America. . . . With our beloved nation at peace, we are in the midst of a springtime of hope for America."[18] No major political figure had spoken in such soaring tones about America since John F. Kennedy. In doing so, Reagan revealed how much he was the product of the golden age of the Rooseveltian nation, an age whose spirit— if not its politics—he wanted to restore. "An American President [Franklin Roosevelt] told the generation of the Great Depression that it had 'a rendezvous with destiny,' " Reagan declared at the Republican National Convention in 1980. "I believe this generation of Americans today also has a rendezvous with destiny."[19]

When speaking in this mode, Reagan did not draw racial distinctions. "I ask you," he declared in 1980, "to trust the American spirit which knows no ethnic, religious, social, political, regional, or economic boundaries, the spirit that burned with zeal in the hearts of millions of immigrants from every corner of the earth who came here in search of freedom."[20] Reagan celebrated the role of World War II in ending segregation in the armed forces and thus in allowing African Americans to become full-fledged patriots and heroes. One of his favorite war stories was of a Negro sailor during the Japanese attack on Pearl Harbor who, though officially limited to "kitchen-type duties" on his ship, grabbed a machine gun and "stood at the end of a pier blazing away at Japanese airplanes that were coming down and strafing him."[21] Reagan, as was his wont, got his details wrong, forgetting the sailor's name (it was Dorie Miller) and claiming that the heroic acts of Miller and others led to the ending of military segregation during the war itself. What matters here, however, is that Reagan did, on occasion, open up imaginative space in his proud nation for African Americans and other minorities, a space that a small, but growing, number of conservative African Americans such as Reagan's National Security Advisor Colin Powell, Equal Opportunity Employment Commission director Clarence Thomas, and Civil Rights Commission chairman Clarence Pendleton were eager to occupy.[22]

That Reagan's nationalist ideology, like that of the Roosevelts, contained contradictory elements should come as no surprise. But if the two ideologies both harbored civic and racial elements, the balance between the elements was not the same. Both TR and FDR had embraced the idea of an inclusive America more fervently than did Reagan. One sees in Reagan little of the delight that Theodore Roosevelt, in particular, experienced in meeting diverse groups of Americans, or in bringing cultural or religious diversity to his cabinet. Nor was Reagan troubled, as TR certainly was, by the contradictions between his civic and racist faiths. Reagan, instead, lived comfortably within a Republican Party that was overwhelmingly white and native-born and seems not to have been unsettled by his party's periodic attempts to demonize blacks. In TR's and FDR's thought, the civic nationalist tradition had been a more expansive, challenging, and demanding creed.

In addition, the economic content of Reagan's nation-building program diverged sharply from that of the Roosevelts, especially in its hostility to the liberal idea of a large state ready to regulate capital and assist the poor. Government, in Reagan's eyes, was the enemy of entrepreneurship and abundance, and it had to be torn down. His administration attempted to cut food stamps and related welfare programs; eliminate the Legal Services Corporation (that provided legal assistance to the poor); accelerate the deregulation of financial, transportation, and manufacturing industries that had begun under President Jimmy Carter; and undermine the authority of the government's environmental, workplace, and labor regulatory agencies. When Reagan could not accomplish the work of dismantling and diminishing government agencies directly, he chose to render them ineffective by denying them the funds to carry out their work.[23]

Reagan's political economy reached back to a set of beliefs closely associated with the nineteenth-century Democratic Party, that abhorred state regulation, prizing instead individualism, independence, and the market. Nineteenth-century Democrats admitted that the market and self-interest were not sufficient in themselves to insure the welfare of their nation. Thus they sought to exclude from or subordinate within their polity women, blacks, Indians, and, in some cases, religious or ethnic groups who allegedly lacked the ability, rationality, and self-control of white men. Even white men could not succeed entirely on their own, for they were thought to need the guiding hand of God to keep them virtuous in their private and public lives. Christianity was integral to this nineteenth-century nationalist vision, indispensable not only to individual and group discipline but to giving the American nation a transcendent, even providential, destiny. America was God's country.[24]

Reagan often spoke about America in these terms, even though his own religious convictions did not run very deep. His nation depended critically on the revival of religion as a political force, and he drew a good deal of his support from the Christian right, comprised mostly of evangelical Protestants, and from growing numbers of Catholics. He repeatedly stressed the importance of values and virtue, which, for many of his followers, brought with it ethics anchored in religious truth and obligation. Out of religious faith, too, would come the moral discipline necessary to improve familial and communal life and to restore cohesion and greatness to the American nation. Religion, in other words, would take on the disciplinary role that Rooseveltian nationalists had, at an earlier time, assigned to the state.

Religion gave Reagan's program of national renewal coherence and power, and its emphasis on moral discipline would eventually impel key groups of liberals to begin stressing the importance of moral responsibility and social discipline in their own politics. But in the 1980s it was not clear whether moral discipline or amoral narcissism would come to be seen as the defining characteristic of the Reagan era. Reaganism encouraged a spirit of self-enrichment on the part of both individuals and institutions. The gap between rich and poor widened substantially during this time, and the wealthy flaunted the extravagant riches they had assembled. All kinds of Americans, from a new breed of junk bond dealers to normally reticent savings-and-loan managers, indulged in sprees of financial and real-estate speculation. Meanwhile, conservative Republicans rarely questioned whether these practices or others, such as the massive manufacturing job cutbacks implemented by large corporations that eviscerated urban economies in Midwest cities, served the nation or its moral mission well. Those who were poor were made to feel as though they had no one to blame for their poverty but themselves. Evangelical ministers preached against sinful behavior, but several of the most prominent ones, such as Jimmy Swaggart and Jim Bakker, were shamed by exposure of their own moral and financial corruption.[25]

Not even Reagan's vast military buildup did much to encourage notions of national service or obligation. The army had become thoroughly professionalized, prompting many of its members to think of it as a career path rather than as a higher calling. Gone was the idea of a citizen army, so integral to the World War II– Cold War era, or of any other kind of national service, in which individuals would be called upon to serve their country and, if necessary, sacrifice their comforts and their lives. Thus, in the months leading up to the 1991 Gulf War, a sizable number of reservists were incredulous that they were actually being sent to fight, for they had regarded their National Guard obligation primarily as a second job that occasionally required them to devote a weekend to maneuvers and training. As an Atlanta letter carrier and sergeant in the Georgia Air National Guard remarked, "A lot of people went in the reserves with the attitude that they would make a few extra bucks to help pay for the car . . . or fishing boat. . . . Not many expected something like this."[26] Generals, meanwhile, dreamed of fighting wars in which no American soldier would have to die. The generals' vision was a complex one, drawing both on an old—and commendable—American tradition of keeping military deaths to a minimum and on a new fear of provoking a Vietnam-style public outcry about military misdeeds. But lurking in that vision, too, was a fear of personal and institutional failure that, in earlier periods of American history, would have been labeled cowardice. Reagan's conservative stalwarts in Congress liked to stress their commitment to the military but most of their leaders, such as Dan Quayle and Newt Gingrich, had done as much in their youth to avoid combat as had the anti-Vietnam protesters they maligned. Rhetoric aside, a willingness to sacrifice oneself for one's country was no stronger among most of them than it was among the most multiculturalist of Democrats—a state of affairs that Theodore Roosevelt would have deplored and condemned.[27]

The opposition between the Reaganites and the multiculturalists rendered the country deeply divided, without a common set of attitudes toward the nation that could serve as a consensual or rallying creed. The Republicans had the votes for presidents, but multiculturalists enjoyed support among Democrats in Congress and in education and the media. The divisions were exacerbated by economic distress in many black and white working-class communities that persisted through the early 1990s. Ill feelings between whites and blacks remained high, generating violent clashes in America's cities and an increasingly polarized debate in state legislatures, the courts, and the media over affirmative action, legislative redistricting, and other policies designed by liberals to compensate blacks and other minorities for past mistreatment.[28]

These conflicts, in turn, set the stage for a series of spectacular "culture wars" that would rivet the nation's attention in the late 1980s and early 1990s. These wars were waged over the multicultural character of public school curricula in New York and California; over the related case of a multiculturalist-influenced set of U.S. History Standards funded by the National Endowment for the Humanities (NEH) and designed by the UCLA-based National Center for History in the Schools; over an exhibit on the American West at the National Portrait Gallery that portrayed that region less in terms of its great beauty and freedom than as a place in which Indians and Mexican residents suffered the effects of Anglo expansion; over the very existence of the NEH and National Endowment for the Arts, public institutions attacked by conservative critics as promoters of immoral and anti-American scholarship and art; and, finally, over a proposed exhibit on the Enola Gay at the Smithson-

ian Air and Space Museum that intended to interrogate the morality and politics of the American decision to drop atomic bombs
on Japan in 1945. Each of these culture wars was, in some ways,
different. But all addressed a common, key issue: Was America to
be portrayed as a special nation that aspired to treat all people
fairly before the law and in which the promise of liberty and opportunity was greater than any other place on earth? Or was America
to be depicted as a nation compromised by racial exclusion, capitalist exploitation, and the impulse toward world power and domination? Compounding conservative fury was the apparent effort on
the part of multiculturalists to use nation-building institutions—
schools and museums—to advance a perspective conservatives regarded as harmful to the nation's interests and well-being.[29]

REVIVING THE LIBERAL NATION

This stark political and cultural standoff began to give way in the
1990s. The information technology revolution, unfolding since the
1970s, thrust America to the economic fore once again, giving it
the longest continuous economic boom in the country's history.
The boom was so large and sustained that even African Americans
benefited; unemployment rates among black youths, by the late
1990s, had plummeted sharply downward.[30] Meanwhile, a significant group of liberals had ceased to advocate, or acquiesce to, the
hard multicultural position, calling for a renewed respect for
America and a rejection of cultural programs that celebrated minorities at the nation's expense and of political programs that "indulged" minorities instead of applying universal moral principles
sternly. These new liberal moralists emphasized that all individuals,
irrespective of race, should be expected to behave responsibly, civilly, lawfully. Those who did not were to be punished. No leeway
was to be given to those who might blame their lawless or uncivil
behavior—or simply their lack of academic achievement—on racial exploitation. This view, if widely enough accepted, they argued, would give America the best chance of realizing the country's

civic nationalist creed, by which they meant an opportunity for all of America's citizens to enjoy the protection of the laws and the opportunity to prosper.

Among the most influential in this group have been intellectuals such as Arthur Schlesinger Jr., Diane Ravitch, Jim Sleeper, Fred Siegel, Alan Wolfe, E. J. Dionne, Stanley Crouch, and Shelby Steele. Their views overlap with those of Todd Gitlin, John Judis, and Randall Kennedy on the social democratic left, with those of William Galston, Michael Sandel, Mary Ann Glendon, Stephen Carter, and Amitai Etzioni in the communitarian center, and with those of Michael Lind, Glenn Loury, and Stephan and Abigail Thernstrom on the right.[31] These intellectuals have their counterparts in Congress, too, evident in the number of Democrats who have supported laws restricting access to welfare and stripping benefits from aliens who refuse to become citizens. Less visible but significant has been growing sentiment among state Democrats to scale back affirmative action and curtail bilingual education in favor of demands that the children of immigrants learn English as quickly as they possibly can. Theodore Roosevelt would have recognized in these policies a long overdue and necessary disciplinary project— the revival of the liberal nation.

Reagan and his supporters were the inspiration for these policies, and some of the thinkers just mentioned have converted to Republicanism or are in the process of doing so. But others remain committed liberals. Some are rediscovering the accomplishments of Theodore Roosevelt and the progressives and are calling for a New Nationalist state modeled on theirs.[32] A larger group of liberals has emphasized its support for a more modest regulatory state, a soft multiculturalism, and for some forms of affirmative action. The unlikely leader of this group has been Bill Clinton, unlikely because so many questions have attended to his own ability to behave responsibly, civilly, and lawfully. But Clinton successfully repositioned the Democratic Party as a force for law and order, as the opponent of welfare loafers and cheats, and even as a force for family values. He did so while continuing to insist that the government not release the market from all forms of regulation. He also demon-

strated a remarkable ability to lower the temperature of racial disputes through his obvious personal comfort with African Americans, his continuing commitment to affirmative action and soft
multiculturalism, and his determination to include all racial minorities in his nation. Many African Americans felt so at ease with Clinton that they privately regarded him as the first "black president."
This sentiment certainly has no precedent in American history.[33]

While the liberal effort to resuscitate civic nationalist principles
continues to gather force, the kind of nation it is likely to produce
in the new century is still unclear. The civic nationalism of these
liberals aspires to what is best in the American inheritance—the
creation of a society of equal opportunity in which no one suffers
on account of race, religion, gender, or creed. And although its
proponents see the necessity of disciplinary campaigns, most are
not calling for the elimination of all forms of ethnic and cultural
difference, as Theodore Roosevelt was demanding a hundred years
ago. To the contrary, they acknowledge the value of diversity
within a national community.

The plans of these liberal civic nationalists deserve a fair hearing.
If the ethnic and religious turmoil that is currently engulfing many
nations, including Mexico, Indonesia, Russia, Yugoslavia, Turkey,
Rwanda, Zaire, the Sudan, and Sri Lanka, is evidence that nation-
states are losing their power and prestige, it is not necessarily signaling the birth of a postnational world. Those rebelling against
their nations are not, by and large, calling for a world of the sort
imagined by hybridic multiculturalists—one without strong national borders and one in which different peoples share their traditions and construct complex and multicultural identities. To the
contrary, they are intent on creating their own nations, nations that
are likely to be small and to define their identities in terms of the
ethnic or religious group that dominates its population. In fact,
many dream about creating a thoroughly homogeneous citizenry,
composed entirely of Serbs, or Albanian Kosovars, or Chechnians,
or Tutsis, or Tamilese. Such dreams too often skirt the problem of
minorities, by simply pretending that there will be none. But if any
law of nationhood has worked universally across the twentieth

century it is this: the people living within a set of national borders are never homogeneous, and the problems associated with ethnic or religious difference will inevitably arise. In such a world, the demonstration that a civic nationalist ideal can still flourish as an organizing political principle is a vitally important project. Ironically, it is those who practice a minority identity politics hostile to nationalism or who cherish a diasporic existence who may need that project the most, for, in order to thrive, they require the kind of cultural toleration and protection of minority rights that civic nationalist regimes excel at providing. Until recently, advocating an Albanian diasporic politics in a place like Serbia entailed imprisonment or death.

But is the United States in a position to rebuild a civic nationalist dream without, at the same time, reinvigorating its own traditions of exclusion? Specifically, has the tradition of racial nationalism really been vanquished? The evidence on this matter is ambiguous. Good news certainly abounds. Overt practices of racial discrimination have been largely eliminated, and racialist discourses delegitimated, except among a resurgent far right fringe. African Americans and other minorities occupy positions of visibility and influence in politics, media, education, the military, and the entertainment industry that would have been unimaginable fifty years ago. The transformation of the military, and especially of the army, has been nothing short of startling in this regard, given that institution's historic role in reinforcing America's character as a racialized nation. By the mid-1990s, African Americans made up more than a quarter of the army, including 35 percent of its noncommissioned officers, 12 percent of its commissioned officers, and 7 percent of its generals. In 1989 an African American army general, Colin Powell, became chairman of the Joint Chiefs of Staff, arguably the most powerful military position in the world. These advances, moreover, have generally been accomplished with far less racial recrimination and anger than that which accompanied parallel efforts in the 1980s and 1990s to desegregate schools, universities, and workplaces. To be sure, the military today is not held in the same high regard as the World War II military once was. But that has more to do with the military's transformation from a civic to a professional organization than with the rise of blacks within its ranks. Internally, the military has certainly recovered the élan that it had lost during Vietnam.[34]

Other liberal racial remedies instituted in the 1960s, especially affirmative action, despite decades of attack by conservatives, have survived long enough to create a large and dynamic black middle class. In the United States, the creation of such a class within a particular ethnic or racial group historically has been a prerequisite for a more generalized advance in a group's economic and social welfare. African Americans appear to be poised for such a leap today, especially if the current economic boom lasts a few more years (or if the inevitable downturn turns out to be relatively mild). The positive consequences of such a leap for national cohesion would be enormous.

Moreover, rates of intermarriage between white and black Americans have risen significantly over the past generation, quadrupling from a mere 3 percent in 1970 to 12 percent in 1993. The percentages are even higher in sectors, such as academia and the military, where integration is well advanced. Interracial marriage is arguably the most powerful form of integration. The more it occurs, the more whites and blacks will be able to imagine that they both belong to the same national community.[35]

But there is plenty of bad news, too. Most blacks and whites live in neighborhoods that are almost entirely segregated, in some cases to a degree exceeding that which prevailed fifty years ago. A disproportionate part of the black population, meanwhile, remains poor, confined to desperately inferior schools and to labor markets where minimum-wage jobs offer the only employment. Young black men are heavily overrepresented in the nation's huge jail population. Even the intermarriage data is cause for worry, for it turns out that the rate of white-black intermarriage is only one-fourth to one-third the rates of Latino-white and Asian-white unions. The 1990 census revealed that approximately half of Asian immigrants and about one-third of Latino immigrants aged twenty-five to thirty-four had married outside their group. Moreover, rates of intermar-

Fig. 34. A New Nation for the Twenty-First Century? A patriotic and multicultural group of American schoolchildren watching a parade. What will be the place of race in their nation in the twenty-first century? (Courtesy Tony Stone Images)

riage between Asians and African Americans and between Latinos and African Americans are so low that they are barely discernible. Blacks may simply have more catching up to do, and the 2000 census may show their rate of intermarriage converging with those of other non-European groups. But a familiar historical pattern may be reestablishing itself: blacks may find their opportunities for integration limited even as white Americans open their arms (literally, in the case of marriage) to nonblack immigrants. In this way, Asian and Latino immigrants may, at some point, come to define their Americanness in terms of being white or, at least, not black. These patterns suggest that "whiteness" and "blackness" are still charged with meaning, and that, under certain circumstances, the rehabilitation of the racial nationalist tradition would not be that difficult to arrange.[36]

But let us suppose that the tradition of racialized nationalism has been laid to rest. Can civic nationalism regain its older authority without resorting to new patterns of exclusion? The question is even more pressing because America can no longer appeal to the other major tradition of exclusion—anticommunism—that guided nation-building efforts through much of the twentieth century. The Soviet Union is gone and the Communist ideology that undergirded it is dead. We can imagine a resurgent Russian nationalist, and nuclear-equipped, state lashing out at Western imperialism, or an Islamic fundamentalist campaign to terrorize U.S. allies or the United States itself. Other countries, too, are beginning to oppose American economic might and cultural influence, seeing in them pernicious new forms of American imperialism. Most concretely, there is the possibility of a major clash with China over Taiwan, trade, espionage, human rights, or even communism, a faith to which the Chinese leadership remains nominally committed. Tensions with China or Islamic fundamentalist groups abroad, of course, could easily generate antagonism toward Chinese and Muslim Americans living in the United States, thus aiding those seeking to sharpen the sense of American national identity.

Some liberal advocates of the new civic nationalism argue that we are beyond the need for such enemies, that we have learned from past mistakes, and can now be secure in, even relaxed about, our national identity. But if this is true, then the American nation of the future will be different than it has been in the past.[37] Specifically, a nationalism that has no enemies may well lose its ability to arouse its people and to command their loyalty and passion. A less commanding nationalism may sound like a positive development, for nations, in the past, have often commanded their peoples to hate, to conquer, and to slaughter. In some places they still do. But that command has also been turned to more positive purposes as evidenced by the success of the United States government in rallying Americans against the Nazis in the Second World War. And the hold that the national imaginary once exercised over the American people made the civic nationalist creed particularly powerful and capacious. Thus, the labor movement of the 1930s and the civil rights movement of the 1950s and early 1960s both depended for their success not just on the mass mobilization of workers and blacks but on their ability to convince large numbers of Americans that the nation owed workers and African Americans certain rights and opportunities. In a society in which the nationalist ideal is weaker or more diffuse, how will those suffering discrimination press their claims? Why should members of a more prosperous class, a powerful ethnic group or region, or a dominant race express solidarity with the less fortunate? There are, of course, alternative bases of human solidarity rooted in religion and the more secularized form of ethics that have become so manifest in the current international human rights movement.[38] But it is not at all clear that these forms of social solidarity are adequate substitutes for that which was once rooted in nationalism.

Evidence from the last few years does suggest that the renascent civic nationalism is weaker than its Rooseveltian predecessor. Thus, for example, those liberals seeking to use the civic nationalist creed to raise questions about economic inequality and to insist that the more fortunate Americans have a duty to the less fortunate have made little headway in politics. In the 1998–99 war against the Serbs over the future of Kosovo, Clinton did not dare to make a case for national obligation, service, or sacrifice, and the war had to be fought without risking American casualties. It may well be that our reasons for intervening in Yugoslavia were so mired in ambiguity that the war cannot be considered a true test of American resolve. But will American resolve be greater in a different kind of war, in which the threat to America might seem more obvious?[39]

An older nationalist perspective does survive in America, most visibly in the two presidential campaigns that the Republican Patrick Buchanan mounted in the 1990s. In insisting that a primary purpose of the nation is to protect the wages and livelihoods of American workers, Buchanan powerfully deployed nationalism on behalf of economic justice.[40] But the allure of his nationalism depended, too, on the revival of exclusionary notions of America as a white, Christian fortress that should close its doors to immigrants and corral blacks, Jews, and other minorities already in its midst. Through him, and through the fringe groups that attach themselves to him, we can glimpse the dangers that will always be present when a strong nationalism seeks to reassert itself.[41]

A vigorous civic nation that is both tolerant of difference and generative of social solidarity would be a wonderful place in which to live. But the history contained in this book should remind us how difficult it has been and will be to create that kind of society. Most individuals, including Senator John McCain of Arizona (Republican), seeking to resurrect Theodore Roosevelt's legacy have tellingly avoided a discussion of the racial nationalism on which much of the Rooseveltian nation's social solidarity rested.[42] Those who are aware of that older racial nationalism have labored imaginatively but not altogether persuasively to demonstrate how we might enjoy the social solidarity of a strong American nation without restoring old exclusions or creating new ones.[43] I do not share their faith that a new American civic nation, strong but tolerant, is within reach. More likely, the future will witness either the resurgence of a strong, solidaristic, and exclusionary national identity of the sort that has existed in the past; or, in the interests of tolerance and diversity, we will continue to opt for a weaker identity, one that makes fewer claims on us, that allows us to cultivate strong ethnic, religious, regional, or transnational identities, but that is capable of generating only thin loyalty to nationalist ideals and limited ties of feeling and obligation to Americans outside our core identity groups. Each option has costs attached to it, the first in its revival of exclusionary traditions and the latter in its lack of social solidarity. Neither will render the American nation the exceptional entity that so many Americans have always believed it could be. We should nevertheless labor to strengthen the civic component of our nationhood, even as we recognize that no special providence or manifest destiny will guide our way. To the contrary, we will continue to be what we have been—a nation among nations, struggling, like many other peoples, with the complexities, contradictions, and burdens of our nationhood.

Notes

INTRODUCTION

1. Israel Zangwill, *The Melting-Pot* (1909; New York, 1923), 33; Arthur M. Schlesinger Jr., *The Disuniting of America: Reflections on a Multicultural Society* (New York, 1992), 13; Gunnar Myrdal, *An American Dilemma: The Negro Problem and Modern Democracy,* 2 vols. (1944; New York, 1972), 1:esp. 3–4, 6; Michael Ignatieff, *Blood and Belonging: Journeys into the New Nationalism* (New York, 1993), 5–6.

2. Representative Elton Watkins of Oregon (Democrat) made the first statement, Harry H. Laughlin the second. *Congressional Record,* February 2, 1924, 1895; Harry H. Laughlin, "Analysis of America's Modern Melting Pot," Statement to U.S. Congress, House, Committee on Immigration and Naturalization, 67th Cong., 3rd sess., November 21, 1922, Serial 7-C (Washington, D.C., 1923), 738.

3. Malcolm X, "The Ballot or the Bullet" (April 1964), in *Malcolm X Speaks: Selected Speeches and Statements*, ed. George Breitman (New York, 1965), 26.

4. Herbert Croly, *The Promise of American Life* (1909; Boston, 1989); Theodore Roosevelt, *The New Nationalism* (New York, 1910).

5. Benedict Anderson, *Imagined Communities: Reflections on the Origin and Spread of Nationalism* (1983; London, 1991), 4. See also Eric Hobsbawm, *Nations and Nationalism since 1780: Programme, Myth, Reality* (New York, 1990); Anthony D. Smith, *The Ethnic Origins of Nations* (Oxford, 1986); Ignatieff, *Blood and Belonging*; Rogers Brubaker, *Citizenship and Nationhood in France and Germany* (Cambridge, Mass., 1992); Linda Colley, *Britons: Forging the Nation, 1707–1837* (New York, 1992); John Breuilly, *Nationalism and the State* (1982; Chicago, 1994); Partha Chatterjee, *The Nation and Its Fragments: Colonial and Postcolonial Histories* (Princeton, 1993); Prasenhit Duara, *Rescuing History from the Nation: Questioning Narratives of Modern China* (Chicago, 1995); Stuart Hall, "Cultural Identity and Diaspora," in Jonathan Rutherford, ed., *Identity: Community, Culture, Difference* (London, 1990), 222–37; Homi K. Bhabha, ed., *Nation and Narration* (London, 1990); Paul Gilroy, *The Black Atlantic: Modernity and Double Consciousness* (Cambridge, Mass., 1993); Nira Yuval-Davis, *Gender and Nation* (London, 1997); Florencia Mallon, *Peasant and Nation: The Making of Postcolonial Mexico and Peru* (Berkeley, 1995); Jeffrey L. Gould, *To Die in this Way: Nicaraguan Indians and the Myth of Mestizaje, 1880–1965* (Durham, N.C., 1998).

6. W.E.B. Du Bois, *Black Reconstruction in America, 1860–1880* (1995; New York, 1935); Edmund S. Morgan, *American Slavery, American Freedom: The Ordeal of Colonial Virginia* (New York, 1975); David R. Roediger, *The Wages of Whiteness: Race and the Making of the American Working Class* (London, 1991), and *Towards the Abolition of Whiteness: Essays on Race, Politics, and Working Class History* (New York, 1994).

7. On the marginalization and recovery of Du Bois, see Ira Katznelson, "Du Bois's Century," *Social Science History* 23 (Winter 1999): 459–74. See also David R. Roediger, introduction to *Black on White: Black Writers on What It Means to Be White* (New York, 1998), 3–26. On the centrality of race to the consciousness of American workers, consult Bruce Nelson, *Divided We Stand: American Workers and the Struggle for Black Equality* (Princeton, 2001), and Alexander Saxton, *The Rise and Fall of the White Republic: Class Politics and Mass Culture in Nineteenth-Century America* (New York, 1990). Other important contributions to the whiteness school include Matthew Frye Jacobson, *Whiteness of a Different Color: European Americans and the Alchemy of Race* (Cambridge, Mass., 1998); Noel Ignatiev, *How the Irish Became White* (London, 1995); Reginald Horsman, *Race and Manifest Destiny: The Origins of American Racial Anglo-Saxonism* (Cambridge, Mass., 1981); Ronald Takaki, *Iron Cages: Race and Culture in Nineteenth-Century America* (Berkeley, 1971); George Lipsitz, *The Possessive Investment in Whiteness: How White People Profit from Identity Politics* (Philadelphia, 1998); Michael Rogin, *Blackface, White Noise: Jewish Immigrants in the Hollywood Melting Pot* (Berkeley, 1996); Maria Mazzenga, "Inclusion, Exclusion, and the National Experience: European- and African-American Youth in World War

Two Baltimore" (Ph.D. dissertation, Catholic University of America, 1999); Neal Foley, *The White Scourge: Mexicans, Blacks, and Poor Whites in Texas Cotton Culture* (Berkeley, 1997); Karen Sacks, *How Jews Became White Folks and What That Says about Race in America* (New Brunswick, N.J., 1998); Theodore W. Allen, *The Invention of the White Race*, vol. 1, *Racial Oppression and Social Control* (New York, 1994); Grace Elizabeth Hale, *Making Whiteness: The Culture of Segregation in the South, 1890–1940* (New York, 1998); Ruth Frankenberg, *White Women, Race Matters: The Social Construction of Whiteness* (Minneapolis, 1993).

8. Eric Foner, *The Story of American Freedom* (New York, 1998); Rogers M. Smith, *Civic Ideals: Conflicting Visions of Citizenship in U.S. History* (New Haven, 1997). My book probably bears the closer resemblance to Smith's, though he concentrates on the nineteenth century and I on the twentieth. Smith and I both build our analysis around the interplay of conflicting nationalist traditions. We define the array of traditions somewhat differently; he accords republicanism an autonomy that I do not, and, rather than treat racial nationalism on its own, he incorporates it in a broader category that he labels "ascriptive Americanism." The use of this latter category allows Smith to study the effects of gender more systematically than I do, but it also makes the influence of race more diffuse. Smith focuses less than do I on the work of exclusion done by the civic tradition itself, and thus has less to say about the role of political radicalism and antiradicalism in constituting the American nation.

The historiography of American nationalism and nationhood is still young. Until recently, the most important work in this field was John Higham, *Strangers in the Land: A History of American Nativism, 1860–1925* (1955; New Brunswick, N.J., 1992), now almost fifty years old. It has long been an inspiration and guide to me. For other older works on American nationalism, see Merle Curti, *The Roots of American Loyalty* (New York, 1946); Hans Kohn, *American Nationalism: An Interpretive Essay* (New York, 1957); and Yehoshua Arieli, *Individualism and Nationalism in American Ideology* (Cambridge, Mass., 1964).

More recent work from which I have benefited includes Cecilia Elizabeth O'Leary, *To Die For: The Paradox of American Nationalism* (Princeton, 1998); Stuart McConnell, "Nationalism," in Stanley Kutler, ed., *Encyclopedia of the United States in the Twentieth Century* (New York, 1996), 1:251–71; John Bodnar, *Remaking America: Public Memory, Commemoration, and Patriotism in the Twentieth Century* (Princeton, 1992); John Bodnar, ed., *Bonds of Affection: Americans Define Their Patriotism* (Princeton, 1996); Michael Kammen, *Mystic Chords of Memory: The Transformation of Tradition in American Culture* (New York, 1993); Wilbur Zelinsky, *Nation into State: The Shifting Symbolic Foundations of American Nationalism* (Chapel Hill, 1988); Richard Slotkin, *Gunfighter Nation: The Myth of the Frontier in Twentieth-Century America* (New York, 1992); Gail Bederman, *Manliness and Civilization: A Cultural History of Gender and Race in the United States, 1880–1917* (Chicago, 1995); David A. Hollinger, *Postethnic America: Beyond Multiculturalism* (New York, 1995); Michael Lind, *The Next American Nation: The New Nationalism and the Fourth American Revolution* (New York, 1995); Jennifer L. Hochschild, *Facing Up to the American*

Dream: Race, Class, and the Soul of the Nation (Princeton, 1995); Lary May, *The Big Tomorrow: Hollywood and the Politics of the American Way* (Chicago, 2000); Desmond King, *Making Americans: Immigration, Race, and the Origins of the Diverse Democracy* (Cambridge, Mass., 2000); Nina Silber, *The Romance of Reunion: Northerners and the South, 1865–1900* (Chapel Hill, 1993); Stuart McConnell, *Glorious Contentment: The Grand Army of the Republic, 1865–1900* (Chapel Hill, 1992); Russell A. Kazal, "Becoming 'Old Stock': The Waning of German-American Identity in Philadelphia, 1900–1930," (Ph.D. dissertation, University of Pennsylvania, 1998); Keith Fitzgerald, *The Face of the Nation: Immigration, the State, and National Identity* (Stanford, 1996); Mae M. Ngai, "Illegal Aliens and Alien Citizens: United States Immigration Policy and Racial Formation, 1924–1965" (Ph.D. dissertion, Columbia University, 1997).

CHAPTER 1

1. Theodore Roosevelt, *The Winning of the West: An Account of the Exploration and Settlement of Our Country from the Alleghanies to the Pacific* (1890), in *The Works of Theodore Roosevelt, National Edition*, ed. Hermann Hagedorn, 20 vols. (New York, 1926), vol. 8, 9. In addition to Roosevelt's own writings, the following account draws on Thomas Dyer, *Theodore Roosevelt and the Idea of Race* (Baton Rouge, 1980); George Sinkler, *The Racial Attitudes of American Presidents: From Abraham Lincoln to Theodore Roosevelt* (Garden City, N.Y., 1971), 308–73; Richard Slotkin, *Gunfighter Nation: The Myth of the Frontier in Twentieth-Century America* (New York, 1992), 29–122; Gail Bederman, *Manliness and Civilization: A Cultural History of Gender and Race in the United States, 1880–1917* (Chicago, 1995), 170–215; Alexander Saxton, *The Rise and Fall of the White Republic: Class Politics and Mass Culture in Nineteenth-Century America* (London, 1996).
2. *Winning of the West*, 8:6.
3. Slotkin, *Gunfighter Nation*, 39–44.
4. *Winning of the West*, 8:3.
5. Ibid., 100–101.
6. Ibid., 123.
7. "Manhood and Statehood" (1901), in *Works*, 13:455.
8. *Winning of the West*, 8:32–38.
9. Ibid., 89.
10. Ibid., 84.
11. Hector St. John de Crèvecoeur, *Letters from an American Farmer* (1782; New York, 1912), 43.
12. In *Letters from an American Farmer*, Crèvecoeur wrote a good deal about the Indians he encountered in his travels through Nantucket and Martha's Vineyard and the black slaves he observed in South Carolina. The decline of the Indian population and civilization in New England troubled him, and chattel slavery, especially as it was practiced in the southern states, appalled him. But even as he

recognized the humanity of Indians and Africans, he could not envision them as Americans. Ibid., esp. 102–9, 160–73.

13. *Winning of the West*, 8:8.

14. Roosevelt to Albion Winegar Tourgee, November 8, 1901, in *The Letters of Theodore Roosevelt*, 8 vols., ed., Elting E. Morison (Cambridge, Mass., 1951–54) 3:190–91.

15. "National Life and Character," *The Sewanee Review* (August 1894), in *Works*, 13:212–13. Many white workers shared this class analysis of the origins of the slave trade. See Saxton, *The Rise and Fall of the White Republic*.

16. "National Life and Character," in *Works*, 13:212–13.

17. Roosevelt to Tourgee, November 8, 1901, in *Letters*, 3:190–91.

18. "National Life and Character," in *Works*, 13:212–13; on Chinese exclusion, see Saxton, *The Rise and Fall of the White Republic*, and Andrew Gyory, *Closing the Gate: Race, Politics, and the Chinese Exclusion Act* (Chapel Hill, 1998).

19. *The Winning of the West*, 8:83–159.

20. Ibid., 157–58.

21. "The Manly Virtues and Practical Politics," *The Forum* (July 1894), in *Works*, 13:32.

22. "True Americanism," *The Forum* (April 1894), in *Works*, 13:19. TR lambasted those Americans trying to emulate European aristocrats, living in Europe, becoming "over-civilized, over-sensitive, over-refined, and . . . [losing] the hardihood and manly courage by which alone he can conquer in the keen struggle of our national life." Roosevelt, *The Strenuous Life* (1899), in ibid., 319.

23. "American Ideals," 1895, in *Works*, 13:3–4; "Grant" (1900), speech, in ibid., 430–41.

24. Walter LaFeber, *The New Empire: An Interpretation of American Expansion, 1860–1898* (Ithaca, 1963), 80–101.

25. William H. Harbaugh, *The Life and Times of Theodore Roosevelt* (1961; New York, 1975), 99; see also Kristin L. Hoganson, *Fighting for American Manhood: How Gender Politics Provoked the Spanish-American and Philippine-American Wars* (New Haven, 1998).

26. Harbaugh, *Theodore Roosevelt*, 104; Edmund Morris, *The Rise of Theodore Roosevelt* (New York, 1979), 612.

27. Theodore Roosevelt, *The Rough Riders* (New York, 1902), 22–23.

28. Ibid., 17–22, 28–32, 50, 52; Roosevelt to Henry Fairfield Osborn, December 21, 1908, *Letters*, 6:1434–36; Morris, *The Rise of Theodore Roosevelt*, 618. The Indians were segregated in their own company. Slotkin, *Gunfighter Nation*, 103.

29. Here my interpretation diverges from Slotkin's, who sees in the Rough Riders a replication of the racial mix that had conquered the frontier. Slotkin, *Gunfighter Nation*, 104.

30. The only black in the regiment was Roosevelt's body-servant, identified only as "Marshall"; Roosevelt, *Rough Riders*, 67.

31. Ibid., 18, 51.

32. Ibid., 52.

33. Morris, *The Rise of Theodore Roosevelt*, 620–21, 639–40, 647; Harbaugh, *Theodore Roosevelt*, 106; Roosevelt, *Rough Riders*, 116–17.

34. Morris, *The Rise of Theodore Roosevelt*, 623; Roosevelt, *Rough Riders*, 46–78.

35. For a history of the war, see David F. Trask, *The War with Spain in 1898* (New York, 1981), and Philip S. Foner, *The Spanish-Cuban-American War and the Birth of American Imperialism, 1895–1902*, 2 vols. (New York, 1972).

36. Gerald Linderman, *The Mirror of War: American Society and the Spanish-American War* (Ann Arbor, 1974), 114–73.

37. Roosevelt, *Rough Riders*, 95.

38. Ibid., 110.

39. Ibid., 115.

40. Richard Harding Davis, *Notes of a War Correspondent* (New York, 1910), 96; Roosevelt, *Rough Riders*, 119–64; Morris, *The Rise of Theodore Roosevelt*, 650–56.

41. The desertion and alcoholism rates among black regulars were considerably lower than among their white counterparts. William Leckie, *The Buffalo Soldiers: A Narrative of the Negro Cavalry in the West* (Norman, Okla., 1967); Albert L. Scipio II, *Last of the Black Regulars: A History of the Twenty-fourth Infantry Regiment, 1869–1951* (Silver Spring, Md., 1983); Anthony Lukas, *Big Trouble: A Murder in a Small Western Town Sets Off a Struggle for the Soul of America* (New York, 1997), 118–32.

42. Roosevelt, *Rough Riders*, 132–64; Theophilus G. Steward, *The Colored Regulars in the United States Army* (Philadelphia, 1904); Marvin Edward Fletcher, "The Negro Soldier and the United States Army, 1891–1917" (Ph.D. dissertation, University of Wisconsin, 1968), chap. 8.

43. Roosevelt, *Rough Riders*, 145–52; John Hope Franklin and Alfred A. Moss Jr., *From Slavery to Freedom: A History of Negro Americans*, 6th ed. (New York, 1988), 271; unsigned letter to *Illinois Record* by a member of the Tenth Cavalry (probably John E. Lewis), reproduced in William B. Gatewood, *"Smoked Yankees" and the Struggle for Empire: Letters from Negro Soldiers, 1898–1902* (Urbana, Ill., 1971), 76–77; Lukas, *Big Trouble*, 137.

44. Quoted in Frank Friedel, *The Splendid Little War* (Boston, 1958), 173.

45. Roosevelt, *Rough Riders*, 145.

46. Amy Kaplan, "Black and Blue on San Juan Hill," in Amy Kaplan and Donald E. Pease, eds., *The Cultures of United States Imperialism* (Durham, N.C., 1993), 219–36.

47. Roosevelt, *Rough Riders*, 149.

48. Ibid., 150–52.

49. Letter from Presley Holliday to the *New York Age*, May 11, 1899, reproduced in Gatewood, *"Smoked Yankees,"* 92–97.

50. Ibid., 95–96.

51. Lukas, *Big Trouble*, 134–35; Letters to *Illinois Record*, unsigned, from two members of the Tenth Cavalry, September 10 and October 1, 1898, and letter from Presley Holliday, reproduced in Gatewood, *"Smoked Yankees,"* 72–73, 76–81, 97.

52. *Plessy v. Ferguson*, 163 U.S. 537 (1896); John W. Cell, *The Highest State of White Supremacy: The Origins of Segregation in South Africa and the American South* (Cambridge, 1982); Kenneth L. Kusmer, *A Ghetto Takes Shape: Black Cleveland, 1870–1930* (Urbana, Ill., 1976), 53–90.

53. See, for example, letters from two African American cavalrymen to the *Illinois Record*, October 8 and November 12, 1898, in Gatewood, *"Smoked Yankees,"* 79–81, 87.

54. William B. Gatewood Jr., *Black Americans and the White Man's Burden* (Urbana, Ill., 1975); Bernard C. Nalty, *Strength for the Fight: A History of Black Americans in the Military* (New York, 1986), 78–124; Ann J. Lane, *The Brownsville Affair: National Crisis and Black Reaction* (Port Washington, N.Y., 1971).

55. Cecilia Elizabeth O'Leary, *To Die For: The Paradox of American Nationalism* (Princeton, 1998), chap. 8; Roosevelt, "The Reunited People," 1902, in *Works*, 16:27–32.

56. Roosevelt, *Rough Riders*, 81; Morris, *The Rise of Theodore Roosevelt*, 646; Kaplan, "Black and Blue on San Juan Hill," 223–26; Linderman, *The Mirror of War*, 114–47.

57. Stuart Creighton Miller, *"Benevolent Assimilation": The American Conquest of the Philippines, 1899–1903* (New Haven, 1982); Richard Drinnon, *Facing West: The Metaphysics of Indian-Hating and Empire Building* (New York, 1980), esp. chaps. 21, 22; Slotkin, *Gunfighter Nation*, 106–22; Paul Kramer, "U.S. Anthropology and Colonial Politics in the Occupied Philippines, 1898–1916" (Ph.D. dissertation, Princeton University, 1998); Louis A. Perez, *The War of 1898: The United States and Cuba in History and Historiography* (Chapel Hill, 1998).

58. Foner, *The Spanish-Cuban-American War*; James H. Hitchman, *Leonard Wood and Cuban Independence, 1898–1902* (The Hague, 1971); Louis A. Perez, *Cuba under the Platt Amendment, 1902–1934* (Pittsburgh, 1986).

59. Matthew Frye Jacobson, *Special Sorrows: The Diasporic Imagination of Irish, Polish, and Jewish Immigrants in the United States* (Cambridge, Mass., 1995), 181–216; Richard Hofstadter, "Cuba, the Philippines, and Manifest Destiny," in Richard Hofstadter, *The Paranoid Style of American Politics and Other Essays* (New York, 1965), 145–87.

60. Morris, *The Rise of Theodore Roosevelt*, 665.

61. Slotkin, *Gunfighter Nation*, 69–87.

CHAPTER 2

1. On the history of ethnic nationalism in Europe, see Rogers Brubaker, *Citizenship and Nationhood in France and Germany* (Cambridge, Mass., 1992); Michael Ignatieff, *Blood and Belonging: Journeys in the New Nationalism* (New York, 1993); Anthony D. Smith, *The Ethnic Origins of Nations* (Oxford, 1986).

2. See, for example, Nancy Maclean, *Behind the Mask of Chivalry: The Making of the Second Ku Klux Klan* (New York, 1994); Katherine M. Blee, *Women of the Klan: Racism and Gender in the 1920s* (Lexington, Ky., 1991).

3. Roosevelt, "True Americanism," *The Forum* (April 1894), in *The Works of Theodore Roosevelt, National Edition,* ed. Hermann Hagedorn, 20 vols. (New York, 1926), 13:24–25. See also Roosevelt, *The Winning of the West,* in ibid., 8:17.

4. Quoted in Richard Slotkin, *Gunfighter Nation: The Myth of the Frontier in the Twentieth Century* (New York, 1992), 97; original source: Ben Merchant Vorpahl, *My Dear Wister: The Frederick Remington-Owen Wister Letters* (Palo Alto, Calif., 1972), 30. See also G. Edward White, *The Eastern Establishment and the Western Experience: The West of Frederic Remington, Theodore Roosevelt, and Owen Wister* (New Haven, 1968).

5. Ignatieff, *Blood and Belonging,* 5.

6. Ibid.

7. Roosevelt, "Religion and the Public Schools" (1893), speech in *Works,* 13:275.

8. Roosevelt, "True Americanism," 13:25.

9. Roosevelt to James Andrew Drain, June 27, 1911, in *The Letters of Theodore Roosevelt,* ed. Elting E. Morison, 8 vols. (Cambridge, Mass., 1951–54), 7:299–300.

10. Roosevelt to Raymond Robins, June 3, 1915, in *Letters,* 8:927–35.

11. Theodore Roosevelt, *An Autobiography* (1913; New York, 1927), 185. See also Roosevelt, "The Ethnography of the Police," *Munsey's Magazine* 127 (June 1897): 395–99.

12. William H. Harbaugh, *The Life and Times of Theodore Roosevelt* (1961; New York, 1975), 13–49, 69–92.

13. Roosevelt, *Autobiography,* 173.

14. Ibid., 174–75.

15. Roosevelt to Anna Roosevelt, June 16, 1895, in *Letters,* 1:463.

16. Jacob A. Riis, *How the Other Half Lives: Studies among the Tenements of New York* (1890; New York, 1971).

17. H. Paul Jeffers, *Commissioner Roosevelt: The Story of Theodore Roosevelt and the New York City Police, 1895–1897* (New York, 1994), 135–36.

18. Ibid., 136.

19. Slotkin, *Gunfighter Nation,* 189–92.

20. Israel Zangwill, *The Melting-Pot: Drama in Four Acts* (1909; New York, 1923).

21. Mendel, Zangwill adds, possesses "a fine Jewish face, pathetically furrowed by misfortunes, and a short grizzled beard." Ibid., 2.

22. By casting both Mendel and David as lovers of European classical music, Zangwill shows how much these "lowly" immigrants want to assimilate to the highest standards of Western culture. Zangwill contrasts Frau Quixano's sad, pathetic parochialism with the worldliness of both Mendel and David. The latter are not only lovers of classical music but avid readers of Shelley, Tennyson, and Nietzsche.

23. Zangwill, *The Melting-Pot,* 33.

24. Roosevelt to Israel Zangwill, October 15, 1908, in *Letters,* 6:1288.

25. Roosevelt to Michael A. Schaap, January 24, 1913, in *Letters,* 7:696–701.

26. Ibid.; Annelise Orleck, *Common Sense and a Little Fire: Women and Working-Class Politics in the United States, 1900–1965* (Chapel Hill, 1995), 77–78.

27. Roosevelt, "True Americanism," 13:20–21.

28. Ibid., 23–24.

29. Roosevelt, "The Monroe Doctrine," *The Bachelor of Arts* (March 1896), in *Works*, 13:172.

30. Roosevelt, "True Americanism," 13:17–20.

31. The effeminacy of the captains of industry—their concern for materialism and leisure to the exclusion of idealism and manliness—would become a reason for Roosevelt to have his New Nationalist state regulate their economic behavior.

32. On manhood and the Spanish-American War, see Kristin L. Hoganson, *Fighting for American Manhood: How Gender Politics Provoked the Spanish-American and Philippine-American Wars* (New Haven, 1998).

33. Roosevelt, "True Americanism," 13:20–23.

34. See, for example, Roosevelt, "Fifth Annual Message," December 5, 1905, in *Works*, 15:317–20.

35. John R. Jenswold, "Leaving the Door Ajar: Politics and Prejudices in the Making of the 1907 Immigration Law," *Mid-America: An Historical Review* 67 (January 1985): 5; *Harvard Encyclopedia of American Ethnic Groups*, s.v. "Naturalization and Citizenship," 740.

36. Jenswold, "Leaving the Door Ajar," 11, 15–16.

37. Candice Lewis Bredbenner, *A Nationality of Her Own: Women, Marriage, and the Law of Citizenship* (Berkeley, 1998), 45–79; Nancy F. Cott, "Marriage and Women's Citizenship in the United States, 1830–1934," *American Historical Review* 103 (December 1998): 1461–64.

38. Jenswold, "Leaving the Door Ajar," 20.

39. *Harvard Encyclopedia of American Ethnic Groups*, s.v. "Naturalization and Citizenship," 740.

40. Lucy Salyer, *Laws Harsh as Tigers: Chinese Immigrants and the Shaping of Modern Immigration Law* (Chapel Hill, 1995), 94–138.

41. Roosevelt, "True Americanism," 13:20–23; Roosevelt, "Religion and the Public Schools," *Works*, 13:275.

42. Roosevelt, "Fifth Annual Message," 15:317; Roosevelt to Joseph Gurney Cannon, January 12, 1907, in *Letters*, 5:550; Jenswold, "Leaving the Door Ajar," 11–13.

43. Roosevelt, "True Americanism," 13:22–23.

44. Ibid., 18.

45. And, Roosevelt believed, the immigrant who refused Americanness would not retain his Europeanness anyway; he "becomes nothing at all." Ibid., 22.

46. See, for example, Eugene Weber, *Peasants into Frenchmen: The Modernization of Rural France, 1870–1914* (Stanford, 1976); Linda Colley, *Britons: Forging the Nation, 1707–1837* (New Haven, 1992); Brubaker, *Citizenship and Nationhood in France and Germany*; John Riddell, ed., *The Communist International in Lenin's Time: The German Revolution and the Debate on Soviet Power. Documents: 1918–1919, Preparing the Founding Congress* (New York, 1986), 299–404; Dipesh Chakraparty, *Rethinking Working-Class History: Bengal, 1890–*

1940 (Princeton, 1989), chap. 7; Jeffrey L. Gould, *To Die in This Way: Nicara-guan Indians and the Myth of Mestizaje, 1880–1965* (Durham, N.C., 1998).

47. Arnaldo Testi, "The Gender of Reform Politics: Theodore Roosevelt and the Culture of Masculinity," *Journal of American History* 81 (March 1995): 1509–33; Robyn Muncy, "Trustbusting and White Manhood in America, 1898–1914," *American Studies* 38 (Fall 1997): 21–42; Paula Baker, "The Domestication of Politics: Women and American Political Society, 1780–1920," *American Historical Review* 89 (June 1984): 620–47; Roosevelt, *Autobiography* 161–67; Theodore Roosevelt, *The Foes of Our Own Household* (New York, 1917), esp. 232–73; Hoganson, *Fighting for American Manhood*; Gail Bederman, *Manliness and Civilization: A Cultural History of Gender and Race in the United States, 1880–1917* (Chicago, 1995), 170–215; Cott, "Marriage and Women's Citizenship in the United States, 1830–1934," 1440–74; Nira Yuval-Davis, *Gender and Nation* (London, 1997).

48. Roosevelt to Arthur Hamilton Lee, March 7, 1908, in *Letters*, 6:965.

49. Salyer, *Laws Harsh as Tigers*; Andrew Gyory, *Closing the Gate: Race, Politics, and the Chinese Exclusion Act* (Chapel Hill, 1998).

50. Roosevelt to George Otto Trevelyan, September 12, 1905, in *Letters*, 5:22.

51. Roosevelt to John St. Loe Strachey, February 22, 1907, in *Letters*, 5:597–98.

52. Roosevelt to Kogoro Takahira, April 28, 1907, in *Letters*, 5:656.

53. Roy L. Garis, *Immigration Restriction* (New York, 1927), chap. 10.

54. Roosevelt to Philander Chase Knox, February 8, 1909, in *Letters*, 6:1511–12; and to Henry C. Lodge, July 10, 1907, ibid., 5:710.

55. Roosevelt to Owen Wister, April 27, 1906, in *Letters*, 5:226.

56. Alfred Holt Stone, *Studies in the American Race Problem* (New York, 1908), 313.

57. Ann J. Lane, *The Brownsville Affair: National Crisis and Black Reaction* (Port Washington, N.Y., 1971). On Roosevelt's attitudes toward blacks, see also George Sinkler, *The Racial Attitudes of American Presidents: From Abraham Lincoln to Theodore Roosevelt* (Garden City, N.Y., 1971), 308–73.

58. Stone, *American Race Problem*, 243–49, 315 (quotation), 319 (quotation).

59. Ibid., 312.

60. Harbaugh, *Theodore Roosevelt*, 127–28.

61. Joel Williamson, *The Crucible of Race: Black-White Relations in the American South since Emancipation* (New York, 1984), 354.

62. Roosevelt to Albion Winegar Tourgee, November 8, 1901, in *Letters*, 3:190–91.

63. Roosevelt to Owen Wister, April 27, 1906, in *Letters*, 5:228.

64. Stone, *American Race Problem*, 286–87.

65. George Mowry, *Theodore Roosevelt and the Progressive Movement* (Madison, Wis., 1946); Arthur S. Link, *Woodrow Wilson and the Progressive Era, 1910–1917* (New York, 1954), 1–24.

66. Herbert Croly, *The Promise of American Life* (1909; Boston, 1989).

67. Ibid., 210.

68. Harbaugh, *Theodore Roosevelt*, 355–71.

69. Howard Lawrence Hurwitz, *Theodore Roosevelt and Labor in New York State, 1880–1900* (New York, 1943). Roosevelt would never forget the drubbing he took from labor in the 1886 New York City mayoralty election. Afterward, according to Hurwitz (289), he would no longer "publicly disparage organized labor"; as a result of these and similar encounters, he began to revise his civic nationalism to include social as well as civic rights.

70. These social rights, according to Marshall, encompassed "the whole range from the right to a modicum of economic welfare and security to the right to share to the full in the social heritage and to live the life of a civilised being according to the standards prevailing in the society." T. H. Marshall, "Citizenship and Social Class," in Marshall, *Citizenship and Social Class and Other Essays* (Cambridge, 1950), 11.

71. Theodore Roosevelt, "The New Nationalism," in Roosevelt, *The New Nationalism* (New York, 1910), 11.

72. Ibid., 5–7.

73. Roosevelt to William Allen White, August 9, 1910, in *Letters*, 7:108.

74. Roosevelt, "New Nationalism," 17, 12.

75. Ibid., 29.

76. Ibid., 12.

77. Ibid., 23–24.

78. Ibid., 18.

79. Ibid., 21.

80. Ibid., 25–26.

81. Quoted in Hurwitz, *Theodore Roosevelt and Labor*, 283. After learning of the Haymarket debacle, Roosevelt had written from his ranch in North Dakota that "nothing would give" his cowboys "greater pleasure than a chance with their rifles at one of the [Haymarket] mobs." Quoted in ibid., 111.

82. In moments of fury, Roosevelt expanded his enemies-of-the-nation list well beyond those who were card-carrying revolutionists to include Governor Peter Altgeld of Illinois, who had pardoned the Haymarket anarchists, William Jennings Bryan, populist leader, anti-imperialist, and Democratic Party standard-bearer, and other populists as well. His New Nationalism would not be fully achieved until such radicalism had been extinguished from the body politic. Ibid., 181; Slotkin, *Gunfighter Nation*, 106–7, 121–22.

83. Roosevelt, "American Ideals," *The Forum* (February 1895), in *Works*, 13:7. "Orderly liberty" and "ordered liberty" were two of Roosevelt's favorite expressions.

84. Roosevelt, "New Nationalism," 7–9.

85. Roosevelt, "Nationalism and Popular Rule," in *Works*, 17:53.

86. Mowry, *Theodore Roosevelt*, 142–43, 147.

87. Roosevelt, "New Nationalism," 27.

88. John Allen Gable, *The Bull Moose Years: Theodore Roosevelt and the Progressive Party* (Port Washington, N.Y., 1978), 6, 40.

89. Jane Addams, *Twenty Years at Hull House* (New York, 1910); Rivka Shpak Lissak, *Pluralism and the Progressives: Hull House and the New Immigrants, 1890–1919* (Chicago, 1919); Catherine Kerr, "Race in the Making of American

Liberalism, 1912–1965" (Ph.D. dissertation, Johns Hopkins University, 1995). On the progressives' engagement with the new immigrants and their problems, see also Margaret Byington, *Homestead: Households of a Mill Town* (New York, 1910), and Paul U. Kellogg, ed., *The Pittsburgh District, The Civic Frontage* (New York, 1914). Both volumes were published as part of the six-volume Pittsburgh Survey, an exhaustive examination of the lives of immigrants in Pittsburgh. For a brief introduction to this project, see Paul U. Kellogg, ed., "The Pittsburgh Survey," *Charities and the Commons* 2 (January 2, 1909): 517–26.

90. Quoted in Daniel Levine, *Jane Addams and the Liberal Tradition* (Madison, Wis., 1971), 190–91.

91. Mowry, *Theodore Roosevelt*, 146.

92. Levine, *Jane Addams*, 192.

93. Thomas J. Knock, *To End All Wars: Woodrow Wilson and the Quest for a New World Order* (New York, 1992), 15–30.

94. Mowry, *Theodore Roosevelt*, 264, 273.

95. Martin J. Sklar, *The Corporate Reconstruction of American Capitalism, 1890–1916: The Markets, the Law, and Politics* (New York, 1988); Alan Dawley, *Struggles for Justice: Social Responsibility and the Liberal State* (Cambridge, Mass., 1991), 136.

96. Gable, *The Bull Moose Years*, 60–74.

97. Ibid; George E. Mowry, "The South and the Progressive Lily White Party of 1912," *Journal of Southern History* 6 (May 1940): 237–47; Dewey W. Grantham Jr., "The Progressive Movement and the Negro," *South Atlantic Quarterly* 54 (October 1955): 461–77; Arthur S. Link, "The Negro as a Factor in the Campaign of 1912," *Journal of Negro History* 32 (January 1947): 81–99.

98. Arthur S. Link, ed., "Correspondence Relating to the Progressive Party's 'Lily White' Policy in 1912," *Journal of Southern History* 10 (November 1944): 483–84.

99. Ibid., 485–88; Roosevelt, "The Progressives and the Colored Man," *The Outlook*, August 24, 1912, in *Works*, 17:304–5.

100. Jane Addams, "The Progressive Party and the Negro," *Crisis*, November 1912, 30–31.

101. Levine, *Jane Addams*, 192.

102. Roosevelt, in Link, "Correspondence Relating to the Progressive Party's 'Lily White' Policy," 482.

103. Mowry, "The South and the Progressive Lily White Party of 1912," 246.

CHAPTER 3

1. At least one parent in each of these families had been born abroad. David Kennedy, *Over Here! The First World War and American Society* (New York, 1980), 24.

2. Bruce White, "The American Military and the Melting Pot in World War I," in J. L. Granatstein and R. D. Cuff, eds., *War and Society in North America*

(Toronto, 1971), 39; Leonard Wood, "Heating Up the Melting Pot," *Independent*, July 3, 1916, 15.

3. Quoted in Kennedy, *Over Here*, 17; from Chase C. Mooney and Martha E. Lyman, "Some Phases of the Compulsory Military Training Movement, 1914–1920," *Mississippi Valley Historical Review* 38 (1952): 41.

4. Theodore Roosevelt, "The Square Deal in Americanism," in *The Great Adventure: Present-Day Studies in American Nationalism* (New York, 1918), in *The Works of Theodore Roosevelt, National Edition*, ed. Hermann Hagedorn, 20 vols. (New York, 1926), 19:313.

5. Frederick C. Luebke, *Bonds of Loyalty: German-Americans and World War I* (DeKalb, Ill., 1974); H. C. Peterson, *Propaganda for War: The War against American Neutrality, 1914–1917* (Norman, Okla., 1939); George Sylvester Viereck, *Spreading Germs of Hate* (New York, 1930); Christopher Gildemeister, "My Four Years in Germany: Progressivism, Propaganda and American Film in World War I" (unpublished seminar paper, Catholic University of America, 1994); Kennedy, *Over Here!*, 212–13.

6. Wilson, in Roosevelt's eyes, never showed the proper appreciation for the virtues of combat itself or for war as an instrument of national or racial fulfillment.

7. Thomas J. Knock, *To End All Wars: Woodrow Wilson and the Quest for a New Moral Order* (Oxford, 1992); John Milton Cooper Jr., *The Warrior and the Priest: Woodrow Wilson and Theodore Roosevelt* (Cambridge, Mass., 1983).

8. There were also obvious physical dangers in allowing a man of nearly sixty years and in poor health to command a regiment in battle. Kennedy, *Over Here!*, 19–20.

9. Ibid., 192–93, 199; Robert H. Ferrell, *Woodrow Wilson and World War I, 1917–1921* (New York, 1985), 20.

10. Daniel H. Kevles, "Testing the Army's Intelligence: Psychologists and the Military in World War I," *Journal of American History* 55 (December 1968): 565–82.

11. Kennedy, *Over Here!*, 218–21. See discussion of story by Samuel McCoy, "Eight American Soldiers," in *Congressional Record* (hereafter CR), April 5, 1924, 5656.

12. See, for example, Ernest Hemingway, *A Farewell to Arms* (New York, 1929); Erich Maria Remarque, *All Quiet on the Western Front* (1929; New York, 1982), and the 1930 movie by the same title it inspired, which won Academy Awards for best picture and best director. On the rise of the 1920s peace movement, see Charles DeBenedetti, *Origins of the Modern Peace Movement, 1915–1929* (Millwood, N.Y., 1978).

13. Knock, *To End All Wars*; DeBenedetti, *Origins of the Modern Peace Movement*.

14. Stephen Vaughn, *Holding Fast the Inner Lines: Democracy, Nationalism, and the Committee on Public Information* (Chapel Hill, 1980); George Creel, *How We Advertised America* (New York, 1920); James R. Mock and Cedric Larson, *Words That Won the War* (Princeton, 1939).

15. David Montgomery, *The Fall of the House of Labor: The Workplace, the State, and American Labor Activism, 1865–1925* (New York, 1987), 330–410; Joseph A. McCartin, *Labor's Great War: The Struggle for Industrial Democracy and the Origins of Modern American Labor Relations, 1912–1921* (Chapel Hill, 1997); Nell Irvin Painter, *Standing at Armageddon: The United States, 1877–1919* (New York, 1987), 283–380; Ronald Schaffer, *America in the Great War: The Rise of the War Welfare State* (New York, 1991), 64–95; John Higham, *Strangers in the Land: Patterns of American Nativism, 1865–1925* (New Brunswick, N.J., 1955), 194–263; James Weinstein, *The Decline of Socialism in America: 1912–1925* (1967; New Brunswick, N.J., 1984), 27–176; Anne Firor Scott and Andrew MacKay Scott, *One Half the People: The Fight for Woman's Suffrage* (Urbana, Ill., 1982); Christine A. Lunardini, *From Equal Suffrage to Equal Rights: Alice Paul and the National Women's Party, 1912–1920* (New York, 1986); Maurine W. Greenwald, *Women, War, and Work* (Westport, Conn., 1980); David Levering Lewis, *W.E.B. Du Bois: Biography of a Race* (New York, 1993), 535–80.

16. Luebke, *Bonds of Loyalty*; Higham, *Strangers in the Land*, 194–263; Yuji Ichioka, *The Issei: The World of First Generation Japanese Immigrants, 1880–1924* (New York, 1988); Kennedy, *Over Here!*, 3–92.

17. Lucy Salyer, *Laws Harsh as Tigers: Chinese Immigrants and the Shaping of Modern Immigration Law* (Chapel Hill, 1995); William Preston Jr., *Aliens and Dissenters: Federal Suppression of Radicals, 1903–1933* (1963; Urbana, Ill., 1994).

18. Richard Polenberg, *Fighting Faiths: The Abrams Case, the Supreme Court, and Free Speech* (New York, 1987), 164–65; Richard Gid Powers, *Secrecy and Power: The Life of J. Edgar Hoover* (New York, 1987), 36–129; Athan G. Theoharis and John Stuart Cox, *The Boss: J. Edgar Hoover and the Great American Inquisition* (Philadelphia, 1988), 51–70.

19. Polenberg, *Fighting Faiths*, 167–68; Richard D. Challener, ed., *United States Military Intelligence, 1917–1927* (New York, 1978), 1:v–xii; Theodore Kornweibel, ed., *Federal Surveillance of Afro-Americans, 1917–1925: The First World War, the Red Scare and the Garvey Movement*, microfilm (Frederick, Md., 1985).

20. Polenberg, *Fighting Faiths*, 170.

21. Ibid., 163–64.

22. Kennedy, *Over Here!*, 81–83; Stephen Meyer III, *The Five Dollar Day: Labor Management and Social Control in the Ford Motor Company, 1908–1921* (Albany, N.Y., 1981), 169–94.

23. Ellis Hawley, *The Great War and the Search for Modern Order: A History of the American People and Their Institutions, 1917–1933* (New York, 1979); Robert D. Cuff, *The War Industries Board: Business-Government Relations during World War I* (Baltimore, 1973); Alan Dawley, *Struggles for Justice: Social Responsibility and the Liberal State* (Cambridge, 1991), 194–96.

24. An American Legion member noted in 1919 that when "the Legion officials needed anything, they called on the Governor, the Adjutant General, the Attorney General, and they got what they wanted RIGHT ON THE SPOT." Quoted in

William Pencak, *For God and Country: The American Legion, 1919–1941* (Boston, 1989), 66, 121. On the rebirth of the Klan, see Nancy MacLean, *Behind the Mask of Chivalry: The Making of the Second Ku Klux Klan* (New York, 1994), and Kathleen M. Blee, *Women of the Klan: Racism and Gender in the 1920s* (Berkeley, 1991).

25. John C. Burnham, *Bad Habits: Drinking, Smoking, Taking Drugs, Gambling, Sexual Misbehavior, and Swearing in American History* (New York, 1993), 28–29.

26. Hoover was even forced to dismantle the General Intelligence Division in 1924. Kenneth Reilly, *Hoover and the Un-Americans: The FBI, HUAC, and the Red Menace* (Philadelphia, 1983), 18. The wartime sedition law expired soon after the war ended. Also, funds for the army's Military Intelligence Unit dried up after the war, forcing it to curtail its activities. Challener, *United States Military Intelligence*, 1:v–xii.

27. *Meyer v. State of Nebraska*, 262 U.S. 390 (1923); *Pierce, Governor of Oregon, et al. v. The Society of Sisters*, 268 U.S. 510 (1925); *Farrington, Governor of Hawaii, et al. v. Tokushige et al.*, 284 U.S. 298 (1926); Lawrence H. Fuchs, *The American Kaleidoscope: Race, Ethnicity, and the Civic Culture* (Hanover, N.H., 1990), 70–71.

28. Polenberg, *Fighting Faiths*, 158.

29. Salyer, *Laws Harsh as Tigers*; Preston, *Aliens and Dissenters*.

30. Higham, *Strangers in the Land*; Robert A. Divine, *American Immigration Policy, 1924–1952* (New Haven, 1957); Salyer, *Laws Harsh as Tigers*; John R. Jenswold, "Leaving the Door Ajar: Politics and Prejudices in the Making of the 1907 Immigration Law," *Mid-America: An Historical Review* 67 (January 1985): 3–22. The 1907 law actually had not been the first to establish the principle of individual exclusion. The 1882 law excluded convicts, lunatics, and those unable to care for themselves; an 1891 law added to the list polygamists, people with contagious diseases, and those likely to become public charges. Salyer, *Laws Harsh as Tigers*, 26; for more on the 1907 law, see chapter 2.

31. Roosevelt never got a chance to veto it, for, during his presidency, the literacy test was defeated in Congress; Jenswold, "Leaving the Door Ajar."

32. For veto messages, see *CR*, March 25, 1916, 4876.

33. The 1917 law mandated that entry to America would be limited to those individuals who could read thirty or forty commonly used words in any language. Anyone who failed the test would be shipped back to Europe.

34. By Dillingham's count, the illiteracy rate among so-called old immigrants in the years from 1899 to 1909 was 3 percent, while the rate for new immigrants was 36 percent. The rates for specific groups among the new immigrants were as follows: southern Italians, 54 percent; Croatians and Slovenians, 36 percent; Poles, 35 percent; Russians, 35 percent; Hebrews, 26 percent; northern Italians, 12 percent; Hungarians, 11 percent; *CR*, August 17, 1916, 12771–75. See also Divine, *American Immigration Policy*, 5.

35. U.S. Department of Commerce, Bureau of the Census, *Historical Statistics of the United States, Colonial Times to 1970* (White Plains, N.Y., 1989), 1:105. The actual numbers were 430,001 in 1920 and 805,228 in 1921. In 1920 more

than half came from Europe and about one-third came from eastern and southern Europe. In 1921, more than four-fifths came from Europe and almost two-thirds from southern and eastern Europe; 222,260 (28 percent) came from Italy alone.

36. The Asiatic Barred Zone did not include Japan. Immigration from Japan was already restricted by the Gentlemen's Agreement of 1907, which obligated the Japanese government to limit emigration of its nationals to the United States. This policy had curtailed the number of Japanese male laborers arriving in the United States, but it had not shut the door to Japanese immigration altogether. Moreover, many anti-Japanese groups in the United States were outraged that the agreement had vested the power to restrict Japanese immigration in the Japanese, rather than the American, government. Sidney L. Gulick, *American Democracy and Asiatic Citizenship* (New York, 1918), 14–29, 51–52.

37. Mark Mazower, *Dark Continent: Europe's Twentieth Century* (London, 1998), 1–39.

38. Steven Fraser, *Labor Will Rule: Sidney Hillman and the Rise of American Labor* (New York, 1991), 114–45; Cooper, *The Warrior and the Priest*, 264; Woodrow Wilson cable to Congress, May 20, 1919, in *Woodrow Wilson Presidential Papers*, ed., Arthur S. Link (Princeton, 1966–94), 5:486–87; N. Gordon Levin Jr., *Woodrow Wilson and World Politics: America's Response to War and Revolution* (New York, 1968); Lloyd C. Gardner, *Safe for Democracy: The Anglo-American Response to Revolution, 1913–1923* (New York, 1984).

39. Cooper, *The Warrior and the Priest*, 264.

40. Preston, *Aliens and Dissenters*, 182–83.

41. Ibid., passim; H. C. Peterson and Gilbert C. Fite, *Opponents of War, 1917–1918* (Madison, Wis., 1957).

42. The precise percentages are as follows: sugar refining, 85 percent; clothing manufacture, 72 percent; cotton goods and oil refining, 67 percent; woolen goods and coal mining, 62 percent; meat-packing, 61 percent; and iron and steel, 58 percent. *CR*, January 17, 1920, 1654. On the immigrant character of the working class during this period, see Montgomery, *The Fall of the House of Labor*.

43. *CR*, January 31, 1920, 2299.

44. *CR*, May 25, 1920, 7607; see also *CR*, December 20, 1919, 991.

45. *CR*, December 20, 1919, 987.

46. This was the claim of Representative John Raker of California (Democrat), and it was immediately disputed by Representative Nathan Perlman of New York (Republican), who argued that only 0.5 percent of the Russian Jewish population was Bolshevik at that time. *CR*, April 20, 1921, 551.

47. Adolf Hitler, *Mein Kampf* (1925–27; New York, 1939); Arno J. Mayer, *Why Did the Heavens Not Darken? The "Final Solution" in History* (New York, 1988), 39–109; Omer Bartov, "Defining Enemies, Making Victims: Germans, Jews, and the Holocaust," *American Historical Review* 103 (June 1998): 771–816.

48. A total of 600,000 Russians, 70,000 Poles, and 300,000 Italians applied for passports and visas in the early postwar years; many of the Russians and Poles were Jews. U.S. Congress, House, "Report on Restriction of Immigration," *House Reports*, 67th Cong., 1st sess., 1921, vol. 1, 9–16; *CR*, April 5, 1924,

5648. Passports were first required of immigrants wishing to enter the United States during the First World War. This procedure was formally extended in the postwar period by the Passport Control Extension Bill, passed by Congress in October 1919. *CR*, January 8, 1921, 1163.

49. House, "Report on Restriction of Immigration," 12–13.

50. *CR*, December 20, 1919, 990–91.

51. Alice Wexler, *Emma Goldman: An Intimate Life* (New York, 1984).

52. Almost 1 million Americans would soon vote for another jailbird, the Socialist leader Eugene Victor Debs, who ran his 1920 presidential campaign from the Atlanta Federal Penitentiary. Nick Salvatore, *Eugene V. Debs: Citizen and Socialist* (Urbana, Ill., 1982): esp. 183–219 (on Victor Berger); 321–26 (on Debs's 1920 presidential campaign).

53. *CR*, December 20, 1919, 994.

54. For divergent interpretations of the Sacco-Vanzetti affair, see Francis Russell, *Tragedy in Dedham: The Story of the Sacco-Vanzetti Case* (New York, 1962), and Roberta Strauss Feuerlicht, *Justice Crucified: The Story of Sacco and Vanzetti* (New York, 1977). In *Sacco-Vanzetti: The Anarchist Background* (Princeton, 1991), Paul Avrich reconstructs the milieu from which these two anarchists emerged.

55. Humbert Nelli, *The Business of Crime: Italians and Syndicate Crime in the United States* (New York, 1976).

56. *CR*, May 3, 1921, 968. The bill passed in the Senate 78–1; soon after, the bill passed in the House, 276–33. *CR*, May 13, 1921, 1442–43.

57. This method was actually a compromise between the Senate, which wanted national quotas set at 5 percent, and the House, which wanted to halt immigration altogether for at least a year while permitting unlimited immigration for purposes of family reunification.

58. *CR*, February 19, 1921, 3457; February 26, 1921, 3812; May 3, 1921, 968; May 13, 1921, 1442–43; January 23, 1924, 580. The text of the bill can be found in *CR*, May 13, 1921, 1427–28. The bill did not affect immigration law toward Asians. Thus the Chinese Exclusion Act, the Gentleman's Agreement, and the Asiatic Barred Zone continued in effect. All Western Hemispheric nations were exempted from the provisions of this act. The 1921 law could have been worse: a proposal to restrict immigrants to 3 percent of the *naturalized* population (which would have limited southern and eastern European immigrants to 27,000 a year) was defeated. *CR*, February 19, 1921, 3457.

59. The precise figures were 64 and 29 percent. Bureau of the Census, *Historical Statistics*, 1:105–7. Total immigration actually rose from 1922 to 1923, chiefly because 200,000 had come to the United States from Western Hemispheric countries that were exempted from the 3 percent rule. But because almost two-thirds of this "North American" immigration (59 percent) came from Canada and Newfoundland, it raised few worries. It is true, however, that a certain percentage of those "North Americans" were eastern and southern Europeans sneaking into the country under false identities.

60. Harry H. Laughlin, "Analysis of America's Modern Melting Pot," Statement to U.S. Congress, House, Committee on Immigration and Naturalization,

67th Cong., 3rd sess., November 21, 1922, Serial 7-C (Washington, D.C., 1923), 727–831. Laughlin's report suffered from numerous methodological and interpretive flaws that rendered his findings suspect. For data, it relied exclusively on that part of the "degenerate" population that had been institutionalized in federal and state institutions. It therefore did not include those who were in the care of private institutions or who remained with their families. It took no account of disparities in wealth and living conditions between the different groups and how these differences may have influenced rates of degeneracy. Poverty, when it was considered at all, was treated simply as another sign of racial degeneracy rather than as a function of exploitation or lack of education—circumstances that could be reversed through social policy and schooling.

Even if the report is accepted on its own terms, its findings are highly ambiguous. New immigrants displayed higher rates of "degeneracy" than old immigrants in some areas, such as crime, but lower rates in other areas, such as insanity and dependency. The Irish rate of insanity exceeded that of every other group of Europeans except the Serbs, while British, French, and Irish immigrants tallied the highest rates of dependency. Overall, Laughlin's data show that the rate of degeneracy among eastern and southern European immigrants was virtually indistinguishable from that of northwestern European immigrants. But Laughlin was not about to call attention to this embarrassing finding. Instead, he concocted an argument that maintained the fiction that a racial divide separated the new immigrants from the old. And the idea of innate racial difference between old and new immigrants was all that many members of Congress wanted to hear.

61. *CR*, March 17, 1924, 4389.

62. *CR*, April 8, 1924, 5872. Kenneth Roberts, a popular writer for the *Saturday Evening Post*, made similar kinds of arguments in a series of articles on immigration and the failure of the melting pot. See, for example, Kenneth L. Roberts, "The Goal of Central Europeans," and "Plain Remarks on Immigration for Plain Americans," *Saturday Evening Post*, November 6, 1920, and February 12, 1921.

63. *CR*, April 5, 1924, 5685.

64. *CR*, February 2, 1924, 1895.

65. *CR*, April 5, 5683–84.

66. *CR*, April 8, 1924, 5868–69. Congressman Ira G. Hersey of Maine (Republican) uttered these words.

67. *CR*, April 5, 5693.

68. Laughlin, "Analysis of America's Modern Melting Pot," 738.

69. *CR*, April 4, 1924, 5641.

70. Ibid.

71. The figures have been drawn from U.S. Department of Commerce, Bureau of the Census, *Statistical Abstract of the United States* (Washington, D.C., 1929), 100.

72. Laughlin, "Analysis of America's Modern Melting Pot," table 8, between pp. 750 and 751. The Japanese rate of degeneracy was almost 50 percent lower than that of the British, the Germans, and native-born Americans of native parentage. Only the Swiss showed a lower rate of degeneracy.

73. *CR*, April 8, 1924, 5883.

74. *CR*, April 7, 1924, 5743.

75. *CR*, July 14, 1916, 11017–18.

76. *CR*, April 5, 1924, 5696.

77. *CR*, July 14, 1916, 11017–18.

78. *CR*, April 8, 1924, 5883.

79. *CR*, July 14, 1916, 11017–18.

80. *CR*, April 8, 1924, 5883.

81. Ibid., 5805.

82. *Ozawa v. United States*, 160 U.S. 178 (1922); *United States v. Thind* 261 U.S. 204 (1923); Ian F. Haney Lopez, *White by Law: The Legal Construction of Race* (New York, 1996), 86–118; Ichioka, *The Issei*; Bill Ong Hing, *Making and Remaking Asian America through Immigration Policy, 1850–1990* (Stanford, 1993); Joan Jensen, *Passage from India* (New Haven, 1988); Matthew Frye Jacobson, *Whiteness of a Different Color: European Americans and the Alchemy of Race*, (Cambridge, Mass., 1998) 223–45; Roger Daniels, *Not Like Us: Immigrants and Minorities in America, 1890–1924* (Chicago, 1997), 136.

83. On the withdrawal of corporations from immigration restriction debates, see Higham, *Strangers in the Land*, 316–18, and Daniels, *Not Like Us*.

84. Ichioka, *The Issei*, 226–43.

85. Pascoe, "Miscegenation Law, Court Cases, and Ideologies of 'Race' in Twentieth-Century America," *Journal of American History* 83 (June 1996): 49, 59.

86. Polenberg, *Fighting Faiths*; Samuel Walker, *In Defense of American Liberties: A History of the ACLU* (New York, 1990); Fuchs, *The American Kaleidoscope*, 67–69; Gary Gerstle, *Working-Class Americanism: The Politics of Labor in a Textile City, 1914–1960* (New York, 1989), chaps. 1–2; Gerstle, "The Politics of Patriotism: Americanization and the Formation of the CIO," *Dissent* (Winter 1986): 84–92.

87. James Kettner, *The Development of American Citizenship, 1608–1870* (Chapel Hill, 1978), 342–51. The key court case affirming the citizenship of Chinese American children born to parents ineligible for citizenship was *United States v. Wong Kim Ark*, 169 U.S. 649 (1898).

88. State legislatures did agitate in this direction. In 1920, Oregon's legislature sent Congress a petition requesting Congress to submit "to the legislatures of the several States a proposed amendment to the fourteenth amendment to the Constitution of the United States, so that such amendment shall provide, when amended, that children born in the United States, or in territory subject to the jurisdiction thereof, and whose parents are not citizens and can not under existing laws acquire citizenship by naturalization, shall retain the citizenship of the parents and shall not become citizens by reason of birth in the United States or in territory subject to the jurisdiction thereof." *CR*, January 31, 1920, 2296.

89. *CR*, April 8, 1924, 5893. For Dickstein's espousal of civic nationalism, see, *CR*, March 20, 1924, 4570–73.

90. *CR*, April 5, 1924, 5647; see also Rep. Perlman's comments, ibid., 5651.

91. *CR*, April 8, 1924, 5872.

92. *CR*, April 5, 1924, 5649.

93. Ibid., 5656.

94. Ibid., 5667.

95. Ibid. Antirestrictionists did not rest their case entirely on these Roosevelt-style war stories. They also poked holes in the racialist arguments of the restrictionists. One congressman identified methodological weaknesses in Laughlin's report, while another ridiculed it, pointing out that the first syllable of Laughlin's name spelled "L-a-u-g-h." Still others lampooned the racialist theories of the restrictionists, pointing out the utterly mongrel origins of the "pure" British, German, and American peoples. They even forced some restrictionists, such as Senator Henry Cabot Lodge of Massachusetts (Republican), to concede that virtually every "race" in Europe, including the Germans and the British, had been the product of extensive ethnic mixing. Theodore Roosevelt had regarded the hybridized origins of the German and British peoples as a chief reason for their virtue, but his good friend Lodge took no satisfaction in that knowledge. Lodge and others continued to insist on passing a law that they knew to be based on spurious notions of racial purity. CR, January 23, 1924, 1329; March 14, 1924, 4177; April 3, 1924, 5461; April 5, 1924, 5647.

The critique of the antirestrictionists, and their advocacy of a civic rather than racial nationalism, did prompt the restrictionist majority to search for ways to write an anti-immigrant law that would seem less arbitrary, less racialist, and thus less insulting to the new immigrants than the Immigration Act of 1924. Thus, in 1927, this majority passed the National Origins Act, which granted to each country an annual quota that, in percentage terms, equaled the contribution that that country had made, in terms of numbers of immigrants and their descendants, to the 1920 American population. This law was rigged to yield the *same* discriminatory quota distribution as the 1924 act, but it justified the distribution of immigrant slots as a way of preserving the country's existing mix of "national stocks" rather than in terms of barring inferior immigrant streams. This law, in other words, continued to exclude southern and eastern European immigrants, but not in an overtly racist fashion. It altered the language, but not the substance, of immigration restriction. It took effect fully in 1929. See Divine, *American Immigration Policy*, 26–51; Mae M. Ngai, "The Architecture of Race in American Immigration Law: A Reexamination of the Immigration Act of 1924," *Journal of American History* 86 (June 1999): 67–92; Desmond King, *Making Americans: Immigration, Race, and the Origins of the Diverse Democracy* (Cambridge, Mass., 2000), 199–228.

96. CR, April 4, 1924, 5586. If immigration policy toward Japan had been his to devise, Hughes simply would have maintained the Gentleman's Agreement; but he—and his westernizing supporters in Japan—regarded the quota system as an acceptable alternative.

97. Only Senators David Reed of Pennsylvania (Republican), the Senate's sponsor of the 1924 bill, Joseph T. Robinson of Arkansas (Democrat), and LeBaron Colt of Rhode Island (Republican) supported Hughes's proposal. CR, April 8, 1924, 5809; April 2, 1924, 5415. Congressmen Celler and LaGuardia seemed willing to consider supporting this position as well. CR, March 14, 1924, 4174; April 5, 1924, 5681. This issue prompted numerous individuals and organizations

to write to Congress, but, of the letters printed in the *CR*, only the ones from the Japanese American community itself and the Federal Council of Churches protested Japanese exclusion.

98. *CR*, March 13, 1924, 4073.

99. *CR*, April 5, 1924, 5681.

100. *CR*, April 8, 1924, 5889.

101. *CR*, April 5, 1924, 5681. Emanuel Celler may also have been more willing to support a more liberal position on the Japanese question.

102. *CR*, August 17, 1916, 12775; January 23, 1924, 1331; April 3, 1924, 5468; April 5, 1924, 5696, 5703.

103. *CR*, April 8, 5843, 5886. A full-fledged fight about Mexican immigration never erupted in debates about the 1924 law; Mexicans had yet to come in sufficient numbers to raise a level of concern similar to that expressed about the new immigrants. Agricultural interests in the Southwest, meanwhile, squashed whatever opposition did arise, for they were heavily dependent on Mexican labor. But the fight could only be postponed, not circumvented; it broke out, with fury, in the late 1920s and climaxed in 1930. The restrictionists lost. Divine, *American Immigration Policy*, 52–68.

104. This was in fact how moderate restrictionists within Congress and many liberals outside its halls rationalized their own tacit support for this racist legislation. For a moderate restrictionist viewpoint in Congress, see the speech of Representative Charles Stengle of New York in *CR*, April 8, 1924, 5848; on liberals' tacit support for immigration restriction, see Gary Gerstle, "The Protean Character of American Liberalism," *American Historical Review* 99 (October 1994): 1043–73.

105. Hawley, *The Great War and the Search for a Modern Order*; Schaffer, *America in the Great War*, 31–74; Cuff, *The War Industries Board*; Dawley, *Struggles for Justice*, 194–96; McCartin, *Labor's Great War* 65–146.

106. Alan Brinkley, "The Two World Wars and the Idea of the State," in John Patrick Diggins, ed., *The Liberal Persuasion: Arthur Schlesinger Jr., and the Challenge of the American Past* (Princeton, 1997), 127–141; William E. Leuchtenberg, "The New Deal and the Analogue of War," in John Braeman, Robert H. Bremner, and Everett Walters, eds., *Change and Continuity in Twentieth-Century America* (Columbus, Ohio, 1964), 81–144.

107. Hawley, *The Great War and the Search for a Modern Order*; Ellis Hawley, ed., *Herbert Hoover as Secretary of Commerce: Studies in New Era Thought and Practice* (Iowa City, Iowa, 1981); Dawley, *Struggles for Justice*, 297–333.

108. Corporations, of course, believed that they could achieve economic opportunity, prosperity, and social harmony on their own by offering employees generous wage and benefit packages, implementing fair personnel practices, and sponsoring athletic leagues, picnics, and other recreational events. But these programs were not widespread or durable enough in the 1920s to achieve the desired goals. Lizabeth Cohen, *Making a New Deal: Industrial Workers in Chicago, 1919–1939* (New York, 1990), 159–211; Sanford M. Jacoby, *Employing Bureaucracy: Managers, Unions, and the Transformation of Work in American Industry, 1900–1945* (New York, 1985).

CHAPTER 4

1. Geoffrey C. Ward, *A First-Class Temperament: The Emergence of Franklin Roosevelt* (New York, 1989), 254.

2. Ibid., 88, 152–53; Frank Friedel, *Franklin D. Roosevelt: A Rendezvous with Destiny* (Boston, 1990), 3–22; James MacGregor Burns, *Roosevelt: The Lion and the Fox* (1956; Orlando, Fla., 1986), 25.

3. Ward, *First-Class Temperament*, 84–123; Friedel, *Franklin D. Roosevelt*, 17–32; Burns, *The Lion and the Fox*, 22–80.

4. Roosevelt, "Address at the Dedication of the Theodore Roosevelt Memorial," January 19, 1936, in *Public Papers and Addresses of Franklin D. Roosevelt*, ed. Samuel I. Rosenman, 13 vols. (Washington, D.C., 1938–1950), 5:64.

5. On Peabody, see Geoffrey C. Ward, *Before the Trumpet: Young Franklin Roosevelt, 1882–1905* (New York, 1985), 189–95; Ward, *A First-Class Temperament*, 88–90; Burns, *The Lion and the Fox*, 163, 468. Peabody assisted with church services on the morning of FDR's inauguration; FDR mourned his death in 1944.

6. John Milton Cooper Jr., *The Warrior and the Priest: Woodrow Wilson and Theodore Roosevelt* (Cambridge, Mass., 1983), 350.

7. Roosevelt, "Presidential Statement on N.I.R.A.," June 16, 1933, in *Public Papers*, 2:252–53.

8. Roosevelt, "Inaugural Address," March 4, 1933, in *Public Papers*, 2:14. See also, Roosevelt, "Address at Jefferson Day Dinner," St. Paul, Minnesota, April 18, 1932, ibid., 1:631–32; William E. Leuchtenberg, "The New Deal and the Analogue of War," in John Braeman, Robert H. Bremner, and Everett Walters, eds., *Change and Continuity in Twentieth-Century America* (Columbus, Ohio, 1964), 81–144.

9. Johnson had also helped to organize conscription in the First World War.

10. Roosevelt, "The Third 'Fireside Chat,' " July 24, 1933, in *Public Papers*, 1:300.

11. Ward, *First-Class Temperament*, 160–61.

12. *Public Papers*, 2:12.

13. See, for example, Robert McElvaine, *The Great Depression: America, 1929–1941* (New York, 1984) 73–94.

14. Roosevelt, "Address at Roosevelt Park," New York City, October 28, 1936, in *Public Papers*, 5:544–55.

15. Roosevelt, "Address on the Occasion of the Fiftieth Anniversary of the Statue of Liberty," New York City, October 28, 1936, in *Public Papers*, 5:542–43.

16. See, for example, Kristi Anderson, *The Creation of a Democratic Majority, 1928–1936* (Chicago, 1979); Paul Kleppner, *Who Voted? The Dynamics of Electoral Turnout, 1870–1980* (New York, 1982), 83–111; and Gary Gerstle, *Working-Class Americanism: The Politics of Labor in a Textile City, 1914–1960* (New York, 1989), 41–60.

17. Irving Bernstein, *The Turbulent Years: A History of the American Worker, 1933–1941* (Boston, 1969); Melvyn Dubofsky and Warren Van Tine, *John L. Lewis: A Biography* (New York, 1977).

18. See, for example, Robert S. McElvaine, ed., *Down and Out in the Great Depression: Letters from the Forgotten Man* (Chapel Hill, 1983), and Jacquelyn Dowd Hall, James Leloudis, Robert Korstad, Mary Murphy, Lu Ann Jones, and Christopher B. Daly, *Like a Family: The Making of a Southern Cotton Mill World* (Chapel Hill, 1987), 289–357.

19. Bernstein, *The Turbulent Years*; Farrell Dobbs, *Teamster Rebellion* (New York, 1972); Charles Rumford Walker, *An American City: A Rank and File History* (New York, 1937); Elizabeth Faue, *Community of Suffering and Struggle: Women, Men, and the Labor Movement in Minneapolis, 1915–1945* (Chapel Hill, 1991); Bruce Nelson, *Workers on the Waterfront: Seamen, Longshoremen, and Unionism in the 1930s* (Urbana, Ill., 1988).

20. Gerstle, *Working-Class Americanism*, 127–50; Hall et al., *Like a Family*, 289–357; James A. Hodges, *New Deal Labor Policy and the Southern Cotton Textile Industry, 1933–1941* (Knoxville, Tenn., 1986), 3–78.

21. The Democrats increased their majority, from 310 to 319 (out of 432) in the House, and from 60 to 69 (out of 96) in the Senate. McElvaine, *The Great Depression*, 229; Gerstle, *Working-Class Americanism*, 127–50, 232–47. On South Carolina politics, see Bryant Simon, *A Fabric of Defeat: The Politics of South Carolina Millhands, 1910–1948* (Chapel Hill, 1998).

22. McElvaine, *The Great Depression*, 224–49.

23. McElvaine, *Down and Out in the Great Depression*, 223.

24. Albert Pelchat to President Roosevelt, September 14, 1934, Woonsocket Rayon Co. file, Record Group 9, Entry 402, National Archives, Washington, D.C.

25. John L. Lewis, *The Miners' Fight for American Standards* (Indianapolis, 1925), 179–80.

26. For an example of his use of the language of industrial democracy, see John L. Lewis, "Industrial Democracy in Steel," *United Mine Workers Journal* 47 (July 1936): 3. A key ideological influence on Lewis in the 1920s and 1930s was W. Jett Lauck, a member of the UMW brain trust. In 1926, Lauck published *Political and Industrial Democracy: 1776–1926* (New York, 1926), which became a blueprint for the CIO's industrial democracy campaign in the 1930s.

27. Quoted in *ITU News*, October 1940, 6.

28. For this reason, he had changed the name of his journal from *The Socialist Review* to *Labor Age*. A. J. Muste, *The Essays of A. J. Muste*, ed. Nat Hentoff (Indianapolis, 1967), 116–23.

29. Roy Rosenzweig, "Radicals and Mass Movements: The Musteites and the Unemployed Leagues, 1932–1936" (unpublished paper, Cambridge University, 1972), 16–17. On Muste, see Muste, "Sketches for an Autobiography," in *The Essays of A. J. Muste*, 116–67.

30. Rosenzweig, "Radicals and Mass Movements," 50–51, 68. For a condensed version of this paper, see Roy Rosenzweig, "Radicals and the Jobless: Musteites and the Unemployed Leagues, 1932–1936," *Labor History* 16 (Winter 1975): 52–77. The use of the phrase "Declaration of the Rights" was meant to

tie the document, too, to the French Revolution and its manifesto, "The Declaration of the Rights of Man."

31. "Continental Congress of Workers and Farmers for Economic Reconstruction, a Call for Delegates," *Minutes of Continental Congress for Economic Reconstruction,* May 6–7, 1933, David P. Saposs Papers, MSS 133, box 22, folders 19 and 20, Wisconsin State Historical Society, Madison, Wisconsin. See also David Shannon, *The Socialist Party of America: A History* (New York, 1955), 227–28 (quotation), and Bernard K. Johnpoll, *Pacifist's Progress: Norman Thomas and the Decline of American Socialism* (Chicago, 1970).

32. Irving Howe and Lewis Coser, *The American Communist Party: A Critical History* (New York, 1957), esp. 339–40 and 319–86; see also Irving Howe, "The Brilliant Masquerade: A Note on Browderism," in Howe, *Socialism and America* (New York, 1985), 87–104.

33. Membership fell in the years from 1939 to 1941, as the Stalin-Hitler Pact forced Communist parties in most countries to abandon their popular fronts. These popular fronts resurged after Hitler attacked the Soviet Union in June 1941.

34. Howe and Coser, *The American Communist Party,* 319–86; Harvey Klehr, *The Heyday of American Communism: The Depression Decade* (New York, 1984); Sam Tanenhaus, *Whittaker Chambers* (New York, 1997); Michael Denning, *The Cultural Front: The Laboring of American Culture in the Twentieth Century* (New York, 1996).

35. American socialists and syndicalists, like their Italian counterparts, were exceptional in maintaining their opposition to war and nationalism. See Irving Howe, "The Era of Debs," in Howe, *Socialism and America,* 3–48.

36. It is true, however, that, by the 1920s, Lenin and Stalin were making distinctions between "progressive" and "reactionary" nationalisms. The progressive nationalisms were those of oppressed groups for whom "national liberation" could be conjoined with socialist revolution; reactionary nationalisms were those that sought to contain and destroy revolutionary movements. See Gary Gerstle, "The Changing Language of American Labor, 1900–1940" (unpublished paper in author's possession); John Riddell, ed., *The Communist International in Lenin's Time: The German Revolution and the Debate on Soviet Power. Documents: 1918–1919, Preparing the Founding Congress* (New York, 1986), 299–404; Richard Pipes, *The Formation of the Soviet Union: Communism and Nationalism, 1917–1923* (Cambridge, Mass., 1964).

37. Robert Darnton, "What Was Revolutionary about the French Revolution?" *New York Review of Books,* January 19, 1989, 3.

38. Radicals abandoned the "Marseillaise" for the "Internationale" in the late nineteenth century. Eric Hobsbawm, *Nations and Nationalism since 1870: Programme, Myth, Reality* (New York, 1990), 145 and, more generally, 131–62.

39. By contrast, those radicals, such as the Trotskyists, who remained insistently internationalist and antinationalist in these years sank into oblivion. So did virtually every other antinationalist movement in the United States in these years.

40. Franklin D. Roosevelt, "Acceptance of the Renomination for the Presidency," June 27, 1936, in *Public Papers,* 5:230–36.

41. McElvaine, *The Great Depression*, 281, and, more generally, 275–81; William E. Leuchtenberg, *Franklin D. Roosevelt and the New Deal, 1932–1940* (New York, 1963), 143–96.

42. Steve Fraser, "The 'Labor Question,' " in Steve Fraser and Gary Gerstle, *The Rise and Fall of the New Deal Order, 1930–1980* (Princeton, eds., 1989), 55–84.

43. Ibid.; Nelson Lichtenstein, "From Corporatism to Collective Bargaining: Organized Labor and the Eclipse of Social Democracy in the Postwar Era," in Fraser and Gerstle, *The Rise and Fall of the New Deal Order*, 122–52.

44. Sidney Fine, *Sit-Down: The General Motors Strike of 1936–1937* (Ann Arbor, Mich., 1969), 312.

45. Victor G. Reuther, *The Brothers Reuther and the Story of the UAW: A Memoir* (Boston, 1976), 148.

46. Gerstle, *Working-Class Americanism*, 153–95.

47. Richard Pells, *Radical Visions and American Dreams: Culture and Social Thought in the Depression Years* (New York, 1973); Barbara Melosh, *Engendering Culture: Manhood and Womanhood in New Deal Public Art and Theater* (Washington, D.C., 1991); Denning, *The Cultural Front*, 283–309; Harry Goldman, "When Social Significance Came to Broadway: 'Pins and Needles' in Production," *Theatre Quarterly* 7 (Winter 1977–78): 25–39; Clifford Odets, "Waiting for Lefty," in Odets, *Six Plays of Clifford Odets* (New York, 1979), 1–32; Gerald Weales, *Clifford Odets, Playwright* (New York, 1971), 35–55.

48. Only the movie ends with that line; the novel does not. John Ford, director, *The Grapes of Wrath* (1940); John Steinbeck, *The Grapes of Wrath* (1939; New York, 1985); Frank Capra, director, *Mr. Deeds Goes to Town* (1936) and *Mr. Smith Goes to Washington* (1939); Pells, *Radical Visions and American Dreams*, 215–19; Denning, *The Cultural Front*, 259–82.

49. Lawrence H. Fuchs, *The Political Behavior of American Jews* (Glencoe, Ill., 1956), 71–81.

50. Geoffrey Ward estimates that Jews eventually formed about 15 percent of Roosevelt's top appointments at a time when they formed only 3 percent of the population; Ward, *First-Class Temperament*, 254.

51. See Gerstle, *Working-Class Americanism*, 127–229; David Brody, "Workplace Contractualism in Comparative Perspective," in Nelson Lichtenstein and Howell John Harris, eds., *Industrial Democracy in America: The Ambiguous Promise* (New York, 1993), 200–201; Lizabeth Cohen, *Making a New Deal: Industrial Workers in Chicago, 1919–1939* (New York, 1990).

52. A hard class logic was at work among these minority groups, who understood that they stood to gain more economic benefits from the policies of the Democrats than those of the Republicans. Nancy J. Weiss, *Farewell to the Party of Lincoln: Black Politics in the Age of FDR* (Princeton, 1983); George J. Sanchez, *Becoming Mexican American: Ethnicity, Culture, and Identity in Chicano Los Angeles, 1900–1945* (New York, 1993), 227–69.

53. This subject will be explored in chapter 5.

54. From November 1936 to July 1937, Detroit workers alone staged 147 sit-down strikes. Walter Goodman, *The Committee: The Extraordinary Career of the House Committee on Un-American Activities* (New York, 1968), 49.

55. Robert Zieger, *The CIO, 1935–1955* (Chapel Hill, 1995), 1–110; Christopher L. Tomlins, *The State and the Unions: Labor Relations, Law, and the Organized Labor Movement in America, 1880–1960* (New York, 1985); James Patterson, *Congressional Opposition to the New Deal: The Growth of the Conservative Coalition in Congress, 1933–1939* (Lexington, Ky., 1967); Gerstle, *Working-Class Americanism*, 196–259; Steven Fraser, *Labor Will Rule: Sidney Hillman and the Rise of American Labor* (New York, 1991), 373–406.

56. Once again, FDR was following in TR's footsteps. Although TR had never made so brash a proposal, he regularly attacked the Supreme Court for thwarting the people's will by invalidating progressive state and federal legislation. See, for example, Theodore Roosevelt, "Criticism of the Courts," in Roosevelt, *The New Nationalism* (New York, 1910), 245–58.

57. Leuchtenberg, *Franklin D. Roosevelt and the New Deal*, 231–74; McElvaine, *The Great Depression*, 282–86.

58. Roosevelt had partly himself to blame for this too, for, in an effort to balance the federal budget, he had scaled back the New Deal programs of 1935 and 1936 that had been pumping money into the economy and stimulating a recovery.

59. McElvaine, *The Great Depression*, 297–300.

60. Ibid., 297–305; Leuchtenberg, *Franklin D. Roosevelt and the New Deal*, 252–74; Gerstle, *Working-Class Americanism*, 230–59; Fraser, *Labor Will Rule*, 407–40; Patterson, *Congressional Opposition to the New Deal*.

61. Goodman, *The Committee*, esp. 20; August Raymond Ogden, *The Dies Committee: A Study of the Special House Committee for the Investigation of Un-American Activities, 1938–1944* (Washington, D.C., 1945).

62. They were Donald W. Smith, NLRB member, and Nathan Witt, NLRB executive secretary.

63. Martin Dies, *The Trojan Horse in America* (New York, 1940), 292.

64. Thus, one of the committee's first public acts was to release a Washington area "membership" list of the American League against War and Fascism's Washington chapter. The league was a prominent Popular Front organization. Dies charged that all 563 people on this list, many of whom were government officials, were Communists or Communist supporters. But Dies knew nothing else about the people on this list, nor was he even sure whether the list was an actual membership list or just a mailing list. Goodman, *The Committee*, 3–88, esp. 71; Ogden, *The Dies Committee*, 38–113.

65. Dies, *Trojan Horse*, 353–54.

66. Ibid., 355.

67. Ibid., 361–62.

68. Ibid., 353–55, 361–62. In charging that the New Deal was communistic, Dies was anticipating the charges that would be hurled at the New Deal by Republicans in the early years of the Cold War. He also anticipated the conservative critique of the New Deal that emerged in the 1970s and 1980s. In 1937 Dies had said this about the threat of the New Deal to American liberties: "The steady day-

by-day tendency to throw 'one restriction after another around the freedom and independence of the American people' was leading to 'fascism' in the United States; for 'when men are compelled to constantly comply with innumerable rules and regulations of some board, when they are compelled to watch every step and every move for the mere right, a right which our fathers fought and died for, to engage in business without being continually hamstrung by the Government or by boards, or by bureaus, they become discontented.' " William Gellermann, *Martin Dies* (New York, 1944), 39. *Congressional Record* (hereafter *CR*), April 21, 1937, 3692–94; June 14, 1937, 5667, 5677–82.

69. Even Roosevelt came under suspicion; the Jew-haters pointed out that his family name had originally been "Van Rosenvelt," which, they charged, was a Jewish name. Friedel, *Franklin D. Roosevelt*, 4.

70. Dies, "Have We Forgotten Washington's Advice?" speech before Mass Meeting for America, Madison Square Garden, N.Y., November 29, 1939, *Vital Speeches of the Day* 6 (1939–40): 155.

71. *CR*, April 17, 1935, 5849–53. The figure of 3.5 million illegal aliens is undoubtedly an exaggeration; a more reliable figure is 500,000.

72. *CR*, May 10, 1935, 7319–20.

73. Dies, "Have We Forgotten Washington's Advice?" 153; *CR*, March 10, 1936, 3532–33.

74. *CR*, February 3, 1936, 1367–68.

75. Henry L. Feingold, *The Politics of Rescue: The Roosevelt Administration and the Holocaust, 1938–1945* (New Brunswick, N.J., 1970), 130, 136, 148, 296. See also David S. Wyman, *The Abandonment of the Jews: America and the Holocaust, 1941–1945* (New York, 1985).

76. Feingold, *The Politics of Rescue*, 8.

77. See, for example, Bruno Bettelheim and Morris Janowitz, *Dynamics of Prejudice: A Psychological and Sociological Study of Veterans* (New York, 1950).

78. "Gallup and Fortune Polls," *Public Opinion Quarterly* 4 (March 1940): 95.

79. The Dies committee not only would support the internment of Japanese Americans in World War II but also would argue that the entire Japanese American population ought to be permanently expelled from the country. Goodman, *The Committee*, 118–66.

80. Harvard Sitkoff, *A New Deal for Blacks* (New York, 1978); John B. Kirby, *Black Americans in the Roosevelt Era: Liberalism and Race* (Knoxville, Tenn., 1980); Sanchez, *Becoming Mexican American*; Cletus E. Daniel, *Bitter Harvest: A History of California Farmworkers, 1870–1941* (Ithaca, N.Y., 1981); Robin D. G. Kelley, *Hammer and Hoe: Alabama Communists during the Great Depression* (Chapel Hill, 1990); Mae Ngai, "Illegal Aliens and Alien Citizens: United States Immigration Policy and Racial Formation, 1924–1965" (Ph.D. dissertation, Columbia University, 1997); Gail Radford, *Modern Housing for America: Policy Struggles in the New Deal Era* (Chicago, 1996); Linda Gordon, *Pitied but Not Entitled: Single Mothers and the History of Welfare* (New York, 1994); Anthony J. Badger, *The New Deal: The Depression Years, 1933–1940* (New York, 1989), 190–244.

81. Robert L. Zangrando, *The NAACP Crusade against Lynching, 1909–1950* (Philadelphia, 1980); Abraham Hoffman, *Unwanted Mexican Americans in the Great Depression: Repatriation Pressures, 1929–1939* (Tucson, Ariz., 1974); Roger Daniels, *Asian America: Chinese and Japanese in the United States since 1850* (Seattle, 1988), 67–99, 155–85; Ronald Takaki, *Strangers from a Different Shore: A History of Asian Americans* (New York, 1989), 197–229, 257–69; David G. Gutierrez, *Walls and Mirrors: Mexican Americans, Mexican Immigrants, and the Politics of Ethnicity* (Berkeley, 1995), 69–116.

82. Vicki Ruiz, *Cannery Women/Cannery Lives: Mexican Women, Unionization, and the California Food Processing Industry, 1930–1950* (Albuquerque, N.M., 1987); Kelley, *Hammer and Hoe*; Sanchez, *Becoming Mexican American,* 227–69; Lizabeth Cohen, *Making a New Deal,* 333–49; Dorothy Ray Healey and Maurice Isserman, *California Red: A Life in the Communist Party* (Urbana, Ill., 1993).

83. Efforts of Communists to integrate blacks into their organization and personal lives generated new tensions, of course. Blacks who were recruited and promoted sometimes felt as though they were regarded more as symbols of struggle than as true comrades. Also romantic and sexual liaisons between black men and white women were far more common than those between white men and black women, suggesting that Communist men, at least, equated female beauty with whiteness. See Ralph Ellison, *Invisible Man* (New York, 1947), and Mark Naison, *Communists in Harlem in the Great Depression* (Urbana, Ill., 1983), esp. 136–73.

84. Gellermann, *Martin Dies,* 76.

85. Denning, *The Cultural Front,* 323–61; Lewis A. Erenberg, *Swingin' the Dream: Big Band Jazz and the Rebirth of American Culture* (Chicago, 1998); David A. Stowe, *Swing Changes: Big-Band Jazz in New Deal America* (Cambridge, Mass., 1994).

86. Denning, *The Cultural Front,* esp. 336; Erenberg, *Swingin' the Dream,* 120–49.

87. The literature on the ethnic or racialized character of left-wing representations of the working class is rather weak. It is much stronger on the gendered character of representations, and these works are suggestive of ways of thinking about their ethnoracial dimensions. See, for example, Eric Hobsbawm, "Man and Woman in Socialist Iconography," *History Workshop Journal* 6 (Autumn 1978): 121–38; Faue, *Community of Suffering and Struggle,* 73–95; Maurice Agulhon, *Marianne into Battle: Republican Imagery and Symbolism in France, 1789–1900* (New York, 1981); Lynn Hunt, *Politics, Culture and Class in the French Revolution* (Berkeley, 1984).

88. Harvey Klehr, *The Heyday of American Communism: The Depression Decade* (New York, 1984), 26; Steve Nelson, James R. Barrett, and Rob Ruck, *Steve Nelson, American Radical* (Pittsburgh, 1981), 3; Maurice Isserman, *Which Side Were You On? The American Communist Party during the Second World War* (Middletown, Conn., 1982), 12; Healey and Isserman, *California Red,* 15; Mari Jo Buhle, Paul Buhle, and Dan Georgakas, eds., *Encyclopedia of the American Left* (New York, 1990), 274, 287. Healey acquired the Healey name from her

second husband, but the "Ray" seems to represent a modification and erasure of Rosenblum. There was an alternate tradition among Communists of preserving and celebrating ethnicity, but it had peaked in the 1920s and then went into decline. See Paul Buhle, "Jews and American Communism: The Cultural Question," *Radical History Review* 23 (Spring 1980): 9–33.

89. David Saposs Papers, MSS 113, box 27, folder 2, unpublished, untitled manuscript on the steel strike of 1919, 1; Wisconsin State Historical Society, Madison, Wisconsin.

90. On whiteness and its peculiarities, see David R. Roediger, *The Wages of Whiteness: Race and the Making of the American Working Class* (New York, 1991), and *Towards the Abolition of Whiteness: Essays on Race, Politics, and Working Class History* (London, 1994), 181–99; Robert Orsi, "The Religious Boundaries of an Inbetween People: Street Feste and the Problem of the Dark-Skinned 'Other' in Italian Harlem, 1920–1990," *American Quarterly* 44 (September 1992): 313–47; Matthew Frye Jacobson, *Whiteness of a Different Color: European Immigrants and the Alchemy of Race* (Cambridge, Mass., 1998); James R. Barrett and David Roediger, "Inbetween Peoples: Race, Nationality, and the 'New Immigrant' Working Class," *Journal of American Ethnic History* 16 (Spring 1997): 3–44; Mae Ngai, "Illegal Aliens and Alien Citizens"; Bruce Nelson, *Divided We Stand: American Workers and the Struggle for Racial Equality* (Princeton, 2001).

91. Carl Sandburg, *Abraham Lincoln: The War Years* (New York, 1939).

92. Nelson, *Divided We Stand*, chap. 4.

93. Gerstle, *Working-Class Americanism*, esp. 158–66; see also Peter Friedlander, *The Emergence of a UAW Local* (Pittsburgh, 1976).

94. Thomas Bell, *Out of This Furnace: A Novel of Immigrant Labor in America* (1941; Pittsburgh, 1976), 384–85.

95. Werner Sollors, *Beyond Ethnicity: Consent and Descent in American Culture* (New York, 1986). For my critique of this view, see Gary Gerstle, "Liberty, Coercion and the Making of Americans," *Journal of American History* 84 (September 1997): 524–58.

96. On Jews in Hollywood, see Neal Gabler, *An Empire of Their Own: How the Jews Invented Hollywood* (New York, 1989).

97. For an introduction to Capra, see Robert Sklar, *Movie-Made America: A Cultural History of American Movies* (New York, 1975), 205–14. For a more sympathetic treatment of the populist character of his movies, see, Leonard Quart, "A Populist in Hollywood," *Socialist Review* 68 (March–April 1983): 59–74; Leonard Quart, "Frank Capra and the Popular Front," *Cineaste* 8 (Summer 1977): 4–7.

98. Frank Capra, *The Name above the Title: An Autobiography* (New York, 1971), 259.

99. Guliana Muscio, *Hollywood's New Deal* (Philadelphia, 1997), 43.

100. They are identifiable through their strongly accented English.

101. In 1936, more than 2 million Jews lived in New York City, forming 30 percent of the city's population. The number of Italians in New York City was almost as large. "Jews in America," *Fortune* 13 (February 1936): 130. See also

Brian Neve, *Film and Politics in America: A Social Tradition* (New York, 1992), 2–3.

102. Raymond Carney, *American Vision: The Films of Frank Capra* (New York, 1986), 300; Gabler, *An Empire of Their Own*, 405.

103. The movie does nod in the direction of racial liberalism by including a black boy in Jefferson Smith's band of Boy Rangers, but this gesture was not likely to upset the guardians of racial separation; even Southerners tolerated some degree of play between black and white children.

104. Capra, *The Name above the Title*, 260.

105. Ibid., 256, 259.

106. Ibid., xi.

107. Ibid., 3–6.

108. Ibid., 494.

109. Barrett and Roediger, "Inbetween Peoples," 32; see also Orsi, "The Religious Boundaries of an Inbetween People."

110. For a similar analysis of Jewish filmmakers in the interwar years, see Michael Rogin, *Blackface, White Noise: Jewish Immigrants in the Hollywood Melting Pot* (Berkeley, 1996).

111. Capra actually explored racial mixing in one of his 1930s films, *The Bitter Tea of General Yen* (1933), in which a prudish New England missionary, caught in the chaos of China's civil war, finds sexual awakening and love with a Chinese warlord (though consummation through sex or marriage is impossible, and the warlord must die lusting after his white woman). For Capra, this was a self-consciously "art" film that always remained one of his favorites. It failed at the American box office and received few accolades in the industry; its treatment of interracial romance prompted British censors to ban it throughout Great Britain and the Commonwealth. Afterward, Capra was reluctant to do films on similar themes. Whether Capra would have pursued stories of interracialism in the United States had this movie been more of a success is, of course, impossible to know. But the failure of this movie does illustrate the pressure on Capra and other filmmakers to produce films that were deemed socially acceptable. The pressure was formalized in 1934 in the Production Code Administration (PCA), headed by a Joseph Breen, who was given, according to Robert Sklar, "absolute power to approve, censor or reject movies made or distributed by Hollywood studios." Among the topics prohibited from appearing on screen were homosexuality, interracial sex, abortion, incest, and drugs. The PCA also issued strict rules against the use of profane and vulgar words. Sklar has argued that 1930s filmmakers developed the "screwball comedy" as a way of sustaining Hollywood's iconoclastic interest in "satire, self-mockery, and sexual candor" in a prudish age. Nothing in the code itself explicitly prevented Capra from exploring his brother's interracial experience in the United States as a stepping-stone to the reunification of his immigrant family in the United States and Capra's own subsequent success as a filmmaker. But there can be no doubt that the code discouraged filmmakers from exploring themes of interracialism and increased the pressure on them to conform to prevailing social mores.

See Victor Scherle and William Turner Levy, *The Films of Frank Capra* (Secaucus, N.J., 1977), 110–15; Capra, *The Name above the Title*, 140–44; Carney, *American Vision*, 187–22; Sklar, *Movie-Made America*, 173–75, 187–94, 206–7; Gregory D. Black, *Hollywood Censored: Morality Codes, Catholics, and the Movies* (New York, 1994); Frank Walsh, *Sin and Censorship: The Catholic Church and the Motion Picture Industry* (New Haven, 1996); Marybeth Hamilton, *"When I'm Bad, I'm Better": Mae West, Sex, and American Entertainment* (New York, 1993).

112. I am indebted to Christopher Gildemeister for bringing this aspect of Superman to my attention and for sharing with me his unparalleled knowledge of 1930s comic books. See Christopher Gildemeister, "Isolationism, Wartime Patriotism and American Popular Culture, 1935–1950" (Master's thesis, University of Wisconsin, River Falls, 1993), 21–22. See also Ian Gordon, *Comic Books and Consumer Culture, 1890–1945* (Washington, D.C., 1998), 131–39; Thomas Andrae, "Of Superman and Kids with Dreams: An Interview with the Creators of Superman, Jerry Siegel and Joe Shuster," *Nemo* (August 1983): 6–19; Thomas Andrae, "From Menace to Messiah: The History and Historicity of Superman," in Donald Lazure, ed., *America Media and Mass Culture: Left Perspectives* (Berkeley, 1987), 124–38; Dennis Dooley, "The Man of Tomorrow and the Boys of Yesterday," in Dennis Dooley and Gary Engle, eds., *Superman at Fifty! The Persistence of a Legend* (Cleveland, 1987), 19–36; Coulton Waugh, *The Comics* (1947; Jackson, Miss., 1990); *Superman: From the Thirties to the Seventies*, with an introduction by E. Nelson Bridwell (New York, 1971); Michael L. Fleisher, *The Encyclopedia of Superheroes*, vol. 3, *The Great Superman Book* (New York, 1978); and Richard O'Brien, *The Golden Age of Comic Books, 1937–1945* (New York, 1977).

113. For some casual but suggestive remarks on Superman's "Jewish origins," see Scott Rabb, "Is Superman Jewish?" in Dooley and Engle, *Superman at Fifty!*, 167–68.

114. For some suggestive comments on how unemployment exacerbated male vulnerability during the Great Depression, see E. Wight Bakke, *The Unemployed Man: A Social Study* (New York, 1934).

115. Bell, *Out of this Furnace*, 259–413; Linda Gordon, *Pitied but Not Entitled: Single Mothers and the History of Welfare, 1890–1935* (New York, 1994), 183–306; Winifred Wandersee, *Women's Work and Family Values, 1920–1940* (Cambridge, Mass., 1981); Alice Kessler-Harris, *Out to Work: A History of Wage-Earning Women in the United States* (New York, 1982), 250–72, esp. 256; Robyn Muncy, *Creating a Female Dominion in American Reform, 1890–1935* (New York, 1991); Barbara Melosh, *Engendering Culture: Manhood and Womanhood in New Deal Public Art and Theatre* (Washington, D.C., 1991); Faue, *Community of Suffering and Struggle*; Gwendolyn Mink, *Wages of Motherhood: Inequality in the Welfare State, 1917–1942* (Ithaca, N.Y., 1995); Alice Kessler-Harris, "In the Nation's Image: The Gendered Limits of Social Citizenship in the Depression Era," *Journal of American History* 86 (December 1999): 1251–79.

116. The literature on official New Deal culture is enormous, but very little of it deals with the erasure of ethnicity and race that is so central to much of it. For

one effort to address this erasure, see Gary Gerstle, "The Protean Character of American Liberalism," *American Historical Review* 99 (October 1994): esp. 1068–69. The virtually complete absence of references to ethnicity and race in Warren Susman's encyclopedic essays on 1930s culture further underscores my point. See Susman, "The Culture of the Thirties," and "Culture and Commitment," in his *Culture as History: The Transformation of American Society in the Twentieth Century* (New York, 1984), 150–211. Artists and intellectuals of the decade actually did assemble considerable material on racial and ethnic minorities (one outstanding example being the Works Projects Administration [WPA] interviews with ex-slaves), archives that present-day historians are using to render a far more complex portrait of 1930s society and culture. But this material had little effect on liberal perceptions of the American people at the time. For example, none of the WPA ex-slave narratives were published during the 1930s, and most received no scholarly or popular attention before the late 1960s. See George P. Rawick, *From Sundown to Sunup: The Making of the Black Community* (1972), in George P. Rawick, gen. ed., *The American Slave: A Composite Autobiography*, 12 vols. (Westport, Conn., 1972-74), 1:xiii–xxi; see also Ira Berlin, Marc Favreau, and Stephen F. Miller, *Remembering Slavery: African Americans Talk about Their Personal Experiences of Slavery and Freedom* (New York, 1998). For a fascinating glimpse of how "emulation of the Nordic" shaped views of beauty among New York City high school youngsters, see Paula S. Fass, *Outside In: Minorities and the Transformation of American Education* (New York, 1989), 73–111.

117. Gordon, *Pitied but Not Entitled*; Kessler-Harris, *Out to Work*; Muncy, *Creating a Female Dominion*. This view has been challenged to some extent by Susan Ware, who finds in the 1930s more options and opportunities for women. See, for example, Susan Ware, *Beyond Suffrage: Women in the New Deal* (Cambridge, Mass., 1988); Ware, *Partner and I: Molly Dewson, Feminism and New Deal Politics* (New Haven, 1987); and Ware, *Still Missing: Amelia Earhart and the Search for Modern American Feminism* (New York, 1993).

118. On strength of anti-Semitism in the 1930s, and on growth of Nazi support in the United States, see Feingold, *Politics of Rescue*, 3–21; Wyman, *Abandonment of the Jews*, 5–15; Michael Selzer, ed., *"Kike!" A Documentary History of Anti-Semitism in America* (New York, 1972), 167–200; Alan Brinkley, *Voices of Protest: Huey Long, Father Coughlin and the Great Depression* (New York, 1982); Leo Ribuffo, *The Old Christian Right: The Protestant Far Right from the Great Depression to the Cold War* (Philadelphia, 1983).

119. The American "racial hierarchy," Michael Rogin has written, "placed such pressure on the idea of equality . . . that even representations intending to include peoples of color within the Declaration of Independence still often reproduced racialized images." Rogin, *Blackface, White Noise*, 17.

120. Quoted in Goodman, *The Committee*, 20.

121. Quoted in Fraser, *Labor Will Rule*, 530.

122. Wyman, *Abandonment of the Jews*, 150–51; William D. Hassett, *Off the Record with F.D.R., 1942–1945* (New Brunswick, N.J., 1958), 209–10; Ward, *First-Class Temperament*, 254–55.

123. Quoted in Ward, *First-Class Temperament*, 255; Henry Morgenthau, Jr., Papers, Presidential Diary, vol. 5, January 27, 1942 (microfilm version), Franklin D. Roosevelt Presidential Library, Hyde Park, New York. In these matters, FDR was less liberal than TR. The former had not grown up in New York City and never delighted in the melting pot idea quite as much as TR. He lived a more sheltered existence.

CHAPTER 5

1. The phrase, "good war," seems to have come into common usage only after the war had ended. Studs Terkel reports that it "is a phrase . . . frequently voiced by men . . . of my generation, to distinguish that war from other wars, declared and undeclared." Studs Terkel, *"The Good War": An Oral History of World War II* (New York, 1984); the quotation is from a page of frontmatter.

2. John P. Diggins, *The Proud Decades: America in War and Peace, 1941–1960* (New York, 1988), 25.

3. John Whiteclay Chambers II, *To Raise an Army: The Draft Comes to Modern America* (New York, 1987), 213, 343. Desertion rates did rise in 1944 and 1945, however. Richard A. Gabriel and Paul L. Savage, *Crisis in Command: Mismanagement in the Army* (New York, 1978), table 1, 181.

4. Mason Wade, *The French Canadians, 1760–1967*, 2 vols. (1945; Toronto, 1976), 1:708–80.

5. A. J. Muste, "War Is the Enemy," in *The Essays of A. J. Muste*, ed. Nat Hentoff, (Indianapolis, 1967), 261–78; Jo Ann Robinson, *Abraham Went Out: A Biography of A. J. Muste* (Philadelphia, 1981); Jervis Anderson, *Bayard Rustin: Troubles I've Seen: A Biography* (New York, 1997).

6. Robin D. G. Kelley, "The Riddle of the Zoot: Malcolm Little and Black Cultural Politics in World War II," in Joe Wood, ed., *Malcolm X: In Our Own Image* (New York, 1992), 155–82; George Q. Flynn, "Selective Service and American Blacks during World War II," *Journal of Negro History* 69 (Winter 1984): 14–25; Mauricio Mazon, *Zoot Suit Riots: The Psychology of Symbolic Annihilation* (Austin, Tex., 1984); David G. Gutierrez, *Walls and Mirrors: Mexican Americans, Mexican Immigrants, and the Politics of Ethnicity* (Berkeley, 1995), 121–30.

7. See George Lipsitz, " 'Frantic to Join . . . the Japanese Army': Beyond the Black-White Binary," in Lipsitz, *The Possessive Investment in Whiteness: How White People Profit from Identity Politics* (Philadelphia, 1998), 184–210; Ernest Allen Jr., "Waiting for Tojo: The Pro-Japan Vigil of Black Missourians, 1932–1943," *Gateway Heritage* 15 (Fall 1994), 16–33, and "When Japan Was 'Champion of the Darker Races': Satokata Takahishi and the Flowering of Black Messianic Nationalism," *Black Scholar* 24 (Winter 1994): 23–46; Quintard Taylor, "Blacks and Asians in a White City: Japanese Americans and African Americans in Seattle, 1890–1940," *Western Historical Quarterly* 22 (November 1991): 401–29.

8. Willam Pickens, "The American Negro and His Country in World War," n.d., reel 3, box 6, William Pickens Record Group, microfilm, Schomburg Collec-

tion of Negro Literature and History, New York Public Library. See also Clayton R. Koppes and Gregory D. Black, *Hollywood Goes to War: How Politics, Profits, and Propaganda Shaped World War II Movies* (New York, 1987), 86; John Hope Franklin, "Their War and Mine," *Journal of American History* 77 (September 1990): 576–79.

9. Roger Daniels, *Concentration Camps, USA: Japanese Americans and World War II* (New York, 1971); Ronald Takaki, *Double Victory: A Multicultural History of America in World War II* (Boston, 2000), 131–37, 149–65. Arnold Krammer, *Undue Process: The Untold Story of America's German Alien Internees* (London, 1997).

10. Robert Dallek, *Franklin D. Roosevelt and American Foreign Policy, 1932–1945* (New York, 1979); Wayne S. Cole, *Roosevelt and the Isolationists, 1932–1945* (Lincoln, Neb., 1983); Manfred Jonas, *Isolationism in America, 1935–1941* (Ithaca, N.Y., 1966); Robert Divine, *The Reluctant Belligerent: American Entry into World War II* (1965; New York, 1979); David M. Kennedy, *Freedom from Fear: The American People in Depression and War, 1929–1945* (New York, 1999), 426–515.

11. Dallek, *Franklin D. Roosevelt and American Foreign Policy.*

12. Gary Gerstle, "The Protean Character of American Liberalism," *American Historical Review* 99 (October 1994): 1043–73, esp. 1070.

13. Reinhold Niebuhr, *The Children of Light and Darkness: A Vindication of Democracy and a Critique of Its Traditional Defence* (New York, 1944); Niebuhr, "Jews after the War, I," *Nation*, February 21, 1942, 214–16; Niebuhr, "Jews after the War, II," *Nation*, February 28, 1942, 253–55; Ashley Montagu, *Man's Most Dangerous Myth: The Fallacy of Race* (New York, 1942); Ruth Benedict, *The Races of Mankind* (New York, 1943); Gunnar Dahlberg, *Race, Reason and Rubbish* (New York, 1942).

14. Gunnar Myrdal, *An American Dilemma: The Negro Problem and Modern Democracy* (1944; New York, 1972), 1:3–4, 6. On the reception and influence of this book, see Walter A. Jackson, *Gunnar Myrdal and America's Conscience: Social Engineering and Racial Liberalism, 1938–1987* (Chapel Hill, 1990). See also William S. Bernard, ed., *American Immigration Policy: A Reappraisal* (New York, 1950); Philip Gleason, "Americans All," in Gleason, *Speaking of Diversity: Language and Ethnicity in Twentieth-Century America* (Baltimore, 1992), 153–87; Richard W. Steele, "The War on Intolerance: The Reformulation of American Nationalism, 1939–1941," *Journal of American Ethnic History* 9 (1989): 11–33; Harvard Sitkoff, *The Struggle for Black Equality, 1954–1980* (New York, 1981).

15. *Common Ground* 1 (Autumn 1940): 2; see also Steele, "The Reformulation of American Nationalism"; Gleason, "Americans All"; Gary Gerstle, *Working-Class Americanism: The Politics of Labor in a Textile City, 1914–1960* (New York, 1989), 289–309.

16. John W. Dower, *War without Mercy: Race and Power in the Pacific War* (New York, 1986).

17. On the emergence of an anticolonial movement among African Americans, see Penny M. Von Eschen, *Race against Empire: Black Americans and Anticolonialism, 1937–1957* (Ithaca, N.Y., 1996), and Jonathan Rosenberg, " 'How Far the

Promised Land?' World Affairs and the American Civil Rights Movement from the First World War to Vietnam" (Ph.D. dissertation, Harvard University, 1997), chap. 5. NAACP figures come from Rosenberg, 273. See also Brenda Gayle Plummer, *Rising Wind: Black Americans and U.S. Foreign Affairs, 1935–1960* (Chapel Hill, 1996).

18. Gleason, "Americans All"; Steele, "The Reformulation of American Nationalism"; Gerstle, "The Protean Character of American Liberalism"; Philip Gleason, "The Odd Couple: Pluralism and Assimilation," in Gleason, *Speaking of Diversity*, 47–90; Margaret Mead, "Anthropological Contributions to National Policies during and Immediately after World War II," in Walter Goldschmidt, ed., *The Uses of Anthropology*, American Anthropological Association Special Publication 11 (Washington, D.C., 1979), 145–57; Virginia Yans-McLaughlin, "Science, Democracy, and Ethics: Mobilizing Culture and Personality for World War II," in George W. Stocking Jr., ed., *Malinowski, Rivers, Benedict and Others: Essays on Culture and Personality*, History of Anthropology, vol. 4 (Madison, Wis., 1986), 184–217; Brian Urquhart, *Ralph Bunche: An American Life* (New York, 1993). For Roosevelt's elaboration of the Four Freedoms, see Roosevelt, "The Annual Message to Congress, January 6, 1941," in *The Public Papers and Addresses of Franklin D. Roosevelt*, ed. Samuel I. Rosenman, 13 vols. (Washington, D.C., 1938–50), 9:672.

19. Koppes and Black, *Hollywood Goes to War*, 283.

20. Gerstle, *Working-Class Americanism*, 289–309, and "The Working Class Goes to War," in Lewis A. Erenberg and Susan E. Hirsch, eds., *The War in American Culture: Society and Consciousness during World War II* (Chicago, 1996), 105–27.

21. Gerald F. Linderman, *The World within War: America's Combat Experience in World War II* (New York, 1997), 1.

22. See, for example, Marc Scott Miller, *The Irony of Victory: World War II and Lowell, Massachusetts* (Urbana, Ill., 1988), and Gerstle, *Working-Class Americanism*, 289–309.

23. *ITU News*, July 12, 1944; the Lowell quotation is from Miller, *The Irony of Victory*, 81. See also Samuel G. Freedman, *The Inheritance: How Three Families and America Moved from Roosevelt to Reagan and Beyond* (New York, 1996), 119–25.

24. Lawrence R. Samuel, *Pledging Allegiance: American Identity and the Bond Drive of World War II* (Washington, D.C., 1997), xiv, 73. The 85 million bonds were bought by an adult population (eighteen and over) that numbered 95.8 million in 1943—in other words, by almost nine of every ten adult Americans (on average). The total American population that year was 136,739,000. See U.S. Department of Commerce, Bureau of the Census, *Historical Statistics of the United States, Colonial Times to 1970* (White Plains, N.Y., 1989), pt. 1, 10. Samuel determined that eight out of thirteen Americans bought war bonds (62 percent), but his calculation is based on the entire American population, including children under the age of eighteen. Samuel, *Pledging Allegiance*, 45.

25. Samuel, *Pledging Allegiance*, 89–92.

26. Estimates of African American contributions in 1944 alone, however, exceeded $1 billion dollars. Samuel, *Pledging Allegiance*, esp. 189.

27. Ibid., Gerstle, *Working-Class Americanism*, 289–309.

28. Samuel, *Pledging Allegiance*; Gerstle, "The Working Class Goes to War," 110–12.

29. John Morton Blum, *V Was for Victory: Politics and American Culture during World War II* (New York, 1976); Robert B. Westbrook, " 'I Want a Girl, Just like the Girl That Married Harry James': American Women and the Problem of Political Obligation in World War II," *American Quarterly* 42 (December, 1990): 587–614; Frank W. Fox, *Madison Avenue Goes to War: The Strange Military Career of Advertising* (Provo, Utah, 1975).

30. Nelson Lichtenstein, "The Making of the Postwar Working Class: Cultural Pluralism and Social Structure in World War II," *History Today* 51 (1988): 42–63; Geoffrey Perrett, *Days of Sadness, Years of Triumph: The American People, 1939–1945* (1973; Madison, Wis., 1985), 325–56; Howell John Harris, *The Right to Manage: Industrial Relations Policies of American Business in the 1940s* (Madison, Wis., 1982), 41–89.

31. Nelson Lichtenstein, *Labor's War at Home: The CIO in World War II* (New York, 1982); Perrett, *Days of Sadness, Years of Triumph*; Blum, *V Was for Victory*; Miller, *The Irony of Victory*; Alan Clive, *State of War: Michigan in World War II* (Ann Arbor, Mich., 1979).

32. Lichtenstein, "The Making of the Postwar Working Class"; Gerstle, "The Working Class Goes to War"; Harris, *The Right to Manage*; Blum, *V Was for Victory*; David R. B. Ross, *Preparing for Ulysses: Politics and Veterans during World War II* (New York, 1969); Gabriel Kolko, *Wealth and Power in America: An Analysis of Social Class and Income Distribution* (New York, 1962), 14.

33. Blum, *V Was for Victory*; Nelson Lichtenstein, "From Corporatism to Collective Bargaining: Organized Labor and the Eclipse of Social Democracy in the Postwar Era," in Steve Fraser and Gary Gerstle, eds., *The Rise and Fall of the New Deal Order, 1930–1980* (Princeton, 1989), 122–52; Steven Fraser, *Labor Will Rule: Sidney Hillman and the Rise of American Labor* (New York, 1991), 441–538; Harris, *The Right to Manage*; Alan Brinkley, *The End of Reform: New Deal Liberalism in Recession and War* (New York, 1995), 175–271; Gerstle, *Working-Class Americanism*, 310–36. On the Economic Bill of Rights, see Roosevelt, "Message to the Congress on the State of the Union," January 11, 1944, *Public Papers*, 12:40–42.

34. Dower, *War without Mercy*, 3.

35. Samuel Eliot Morison, *The Struggle for Guadalcanal, August 1942–February 1943: History of the United States Naval Operations in World War II* (Boston, 1999), 5:187.

36. Dower, *War without Mercy*, 54.

37. Ibid., 33–73 in particular.

38. Ibid. See also Linderman, *The World within War*, 143–84.

39. Morison, *The Struggle for Guadalcanal*, 187. For contemporary descriptions of Japanese-American battles and troop behavior, consult Library of

America, *Reporting World War II*, 2 vols. (New York, 1995), an anthology of World War II dispatches written by American journalists.

40. Bernard C. Nalty, *Strength for the Fight: A History of Black Americans in the Military* (New York, 1986), 143–203; Morris J. MacGregor Jr., *Integration of the Armed Forces, 1940–1965* (Washington, D.C., 1981), 3–122; Richard M. Dalfiume, *Desegregation of the U.S. Armed Forces: Fighting on Two Fronts, 1939–1953* (Columbia, Mo., 1969). Japanese American and Filipino American soldiers also fought in segregated units. See Ronald Takaki, *Strangers from a Different Shore: A History of Asian Americans* (New York, 1989), 357–405, and *Double Victory*.

41. Mexicans, legally defined as white, Native Americans, and Chinese were allowed to serve with Euro-American troops.

42. Theodore Roosevelt, "The Square Deal in Americanism," in *The Great Adventure: Present-Day Studies in American Nationalism* (New York, 1918), in *The Works of Theodore Roosevelt, National Edition*, ed. Hermann Hagedorn (New York, 1926), 19:313.

43. I have compiled this list from my own viewing of World War II movies and in consultation with Stephen Nordhoff, "American Nationalism: Civic Identity in World War II" (unpublished seminar paper, Catholic University of America, 1997), in author's possession.

44. The religious basis to this trinity also opened up the possibility of including non-European Catholics, such as Mexicans and Filipinos, in the platoon, a development that did begin to happen in the war years. See, for example, *Bataan*, where the platoon includes a Filipino, and *Guadalcanal Diary*, where it includes a Mexican.

45. Jungle warfare is not, however, essential to this transformation. Some movies, such as *Battle in the North Atlantic*, portray airplane, ship, and submarine crews being thrown into the crucible of battle.

46. Sometimes the sacrifice is presented in melodramatic, cross-ethnic or cross-racial terms—the crucifixion of a Jewish soldier in *Operation Burma*, the gunning down of a brave Sudanese corporal in *Sahara*, etc.

47. Neil Gabler, *Empire of Their Own: How the Jews Invented Hollywood* (New York, 1988); Michael Denning, *The Cultural Front: The Laboring of American Culture in the Twentieth Century* (New York, 1996), 403–22; Lary May, *The Big Tomorrow: Hollywood and the Politics of the American Way* (Chicago, 2000).

48. Lawson worked on *Action in the North Atlantic* and *Sahara*, Trumbo on *30 Seconds over Tokyo*, Bessie on *Operation Burma*. After the war, all three would become part of the "Hollywood Ten," a group of directors and screenwriters who, because they refused to answer questions about their alleged Communist affiliations, were held in contempt of Congress and then blacklisted. Clayton R. Koppes and Gregory D. Black, *Hollywood Goes to War*, esp. 70, 115, 266–67, 301–2; Gabler, *Empire of Their Own*, 311–86.

49. The standard history of the OWI is Allan W. Winkler, *The Politics of Propaganda: The Office of War Information, 1942–1945* (New Haven, 1978), but Koppes and Black, *Hollywood Goes to War*, is essential for understanding the OWI's

role in shaping Hollywood's World War II movies. The account that follows draws on the latter.

50. Nalty, *Strength for the Fight*, 143–203.

51. Viewers of the time would have seen in this physical struggle a reprise of the second heavyweight fight between Joe Louis and the German Max Schmeling (1938), a fight that ended with a smashing Louis victory and that was interpreted by many as a symbolic victory for racial egalitarianism against the Aryan Nazis. See Thomas Doherty, *Projections of War: Hollywood, American Culture, and World War II* (New York, 1993), 211.

52. Tamdul actually saves the platoon twice: before his mortal combat with the German, he discovers a well whose water will sustain the platoon for several critical days.

53. Koppes and Black, *Hollywood Goes to War*, 301–4.

54. Ibid., 115.

55. Sometimes, the OWI ruled that a film did strike the right balance between black subservience and independence. *Bataan* (1943) was one such example. The screenwriters inserted an African American in a multiracial and multinational platoon (the group also included a Mexican American and two Filipinos) charged with holding a bridge against Japanese advance. The bridge becomes their last stand, and they all die. But while the black private dies with the rest, sealing his inclusion in this sacred American community, he is portrayed in ways that render him inferior to white soldiers. He contributes less than other soldiers to fashioning a defense strategy against the Japanese, and, though he sets an explosive charge to blow up a critical bridge, he is not trusted with pushing the plunger, a task given to his white partner. OWI censors let these subtle messages of subservience pass, choosing instead to celebrate the film for its inclusion of a black soldier on what they regarded as equal terms. See Daniel Leab, *From Sambo to Superspade: The Black Experience in Motion Pictures* (Boston, 1975), 126; Koppes and Black, *Hollywood Goes to War*, 180, 302–4. See also Richard Slotkin, *Gunfighter Nation: The Myth of the Frontier in Twentieth-Century America* (New York, 1993), 322–24.

56. Koppes and Black, *Hollywood Goes to War*, 260.

57. The black press's coverage of blacks in the military can be followed in the *Tuskegee Institute News Clippings File* (Division of Behavioral Science Research, Carver Research Foundation, Tuskegee Institute, microfilm, 1976) and in the "Records of the Office of the Civilian Aide to the Secretary of War" (hereafter OCA records), Record Group 107, National Archives, Washington, D.C. For the duration of the war, the Office of the Civilian Aide published a weekly "Report on Trends in the Negro Press," which offered digests and excerpts of virtually all material appearing in the black press pertaining to the blacks in the military. It is an excellent source.

58. Nalty, *Strength for the Fight*, 141.

59. Letter from W. E. Mahon to FDR, July 16, 1941, Army Adjutant General Central Decimal File, 1940–45 (hereafter AG File), RG 407, box 1082, 291.21, 7/1/41–7/31/41 folder, National Archives.

60. Letter from Charles Edwards, Charles Walton, Richard Frazier, and Alfred Friedman to Eleanor Roosevelt, April 10, 1941, ibid., 4/1/41–4/30/41 folder.

61. Letter from William C. Wyatt to President Roosevelt, December 15, 1941, ibid., folder 12/17/41–12/31/41.

62. Letter from Harry A. Hamilton to President Roosevelt, December 28, 1941, ibid., folder 12/17/41–12/31/41.

63. OCA records, RG 107, box 223, Negro Press folder.

64. Quoted in Walter White memo, OCA records, RG 107, box 221, NAACP-1 folder, 16–17.

65. Ibid. The memo that White saw may have been the Command of Negro Troops, War Department Pamphlet No. 20–6, February 1944, referred to in Samuel A. Stouffer, Edward A. Suchman, Leland C. DeVinney, Shirley A. Star, and Robin M. Williams Jr., *The American Soldier: The Adjustment during Army Life*, 2 vols. (Princeton, 1949), 1:597.

66. "Leadership of Negro Troops," OCA, RG 107, box 221, NAACP-1 folder. This memo has no date, but, in 1943, copies of it were circulating among white officers who were commanding U.S. troops in Europe. It may well have been a version of the Command of Negro Troops pamphlet. It contains the suggestion referred to by White, that officers should "occasionally call a man 'Cpl. John' instead of 'Corporal Smith,' " and it is full of the patronizing air that so offended White. Some other examples:

- "The Negro soldier by and large is still a somewhat primitive character who dislikes and is perturbed by strange places and ways."
- "He does not look for work, he must be assigned a specific task that will keep him busy or else he will soon fall asleep."
- "The colored soldier is extremely responsive to compliments. In correcting a man, praise should be given for any point warranting it while requiring correction of the deficiency. 'Sergeant, these look like wonderfully tasteful cookies but I don't think I would like to eat one until you clear that stove properly.' "
- "Many colored soldiers have the unfortunate faculty of convincing themselves that they are right simply by repeating the argument often enough."
- "It's all very well to say that they should be treated like other soldiers but it's necessary to remember that to secure them in proper uniforms generally requires helping them dress."
- "The colored soldier is extremely responsive to what is known as 'color.' He likes to stand out from the crowd, to be distinctive. He is a showman at heart with the general flair for the dramatic. . . . He loves to march and marches well."

67. OCA records, RG 107, box 223, Negro Press folder.

68. Stouffer et al., *The American Soldier*, 1:495. The engineering corps was really a construction corps.

69. Walter White, "Observations and Recommendations of Walter White on Racial Relations in the ETO," 1944, OCA, RG 107, box 221, NAACP-1 folder,

9. See also undated and unsigned letter to NAACP from "land-sailors," OCA, RG 107, box 222, Navy departmental folder.

70. Nalty, *Strength for the Fight*, 154.

71. White, "Observations and Recommendations," 14.

72. Order of the Office of the Assistant Provost Marshall, 47th District EBS, United States Army, APO 644, in OCA, RG 107, box 204, ETO Racial Relations folder.

73. Daniel Kryder, "Race Policy, Race Violence, and Race Reform in the U.S. Army during World War II," *Studies in American Political Development* 10 (Spring 1996): 130–67; Daniel Kryder, "The American State and the Management of Race Conflict in the Workplace and in the Army, 1941–1945," *Polity* 26 (Summer 1994): 601–34; Ulysses Lee, *The Employment of Negro Troops: U.S. Army in World War II*, Special Studies, Office of the Chief of Military History (Washington, D.C., 1966); Nalty, *Strength for the Fight*, 143–203.

74. *Tuskegee Institute News Clipping File*; "Report on Trends in the Negro Press," 1943–45, OCA, RG 107.

75. Memo, undated and unsigned (contents make it clear though that author was a black soldier at the Lancashire base the night the riot began), OCA, RG 107, box 204, ETO Racial Relations folder.

76. Nalty, *Strength for the Fight*, 154–55. The military court-martialed thirty-two blacks for their roles in this uprising, but their sentences were notably light.

77. Kryder, "Race Policy, Race Violence, and Race Reform in the U.S. Army during World War II." On McCloy, see Alan Brinkley, "Icons of the American Establishment," in Brinkley, *Liberalism and Its Discontents* (Cambridge, Mass., 1998), 177–209; Thomas A. Schwartz, *America's Germany: John J. McCloy and the Federal Republic of Germany* (Cambridge, Mass., 1991); and Walter Isaacson and Evan Thomas, *The Wise Men: Six Friends and the World They Made: Acheson, Bohlen, Harriman, Kennan, Lovett, and McCloy* (New York, 1986), 191–202.

78. Nalty, *Strength for the Fight*, 181; MacGregor Jr., *Integration of the Armed Forces, 1940–1965*, 41; OCA, RG 107, boxes 224, 225.

79. Nalty, *Strength for the Fight*, 143, 203.

80. Ibid.

81. Stouffer et al., *The American Soldier*, 2:99. See also, Terkel, "*The Good War*," 39, and Stephen Ambrose, *Band of Brothers: E Company, 506th Regiment, 101st Airborne: From Normandy to Hitler's Eagle's Nest* (New York, 1992); *D-Day, June 6th, 1944: The Climactic Battle of World War II* (New York, 1994); and *Citizen Soldiers: The U.S. Army from the Normandy Beaches to the Bulge to the Surrender of Germany* (New York, 1997).

82. The Bureau of War Records (BWR) of the National Jewish Welfare Board, attempting to compile a complete list of Jewish American servicemen, could only do so by forming BWR committees in the 1,200 American cities and towns where Jews lived and asking each one to gather data on every serviceman and -woman in their area. This Herculean task took four years and cost an enormous amount of money. Simply establishing the fact that 550,000 Jewish-Americans served in the military was considered a great achievement. Isidor Kaufman, *American Jews*

in World War II: The Story of 550,000 Fighters for Freedom (New York, 1947), 2:7–29.

83. William Manchester, *Goodbye Darkness: A Memoir of the Pacific War* (Boston, 1979).

84. Ibid., 138.

85. Linderman, *The World within War*, 193. Robert Rasmus, a World War II rifleman from the Midwest interviewed by Studs Terkel, described his encounter with the army in this way: "The first time I ever heard a New England accent was at Fort Benning [Georgia]. The southerner was an exotic creature to me. People from the farms. The New York street-smarts. You had an incredible mixture of every stratum of society. And you're of that age when your need for friendship is greatest. I still see a number of these people. There's sort of a special sense of kinship." Terkel, "*The Good War*," 39.

86. Manchester, *Goodbye Darkness*, 138.

87. Ibid., 202.

88. Ibid., 353.

89. Ibid., 352–53.

90. Ibid., 382.

91. Ibid., 391.

92. For similar expressions regarding comradeship by ex-GIs, see Eugene B. Sledge, *With the Old Breed at Peleliu and Okinawa* (New York, 1983), esp. 223; Kurt Gabel, *The Making of a Paratrooper* (Lawrence, Kans., 1990), 72; Janice Holt Giles, *The GI Journal of Sergeant Giles* (Boston, 1965), 130–31.

93. A draftee, Gene Gach, wrote about his unit in 1942: "Everyone is called the Dago, the Wop, the Greek, the Jew, the Heinie, the Polack, and there is no bitterness in any of it." Gach, *In the Army Now* (New York, 1942), 61.

94. Manchester, *Goodbye, Darkness*, 100–8. This implicit toleration of homosexuality accords with Allan Bérubé's argument that military units unintentionally offered homosexuals a more comfortable environment than what they had known in their prewar milieux, even as (paradoxically) the military, buoyed by the psychiatrists' claim that homosexuality constituted a severe form of degeneracy, determined that all homosexuals had to be identified, removed from their units, and punished. Bérubé, *Coming Out under Fire: The History of Gay Men and Women in World War Two* (New York, 1990).

95. See, for example, Jon T. Hoffman, *Once a Legend: "Red Mike" Edson of the Marine Raiders* (Novato, Calif., 1994); Burke Davis, *Marine! The Life of Lieutenant General Lewis B. (Chesty) Puller* (Boston, 1992).

96. Manchester, *Goodbye, Darkness*, 132.

97. Ibid., 232–37.

98. On the general issue of officer–enlisted man relations, see Linderman, *The World within War*, 185–234.

99. Manchester, *Goodbye, Darkness*, 198.

100. It is likely that Lefty's decision to deny his identity was influenced as much by growing up in the South (Louisville), where the pressures on Jews to assimilate were extreme, as by what he encountered in Manchester's squad.

101. Leon Uris, *Battle Cry* (New York, 1953); Rona Hirsch, "The Comeback Kid," *Baltimore Jewish Times*, November 3, 1995.

102. On Jews in the World War II military, see also John McCormick, *The Right Kind of War: A Novel* (Annapolis, Md., 1992); Bruno Bettleheim and Morris Janowitz, *Dynamics of Prejudice: A Psychological and Sociological Study of Veterans* (New York, 1950), 124, 127, 132, 134, 137; Studs Terkel, interview with Arno Mayer, in *"The Good War,"* 469–70; and Charles Herbert Stember et al., *Jews in the Mind of America* (New York, 1966), 115–20. Part of the determination of Jewish groups to document meticulously their contribution to the war effort was to defend themselves against charges that they had shirked their duties. Louis Dublin, chairman of the Technical Committee on (Jewish) War Records wrote that "the circumstances of the war period and of the events leading up to it compelled us to do this job and to produce a record that would convince through its reliability even those who would malign us." Kaufman, *American Jews*, 2:13.

103. Letter from Lieutenant General Bernard E. Trainor to author, November 1998, in author's possession.

104. Linderman, *The World within War*, 283–99.

105. Veterans organizations such as the American Legion and Veterans of Foreign Wars played important parts in this recovery, drawing ex-soldiers together, and giving them status and influence in their communities. Even those soldiers who were disinclined to talk about their experiences took comfort in the knowledge that the others knew what they had been through.

106. Bettleheim and Janowitz, *Dynamics of Prejudice*, 140–61.

107. Letter from a white officer to his father in Atlanta, January 21, 1944, OCA, RG 107, box 222, Navy departmental folder.

108. Nalty, *Strength for the Fight*, 195–96, 202.

109. White, "Observations in the North African and Middle Eastern Theatres of Operation," 1.

110. Ibid., 3–4.

111. Ibid., 4.

112. Nalty, *Strength for the Fight*, 149–53.

113. Ibid., 153.

114. "Observations in the North African and Middle Eastern Theatres of Operation," 4.

115. Stouffer et al., *The American Soldier*; Paul Fussell, *Wartime: Understanding and Behavior in the Second World War* (New York, 1989); Westbrook, " 'I Want a Girl, Just like the Girl That Married Harry James.' " See also Benjamin L. Alpers, "This Is the Army: Imagining a Democratic Military in World War II," *Journal of American History* 85 (June 1998): 129–63.

116. Manchester, *Goodbye Darkness*, 382, 391.

117. Ibid., 393.

118. Ibid. It is possible to detect a note of condescension in Manchester's declaration, early in his memoir, that he and his fellow Marines were not fighting "for the right of blacks, who performed menial, if safe, tasks far behind the lines, to bleed alongside us." Ibid., 100.

119. Ibid., 290–97.

120. Anthony Badger, "Fatalism, Not Gradualism: The Crisis of Southern Liberalism, 1945–65," in Brian Ward and Anthony Badger, eds., *The Making of Martin Luther King and the Civil Rights Movement* (London, 1996), 67–68.

121. Ibid., 69.

122. Arnold R. Hirsch, *Making the Second Ghetto: Race and Housing in Chicago, 1940–1960* (New York, 1983), 54–55. Riots had also erupted over the introduction of black veterans at the Airport Homes project in southwest Chicago in 1946; ibid., 56. For an incisive study of how racial notions of exclusion operated on the home front during the war, see Maria Mazzenga, "Inclusion, Exclusion, and the National Experience: European and African-American Youth in World War Two Baltimore" (Ph.D. dissertation, Catholic University of America, 1999).

123. Thomas J. Sugrue, *The Origins of the Urban Crisis: Race and Inequality in Postwar Detroit* (New York, 1996). See also Arnold R. Hirsch, "Massive Resistance in the Urban North: Trumbull Park, Chicago, 1953–1966," and Thomas J. Sugrue, "Crabgrass-Roots Politics: Race, Rights, and the Reaction against Liberalism in the Urban North, 1940–1964," *Journal of American History* 82 (September 1995): 522–50, and 551–78.

124. Gary Gerstle, "Race and the Myth of the Liberal Consensus," *Journal of American History* 82 (September 1995): 579–86.

125. Wallace Terry, *Bloods: An Oral History of the Vietnam War by Black Veterans* (New York, 1984), 6–7.

126. On the extent to which "young boys growing up in the 1950s and early 1960s were captivated by fantasies of warfare," and of World War II fantasies in particular, see Christian G. Appy, *Working-Class War: American Combat Soldiers and Vietnam* (Chapel Hill, 1993), esp. 60–63. See also Tom Engelhardt, *The End of Victory Culture: Cold War America and the Disillusioning of a Generation* (New York, 1995).

127. Ron Kovic, *Born on the Fourth of July* (New York, 1976), 54–57.

CHAPTER 6

1. On Republican acquiescence in the New Deal, see Michael J. Hogan, *Harry S. Truman and the Origins of the National Security State, 1945–1954* (New York, 1998).

2. Ibid.; Ellen Schrecker, *Many Are the Crimes: McCarthyism in America* (Boston, 1998); Melvyn P. Leffler, *A Preponderance of Power: National Security, the Truman Administration, and the Cold War* (Stanford, 1992). HUAC's name had altered slightly since the 1930s, when it had been the House Special Committee on Un-American Activities.

3. Schrecker, *Many Are the Crimes*, esp. 106, 206–11; Stanley I. Kutler, *The American Inquisition: Justice and Injustice in the Cold War* (New York, 1982).

4. Quoted in J. Edgar Hoover, *On Communism* (New York, 1969), 100, 115, from a speech Hoover gave in 1940 and an article he published in 1954.

5. Ibid., and J. Edgar Hoover, *Masters of Deceit: The Story of Communism in America and How to Fight It* (New York, 1958); Athan G. Theoharis and John Stuart Cox, *The Boss: J. Edgar Hoover and the Great American Inquisition* (Philadelphia, 1988), 157–300.

6. Schrecker, *Many Are the Crimes*; Ellen Schrecker, *No Ivory Tower: McCarthyism and the Universities* (New York, 1986); David Caute, *The Great Fear: The Anti-Communist Purge under Truman and Eisenhower* (New York, 1978); David M. Oshinsky, *A Conspiracy So Immense: The World of Joe McCarthy* (New York, 1983); Neal Gabler, *An Empire of Their Own: How the Jews Invented Hollywood* (New York, 1988), 351–86; Bert Cochran, *Between Labor and Communism: The Conflict That Shaped American Unions* (Princeton, 1977); Harvey A. Levenstein, *Communism, Anticommunism, and the CIO* (Westport, Conn., 1981).

7. Alan Brinkley, *The End of Reform: New Deal Liberalism in Depression and War* (New York, 1995); Gary Gerstle, "The Protean Character of American Liberalism," *American Historical Review* 99 (October 1994): 1043–73, and *Working-Class Americanism: The Politics of Labor in a Textile City, 1914–1960* (New York, 1989), 278–330; Alonzo L. Hamby, "The Vital Center, the Fair Deal, and the Quest for a Liberal Political Economy," *American Historical Review* 77 (June 1972): 653–78; Elizabeth A. Fones-Wolf, *Selling Free Enterprise: The Business Assault on Labor and Liberalism, 1945–60* (Urbana, Ill., 1994); Godfrey Hodgson, *America in Our Time* (New York, 1978), 67–98 (source for Roper poll); Daniel T. Rodgers, *Contested Truths: Keywords in American Politics since Independence* (New York, 1987), chap. 6. See also Steve Fraser and Gary Gerstle, eds., *The Rise and Fall of the New Deal Order, 1930–1980* (Princeton, 1989), and Lary May, ed., *Recasting America: Culture and Politics in the Age of the Cold War* (Chicago, 1989).

8. Donald F. Crosby, S.J., *God, Church, and Flag: Senator Joseph R. McCarthy and the Catholic Church, 1950–1957* (Chapel Hill, 1978); David O'Brien, *American Catholics and Social Reform: The New Deal Years* (New York, 1968); Gerstle, *Working-Class Americanism*, 230–309; Joshua B. Freeman and Steve Rosswurm, "The Education of an Anti-Communist: Father John F. Cronin and the Baltimore Labor Movement," *Labor History* 33 (Spring 1992): 217–47; Michael Kazin, *The Populist Persuasion: An American History* (New York, 1995), 165–94; Jerome E. Edwards, *Pat McCarran, Political Boss of Nevada* (Reno, Nev., 1982); William F. Buckley Jr. and L. Brent Bozell, *McCarthy and His Enemies: The Record and Its Meaning* (1954; Washington, D.C., 1995); Robert I. Gannon, S.J., *The Cardinal Spellman Story* (New York, 1962); Louis F. Budenz, *This Is My Story* (New York, 1947), and *Men without Faces: The Communist Conspiracy in the U.S.A.* (New York, 1950); Patrick Allitt, *Catholic Intellectuals and Conservative Politics in America, 1950–1985* (Ithaca, N.Y., 1993); Christopher J. Kauffman, *Faith and Fraternalism: The History of the Knights of Columbus, 1882–1982* (New York, 1982).

9. Adolf Hitler, *Mein Kampf* (1925–27; New York, 1939); Arno Mayer, *Why Did the Heavens Not Darken? The "Final Solution" in History* (New York, 1988).

10. Douglas's husband was Melvyn Douglas, né Melvyn Hesselberg; see Roger Morris, *Richard Milhous Nixon: The Rise of an American Politician* (New York, 1990), 599–600; Greg Mitchell, *Tricky Dick and the Pink Lady: Richard Nixon vs. Helen Gahagan Douglas—Sexual Politics and the Red Scare* (New York, 1998), 139, 230, 234; Stuart Svonkin, *Jews against Prejudice: American Jews and the Fight for Civil Liberties* (New York, 1997), 135–47; Martin Bauml Duberman, *Paul Robeson* (New York, 1988), 363–80. There were other moments, too, when anti-Communists conflated Judaism and Bolshevism: in the espionage accusations leveled at Jewish engineers at Fort Monmouth, New Jersey, and in the 1950 Senate confirmation hearings for Anna M. Rosenberg, Truman's nominee for assistant secretary of defense. See Svonkin, *Jews against Prejudice*, 117–24.

11. Most of these individuals, unlike Robeson and Du Bois, did not stay in or near the party long. Duberman, *Paul Robeson*; Gerald Horne, *Black and Red: W.E.B. Du Bois and the Afro-American Response to the Cold War, 1944–1963* (Albany, N.Y., 1986). See also Elliott M. Rudwick, *W.E.B. Du Bois, Voice of the Black Protest Movement* (1960; Urbana, Ill., 1982); Manning Marable, *W.E.B. Du Bois: Black Radical Democrat* (Boston, 1986); Mark Naison, *Communism in Harlem during the Depression* (Urbana, Ill., 1983); Ralph Ellison, *Invisible Man* (New York, 1947); Arnold Rampersand, *The Life of Langston Hughes*, vol. 1, *1902–1941: I, Too, Sing America* (New York, 1986); Penny von Eschen, *Race against Empire: Black Americans and Anticolonialism, 1937–1957* (Ithaca, N.Y., 1997).

12. Michael Goldfield, *The Decline of Organized Labor in the United States* (Chicago, 1987), and *The Color of Politics: Race, Class, and the Mainsprings of American Politics* (New York, 1997); Barbara Sue Griffith, *The Crisis of American Labor: Operation Dixie and the Defeat of the CIO* (Philadelphia, 1988); Robert Korstad and Nelson Lichtenstein, "Opportunities Found and Lost: Labor, Radicals, and the Early Civil Rights Movement," *Journal of American History* 75 (December 1988): 786–811; Duberman, *Paul Robeson*, 381–464; Robert Rogers Korstad, *Democracy Denied: Black Insurgency and the Metamorphosis of White Supremacy* (Chapel Hill, forthcoming).

13. Mary L. Dudziak, *Cold War Civil Rights: Equality as Cold War Policy, 1946–1968* (Princeton, 2000), chaps. 2–5.

14. Ibid.; Brief for the United States as amicus curiae, 7–8, *Brown v. Board of Education*, 347 U.S. 483 (1954). See also John David Skrentny, "The Effect of the Cold War on African-American Civil Rights: America and the World Audience," *Theory and Society* 27 (1998): 237–85; Brenda Gayle Plummer, *Rising Wind: Black Americans and U.S. Foreign Affairs, 1935–1960* (Chapel Hill, 1996); Jonathan Rosenberg, "How Far the Promised Land? World Affairs and the American Civil Rights Movement from the First World War to Vietnam" (Ph.D. dissertation, Harvard University, 1997).

15. *The Papers of Martin Luther King, Jr.*, ed. Clayborne Carson, 3 vols. to date (Berkeley, 1992–97), 1:109–11; Plummer, *Black Americans and U.S. Foreign Affairs*; Rosenberg, "How Far the Promised Land?"

16. On the benefits offered by the GI Bill, see Keith W. Olson, *The G.I. Bill, the Veterans, and the Colleges* (Lexington, Ky., 1974).

17. Charles Herbert Stember et al., *Jews in the Mind of America* (New York, 1966), 156–70, 208–18. Stember writes that in 1950, "only 4 percent of the respondents [to his survey] spontaneously mentioned Jews when asked whether 'any kind or groups of people . . . [were] more likely than others to be Communists'; during 1953 and 1954, the response actually dropped to 2 and 1 percent respectively" (161).

18. *Congressional Record* (hereafter *CR*), February 20, 1950, 1954; on McCarthy's appointment of Cohn, see Oshinsky, *A Conspiracy So Immense*, 205, 253–54. David H. Bennett has called this attack on native elites "inverted nativism." See his *The Party of Fear: From Nativist Movements to the New Right in American History* (Chapel Hill, 1988), 238–315.

19. Allen Weinstein, *Perjury: The Hiss-Chambers Case* (New York, 1978); Sam Tanenhaus, *Whittaker Chambers: A Biography* (New York, 1997); Walter Goodman, *The Committee: The Extraordinary Career of the House Committee on Un-American Activities* (New York, 1964), 226–96.

20. *CR*, February 20, 1952, 1957. For McCarthy's 60,000-word attack on Marshall, see ibid., June 14, 1951, 6556–6603. On Acheson, see David S. McLellan, *Dean Acheson: The State Department Years* (New York, 1976), and James Chace, *Acheson: The Secretary of State Who Created the World* (New York, 1998).

21. John D'Emilio, "The Homosexual Menace: The Politics of Sexuality in Cold War America," in Kathy Peiss and Christina Simmons, with the assistance of Robert A. Padgug, eds., *Passion and Power: Sexuality in History* (Philadelphia, 1989), 226–40; Allan Bérubé, *Coming Out under Fire: The History of Gay Men and Women in World War II* (New York, 1990).

22. *CR*, February 20, 1950, 1957; see also Kazin, *Populist Persuasion*, 183–90.

23. This theme played itself out not only in World War II movies but in John Ford westerns. See for example, John Ford, director, *Fort Apache* (1948); Richard Slotkin, *Gunfighter Nation: The Myth of the Frontier in Twentieth-Century America* (New York, 1992), 334–43.

24. For a history of this legislation, see Robert A. Divine, *American Immigration Policy, 1924–1952* (New Haven, 1957), 164–91.

25. Edwards, *Pat McCarran*, 132–48.

26. Divine, *American Immigration Policy*, 164–91.

27. *CR*, June 26, 1952, 8218.

28. For the liberal policy alternative to McCarran-Walter, see William S. Bernard, ed., *American Immigration Policy: A Reappraisal* (New York, 1950).

29. *CR*, May 22, 1952, 5773.

30. *CR*, June 25, 1952, 8083.

31. Divine, *American Immigration Policy*, 172–73, 184, 188.

32. *CR*, June 27, 1952, 8254.

33. See Congressman Judd's speech, *CR*, June 26, 1952, 8217.

34. See, for example, Senator Humphrey's speech, *CR*, June 27, 1952, 8260.

35. *CR*, May 16, 1952, 5330.

36. *CR* May 22, 1952, 5772–73.

37. *CR*, May 16, 1952, 5330.

38. *CR*, May 22, 1952, 5772–73. Author's emphasis.

39. *CR*, June 27, 1952, 8263.

40. *CR*, May 16, 1952, 5330.

41. Not only did the act limit the numbers of Asians to 100 per country per year. It also imposed a cumulative Asian ceiling of 2,000 per year.

42. Svonkin, *Jews against Prejudice*, 151–60. This aspect of the Rosenberg case, like every other one, is steeped in controversy. The mainstream Jewish organizations justified their hard line against the Rosenbergs as a necessary reaction to a disingenuous strategy on the part of the Communist Party (and of the Rosenbergs themselves) to present the Rosenbergs as committed Jews and to portray their victimization in anti-Semitic terms. Even if we grant that the Communist Party used this strategy, the mainstream Jewish response still appears excessive, the expression of a group anxious for acceptance in American society. Those readers who wish to immerse themselves in these issues may want to consult the following: for critical views of the Rosenbergs, see Ronald Radosh and Joyce Milton, *The Rosenberg File: A Search for the Truth* (New York, 1983), and S. Andhil Fineberg, *The Rosenberg Case: Fact and Fiction* (New York, 1953). For treatments sympathetic to the Rosenbergs, see Walter Schneir and Miriam Schneir, *Invitation to an Inquest* (1965; New York, 1983); Michael Meeropol, ed., *The Rosenberg Letters: A Complete Edition of the Prison Correspondence of Julius and Ethel Rosenberg* (New York, 1994); Robert Meeropol and Michael Meeropol, *We Are Your Sons: The Legacy of Ethel and Julius Rosenberg* (1975; Urbana, Ill., 1986); and Andrew Ross, *No Respect: Intellectuals and Popular Culture* (New York, 1989), 15–41. For some brief but shrewd insights in the Jewish question during the McCarthy era as it affected Roy Cohn, see Oshinsky, *A Conspiracy So Immense*, 254. See also Deborah Dash Moore, "Reconsidering the Rosenbergs: Symbol and Substance in Second Generation American Jewish Consciousness," *Journal of American Ethnic History* 8 (Fall 1988): 21–37; Jeffrey M. Marker, "The Jewish Community and the Case of Ethel and Julius Rosenberg," *Maryland Historian* 3 (Fall 1972): 105–21; Marc E. Berkson, "The Case of Julius and Ethel Rosenberg: Jewish Response to a Period of Stress" (M.A. thesis, Hebrew Union College–Jewish Institute of Religion, 1978); Radosh and Milton, *Rosenberg File*, 352–55.

43. Svonkin, *Jews against Prejudice*, esp. 112.

44. Quoted in von Eschen, *Race against Empire*, 118–19.

45. Korstad and Lichtenstein, "Opportunities Found and Lost"; von Eschen, *Race against Empire*; Dudziak, *Cold War Civil Rights*; Horne, *Black and Red*; Gerald Horne, *Black Liberation/Red Scare: Ben Davis and the Communist Party* (Newark, Del., 1994), and *Communist Front? The Civil Rights Congress, 1946–1956* (Rutherford, N.J., 1988).

46. Lee Bernstein, "The Greatest Menace: Organized Crime in U.S. Culture and Politics, 1946–1961" (Ph.D. dissertation, University of Minnesota, 1997).

47. George De Gregorio, *Joe DiMaggio: An Informal Biography* (New York, 1981); *Joseph Durso: The Last American Knight* (Boston, 1995).

CHAPTER 7

1. Karl M. Brauer, *John F. Kennedy and the Second Reconstruction* (New York, 1977).
2. Martin Luther King Jr., *Why We Can't Wait* (New York, 1963), 118. On the history of the civil rights movement, consult Harvard Sitkoff, *The Struggle for Black Equality, 1954–1980* (New York, 1981); Robert Weisbrot, *Freedom Bound: A History of America's Civil Rights Movement* (New York, 1990); David J. Garrow, *Bearing the Cross: Martin Luther King, Jr., and the Southern Christian Leadership Conference* (New York, 1986); Taylor Branch, *Parting the Waters: America in the King Years, 1954–63* (New York, 1988), and *Pillar of Fire: America in the King Years, 1963–1965* (New York, 1998); Clayborne Carson, *In Struggle: SNCC and the Black Awakening of the 1960s* (Cambridge, Mass., 1981); George M. Fredrickson, *Black Liberation: A Comparative History of Black Ideologies in the United States and South Africa* (New York, 1995); William H. Chafe, *Civilities and Civil Rights: Greensboro, North Carolina, and the Black Struggle for Freedom* (New York, 1980); Aldon Morris, *The Origins of the Civil Rights Movement: Black Communities Organizing for Change* (New York, 1984); Robert Korstad and Nelson Lichtenstein, "Opportunities Found and Lost: Labor, Radicals, and the Early Civil Rights Movement," *Journal of American History* 75 (December 1988): 786–811; Charles Payne, *I've Got the Light of Freedom: The Organizing Tradition and the Mississippi Freedom Struggle* (Berkeley, 1995).
3. Mary Dudziak, *Cold War Civil Rights: Equality as Cold War Policy, 1946–1968* (Princeton, 2000), chap. 5.
4. *The Autobiography of Martin Luther King, Jr.*, ed. Clayborne Carson (New York, 1998), 112, 114. On King's trip to India, see ibid., 121–34. On Gandhi's influence, see Fredrickson, *Black Liberation*, 225–76; David Halberstam, *The Children* (New York, 1998), 25–50.
5. Stephen B. Oates, *Let the Trumpet Sound: The Life of Martin Luther King, Jr.* (1982; New York, 1985), 114–15.
6. *The Papers of Martin Luther King, Jr.*, ed. Clayborne Carson, 3 vols. to date (Berkeley, 1992–97), 1:109–11.
7. Ibid., 3:71.
8. Martin Luther King Jr., *A Testament of Hope: The Essential Writings of Martin Luther King, Jr.*, ed. James Melvin Washington (San Francisco, 1986), 165.
9. Ibid., 219.
10. Ibid., 208–9.
11. Ibid., 151.
12. King, *Why We Can't Wait*, 136–41; see also Michael Eric Dyson, *I May Not Get There with You: The True Martin Luther King, Jr.* (New York, 2000).

13. King, *Why We Can't Wait*, 120.

14. King, *A Testament of Hope*, 208–9; King, *Why We Can't Wait*, 121. On Myrdal's creed, see Gunnar Myrdal, *An American Dilemma: The Negro Problem and Modern Democracy* (New York, 1944), 1:3–25.

15. King, *Why We Can't Wait*, 121–22, 123–24. On the security of King's upbringing, see the introduction to *The Papers of Martin Luther King, Jr.*, 1:1–37, and Oates, *Let the Trumpet Sound*, 1–50. On King's use of the American dream as a strategy to appeal to white liberals, see August Meier, "On the Role of Martin Luther King," *New Politics* 4 (Winter 1965): 52–59.

16. King, *A Testament of Hope*, 151. Among the scholars who see this moment as a critical juncture are John Higham, in "Multiculturalism and Universalism: A History and a Critique," *American Quarterly* 45 (June 1993): 195–219; Jim Sleeper, *The Closest of Strangers: Liberalism and the Politics of Race in New York* (New York, 1990); Michael Lind, *The Next American Nation: The New Nationalism and the Fourth American Revolution* (New York, 1995).

17. Ira Katznelson, "Was the Great Society a Lost Opportunity?" in Steve Fraser and Gary Gerstle, eds., *The Rise and Fall of the New Deal Order, 1930–1980* (Princeton, 1989), 185–211; Kevin Boyle, *The UAW and the Heyday of American Liberalism, 1945–1968* (Ithaca, N.Y., 1995), 132–205; Nelson Lichtenstein, *The Most Dangerous Man in Detroit: Walter Reuther and the Fate of American Labor* (New York, 1995), 370–419; Nicholas Lemann, *The Promised Land: The Great Black Migration and How It Changed America* (New York, 1991), 109–222; David Stebenne, *Arthur J. Goldberg: New Deal Liberal* (New York, 1996).

18. This point is overlooked by those commentators such as Michael Lind and Jim Sleeper who mourn the failure of a social democratic coalition to emerge in 1963 and 1964. See Sleeper, *The Closest of Strangers*, and Lind, *The Next American Nation*.

19. Thomas Jackson, "Keys to the Dark Ghetto: Understanding and Mobilizing the Urban Poor in the 1960s" (unpublished manuscript, 1999); Dyson, *I May Not Get There with You*.

20. John F. Kennedy, "Radio and Television Report to the American People on Civil Rights," in *Public Papers of the Presidents of the United States, John F. Kennedy, January 1 to November 22, 1963* (Washington, D.C., 1964), 468–69.

21. Brauer, *Kennedy and the Second Reconstruction*, 230–64; Arthur M. Schlesinger Jr., *A Thousand Days: John F. Kennedy in the White House* (New York, 1965), 867–92; Branch, *Pillar of Fire*, 86–117.

22. Tom P. Brady, "Black Monday: Segregation or Amalgmation . . . America Has Its Choice," in Clayborne Carson, David J. Garrow, Gerald Gill, Vincent Harding, and Darlene Clark Hine, eds., *The Eyes on the Prize Civil Rights Reader: Documents, Speeches, and Firsthand Accounts from the Black Freedom Struggle* (New York, 1991), 84–85.

23. Ibid., 89.

24. Oates, *Let the Trumpet Sound*, 83–85; Branch, *Parting the Waters*, esp. 164–67, 201–2, 243–45. The would-be assassin in 1958 was a black woman, identified as Izola Ware Curry, diagnosed as a paranoid schizophrenic, and ordered committed to Matteawan State Hospital for the Criminally Insane.

25. David J. Garrow, *The FBI and Martin Luther King, Jr.: From "Solo" to Memphis* (New York, 1981).

26. Carson, *In Struggle*, 31–82; Branch, *Parting the Waters*, 412–523, 708–55; Halberstam, *The Children*; Payne, *I've Got the Light of Freedom*.

27. Howell Raines, *My Soul Is Rested: The Story of the Civil Rights Movement in the Deep South* (1977; New York, 1983), 238–43, 268–70, 286–90.

28. Ibid., 288; Theodore White, *The Making of the President, 1964* (New York, 1965), reported that thirty people had been killed in Mississippi in 1964 alone. Fannie Lou Hamer claimed in 1965 that thirty-two black churches had been burned in Mississippi; J. H. O'Dell, "Life in Mississippi, An Interview with Fannie Lou Hamer," *Freedomways* (Spring 1965): 238.

29. Quoted in Halberstam, *The Children*, 451. See also Nicolaus Mills, "Heard and Unheard: What Really Happened at the March on Washington?" *Dissent* 35 (Summer 1988): 288–91; Garrow, *Bearing the Cross*, 281–83; Lucy Grace Barber, "Marches on Washington, 1894–1963: National Political Demonstrations and American Political Culture" (Ph.D. dissertation, Brown University, 1996), chap. 5; James Forman, *The Making of Black Revolutionaries: A Personal Account* (Washington, D.C., 1985), 331–37; John Lewis, *Walking with the Wind: A Memoir of the Movement* (New York, 1998), 202–31.

30. On LBJ and civil rights, see Robert Dallek, *Flawed Giant: Lyndon Johnson and His Times, 1961–1973* (New York, 1998), 111–21; Bruce J. Schulman, *Lyndon B. Johnson and American Liberalism* (New York, 1995), 104–24.

31. Nicolaus Mills, *Like a Holy Crusade: Mississippi, 1964: the Turning of the Civil Rights Movement in America* (Chicago, 1992); Payne, *I've Got the Light of Freedom*, esp. 301, 394–96; Raines, *My Soul Is Rested*, 287; Lewis, *Walking with the Wind*, 261–82.

32. For accounts of the MFDP and the 1964 convention, see Godfrey Hodgson, *America in Our Time: From World War II to Nixon, What Happened and Why* (New York, 1976), 213–18; White, *The Making of the President, 1964*, 243–93; Forman, *The Making of Black Revolutionaries*, 386–95; Len Holt, *The Summer That Didn't End* (New York, 1965), 149–83; Lewis, *Walking with the Wind*, 283–299; Lichtenstein, *The Most Dangerous Man in Detroit*, 392–95; Boyle, *The UAW and the Heyday of American Liberalism*, 193–96; Todd Gitlin, *The Sixties: Years of Hope, Days of Rage* (New York, 1987), 151–62; Branch, *Pillar of Fire*, 456–76.

33. Jack Minnis, "The Mississippi Freedom Democratic Party: A New Declaration of Independence," *Freedomways* (Spring 1965): 269.

34. White, *Making of the President*, 279; Gitlin, *The Sixties*, 153; *New York Times*, August 23, 1964, 1, 81. On Hamer, see Chana Kai Lee, *For Freedom's Sake: The Life of Fannie Lou Hamer* (Urbana, Ill., 1999).

35. Stokely Carmichael and Charles V. Hamilton, *Black Power: The Politics of Liberation in America* (New York, 1967), 93.

36. *New York Times*, August 16, 1964, 1, 60.

37. *Taking Charge: The Johnson White House Tapes, 1963–1964*, ed. Michael R. Beschloss (New York, 1997), 526–27.

38. *New York Times*, August 23, 1964, 80.

39. Dallek, *Flawed Giant*, 54–237; Schulman, *Lyndon B. Johnson and American Liberalism*, 81–103.

40. Thomas Byrne Edsall and Mary D. Edsall, *Chain Reaction: The Impact of Race, Rights, and Taxes on American Politics* (New York, 1991).

41. *Taking Charge*, 516.

42. All but seven of the credentials committee members were white. Holt, *The Summer That Didn't End*, 169.

43. Lichtenstein, *The Most Dangerous Man in Detroit*, 392–95; Boyle, *The UAW and the Heyday of American Liberalism*, 193–96; Gitlin, *The Sixties*, 158.

44. *New York Times*, August 26, 1964, 1, 28.

45. *New York Times*, August 28, 1964, 14.

46. *New York Times*, August 26, 1964, 1, 28. It mattered, too, that they had persuaded Martin Luther King Jr., NAACP head Roy Wilkins, and Bayard Rustin, now cast in the role of civil rights moderates, of the virtues of their actions. David Lawrence, himself, had hailed the resolution of the MFDP crisis as a " 'turning point in the history of the Democratic party, which for most of its history has been profoundly influenced by all-white delegations from the Southern States.' "

47. Cleveland Sellers, with Robert Terrell, *River of No Return: The Autobiography of a Black Militant and the Life and Death of SNCC* (New York, 1973), 111.

48. Minnis, "The Mississippi Freedom Democratic Party," 270.

49. Sellers, *River of No Return*, 111.

50. Minnis, "Mississippi Freedom Democratic Party," 277–78. See, also, Forman, *The Making of Black Revolutionaries*, esp. 396–411; Holt, *The Summer That Didn't End*, 168–83; Jean Smith, "I Learned to Feel Black," in Floyd B. Barbour, ed., *The Black Power Revolt* (Boston, 1968), 207–18.

51. On the history of black nationalism, see John Bracey Jr., August Meier, and Elliott Rudwick, eds., *Black Nationalism in America* (Indianapolis, 1970); Theodore Draper, *The Rediscovery of Black Nationalism* (New York, 1969); E. U. Essien-Udom, *Black Nationalism: A Search for an Identity in America* (Chicago, 1962); Frederickson, *Black Liberation*; William L. Van Deburg, *New Day in Babylon: The Black Power Movement in American Culture, 1965–1975* (Chicago, 1992); Forman, *The Making of Black Revolutionaries*. On Communists and black nationalism in the early 1930s, see Robin D. G. Kelley, *Hammer and Hoe: Alabama Communists during the Great Depression* (Chapel Hill, 1990). On Garveyism, see Judith Stein, *The World of Marcus Garvey: Race and Class in Modern Society* (Baton Rouge, La., 1986).

52. Malcolm X, *The Autobiography of Malcolm X* (New York, 1964), esp. 278; C. Eric Lincoln, *The Black Muslims of America*, 2nd ed. (Boston, 1973); Branch, *Pillar of Fire*, esp. 3–20; James H. Cone, *Martin and Malcolm and America: A Dream or a Nightmare* (Maryknoll, N.Y., 1991); Joe Wood, ed., *Malcolm X in Our Own Image* (New York, 1992); Bruce Perry, *Malcolm: The Life of a Man Who Changed Black America* (Barrytown, N.Y., 1991); Peter Goldman, *The Death and Life of Malcolm X*, 2nd ed. (Urbana, Ill., 1979); Michael Eric

Dyson, *Making Malcolm: The Myth and Meaning of Malcolm X* (New York, 1995). See also Nell Irvin Painter, "Malcolm X across the Genres," and Gerald Horne, " 'Myth' and the Making of 'Malcolm X,' " *American Historical Review* 98 (April 1993), 432–39 and 440–50.

53. Malcolm X, "Message to the Grass Roots" (November 1963), in *Malcolm X Speaks: Selected Speeches and Statements*, ed. George Breitman (New York, 1965), 10.

54. Malcolm X, "The Ballot or the Bullet" (April 1964), in ibid., 26.

55. Malcolm X, "Message to the Grass Roots," 16. In his autobiography, Malcolm called it "The Farce on Washington." Malcolm X, *Autobiography*, 278.

56. Malcolm X, *Autobiography*, 200.

57. Malcolm X, "The Ballot or the Bullet," 39–40.

58. Malcolm X, "With Mrs. Fannie Lou Hamer" (December 1964), in *Malcolm X Speaks*, 108.

59. Ibid., 106; Malcolm X, "At the Audubon" (December 1964), 134, in ibid., and "Message to the Grass Roots," 9–10. The goal of such a revolution, Malcolm argued, should be the same as that which he identified as the aim of the American, French, Russian, and all other great revolutions: the conquest of territory. Once in control of their own land, blacks could establish their own nation, free of white, and "American," control. Then the rehabilitation of the black race, the achievement of independence, freedom, and dignity, could proceed. For Malcolm's thoughts on revolution, see "Message to the Grass Roots," 6–9.

60. Van Deburg, *New Day in Babylon*, 2.

61. Quoted in ibid., 32.

62. Carson, *In Struggle*, 265–86; Draper, *Rediscovery of Black Nationalism*, 97–117; Van Deburg, *New Day in Babylon*, 155–66; Eldridge Cleaver, *Soul on Ice* (New York, 1968); David Burner, *Making Peace with the 60s* (Princeton, 1996), 49–83; Hugh Pearson, *Shadow of the Panther: Huey Newton and the Price of Black Power in America* (Reading, Mass., 1994).

63. Malcolm X, *Autobiography*, 311–12.

64. The most comprehensive study of this urban revolt is still the United States Government's *Report of the National Advisory Commission on Civil Disorders* (Washington, D.C., 1968). See also Robert M. Fogelson, *Violence as Social Protest: A Study of Riots and Ghettos* (Garden City, N.Y., 1971); Gerald Horne, *Fire This Time: The Watts Uprising and the Meaning of the 1960s* (Charlottesville, Va., 1995); Sidney Fine, *Violence in the Model City: The Cavanaugh Administration, Race Relations, and the Detroit Riot of 1967* (Ann Arbor, Mich., 1989); Tom Hayden, *Rebellion in Newark: Official Violence and Ghetto Response* (New York, 1967); James W. Button, *Black Violence: Political Impact of the 1960s Riots* (Princeton, 1978); and Robert Conot, *Rivers of Blood, Years of Darkness* (New York, 1967).

65. Frantz Fanon, *Wretched of the Earth* (1961; New York, 1968); Van Deburg, *New Day in Babylon*, 57–59; Carmichael and Hamilton, *Black Power*; Cleaver, *Soul on Ice*. For an analysis of black nationalist attempts to interpret black poverty in terms of internal colonialism, see Michael Katz, *The Undeserving*

Poor: From the War on Poverty to the War on Welfare (New York, 1989), 52–65.

66. Quoted in Carmichael and Hamilton, *Black Power*, xi. See also Cleaver, *Soul on Ice*.

67. G. Louis Heath, *Off the Pigs! The History and Literature of the Black Panther Party* (Metuchen, N.J., 1976); Earl Anthony, *Picking Up the Gun: A Report on the Black Panthers* (New York, 1970); Pearson, *Shadow of the Panther*. Black Panther minister of religion Earl Neil described the Statue of Liberty as a "cold marble figure of some dyke woman covered with pigeon droppings sitting in a polluted Bay in the Atlantic Ocean." Van Deburg, *New Day in Babylon*, 156.

68. Jerald E. Podair, "Like Strangers: Blacks, Whites, and New York City's Ocean Hill–Brownsville Crisis, 1945–1980" (Ph.D. dissertation, Princeton University, 1997); Van Deburg, *New Day in Babylon*, 63–111; Joshua B. Freeman, *Working-Class New York: Life and Labor since World War II* (New York, 2000), 215–27; Donald Alexander Downs, *Cornell '69: Liberalism and the Crisis of the American University* (Ithaca, N.Y., 1999).

69. Heather Ann Thompson, "The Politics of Labor, Race, and Liberalism in the Auto Plants and the Motor City, 1940–1980" (Ph.D. dissertation, Princeton University, 1995); Van Deburg, *New Day in Babylon*, 63–111; James A. Geschwender, *Class, Race, and Worker Insurgency: The League of Revolutionary Black Workers* (New York, 1977); Dan Georgakas, *Detroit, I Do Mind Dying: A Study in Urban Revolution* (New York, 1975); Bernard C. Nalty, *Strength for the Fight: A History of Black Americans in the Military* (New York, 1986), 287–317; Wallace Terry II, "Bringing the War Home," *Black Scholar* 2 (November 1970): 6–19; Jack White, "The Angry Black Soldiers," *Progressive* 34 (March 1970): 22–26; Roberta Ann Johnson, "The Prison Birth of Black Power," *Journal of Black Studies* 5 (June 1975): 395–414; Angela Y. Davis, "Political Prisoners, Prisons and Black Liberation," in Angela Y. Davis, ed., *If They Came in the Morning: Voices of Resistance* (New York, 1971), 19–36; George Jackson, *Soledad Brother: The Prison Letters of George Jackson* (New York, 1970).

70. To Avery Brundage, the American president of the International Olympic Committee, and to the heads of the United States Olympic Committee, there could be no greater embarrassment, and they quickly brought all their powers to bear on the black members of the U.S. team. The USOC suspended Smith and Carlos from the U.S. Olympic team and expelled them from the Olympic Village, threatening to do the same with any other athletes who followed their example. The swiftness of this counterattack had its desired effect. Other black athletes who sympathized with Smith and Carlos expressed a variety of milder protests on the victory stand, wearing black berets (doffed, however, for the national anthem), refusing to shake the hands of USOC officials, and dedicating their victory to their martyred friends. But none dared to repeat what Carlos and Smith had done—"blaspheme" the national anthem with the Black Power salute. Jeremy Larner and David Wolf, "The Protest of the Black Athletes," *Life* 64 (November 1, 1968): 64C–65; Harry Edwards, *The Revolt of the Black Athlete* (New York, 1969), 38–69, 91–114. On background to protests, see *Sports Illustrated: Mexico 68, the Problem Olympics* (Chicago, 1968); "The Olympic Jolt: 'Hell No, Don't Go!' "

NOTES TO CHAPTER EIGHT

Life 64 (March 15, 1968): 20–29; Arnold Hano, "The Black Rebel Who 'Whitelists' the Olympics," *New York Times Magazine*, May 12, 1968, 32–50; Jack Scott, "The White Olympics," *Ramparts* 6 (May 1968): 54–61; "Should Negroes Boycott the Olympics," *Ebony* 23 (March 1968): 110–16; "Olympic Trials: Black Athletes Prepare for Mexico City," *Ebony* 23 (October 1968): 186–190; Dick Schaap, "The Revolt of the Black Athletes," *Look* 32 (August 6, 1968): 72–77.

71. On 1968, see Hodgson, *America in Our Time*, 352–64; Gitlin, *The Sixties*, 285–340; David R. Farber, *Chicago '68* (Chicago, 1988); Arthur M. Schlesinger Jr., *Robert M. Kennedy and His Times* (New York, 1978), 921–83; Paul Berman, *A Tale of Two Utopias: The Political Journey of the Generation of 1968* (New York, 1996).

72. Van Deburg, *New Day in Babylon*, 192–291; Malcolm X, *Autobiography*; Komozi Woodard, *A Nation within a Nation: Amiri Baraka (LeRoi Jones) and Black Power Politics* (Chapel Hill, 1999); Elizabeth Pleck, "Kwaanza: The Making of a Black Nationalist Invented Tradition, 1966–1990" (unpublished paper in author's possession); Thomas Hauser, *Muhammad Ali: His Life and Times* (New York, 1991); Gerald Early, ed., *The Muhammad Ali Reader* (Hopewell, N.J., 1998); Arthur R. Ashe Jr., *A Hard Road to Glory: A History of the African-American Athlete since 1946* (New York, 1988).

73. Carson, *In Struggle*, 262.

74. Ibid., 244–303; Kenneth O'Reilly, *"Racial Matters": The FBI's Secret File on Black America, 1960–1972* (New York, 1989).

CHAPTER 8

1. Marilyn Young, *The Vietnam Wars, 1945–1990* (New York, 1991), 1–88; Stanley Karnow, *Vietnam: A History: The First Complete Account of Vietnam at War* (New York, 1983), 89–239; William Appleman Williams, Thomas McCormick, Lloyd Gardner, and Walter LaFeber, eds., *America in Vietnam: A Documentary History* (1975; New York, 1989), 10–208; George C. Herring, *America's Longest War: The United States and Vietnam, 1950–1975*, 2nd ed. (New York, 1986), 3–72.

2. On centrality of Japan, see Williams et al., *America in Vietnam*, esp. 45–60 and 61–127.

3. Young, *Vietnam Wars*, 60–104.

4. Eric F. Goldman, *The Tragedy of Lyndon Johnson* (New York, 1969).

5. On SNCC and Vietnam, see "SNCC: Statement on Vietnam War," Massimo Teodori, ed., *The New Left: A Documentary History* (Indianapolis, 1969), 251–52; Clayborne Carson, *In Struggle: SNCC and the Black Awakening in the 1960s* (Cambridge, Mass., 1981), 175–90. On the earlier antiwar protests among pacifists and other groups, see Maurice Isserman, *If I Had a Hammer . . . The Decline of the Old Left and the Birth of the New* (New York, 1987), 125–219; and Todd Gitlin, *The Sixties: Years of Hope, Days of Rage* (New York, 1987), 85–104.

6. Young, *Vietnam Wars*, 192–209; Gitlin, *The Sixties*, 177–92, 242–82; Michael S. Foley, "Confronting the War Machine: Draft Resistance during the Vietnam War" (Ph.D. dissertation, University of New Hampshire, 1999); Teodori, *The New Left*, 240–70.

7. Gitlin, *The Sixties*, 285–361, 377–408; Nancy Zaroulis and Gerald Sullivan, *Who Spoke Up? American Protest against the War in Vietnam, 1963–1975* (Garden City, N.Y., 1984); Charles DeBenedetti, with Charles Chatfield, *An American Ordeal: The Antiwar Movement of the Vietnam Era* (Syracuse, N.Y., 1990); Foley, "Confronting the War Machine."

8. See, for example, Paul Potter, "The Incredible War," in Teodori, *The New Left*, 246–48; Paul Cowan, *The Making of an Un-American: A Dialogue with Experience* (New York, 1970).

9. Nicolaus Mills, *Like a Holy Crusade: Mississippi, 1964—The Turning of the Civil Rights Movement in America* (Chicago, 1992); Gitlin, *The Sixties*; Maurice Isserman and Michael Kazin, "The Failure and Success of the New Radicalism," in Steve Fraser and Gary Gerstle, eds., *The Rise and Fall of the New Deal Order, 1930–1980* (Princeton, 1989), 212–42; Michael Kazin, *The Populist Persuasion: An American History* (New York, 1995), 195–220; Burner, *Making Peace with the 60s* (Princeton, 1996), 134–66, 189–216; Godfrey Hodgson, *America in Our Time: From World War II to Nixon, What Happened and Why* (New York, 1976), 274–352, 384–428; Immanuel Wallerstein and Paul Starr, eds., *The University Crisis Reader: The Liberal University under Attack* (New York, 1971), and *The University Crisis Reader: Confrontation and Counterattack* (New York, 1971); Irwin Unger and Debi Unger, *The Movement: A History of the American New Left, 1959–1972* (1974; Lanham, Md., 1988); Thomas Powers, *The War at Home: Vietnam and the American People, 1964–1968* (New York, 1968); Zaroulis and Sullivan, *Who Spoke Up?*; Kenneth J. Heineman, *Campus Wars: The Peace Movement at American State Universities in the Vietnam Era* (New York, 1993); W. J. Rorbaugh, *Berkeley at War: The 1960s* (New York, 1989); Sherry Gerson Gottlieb, *Hell No, We Won't Go: Resisting the Draft during the Vietnam War* (New York, 1991); Foley, "Confronting the War Machine"; DeBenedetti, *An American Ordeal.* On ties of universities to the Cold War, see Noam Chomsky et al., *The Cold War and the University: Toward an Intellectual History of the Postwar Years* (New York, 1997), and Christopher Simpson, ed., *Universities and Empires: Money and Politics in the Social Sciences during the Cold War* (New York, 1998).

10. On the class origins of the New Left, see Cyril Levitt, *Children of Privilege: Student Revolt in the Sixties* (Toronto, 1984); Stephen Goode, *Affluent Revolutionaries: A Portrait of the New Left* (New York, 1974); and B. Bruce Biggs, ed., *The New Class?* (New Brunswick, N.J., 1979).

11. Zaroulis and Sullivan, *Who Spoke Up?*; William H. Chafe, *Never Stop Running: Allard Lowenstein and the Struggle to Save American Liberalism* (New York, 1993), 276–314.

12. John Whiteclay Chambers II, *To Raise an Army: The Draft Comes to Modern America* (New York, 1987), 213, 243.

13. Robert D. Heinl Jr., "The Collapse of the Armed Forces," *Armed Forces Journal*, June 7, 1971, 35.

14. Christian G. Appy, *Working-Class War: American Combat Soldiers and Vietnam* (Chapel Hill, 1993).

15. Heinl, "The Collapse of the Armed Forces," 30.

16. On problems caused by rotation, see Stanley Goff and Robert Sanders with Clark Smith, *Brothers: Black Soldiers in the Nam* (Novato, Calif., 1982), 55.

17. Heinl, "The Collapse of the Armed Forces," 30–31.

18. Ibid., 31.

19. Ibid., 30–31.

20. Richard A. Gabriel and Paul L. Savage, *Crisis in Command: Mismanagement in the Army* (New York, 1978), 29–50, 181–84.

21. Heinl, "The Collapse of the Armed Forces," 31.

22. Charles C. Moskos Jr., "The American Dilemma in Uniform: Race in the Armed Forces," *Annals of the American Academy of Political and Social Science* 406 (March 1973): 94–106.

23. Goff et al., *Brothers*, esp. 60, 131; Moskos, "The American Dilemma in Uniform"; Wallace Terry, *Bloods: An Oral History of the Vietnam War by Black Veterans* (New York, 1984), esp. 25, 27, 41, 60, 62, 115.

24. Moskos, "American Dilemma in Uniform," 103.

25. Bernard C. Nalty, *Strength for the Fight: A History of Black Americans in the Military* (New York, 1986), esp. 301.

26. Wallace Terry II, "Bringing the War Home," *The Black Scholar* 2 (November 1970): 6–19; William Stuart Gould, "Racial Conflict in the U.S. Army," *Race* 15 (July 1973): 1–24; Moskos, "The American Dilemma in Uniform," 95; Jack White, "The Angry Black Soldiers," *Progressive* 34 (March 1970): 22–26. As bad as race relations seem to have become in Vietnam, they were often worse at military camps in the United States and Germany, where the fear of an external enemy was not strong enough, as it sometimes was in Vietnam, to moderate the hostility that black and white soldiers were willing to express toward each other.

27. On censorship in the military in World War II, see George H. Roeder Jr., *The Censored War: American Visual Experience during World War II* (New Haven, 1993). Some scholars, such as Guenter Lewy, have argued that the U.S. military's loss of control over the media, in combination with the rigid control that the North Vietnamese and Vietcong exercised over representations of the military and society in territory that they ruled, contributed to the turn of American public opinion against the war. Guenther Lewy, *America in Vietnam* (New York, 1978), esp. 433–36.

28. Elizabeth Sutherland Martinez and Enriqueta Longeaux y Vasquez, *Viva La Raza! The Struggle of the Mexican-American People* (Garden City, N.Y., 1974); William Wei, *The Asian American Movement* (Philadelphia, 1993); Paul Chaat Smith and Robert Allen Warrior, *Like a Hurricane: The Indian Movement from Alcatraz to Wounded Knee* (New York, 1996).

29. Jerald E. Podair, "Like Strangers: Blacks, Whites, and New York City's Ocean Hill–Brownsville Crisis, 1945–1980," chaps. 3–5. On Bundy's role in the

war, see David Halberstam, *The Best and the Brightest* (New York, 1972), esp. 56–81, 626–50.

30. For a polemical and critical account of liberalism's support for black nationalist perspectives, see Jim Sleeper, *The Closest of Strangers: Liberalism and the Politics of Race in New York* (New York, 1990), and *Liberal Racism* (New York, 1997).

31. Martinez and Longeaux y Vasquez, *Viva La Raza!*; Wei, *The Asian American Movement*; Smith and Warrior, *Like a Hurricane*; Alice Echols, *Daring to Be Bad: Radical Feminism in America, 1965–1975* (Minneapolis, 1989); Andrew Greeley, *Why Can't They Be Like Us? America's White Ethnic Groups* (New York, 1971), esp. 18; Michaela di Leonardo, "White Ethnicities, Identity Politics, and Baby Bear's Chair," *Social Text* 41 (Winter 1994): 165–91.

32. See, for example, Malcolm X, *The Autobiography of Malcolm X* (New York, 1964), 275, 278, 314, 350; Harold Cruse, *The Crisis of the Negro Intellectual* (1967; New York, 1984), 490.

33. Michael Novak, *The Rise of the Unmeltable Ethnics* (1971; New York, 1973); see also Greeley, *Why Can't They Be Like Us?*

34. Novak, *Rise of the Unmeltable Ethics*, 327, 76–78, 199, 250, 302, 307, 311, 314–42.

35. Podair, "Like Strangers." See also Jonathan Kaufman, *Broken Alliance: The Turbulent Times between Blacks and Jews in America* (New York, 1988); Jonathan Rieder, *Canarsie: The Jews and Italians of New York against Liberalism* (Cambridge, Mass., 1985); Paul Berman, ed., *Blacks and Jews: Alliances and Arguments* (New York, 1994).

36. Marc Lindsey Dollinger, "The Politics of Acculturation: American Jewish Liberalism, 1933–1975" (Ph.D. dissertation, University of California at Los Angeles, 1993), chap. 6; Meir Kahane, *The Story of the Jewish Defense League* (Radnor, Pa., 1975); Meir Kahane, *On Jews and Judaism: Selected Articles, 1961–1990* (Jerusalem, 1993). See also Paul Breines, *Tough Jews: Political Fantasies and the Moral Dilemma of American Jewry* (New York, 1990). The Jewish Defense League was founded in 1968.

37. Peter Novick, *The Holocaust in American Life* (New York, 1999), 146–203.

38. Lawrence M. O'Rourke, *Geno: The Life and Mission of Geno Baroni* (New York, 1991); "An Interview with Monsignor Geno Baroni," *Neighborhood: The Journal of City Preservation* 1 (December 1978): 2–7.

39. Geno Baroni, "Ethnicity and Public Policy," in Michael Wenk, S. M. Tomasi, and Geno Baroni, eds., *Pieces of a Dream: The Ethnic Worker's Crisis with America* (New York, 1972), 1–11. In the early 1970s, Baroni was closely allied with Novak.

40. Michael Novak, "New Ethnic Politics vs. Old Ethnic Politics"; George Meany, "New Dimension for Labor's Urban Ethnic Priorities"; Edmund S. Muskie, "Tax Reform and Ethnic Diversity"; Barbara Mikulski, "The Ethnic Neighborhood: Leave Room for a Boccie Ball"; all in Wenk, Tomasi, and Baroni, *Pieces of a Dream*, 53–62, 103–12, 121–42, 203–12. See also O'Rourke, *Geno*, 84–99; Novak, *The Rise of the Unmeltable Ethnics*, 293–303.

41. Peter Cowie, *Coppola: A Biography* (New York, 1990), 78–79.

42. Mario Puzo, *The Godfather* (New York, 1969).

43. Paul D. Zimmerman, " 'The Godfather': Triumph of Brando," *Newsweek*, March 13, 1972, 58.

44. Novak, *Unmeltable Ethnics*, xiv.

45. Stephen Farber, "Coppola and the Godfather," *Sight and Sound* 41 (Autumn 1972): 223.

46. Pauline Kael, "Alchemy," *New Yorker*, March 18, 1972, 138.

47. Farber, "Coppola and the Godfather," 223.

48. Vincent Canby, "Brando's 'Godfather,' " *New York Times*, March 12, 1972.

49. On the making of *Apocalypse Now*, see Cowie, *Coppola*, 119–43, and Albert Auster and Leonard Quart, *How the War Was Remembered: Hollywood and Vietnam* (New York, 1988), esp. 65–71.

50. Joseph Conrad, *Heart of Darkness* (1899; Cambridge, Mass., 1981).

51. The original *Rocky* appeared in 1976; the first Rambo film, *First Blood*, appeared in 1982.

52. Coppola's movies carried in them a conservative streak, discernible not simply in the celebration, in the *Godfather* movies, of white ethnic men but also, in *Apocalypse Now*, in the denigration of people of color. The latter is apparent both in the depiction of the Montagnards as small, dumb, and herdlike colored people lacking individuality and rationality, and in a scene in which black GIs, who had lost their white officers, are portrayed as utterly confused, cowardly, and trigger-happy. The latter scene was brief but long enough to remind viewers of the old and racist belief that blacks, when left on their own, could not be trusted to represent America in combat.

53. On revolt against the state's disciplinary powers, see David Frum, *How We Got Here: The 70's, the Decade That Brought You Modern Life (for Better or Worse)* (New York, 2000).

54. On origins, intent, and effects of affirmative action policies, see Hugh David Graham, *The Civil Rights Era: Origins and Development of National Policy, 1960–1972* (New York, 1990); John David Skrentny, *The Ironies of Affirmative Action: Politics, Culture, and Justice in America* (Chicago, 1996); David A. Hollinger, *Postethnic America: Beyond Multiculturalism* (New York, 1995), 119–50.

EPILOGUE

1. Gordon Wood, "The Losable Past," *New Republic*, November 7, 1994, 48–49.

2. Michael Walzer, *What It Means to Be an American* (New York, 1992); Lawrence Fuchs, *The American Kaleidoscope: Race, Ethnicity, and the Civic Culture* (Hanover, N.H., 1990); Horace M. Kallen, *Culture and Democracy in the United States: Group Psychology of the American Peoples* (New York, 1924), 67–125; Gary Gerstle, "The Protean Character of American Liberalism," *American His-*

torical Review 99 (October 1994): 1043–73; Oscar Handlin, "Group Life within the American Pattern," *Commentary* 8 (November 1949): 411–17; Will Herberg, *Protestant, Catholic, Jew: An Essay in American Religious Sociology* (New York, 1955); Nathan Glazer and Daniel Patrick Moynihan, *Beyond the Melting Pot: The Negroes, Puerto Ricans, Jews, Italians, and Irish of New York City* (Cambridge, Mass., 1963); Jerald E. Podair, "Like Strangers: Blacks, Whites, and New York City's Ocean Hill–Brownsville Crisis, 1945–1980" (Ph.D. dissertation, Princeton University, 1997), chap. 5; John Higham, "Multiculturalism and Universalism: A History and a Critique," *American Quarterly* 45 (June 1993): 195–219.

3. U.S. Congress, House, General Subcommittee on Education of the Committee on Education and Labor, 91st Cong., 2nd sess. Hearings on H.R. 14910, *A Bill to Provide a Program to Improve the Opportunity of Students in Elementary and Secondary Schools to Study Cultural Heritages of the Major Ethnic Groups in the Nation* (Washington, D.C., 1970), 94. For an account of these hearings, see Reed Ueda, *The Permanently Unfinished Country: Immigrants and Diversity in Twentieth-Century America* (New York, forthcoming), chap. 5. See also Lawrence O'Rourke, *Geno: The Life and Mission of Geno Baroni* (New York, 1991). For other works on the evolution of this ethnic-based, soft multiculturalism, see Andrew M. Greeley, *Why Can't They Be Like Us? America's White Ethnic Groups* (New York, 1971); Michael Novak, *The Rise of the Unmeltable Ethnics: Politics and Culture in the 1970s* (New York, 1971). For a critical view, see Orlando Patterson, *Ethnic Chauvinism: The Reactionary Impulse* (New York, 1977). On the "Nation of Nations" exhibit, see Peter C. Marzio, ed., *A Nation of Nations: The People Who Came to America as Seen through Objects and Documents Exhibited at the Smithsonian Institution* (New York, 1976).

4. Molefi K. Asante, *Afrocentricity* (Trenton, N.J., 1988), 6–7; Molefi K. Asante, *The Afrocentric Idea* (Philadelphia, 1987); "African Dreams," *Newsweek*, September 23, 1991, 42 <http:/web.lexis-nexis.com/univers...749b58e795f&taggedDOCS-Z2,2Z1,421>; William Wei, *The Asian- American Movement* (Philadelphia, 1993); Matt S. Meier and Feliciano Rivera, eds., *Readings on La Raza: The Twentieth Century* (New York, 1974); Asa G. Hilliard III, *The Maroon within Us: Selected Essays on African American Community Socialization* (Baltimore, 1995).

5. Janice Radway, "What's in a Name? Presidential Address to the American Studies Association, 20 November, 1998," *American Quarterly* 51 (March 1999): esp. 8, 12. Arjun Appadurai, "Patriotism and Its Futures," *Public Culture* 5 (1993): 411–29; Masao Miyoshi, "A Borderless World? From Colonialism to Transnationalism and the Decline of the Nation-State," *Critical Inquiry* 19 (Summer 1993): 726–51; Kenneth Cmiel, "The Emergence of Human Rights Politics in the United States," *Journal of American History* 86 (December 1999): 1231–50; Robin D. G. Kelley, " 'But a Local Phase of a World Problem': Black History's Global Vision," *Journal of American History* 86 (December 1999): 1045–77; José David Saldívar, *Border Matters: Remapping American Cultural Studies* (Berkeley, 1997); Paul Gilroy, *The Black Atlantic: Modernity and Double Consciousness* (Cambridge, Mass., 1993); Vincent Thompson, *The Making of the African*

Diaspora in the Americas, 1441–1900 (New York, 1987); Linda Basch, Nina Glick-Schiller, and Christina Szanton Blanc, eds., *Nations Unbound: Transnational Projects, Postcolonial Predicaments, and Deterritorialized Nation-States* (Langhorne, Pa., 1994); Robin Cohen, *Global Diasporas: An Introduction* (London, 1995); Floyd Anthias, "Evaluating 'Diaspora': Beyond Ethnicity?" *Sociology* 32 (August 1998): 557–80; Jonathan Rutherford, ed., *Identity: Community, Culture, Difference* (London, 1990), 222–37; Aihwa Ong and Donald Nonini, *Underground Empires: The Cultural Politics of Modern Chinese Transnationalism* (New York, 1997); Pnina Wernber, *The Migration Process: Capital, Gifts and Offerings among British Pakistanis* (Oxford, 1990), and "The Place Which is Diaspora: Chaordic Leapfrogging, Replicating and Transnational Networking" (unpublished conference paper in author's possession); Homi K. Bhaba, "Dissemi-Nation: Time, Narrative, and the Margins of the Modern Nation," in Bhaba, ed., *Nation and Narration* (London, 1990), 291–32; Kwame Anthony Appiah, *In My Father's House: Africa in the Philosophy of Culture* (New York, 1992).

6. Jonathan Rieder, *Canarsie: The Jews and Italians of Brooklyn against Liberalism* (Cambridge, Mass., 1985); Michael B. Katz, *The Undeserving Poor: From the War on Poverty to the War on Welfare* (New York, 1989), 185–240.

7. Quoted in Arthur M. Schlesinger Jr., *The Disuniting of America: Reflections on a Multicultural Society* (New York, 1992), 67.

8. "A Is for Ashanti, B Is for Black," *Newsweek*, September 23, 1991, 45, <http://web.lexis-nexis.com/univers. . .6e8e9a212d8&taggedDocs=Z2,2Z1,4Z1>; Sara Mosle, "Separatist but Equal? Afrocentric Schools Get a Mixed Report," *American Prospect* (Fall 1993): 73–82.

9. David A. Hollinger, *Postethnic America: Beyond Multiculturalism* (New York, 1995), 19–50.

10. Jennifer L. Hochschild, *Facing Up to the American Dream: Race, Class, and the Soul of the Nation* (Princeton, 1995).

11. Margaret A. Hart, *Managing Diversity for a Sustained Competitiveness* (New York, 1997); National Planning Association, *Affirmative Action: A Course for Future Action* (Washington, D.C., 1996).

12. E. J. Hobsbawm, *Nations and Nationalism since 1780: Programme, Myth, Reality* (New York, 1990); Robert B. Reich, *The Work of Nations: Preparing Ourselves for 21st-Century Capitalism* (New York, 1992); the Wilson quotation appears on p. 48. Karl Marx and Frederick Engels, *The German Ideology, Part One with Selections from Parts Two and Three and Supplementary Texts*, ed. C. J. Arthur, (1993; New York, 1947, 1970), esp. 64–68. See also David Harvey, *The Condition of Postmodernity: An Enquiry into the Origins of Cultural Change* (New York, 1990), and William Leach, *Country of Exiles: The Destruction of Place in American Life* (New York, 1999).

13. On the Berkeley episode, see Todd Gitlin, *The Sixties: Years of Hope, Days of Rage* (New York, 1987), 353–61.

14. On Grenada, see Deborah Hart Strober and Gerald S. Strober, *Reagan: The Man and His Presidency* (New York, 1998), 250–97, and Paul Seabury and Walter A. McDougall, eds., *The Grenada Papers* (San Francisco, 1984). On the specifics of Reagan's antiliberal race policies, see Thomas Byrne Edsall and Mary

D. Edsall, *Chain Reaction: The Impact of Race, Rights, and Taxes on American Politics* (New York, 1991), 172–97; Ronnie Dugger, *On Reagan: The Man and His Presidency* (New York, 1983); and Lou Cannon, *President Reagan: The Role of a Lifetime* (New York, 1991), 516–25. For an argument on the interconnectedness of military aggressiveness and racial nationalism in Reagan's ideology, see George Lipsitz, "Whiteness and War," in Lipsitz, *The Possessive Investment in Whiteness: How White People Profit from Identity Politics* (Philadelphia, 1998), 69–98.

15. Only 12 percent of African Americans voted for Reagan in 1980 and 1984; Peter Goldman and Tony Fuller, *The Quest for the Presidency, 1984* (New York, 1985), 456. *New York Times*, October 24, 1988, A1; *New York Times*, August 25, 1992, A18. The National Security Political Action Committee produced the notorious advertisement in 1988. A subsequent Federal Elections Commission investigation found that Larry McCarthy, the advertisement's producer, was a former employee of Roger Ailes, Bush's chief media consultant in 1988, and that the two men had had phone and personal contact during the 1988 campaign. Ailes consistently denied involvement with the advertisement. *Los Angeles Times*, January 17, 1992, A22; *New York Times*, October 3, 1988, A22. On Atwater's role, see John Brady, *Bad Boy: The Life and Politics of Lee Atwater* (Reading, Mass., 1997), 187–94.

16. *Actor, Ideologue, Politician: The Public Speeches of Ronald Reagan*, ed. Davis W. Houck and Amos Kiewe (Westport, Conn., 1993), 165.

17. Ibid., 178.

18. Edsall and Edsall, *Chain Reaction*, 180.

19. *Actor, Ideologue, Politician*, 165.

20. Ibid.

21. Quoted in Garry Wills, *Reagan's America: Innocents at Home* (Garden City, N.Y., 1987), 165.

22. Colin Powell, with Joseph E. Persico, *My American Journey* (New York, 1996), 382–83.

23. Dugger, *On Reagan*.

24. Rogers M. Smith, *Civic Ideals: Conflicting Visions of Citizenship in U.S. History* (New Haven, 1997), 197–242.

25. The worship of wealth and self-indulgence of the 1980s is best captured in novels such as Tom Wolfe, *Bonfire of the Vanities* (New York, 1987). For a nonfiction account of wealth production on Wall Street, see Michael Lewis, *Liar's Poker: Rising through the Wreckage on Wall Street* (New York, 1989). See also Debora Silverman, *Selling Culture: Bloomingdale's, Diana Vreeland, and the New Aristocracy of Taste in Reagan's America* (New York, 1986). On the evisceration of urban economies in Midwest cities, see Barry Bluestone and Bennett Harrison, *The Deindustrialization of America: Plant Closings, Community Abandonment, and the Dismantling of Basic Industry* (New York, 1982). On Jimmy Bakker's financial corruption, sexual promiscuity, and conviction, see *Los Angeles Times*, October 27, 1989, P2; *Toronto Star*, August 29, 1989, A4; and *Washington Post*, August 29, 1989, C1. On the revelations of Swaggart's consorting with prostitutes and his consequent leaving of his ministry, see *Courier-Journal* (Louisville),

October 16, 1991, 2A, and *Atlanta Journal and Constitution*, October 28, 1991, A-02.

26. *New York Times*, August 24, 1990, A1, A9; see also, ibid., January 14, 1991, A12.

27. *New York Times*, August 24, 1990, A1, A9, and January 14, 1991, A12. See Peter D. Feaver and Christopher Gelpi, "How Many Deaths Are Acceptable? A Surprising Answer," *Washington Post*, November 7, 1999, B3, for an interesting survey finding that a refusal to sacrifice one's life ("casualty aversion" in the language of the survey) is much less entrenched among the American people than is usually thought to be the case. The survey also found, however, that military and civilian elites believe that Americans will not tolerate the death of their soldiers on the battlefield, and plan their military engagements accordingly.

28. For an account of black-white clashes in New York (Howard Beach, Yusef Hawkins's murder in Brooklyn, Crown Heights, etc.), albeit a partisan one, see Jim Sleeper, *The Closest of Strangers: Liberalism and the Politics of Race in New York* (New York, 1990). On the Los Angeles riot of 1992 in the wake of the Rodney King riot, see Melvin T. Oliver, James H. Johnson Jr., and Walter C. Farrell Jr., "Anatomy of a Rebellion: A Political-Economic Analysis," in ed. Robert Gooding-Williams, *Reading Rodney King/Reading Urban Uprising* (New York, 1993), 117–41.

29. For accounts of these wars, see, Schlesinger, *The Disuniting of America*; Robert Hughes, "The Fraying of America," *Time Magazine*, February 3, 1992, 44–49; and Nathan Glazer, *We Are All Multiculturalists Now* (Cambridge, Mass., 1997). Peter N. Stearns, "Uncivil War: Current American Conservatives and Social History," 7–16; Richard Jensen, "The Culture Wars, 1965–1995: A Historian's Map," 17–38; Gary B. Nash, "The History Standards Controversy and Social History," 39–50; Jan Lewis, "The Double-Consciousness of the Academic Historian," 51–58; and Barry W. Bienstock, "Everything Old Is New Again: Social History, The National History Standards and the Crisis in the Teaching of High School American History," 59–64; all in *Journal of Social History* 29 (Supplement, 1995). See also Mike Wallace, *Mickey Mouse History and Other Essays in American Memory* (Philadelphia, 1996), esp. 250–318; Edward T. Linenthal and Tom Engelhardt, eds., *History Wars: The Enola Gay and Other Battles for the American Past* (New York, 1996); Eric Foner and Jon Wiener, "Fighting for the West," *Nation*, July 29–August 5, 1991, 163–66; Dinesh D'Souza, *Illiberal Education: The Politics of Race and Sex on Campus* (New York, 1991); Roger Kimball, *Tenured Radicals* (New York, 1990); and Todd Gitlin, *The Twilight of Common Dreams: Why America Is Wracked by Culture Wars* (New York, 1995).

30. *New York Times*, May 23, 1999, 1.

31. Schlesinger, *The Disuniting of America*; Diane Ravitch, "Our Pluralistic Common Culture," John Higham, ed., *Civil Rights and Social Wrongs: Black-White Relations since World War II* (University Park, Pa., 1997), 134–48; Sleeper, *The Closest of Strangers*, and *Liberal Racism* (New York, 1997); Frederick F. Siegel, *The Future Once Happened Here: New York, D.C., L.A., and the Fate of America's Big Cities* (New York, 1997); Alan Wolfe, *Marginalized in the Middle* (Chicago, 1996); Stephan Thernstrom and Abigail Thernstrom, *America in Black*

and White: One Nation Indivisible (New York, 1997); Stanley Crouch, *The All-American Skin Game, or, the Decoy of Race* (New York, 1995); Shelby Steele, *The Content of Our Character: A New Vision of Race in America* (New York, 1990); Gitlin, *Twilight of Common Dreams*; Randall Kennedy, *Race, Crime, and the Law* (New York, 1997); John B. Judis, *The Paradox of American Democracy: Elites, Special Interests, and the Betrayal of Public Trust* (New York, 2000); William A. Galston, *Liberal Purposes: Goods, Virtues, and Diversity in the Liberal State* (New York, 1991); Michael J. Sandel, *Democracy's Discontent: America in Search of a Public Philosophy* (Cambridge, Mass., 1996); Stephen L. Carter, *Civility: Manners, Morals, and the Etiquette of Democracy* (New York, 1988); Mary Ann Glendon, *Rights Talk: The Impoverishment of Political Discourse* (New York, 1991); Amitai Etzioni, *The New Golden Rule: Community and Morality in a Democratic Society* (New York, 1996), and *The Essential Communitarian Reader* (Lanham, Md., 1998); Michael Lind, *The Next American Nation: The New Nationalism and the Fourth American Revolution* (New York, 1995); Glenn C. Loury, *One by One from the Inside Out: Essays and Reviews on Race and Responsibility in America* (New York, 1995)

32. E. J. Dionne Jr., *They Only Look Dead: Why Progressives Will Dominate the Next Political Era* (New York, 1996), esp. 11, 204, 279; Lind, *The Next American Nation*, esp. 9, 301–2; Sandel, *Democracy's Discontent*; Michael J. Sandel, "America's Search for a New Public Philosophy," *Atlantic Monthly*, March 1996, 60–62; Judis, *The Paradox of American Democracy*.

33. Toni Morrison, "Talk of the Town," *New Yorker*, October 5, 1998, 32–33; see also, "Inside Politics," *Washington Times*, September 20, 1999, A9; "Clinton: Blacks Have Second Thoughts," *Independent*, June 23, 1999; Jay Nordlinger, "The Scandal II," *National Review*, March 8, 1999.

34. Charles C. Moskos and John Sibley Butler, *All That We Can Be: Black Leadership and Racial Integration the Army Way* (New York, 1996), esp. 6, 34.

35. Thernstrom and Thernstrom, *America in Black and White*, 526. On the declining significance of race, see also Orlando Patterson, "Race Over," *New Republic*, January 10, 2000, 6.

36. Douglas S. Massey and Nancy A. Denton, eds., *American Apartheid: Segregation and the Making of the Underclass* (Cambridge, Mass., 1993); Reynolds Farley and William H. Frey, "Changes in the Segregation of Whites from Blacks during the 1980s," *American Sociological Review* 59 (February 1994): 23–45; Maria P. P. Root, ed., *Racially Mixed People in America* (Newbury Park, Calif., 1992); Sharon Lee and Keiko Yamanaka, "Patterns of Asian American Intermarriage and Marital Assimilation," *Journal of Comparative Family Studies* 21 (Summer 1990): 287–305; Barry Edmonston, Sharon Lee, and Jeffrey Passell, "U.S. Population Projections for National Group Origins: Taking into Account Ethnicity and Exogamy," in *Proceedings of the American Statistical Association, Social Statistics Section* (Washington, D.C., 1994), 100–105; Matthijs Kalmigh, "Trends in Black/White Intermarriage," *Social Forces* 72 (September 1993): 119–46; George Lipsitz, "California: The Mississippi of the 1990s," in Lipsitz, *The Possessive Investment in Whiteness*, 211–33.

37. Robert B. Reich, "The Nationalism We Need," *American Prospect*, December 6, 1999, <http://www.prospect.org/archives/V11–2/reich.html>; Richard Rorty, *Achieving Our Country: Leftist Thought in Twentieth-Century America* (Cambridge, Mass., 1998); Hollinger, *Postethnic America*.

38. On the human rights movement, see Kenneth Cmiel, "The Emergence of Human Rights Politics in the United States," *Journal of American History* 86 (December 1999): 1231–50.

39. Feaver and Gelpi, in "How Many Deaths Are Acceptable?" argue that their findings demonstrate that Americans would be willing to endure greater sacrifices for causes to which they feel more committed. This remains to be seen.

40. See, for example, Patrick J. Buchanan, "The New Patriotism," speech announcing Buchanan's resignation from the Republican Party, 1999, <www.gopatgo2000.org/speech.htr>. See also Patrick J. Buchanan, *A Republic, Not an Empire* (New York, 1999).

41. George J. Sanchez discerns in 1990s anti-immigrant developments in California additional signs of the revival of an exclusionary nationalism. See his "Face the Nation: Race, Immigration, and the Rise of Nativism in Late-Twentieth-Century America," in Charles Hirschman, Philip Kasinitz, and Josh DeWind, eds., *The Handbook of International Migration: The American Experience* (New York, 1999), 371–82.

42. Walter Schapiro, "Echoes of Reagan, before the Revolution," *USA Today*, February 4, 2000, 13A. Michael Lind constitutes an important exception in this regard; see his *The Next American Nation*, 55–96.

43. Rogers Smith, *Civic Ideals: Conflicting Visions of Citizenship in U.S. History* (New Haven, 1997), 470–506; Hollinger, *Postethnic America*. For a debate on this issue, see Gary Gerstle, "Liberty, Coercion, and the Making of Americans," *Journal of American History* 84 (September 1997): 524–58; David A. Hollinger, "National Solidarity at the End of the Twentieth Century: Reflections on the United States and Liberal Nationalism," *Journal of American History* 84 (September 1997): 559–69; Donna R. Gabaccia, "Liberty, Coercion, and the Making of Immigration Historians," *Journal of American History* 84 (September 1997): 570–75; Gary Gerstle, "The Power of Nations," *Journal of American History* 84 (September 1997): 576–80.

Index